T0270795

Computational Intelligence for Oncology and Neurological Disorders

With the advent of computational intelligence (CI)-based approaches, such as bio-inspired techniques, and the availability of clinical data from various complex experiments, medical consultants, researchers, neurologists, and oncologists, there is huge scope for CI-based applications in medical oncology and neurological disorders. This book focuses on interdisciplinary research in this field, bringing together medical practitioners dealing with neurological disorders and medical oncology along with CI investigators.

The book collects high-quality original contributions, containing the latest developments or applications of practical use and value, presenting interdisciplinary research and review articles in the field of intelligent systems for computational oncology and neurological disorders. Drawing from work across computer science, physics, mathematics, medical science, psychology, cognitive science, oncology, and neurobiology among others, it combines theoretical, applied, computational, experimental, and clinical research. It will be of great interest to any neurology or oncology researchers focused on computational approaches.

Chapman & Hall/CRC Computational Biology Series

About the Series:
This series aims to capture new developments in computational biology, as well as high-quality work summarizing or contributing to more established topics. Publishing a broad range of reference works, textbooks, and handbooks, the series is designed to appeal to students, researchers, and professionals in all areas of computational biology, including genomics, proteomics, and cancer computational biology, as well as interdisciplinary researchers involved in associated fields, such as bioinformatics and systems biology.

Computational Intelligence for Oncology and Neurological Disorders
First Edition
Mrutyunjaya Panda, Ajith Abraham, Biju Gopi, and Reuel Ajith

Stochastic Modelling for Systems Biology
Third Edition
Darren J. Wilkinson

Computational Genomics with R
Altuna Akalin, Bora Uyar, Vedran Franke, Jonathan Ronen

An Introduction to Computational Systems Biology: Systems-level Modelling of Cellular Networks
Karthik Raman

Virus Bioinformatics
Dmitrij Frishman, Manuela Marz

Multivariate Data Integration Using R: Methods and Applications with the mixOmics Package
Kim-Anh LeCao, Zoe Marie Welham

Bioinformatics
A Practical Guide to NCBI Databases and Sequence Alignments
Hamid D. Ismail

Data Integration, Manipulation and Visualization of Phylogenetic Trees
Guangchuang Yu

Bioinformatics Methods
From Omics to Next Generation Sequencing
Shili Lin, Denise Scholtens and Sujay Datta

Systems Medicine
Physiological Circuits and the Dynamics of Disease
Uri Alon

The Applied Genomic Epidemiology Handbook
A Practical Guide to Leveraging Pathogen Genomic Data in Public Health
Allison Black and Gytis Dudas

For more information about this series please visit: https://www.routledge.com/Chapman--HallCRC
-Computational-Biology-Series/book-series/CRCCBS

Computational Intelligence for Oncology and Neurological Disorders

Current Practices and Future Directions

Edited by
Mrutyunjaya Panda, Ajith Abraham, Biju Gopi,
and Reuel Ajith

CRC Press
Taylor & Francis Group
Boca Raton London New York

CRC Press is an imprint of the
Taylor & Francis Group, an **Informa** business

Designed cover image: Shutterstock Images

First edition published 2025
by CRC Press
2385 NW Executive Center Drive, Suite 320, Boca Raton FL 33431

and by CRC Press
4 Park Square, Milton Park, Abingdon, Oxon, OX14 4RN

CRC Press is an imprint of Taylor & Francis Group, LLC

ISBN: 9781032584577 (hbk)
ISBN: 9781032584607 (pbk)
ISBN: 9781003450153 (ebk)

DOI: 10.1201/9781003450153

Typeset in Palatino
by Deanta Global Publishing Services, Chennai, India

Contents

Part 1   Neurological Disorders

Preface

Neurological disorders comprise both fatal and non-fatal disorders and contribute approximately 10 percent of the global burden of the most communicable and non-communicable diseases in today's world. Neurological disorders include a large number of discrete health conditions with their own prevalence of disease characteristics including genetic, biological, social, and psychological determinants. All these can affect the central or peripheral nervous system such as brain, spinal cord, neuromuscular function etc. Due to their chronic course and highly disabling rate, neurological disorder–associated diseases cause significant premature mortality with immense socioeconomic impact not only on human wellness but also on families and society at large. In spite of these alarming situations, which are rising globally, no significant contributions are coming from policymakers to prevent and cure these diseases. Hence, more research, containing structured and exhaustive neurological- disorder data analysis, is called for to present good insights into disease detection, prevention, and cure, along with associated risk factors and solutions to the problem.

Oncology is another life-threatening disease with a high mortality rate worldwide, accounting for nearly one in every six deaths; with nearly 10 million deaths predicted from cancer and 20 million new cases of cancer, more attention need to be paid to better diagnosis and treatment of the disease. This includes (i) medical oncology, where chemotherapy, hormone therapy etc. are used to treat the cancer, (ii) radiation oncology, where radiation therapy by using X-ray or proton radiation is used, and (iii) surgical oncology, where preventive surgery or reconstructive surgery are used to treat the cancer.

With progress being made in artificial intelligence (AI)-based approaches and the availability of clinical data/information from various resources, medical consultants, researchers, neurologists, and oncologists, it is observed that there is huge scope for research in the field of AI-based applications in neurological disorders and oncology.

Since the past few years, advances in AI, along with the availability of structured and unstructured healthcare data and the rapid progress of data analytics techniques, have brought about a paradigm shift in healthcare applications. Further, these pave the way for improved diagnostic and therapeutic methods in precision medicine. Some of the very popular AI methods, such as support vector machine, artificial neural network, deep learning, and natural language processing etc., find wide applications in today's life-threatening diseases such as neurological disorders, oncology, and cardiology for early detection, diagnosis, treatment success rate and prognosis evaluation. Although several measures have been taken by governments to create better patient care for those suffering from these diseases, still substantial challenges remain which urge AI experts and medical practitioners to do collaborative, interdisciplinary research to enhance clinical practices and to save lives.

This book explores recent advances in AI methods to safeguard individuals' wellbeing with sustainable, precision, and personalized healthcare as a part of the fifth industrial revolution, Industry 5.0. The chapters presented in the book will pave the way to deliver personalised healthcare products through an interface of human intelligence, robotic automation technology, and smart systems for patients with neurological disorders and/or oncology symptoms.

This book aims at a collection of interdisciplinary research and review articles in the field of intelligent systems for computational oncology and neurological disorders; an amalgamation of fields of research including computer science, physics, mathematics, medical science, psychology, cognitive science, oncology, and neurobiology, among others, to provide theoretical, applied, computational, experimental, and clinical research.

This book consists of 16 chapters which are presented in two parts. Part 1 has eight chapters (Chapters 1–8) related to neurological disorders and the last eight chapters (Chapters 9–16) related to oncology research are presented in Part 2.

Part 1: Neurological Disorders

Chapter 1 presents AI for mental health exploring autism spectrum disorder, schizophrenia, attention deficit hyperactivity disorder etc. The authors also point out the research gaps and propose future directions to further improve mental health.

Chapter 2 deals with blockchain applications in neurological disorders and oncology. Authors discuss the efficiency of blockchain technology in clinical trials to have more effective disease diagnosis and personalized treatment of the patients with cancer and neurological disorders.

Chapter 3 explores deep scattering wavelet network and marine predators algorithm-based stuttering disfluency detection, which is an automated computer-based diagnostic algorithm to identify two stuttering speech events. The authors use scattering wavelet network for feature extraction and KNN classifier for the detection of stuttering events. Audio samples from a stuttering event database were used for the experiments.

Chapter 4 presents an overview on the diverse array of neurological disorders and the application of artificial intelligence methodologies in the detection and diagnosis of those ailments. The authors illustrate how development of computational intelligence models can facilitate rapid, efficient, and precise identification of neurological illnesses.

Chapter 5 illustrates malformation risk prediction for pregnant women with epilepsy for improving prenatal care. The authors use synthetic oversampling and evaluated six classifiers for detecting congenital malformations accurately.

Chapter 6 presents a comprehensive and comparative review and discusses the effectiveness of the computational intelligence techniques in solving the critical health-related issues pertaining to genomics and proteomics in mutational disease prediction. The authors illustrate how AI methods could be used for the deoxyribonucleic acid sequence to synthesize the genomic data in order to identify the exon location accurately while trying to detect genetic disorder.

Chapter 7 provides a comparative analysis of deep learning models for accurate brain MRI segmentation, for precise medical image analysis and diagnosis using deep learning models, for early detection of neurological disorders.

Chapter 8 narrates a comprehensive review on depression detection based on text from social media posts with an overview on the complex nature of mental disorders with their challenges that affect the society at large.

Part 2: Oncology

Chapter 9 highlights artificial intelligence in radiation oncology specifically to improve treatment planning, image analysis, patient outcome prediction, and adaptive therapy. The author presents a SWOC analysis on the suitability of various AI techniques that are currently being applied in radiation oncology research along with ethical considerations.

Chapter 10 provides a comprehensive overview of AI Applications in radiation oncology and elaborates on the specificities and niche understandings concerning the use of artificial intelligence in general radiation oncology.

Chapter 11 illustrates melanoma skin cancer identification using a lightweight embedded medical assistance device designed through a general-purpose deep learning method based on IoT platform using Raspberry Pi 4. The authors use a digital hair removal model that combines digital hair removal during pre-processing with a pre-trained deep learning model.

Chapter 12 presents a deep hybrid system for effective diagnosis of breast cancer using a light weight deep convolution neural network architecture for feature extraction and random forest classifier for breast cancer classification on ultrasound and mammography datasets.

Chapter 13 highlights the identification of brain cancer using medical hyperspectral image analysis. The authors use in vivo HS data set for brain tumour delineation during surgical procedures.

Chapter 14 illustrates an acute myeloid leukaemia detection system by combining deep learning model and an augmentation approach for better classification efficiency with a reasonable computing cost.

Chapter 15 narrates the effective use of computational biology and artificial intelligence in the domain of medical oncology. The authors illustrate several computational simulations to predict cancer progression and treatment responses, for personalized healthcare.

Chapter 16 depicts computer-aided ensemble method for early diagnosis of coronary artery disease and focuses on the need for efficient and non-invasive computer-aided procedures in order to prevent fatalities resulting from coronary artery disease in cancer patients. The authors discuss the suitability of detecting coronary artery disease in an effective and accurate manner in comparison to other existing approaches.

About the Editors

Dr. Mrutyunjaya Panda holds a PhD in computer science from Berhampur University. He obtained his Master's in communication system engineering from University College of Engineering, Burla, under Sambalpur University (now, VSSUT, Burla), an MBA in HRM from IGNOU, New Delhi, and a Bachelor's degree in electronics and telecommunication engineering from Utkal University. He has 23 years' experience of teaching and research experience and presently works as associate professor and head in the department of computer science and applications, Utkal University, Vani Vihar, Bhubaneswar, Odisha, India. He is a member of KES (Australia), IAENG (Hong Kong), ACEEE (India), IETE (India), CSI (India), and ISTE (India). He has published about 130 research papers in international and national journals and at conferences of repute. He has also published 15 book chapters and edited five books. He is a guest editor for the *International Journal of Computational Intelligence Studies* and has authored two text books on soft computing techniques for Universal Science Press and on modern approaches of data mining for Narosa Publications. He is a program committee member of various international conferences. He acts as a member of editorial boards and is an active reviewer of various international journals and conferences. He is an associate editor of the *International Journal of Cognitive Informatics and Natural Intelligence* and the *Journal of Network and Innovative Computing*. His active areas of research include data mining, granular computing, big data analytics, the Internet of Things, intrusion detection systems, social networking, wireless sensor networks, image processing, text and opinion mining and bioinformatics, and natural language processing.

Dr. Ajith Abraham is presently working as dean of Faculty of Computing and Data Science at FLAME University, Pune India. Dr. Abraham was the founding director of Machine Intelligence Research Labs (MIR Labs), a not-for-profit scientific network for innovation and research excellence connecting industry and academia. The network, with HQ in Seattle, USA, has currently more than 1,000 scientific members from over 100 countries. As an investigator/co-investigator, he has won research grants worth over 100 million US$ from Australia, USA, EU, Italy, Czech Republic, France, Malaysia, and China. Dr. Abraham works in a multi-disciplinary environment involving machine intelligence, cyber-physical systems, Internet of things, network security, sensor networks, Web intelligence, Web services, data mining and applied to various real-world problems. In these areas he has authored/co-authored more than 1,400 research publications out of which there are more than 100 books covering various aspects of computer science. One of his books was translated into Japanese and a few other articles were translated into Russian and Chinese. About 1,200 publications are indexed by Scopus and over 1,000 are indexed by Thomson ISI Web of Science. Some of the articles are available in the ScienceDirect Top 25 articles. He has more than 1,100 co-authors originating from more than 40 countries. Dr. Abraham has nearly 50,000 academic citations (h-index of 104 as per Google Scholar). He has given more than 150 plenary lectures and conference tutorials (in more than 20 countries). For his research, he has won seven best-paper awards at prestigious international conferences held in Belgium, Canada Bahrain, Czech Republic, China, and India. Since 2008, Dr. Abraham has been the chair of IEEE Systems Man and Cybernetics Society Technical Committee on Soft Computing (which has over 200 members) and served as a distinguished lecturer of the IEEE Computer Society representing Europe (2011 to 2013). Dr. Abraham was the editor-in-chief of *Engineering Applications of Artificial Intelligence* and serves/has served the editorial boards of over 15 international journals indexed by Thomson ISI. He is actively involved in the organization of several academic conferences, and some of them are now annual events. Dr. Abraham received a PhD degree in computer science from Monash University, Melbourne, Australia (2001) and a master's degree in science from Nanyang Technological University, Singapore (1998). More information at: http://www.softcomputing.net/

Dr. Biju Gopi holds a MBBS degree from Medical College, Trivandrum (1981) and BCCPM (palliative medicine) from General Hospital, Ernakulam (2020). He was the recipient of the National Fellowship of Palliative Medicine 2021–22, in the Institute of Palliative Medicine, Calicut Medical College, Kozhokode, Kerala, India and the global fellowship program in palliative medicine from Pallium India, Trivandrum, Kerala. He has worked as consultant palliative physician, palliative physician and general practitioner since 1984 till now in several medical colleges and hospitals such as Khorfakkan Hospital, Sharjah, UAE, and the Pain and Palliative Care Dept., Lakeshore Hospital, Nettoor, Ernakulam, Kerala, India, to name a few. He has very rich clinical experiences in and around the globe, including starting the Pain and Palliative Home Care facilities at Lakeshore Hospital during the Covid pandemic; starting a joint venture called "Doctor on Wheels" in association with Signature Aged Care, Chalikkavattom, Ernakulam, Kerala to provide palliative and curative care for elderly patients; working in Peace Mission Centre as palliative physician, in Al Ghail Medical Centre, Al Ghail, RAK as a general practitioner, and in Reem Al Nahda Medical Centre as a general practitioner. He completed a basic life support course as per American Heart Association guidelines conducted by Eduscope International LLC, Dubai Health Care City, Dubai, UAE, and became a BLS Provider in 2016. At present, he is working as consultant palliative physician at the Pain and Palliative Care Dept., Lakeshore Hospital, Nettoor, Ernakulam, Kerala, India. He is a member of the Indian Medical Association, Trivandrum Branch.

Dr. Reuel Ajith finished an MD degree in June 2021 from the Faculty of Medicine in Vilnius University, Lithuania. His research interests are in internal medicine with a focus on neuro-degenerative diseases. He was in a team of researchers that developed the usage of artificial intelligence and free-speech to detect early signs of Parkinson's disease (https://doi.org/10.1016/j.engappai.2018.09.018). The early detection mechanism used signal and speech processing techniques integrated with machine learning algorithms. He is affiliated with Machine Intelligence Research Labs (MIR Labs) dealing with AI and healthcare related projects.

List of Contributors

Ashwani Kumar Aggarwal
Electrical and Instrumentation
  Engineering Department
Sant Longowal Institute of Engineering
  and Technology
Longowal, India

Korra Sathya Babu
Department of Computer Science and
  Engineering
Indian Institute of Information Technology
  Design and Manufacturing
Kurnool, India

Charvi Bannur
Department of Computer Science
PES University
Bangalore, India

Chaitra Bhat
Department of Computer Science
PES University
Bangalore, India

Gajanan K. Birajdar
Department of Electronics Engineering
Ramrao Adik Institute of Technology
DY Patil Deemed to be University
Navi-Mumbai, India

J. K. Das
KIIT
Bhubaneswar, India

Pradeep Kumar Das
School of Electronics and Engineering
  (SENSE)
Vellore Institute of Technology,
Vellore, India

Lopamudra Das
SIT
Bhubaneswar, India

Aloke Datta
Department of Computer Science and
  Engineering
The LNM Institute of Information
  Technology
Jaipur, India

Arka De
Vellore Institute of Technology
Vellore, India

P. L. Deepa
Department of Electronics and
  Telecommunication and Engineering
Mar Baselios College of Engineering and
  Technology
Trivandrum, India

Neel Ghoshal
School of Computer Science and
  Engineering
Vellore Institute of Technology
Vellore, India

Gagan Goutham
Department of Computer Science
PES University
Bangalore, India

Mamatha H.R.
Department of Computer Science
PES University
Bangalore, India

Roohum Jegana
Department of Electronics &
 Communication Engineering
BMS College of Engineering
Bangalore, India

Jisha John
Department of Computer Science and
 Engineering
Mar Baselios College of Engineering and
 Technology
Trivandrum, India

Sada Kakarla
Department of Computer Science
PES University
Bangalore, India

Bhakti Kaushal
Department of Electronics &
 Telecommunication Engineering
Ramrao Adik Institute of Technology
DY Patil Deemed to be University
Navi-Mumbai, India

Nam Kim
Information and Communication
 Engineering
Chungbuk National University
South Korea

Shinde Rupali Kiran
Information and Communication
 Engineering
Chungbuk National University
South Korea

Soumya Ranjan Mahanta
Department of Computer Science
Utkal University
Bhubaneswar, India

Tessy Mathew
Department of Computer Science and
 Engineering
Mar Baselios College of Engineering and
 Technology
Trivandrum, India

Sukadev Meher
Department of Electronics and
 Communication Engineering
National Institute of Technology
Rourkela, India

Shashwati Mishra
B.J.B. (A.) College
Bhubaneswar, India

Arkashree P. Mishra
Department of Computer Science and
 Engineering
Veer Surendra Sai University of
 Technology (VSSUT)
Burla, India

Jesna Mohan
Department of Computer Science and
 Engineering
Mar Baselios College of Engineering and
 Technology
Trivandrum, India

Sarita Nanda
KIIT
Bhubaneswar, India

Mrutyunjaya Panda
Department of Computer Science
Utkal University
Bhubaneswar, India

Gobinda Chandra Panda
BIITM
Bhubaneswar, India

Suvasini Panigrahi
Department of Computer Science and
 Engineering
Veer Surendra Sai University of
 Technology (VSSUT)
Burla, India

Mukesh D. Patil
Department of Electronics &
 Telecommunication Engineering
Ramrao Adik Institute of Technology
DY Patil Deemed to be University
Navi-Mumbai, India

Bibhudatta Sahoo
Computer Science and Engineering
National Institute of Technology
Rourkela, India

Adyasha Sahu
Department of Electronics and Department
  of Electronics and Communication
  Engineering
National Institute of Technology,
Rourkela, India

Sameeksha Saraf
Vellore Institute of Technology
Vellore, India

Gençay Sevim
Antalya Bilim University
Vocational School of Health Services
Department of Medical Services and
  Techniques
Antalya, Türkiye

Raj Bahadur Singh
Department of Computer Science and
  Engineering
The LNM Institute of Information
  Technology
Jaipur, India

Vankayala Tejaswini
Computer Science and Engineering
National Institute of Technology
Rourkela, India

Sanjeev V. Thomas
ICCOONS
Trivandrum, India

Aruna Tripathy
OUTR
Bhubaneswar, India

B.K. Tripathy
School of Information Technology and
  Engineering
Vellore Institute of Technology
Vellore, India

Part 1

Neurological Disorders

1

Advancements in AI for Mental Health: Exploring ASD, ADHD and Schizophrenia, Video Datasets, and Future Directions

Charvi Bannur, Chaitra Bhat, Gagan Goutham, Mamatha H. R., and Sada Kakarla

1.1 Introduction

Mental health disorders, encompassing a diverse range of conditions that affect an individual's cognitive processes, emotions, and behaviours, stand as some of the most pressing challenges of our modern era. The intricate interplay between genetics, environment, and brain function gives rise to a complex spectrum of disorders, each with its unique set of symptoms and manifestations.

Mental health illnesses have a significant economic cost that affects every aspect of society. Families, communities, and economies are all affected, thorough knowledge and creative solutions are needed. However, identifying and treating these illnesses are still difficult undertakings. The subjectivity of symptom reporting, the possibility of a false positive, and the wide range of treatment outcomes highlight the need for accuracy and wisdom in mental health research and practice. A few examples of this diversity include schizophrenia, attention deficit hyperactivity disorder (ADHD), and autism spectrum disorder (ASD), each of which presents a distinct canvas of behavioural manifestations that impact people at all stages of life.

A glimmer of hope has appeared with the development of artificial intelligence (AI), which has shed fresh light on the complexity of mental health illnesses. It is a transformative force that has the ability to significantly alter how we understand and manage mental health issues; it is not restricted to algorithms and lines of code in this context. The potential of artificial intelligence is not just in its computing capability, but also in its ability to understand the complex layers of human behaviour and turn visual clues into useful insights.

Traditionally, these illnesses were diagnosed mostly by clinical observation, subjective judgments, and self-reporting. However, the drawbacks of these approaches are well known, including the possibility of human bias, the difficulty of collecting small behavioural clues, and the difficulty of quantifying complex emotional states. Enter AI, computer vision, and a slew of other technologies that prioritise impartiality, scalability, and precision. AI is capable of deciphering facial expressions, quantifying bodily motions, and analysing patterns that the human eye may miss. It paves the way for automatic detection, objective analysis, and proactive action.

A key element of this revolution is deep learning, a kind of artificial intelligence. The subtleties of visual data are revealed by convolutional neural networks (CNNs), which

DOI: 10.1201/9781003450153-2

take their inspiration from the human visual brain. These networks, which resemble complex neural networks, develop the ability to spot patterns in pictures and movies. Models pre-trained on large datasets learn to detect specific aspects of neurological illnesses by transfer learning, enabling a customised diagnosis in a short amount of time (Boppana et al., 2021). The promise of AI is not, however, without its share of difficulties. The ethical issues loom large, posing concerns about data privacy, prejudice reduction, and the possibility of technological dependency. The delicate balancing act between innovation and ethical responsibility becomes crucial when the algorithms analyse the intricacies of human behaviour. Additionally, the integration of AI into clinical practice requires careful navigation, fostering a symbiotic relationship between technology and the human touch that defines healthcare (Torous et al., 2017).

This chapter embarks on an exploration of the heart of this groundbreaking field, where AI and mental health meet. The chapters that follow will be devoted to talking about AI and its present uses. We'll talk about the mysteries surrounding various neurological conditions and look at the methods for identifying their early warning signs and cues. When examining neurological illnesses, the power of AI in mental health becomes very clear. ASD is an excellent example, with issues in social interaction, communication, and repetitive activities. ADHD brings attentional difficulties and hyperactivity to the forefront, making it difficult for people to perform everyday chores. Schizophrenia, on the other hand, is characterised by a complex interplay of skewed perceptions, disordered thinking, and emotional turpitude (Boppana et al., 2021).

The following sections will delve deeper into how AI is used to treat ASD, ADHD, and schizophrenia as well as the datasets used for the analysis of neurological illnesses. This will shed light on how it may be both a benefit and a difficulty for mental health researchers and doctors. We will also talk about the ethical concerns that arise when AI becomes an essential part of mental health research, practice, and future considerations.

1.2 Artificial Intelligence (AI) Research in Mental Health

1.2.1 Convoluted Nature of Mental Health Disorders

People all around the world are affected by mental health illnesses, which is a complicated and diverse problem. These illnesses cover a wide spectrum of ailments, each displaying a distinct set of symptoms and manifestations due to a complicated interplay of genetic predispositions, environmental factors, and brain dynamics. There is a wide range of mental health issues.

The enigmatic nature of mental health issues is one of its distinguishing features. Mental health illnesses mostly rely on subjective observations and self-reported experiences, as opposed to numerous physical health diseases that may frequently be objectively quantified by biomarkers or diagnostic testing. Accurate diagnosis and efficient treatment are made more difficult by this inherent subjectivity. It can be challenging to measure and categorise the complexity of human emotions, ideas, and behaviours, which can result in incorrect diagnoses and postponed interventions.

1.2.2 AI as a Transformative Force

Machine learning and deep learning are at the forefront of the technologies that make up artificial intelligence (AI). These technologies have the power to analyse enormous volumes of data, spot complex patterns, and derive significant insights that might fundamentally alter how mental health issues are recognised and treated.

Fundamentally, AI has the power to revolutionise mental health research by delivering unbiased, data-driven insights into the complexity of these conditions. AI algorithms may find hidden connections and trends through the examination of numerous data sources, such as neuroimaging, physiological indicators, expression monitoring, speech, behavioural patterns, and other types of data. AI is a potent tool for unravelling the mystery of mental health because of its potential to process and analyse data in a way that exceeds human capability.

1.2.3 Bridging the Gap: Integrating Technology and Mental Healthcare

The use of AI for mental health research creates a link between two hitherto unconnected domains: technology and human well-being. Researchers and practitioners can improve their knowledge of mental health issues by using its capabilities, resulting in more accurate diagnosis and targeted therapies. This combination of technology and mental health knowledge is critical in tackling the specific issues that these conditions present.

The potential of AI in the field of mental health goes beyond diagnosis and treatment. In order to spot indications of distress or potential mental health problems, machine learning algorithms can examine a person's digital footprint, which includes social media posts, text messages, and online activity. Linguistic and emotional cues extracted from social media can provide insights into an individual's mental well-being (Guntuku et al., 2019). By detecting early warning signs, AI can facilitate timely interventions, potentially preventing the escalation of mental health conditions. It has the capacity to streamline data collection and analysis, enabling the identification of early warning signs and risk factors that might otherwise be missed (Figure 1.1).

FIGURE 1.1
Impact of social media on mental and emotional health.

Chatbots powered by AI can provide immediate support, coping strategies, and even crisis intervention. These interventions can be available 24/7, overcoming the limitations of traditional therapy schedules and offering continuous assistance (Fitzpatrick et al., 2017) (Figure 1.2).

Additionally, AI-driven insights can contribute to the development of interventions that are tailored to an individual's unique profile. Technologies such as virtual reality (VR) and augmented reality (AR) have created new opportunities for therapeutic treatments. Exposure treatment for anxiety disorders may be carried out in a controlled VR environment (Freeman et al., 2018) (Figure 1.3).

By progressively exposing patients to their concerns in a safe and regulated way, this immersive method can improve therapy outcomes. Data analytics combined with AI provides a lot of information on trends and patterns in mental health. Large-scale datasets may be analysed by AI to find population-level patterns, which helps with resource allocation and better-informed policy-making for managing public mental health by forecasting mental health trends via digital phenotyping (Mendes et al., 2022) (Figure 1.4).

FIGURE 1.2
AI chatbots can help with immediate preliminary support.

FIGURE 1.3
AR andVR technologies can bring new forms of therapy.

FIGURE 1.4
Digital phenotyping can be used to monitor public health by analysing data.

1.3 The Enigma of Neurological Disorders

1.3.1 Autism Spectrum Disorder (ASD): Unravelling Social Perceptions

Autism spectrum disorder (ASD), a pervasive neurodevelopmental disorder, casts a unique hue on an individual's perception of, and interaction with, the world. Its origins remain enigmatic, stemming from an intricate interplay between genetic predispositions and environmental factors. ASD's hallmark features include challenges in social communication and interaction, coupled with restricted and repetitive behaviours. Individuals with ASD may find it challenging to interpret social signs, engage in reciprocal conversations, and express emotions in ways recognisable to others. These challenges can hinder the formation of relationships and the navigation of social contexts, underscoring the need for specialised support and understanding (Lee et al., 2020). Altered eye contact, unconventional facial expressions, intricate patterns, nonverbal communication, and struggles in deciphering social cues may signal a heightened likelihood of ASD. The significance of early ASD detection cannot be overstated, as it underpins timely interventions and the provisioning of tailored support and therapies to affected individuals.

1.3.2 Attention-Deficit Hyperactivity Disorder (ADHD): Balancing Focus and Impulsivity

Attention-deficit hyperactivity disorder (ADHD) manifests as a complex interplay of cognitive restlessness and impulsivity, significantly disrupting an individual's capacity to focus and sustain attention. This disruption often results in difficulties in engaging with tasks and adhering to routines, hampering daily functioning. A pronounced element of ADHD is hyperactivity, which materialises as an incapacity to remain seated or a propensity for impulsive actions without due forethought. The origins of ADHD are multifaceted, encompassing genetic predisposition, brain morphology, and environmental influences. Notably, imbalances in neurotransmitter systems play a pivotal role in shaping the ADHD phenotype, contributing to the challenges associated with self-regulation and executive functions (Lee et al., 2022).

1.3.3 Schizophrenia: Distorted Realities and Emotional Upheaval

Schizophrenia, a complex and severe mental disorder, casts a shadow over an individual's perception of reality and emotional equilibrium. Hallucinations and delusions are among its defining features, skewing one's interpretation of the external world. Disorganised thinking and impaired emotional expression contribute to the disorder's profound impact on daily functioning (McCutcheon et al., 2020). The etiological landscape of schizophrenia is a complex interplay of genetic susceptibility, altered neural circuitry, and environmental triggers. Dysregulation in neurotransmitter systems, particularly dopamine and glutamate, underpins the cognitive and perceptual distortions characteristic of the disorder (Javitt et al., 2007).

1.4 The Role of AI in Advancing Research on Mental Health

1.4.1 Understanding Artificial Intelligence

Fundamentally, AI is the emulation of human intellectual functions by machines, allowing them to analyse data, derive conclusions, and make defensible judgements. The strength

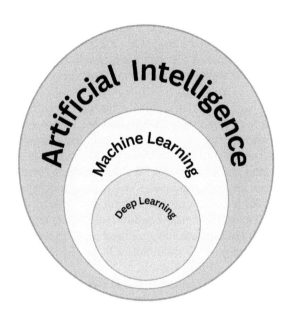

FIGURE 1.5
Understanding AI.

of this technology rests in its capacity to swiftly analyse enormous datasets in order to uncover hidden connections and patterns that may shed new light on neurological and psychiatric problems.

The core of AI's capabilities is machine learning (ML), which enables computers to learn from data and continuously improve their performance. In this field, deep learning dominates, making use of complex neural networks modelled after the architecture of the human brain. The intricacy of mental health problems can be better understood by using convolutional neural networks (CNNs) and recurrent neural networks (RNNs), which are excellent at tasks like image recognition and sequential data analysis. The data-centric aspect of AI sits at the core of its strength. Large datasets may be analysed by AI systems to find patterns that may be invisible to the human eye. The ability to identify complex genetic, physiological, and behavioural signs that lead to disorders like ASD and schizophrenia has revolutionised mental health research (Figure 1.5).

In the past few years, systems powered by AI that support mental health and treatment have made significant advancements. Online platforms provide easily available therapy and counselling services, increasing the population's access to assistance. Apps for measuring mental health use AI algorithms to measure psychological states by examining linguistic patterns and emotions in spoken or written communications. Additionally, a rise in businesses focusing on mental health shows a growing interest in utilising AI's ability to treat this important social issue.

1.4.2 Advanced Technological Methods for the Analysis of Neurological Disorders

Pioneering studies in the field of computer vision (CV) have shown how powerfully CNNs can understand the intricacies of facial expressions linked to neurological diseases (Ahmed et al., 2022). Additionally, the use of CNNs in conjunction with bi-directional long short-term memory (Bi-LSTM) recurrent neural networks has facilitated the correct identification of people suffering from ADHD and ASD (Jaiswal et al., 2018). A novel method that makes use of spatial and temporal data (Jie Huang et al., 2022) focuses on the use of a 3D convolutional neural network for automated identification of schizophrenia from face films. Such advancements highlight CV's ability to capture and interpret complex visual signals with diagnostic value.

Advances in the analysis of textual and aural data have been made possible by the convergence of natural language processing (NLP) and ML approaches. For instance, acoustic signal analysis has shown the capacity to identify emotion-related low-level speech patterns and predict schizophrenia symptoms (Chakraborty et al., 2018). Additionally, research has demonstrated the promise of NLP approaches for deciphering textual and auditory information from multimedia resources by using machine learning algorithms to analyse YouTube videos for telltale symptoms of autism (Fusaro et al., 2014).

Utilising the unique properties of auto-encoder feature representation, the exploitation of electroencephalography (EEG) data has emerged as a cornerstone, propelling the creation of novel models for baby ASD detection (Oh et al., 2021) employing EEG data to anticipate ASD symptoms using brain signals.

In summation, the synergy of advanced technologies – spanning CV, NLP, eye tracking, and EEG – has ushered in a new era of exploration and understanding in the realms of neurological and psychological disorders. This convergence holds promise for early diagnosis, informed interventions, and comprehensive insights into complex conditions that resonate through the annals of mental health research and clinical practice. As AI technology continues to advance, the potential for transformation in this domain remains boundless, igniting hope for brighter horizons in the arena of mental well-being.

1.5 The Intricacies of AI and Datasets in Neurological and Psychological Disorder Analysis

1.5.1 Analysis of ASD, ADHD, and Schizophrenia Using Multimodal Datasets

Multimodal datasets for ADHD, ASD, and schizophrenia involve collecting data from individuals diagnosed with these disorders through various modalities, including clinical assessments, neuroimaging, genetic data, behavioural observations, and more. For ADHD, clinical assessments include standardised assessments like ADHD rating scales, questionnaires, and interviews to gather information about symptoms and impairments.

Neuroimaging involves structural and functional brain-imaging data to identify brain regions associated with ADHD, while genetic data involves DNA samples for genotyping or whole-genome sequencing. Numerous studies have attempted to diagnose ADHD via neuroimaging modalities like magnetic resonance imaging (MRI) (Bohland et al., 2012; Y. Tang et al., 2022), physiological signals like an electroencephalogram (EEG) (Öztoprak et al., 2017; Ahmadi et al., 2021), and electrocardiograms (ECG) (Koh et al., 2022) and other modalities like accelerometers (O'Mahony et al., 2014) and game simulators (Heller et al., 2013).

For ASD, clinical assessments include assessments specific to ASD, such as the autism diagnostic observation schedule (ADOS), to gather information about social communication deficits and restricted behaviours. Genetic data is collected to investigate genetic contributions to ASD, and eye-tracking data quantifies gaze patterns and assesses how individuals with ASD respond to social stimuli. A multimodal dataset for autism intervention analysis (MMASD) is a publicly accessible multimodal dataset (Jicheng Li et al. 2023), featuring diverse scenes collected from therapy interventions for children with autism. This includes multimodal features such as 2D and 3D skeleton data, optical flow, demographic data, and the autism diagnostic observation schedule (ADOS) rating scale, offering a confidential data-sharing approach that can maintain critical motion information, distinguishing itself from existing works by utilising privacy-preserving multimodal features to provide comprehensive representations of full-body movements across a range of diverse themes.

For schizophrenia, the integration of multimodal imaging and genomic data has gained significant traction. This approach combines various sources of information to enhance our understanding of the disorder. Modalities such as functional magnetic resonance imaging (fMRI), structural MRI (sMRI), positron emission tomography (PET) scans, and diffusion tensor imaging (DTI) offer insights into brain structure and function. Simultaneously, genetic aspects are explored through single nucleotide polymorphisms (SNPs), DNA methylations, and gene expression (GE) profiles. These combined datasets have emerged as a powerful tool for uncovering disease-related insights. Notably, both genetic investigations and brain-imaging techniques have yielded valuable contributions to the identification of disease phenotypes (Md. Ashad Alam et al., 2018).

Creating these datasets requires careful planning, ethical considerations, and collaboration with clinicians, researchers, and participants. Careful anonymisation and informed consent are critical to protect participants' privacy and ensure responsible data usage. These datasets hold immense potential for advancing our understanding of these disorders and developing more effective diagnostic and treatment strategies.

1.5.2 Analysis of ASD, ADHD, and Schizophrenia Using Video Datasets

The availability and effective use of a variety of video datasets is integrally linked to the successful use of cutting-edge technology tools for the investigation of neurological and psychiatric problems. Significant progress has been made in the sector as a result of the convergence of cutting-edge technologies and how they interact with these datasets. A number of researchers have achieved significant advancements in the understanding and prediction of ASD, ADHD, and schizophrenia by using a range of machine-learning algorithms on video datasets. The landscape of available video datasets is examined in this part along with how they might be used to better understand the intricacies of these conditions.

Studies looking into ASD have made use of video collections that capture behavioural and facial clues. A dataset of 3,014 face photographs of autistic and typically developing youngsters (Ahmed et al., 2022) to create a deep-learning–based online application for autism screening. With the use of pretrained models like MobileNet, Xception, and InceptionV3, this method produced excellent accuracy. Additionally, by using convolutional neural networks and bi-directional long short-term memory networks, a dynamic deep-learning system (Jaiswal et al., 2018) demonstrated the promise of facial behaviour analysis for ADHD and ASD. It also made use of the KOMAA database, which was specifically curated for these analyses.

The growth of video datasets has greatly improved schizophrenia analysis. By employing video interviews, SchiNet, a unique neural-network architecture (Bishay et al.,

2019) assessed expression-related symptoms. Low-level audio signals were also used (Chakraborty et al., 2018) to forecast emotion-related symptoms and professional subjective assessments in schizophrenia patients. Using video-extracted facial expressions, 3D convolutional neural networks were used to categorise people with schizophrenia (Jie Huang et al., 2022).

Video datasets have permitted groundbreaking studies for ADHD identification. Robot-led ADHD screening games captured video data of children's behaviours (Lee et al., 2022) and accelerometer data were used by Maniruzzaman et al. (2022) to predict ADHD in kids based on behavioural activity patterns.

The combination of AI and video datasets has yielded vital insights into neurological and psychiatric problems. The use of facial expressions, behavioural clues, and interactions collected in these datasets has enabled the creation of highly accurate prediction models, categorisation systems, and diagnostic tools. These findings highlight the revolutionary power of video collections in improving knowledge, diagnosis, and treatment of ASD, ADHD, and schizophrenia (Table 1.1).

1.6 Ethical Considerations and Future Directions

1.6.1 Mindful Integration of AI and Ethical Deliberations

While the potential of AI and computer vision in behavioural analysis is undeniably promising, a host of critical ethical considerations and challenges demand careful attention. One primary concern revolves around data privacy, particularly as these technologies rely on extensive video datasets, potentially revealing sensitive personal information. Striking a balance between harnessing the power of AI for behavioural insights and safeguarding individuals' privacy rights is of paramount importance (Torous et al., 2017). In summation, while the promise of AI and computer vision in behavioural analysis is profound, grappling with these ethical considerations is indispensable. Balancing privacy, interpretability, fairness, and bias reduction is key to unlocking the full potential of AI in revolutionising medical diagnostics and treatments while upholding the highest standards of ethics and patient well-being.

1.6.2 Envisioning a Future Empowered by AI for Mental Health

Harnessing the capabilities of AI techniques holds the potential to revolutionise the field of mental health by enabling the development of advanced pre-diagnosis screening tools and predictive risk models that can gauge an individual's susceptibility or likelihood of developing mental illnesses. To achieve the overarching goal of personalised mental healthcare, it is imperative to tap into computational methodologies optimised for handling extensive datasets, thus facilitating the extraction of meaningful insights from big data. It is of utmost importance to acknowledge that, while AI presents immense possibilities in the realm of mental health, it should be regarded as a supplementary tool that complements rather than replaces human expertise and compassionate care. Ensuring accessibility and fairness across diverse populations, encompassing underserved communities and resource-limited settings, is pivotal to realising the full potential of AI in promoting mental well-being on a global scale.

TABLE 1.1

A Comparison of Some of the Available Datasets and the Published Research Articles Related to the Detection of ASD, ADHD, and Schizophrenia

Sl. No	Title	Authors	Data	Summary	Year
1.	Analysis and Detection of Autism Spectrum Disorder Using Machine Learning Techniques	Suman Raja et al.	UCI Repository, which is publicly available.	Attempt to explore the possibility of using different models for predicting and analysis of ASD in children, adolescents, and adults using various state-of-the-art models like naïve Bayes, support vector machine, logistic regression, KNN, neural network, and convolutional neural network.	2020
2.	Facial Features Detection System to Identify Children with Autism Spectrum Disorder: Deep Learning Models	Zeyad A. T. Ahmed et al.	Publicly available dataset on Kaggle.	Facial features detection system to identify children with autism spectrum disorder: deep learning models.	2022
3.	SchiNet: Automatic Estimation of Symptoms of Schizophrenia from Facial Behaviour Analysis	Mina Bishay et al.	The interviews were recorded either at the patients' homes or at the premises of mental health services. The collected videos have a wide range of camera viewpoints and illumination levels that are representative of the variety of settings found in clinics.	Analysing facial features and emotional features using a novel neural network architecture.	2019
4.	Dynamic Deep Learning for Automatic Facial Expression Recognition and its Application in Diagnosis of ADHD and ASD	Shashank Jaiswal	Evaluated on SEMAINE, BP4D, DISFA, CK+. New dataset is also proposed – KOMAA.	Presents a dynamic deep learning framework for robust automatic facial expression recognition. It also proposes an approach to apply this method for facial-behaviour analysis which can help in the diagnosis of conditions like ADHD and ASD.	2018
5.	Prediction of Negative Symptoms of Schizophrenia from Emotion Related Low-level Speech Signals	Debsubhra Chakraborty et al.	The audio and video of 78 participants (52 patients and 26 healthy controls) from IMH are recorded while they are interviewed by a trained psychometrician.	We used low-level acoustic prosodic signals to predict subjective ratings related to emotion assigned by a trained clinician. We also demonstrated that these prosodic signals alone, or in combination with movement signals, could distinguish individuals with schizophrenia from healthy individuals with a high accuracy.	2018

(Continued)

TABLE 1.1 (CONTINUED)

A Comparison of Some of the Available Datasets and the Published Research Articles Related to the Detection of ASD, ADHD, and Schizophrenia

Sl. No	Title	Authors	Data	Summary	Year
6.	Selective Impairment of Basic Emotion Recognition in People with Autism: Discrimination Thresholds for Recognition of Facial Expressions of Varying Intensities	Yongning Song et al.	A new highly sensitive test (included six basic emotions) of facial emotion recognition was used that measured the intensity of stimuli required to make accurate judgements about emotional expressions.	The study used a sensitive facial-emotion test with six emotions. People with ASD needed stronger cues to identify anger, disgust, and fear.	2017
7.	A Gesture Recognition System for Detecting Behavioral Patterns of ADHD	Miguel Ángel Bautista et al.	Tested on a novel multimodal dataset (RGB plus depth) of ADHD children's recordings with behavioural patterns.	Dynamic time-warping plus a set of gesture samples of a certain gesture category using either Gaussian mixture models or an approximation of convex hulls.	2016
8.	Early and Objective Evaluation of the Therapeutic Effects of ADHD Medication Through Movement Analysis Using Video Recording Pixel Subtraction	Ying-Han Lee et al.	The study enrolled 25 patients (23 boys and 2 girls) to assess the therapeutic effects of ADHD medication, utilising SNAP-IV scores and movement analysis. The majority of our participants had ADHD-C, and there was an uneven gender distribution in our cohort.	The study found that parents reported significantly lower SNAP scores compared to teachers. It showed that using pixel subtraction from video images is an objective way to quantitatively assess the early effectiveness of ADHD medication.	2022
9.	Deep Learning Approach for an Early Stage Detection of Neurodevelopmental Disorders	Lakshmi Boppana et Al.	The proposed system is trained using ABIDE, ADHD 200, COBRE, UCLA, WUSTL Datasets.	The input fMRI data is pre-processed using FSL tool and features are extracted using Craddock 400 brain atlas to form a functional connectivity matrix, which is fed to the AlexNet model.	2021
10.	Mental Status Detection for Schizophreni a Patients via Deep Visual Perception	Bing-Jhang Lin et al.	A series of experiments on several benchmark datasets, the results show that the proposed learning framework boosts state-of-the-art (SOTA) methods significantly.	For the learning part, a multi-task learning framework is designed and trained to perform emotion recognition and depression estimation simultaneously. For the detection part, we apply the learned multi-task model to infer the mental state of the patient.	2022

Reference list

Boppana, Lakshmi, Nikhat Shabnam, and Tadikonda Srivatsava. "Deep Learning Approach for an early-stage detection of Neurodevelopmental Disorders." In 2021 IEEE 9th Region 10 Humanitarian Technology Conference (R10-HTC), pp. 1–6. IEEE, 2021.

Torous, John, and Laura Weiss Roberts. "Needed innovation in digital health and smartphone applications for mental health: Transparency and trust." JAMA psychiatry 74, no. 5 (2017): 437–438.

Guntuku, Sharath Chandra, J. Russell Ramsay, Raina M. Merchant, and Lyle H. Ungar. "Language of ADHD in adults on social media." Journal of attention disorders 23, no. 12 (2019): 1475–1485.

Fitzpatrick, Kathleen Kara, Alison Darcy, and Molly Vierhile. "Delivering cognitive behavior therapy to young adults with symptoms of depression and anxiety using a fully automated conversational agent (Woebot): A randomized controlled trial." JMIR mental health 4, no. 2 (2017): e7785.

Freeman, Daniel, Polly Haselton, Jason Freeman, Bernhard Spanlang, Sameer Kishore, Emily Albery, Megan Denne, Poppy Brown, Mel Slater, and Alecia Nickless. "Automated psychological therapy using immersive virtual reality for treatment of fear of heights: A single-blind, parallel-group, randomised controlled trial." The Lancet Psychiatry 5, no. 8 (2018): 625–632.

Mendes, Jean PM, Ivan R. Moura, Pepijn Van de Ven, Davi Viana, Francisco JS Silva, Luciano R. Coutinho, Silmar Teixeira, Joel JPC Rodrigues, and Ariel Soares Teles. "Sensing apps and public data sets for digital phenotyping of mental health: Systematic review." Journal of medical Internet research 24, no. 2 (2022): e28735.

Lee, Jung Hyuk, Geon Woo Lee, Guiyoung Bong, Hee Jeong Yoo, and Hong Kook Kim. "Deep-learning-based detection of infants with autism spectrum disorder using auto-encoder feature representation." Sensors 20, no. 23 (2020): 6762.

Lee, Ying-Han, Chen-Sen Ouyang, Yi-Hung Chiu, Ching-Tai Chiang, Rong-Ching Wu, Rei-Cheng Yang, and Lung-Chang Lin. "Early and objective evaluation of the therapeutic effects of ADHD medication through movement analysis using video recording pixel subtraction." International Journal of Environmental Research and Public Health 19, no. 6 (2022): 3163.

McCutcheon, Robert A., Tiago Reis Marques, and Oliver D. Howes. "Schizophrenia—An overview." JAMA psychiatry 77, no. 2 (2020): 201–210.

Javitt, Daniel C. "Glutamate and schizophrenia: Phencyclidine, N-methyl-d-aspartate receptors, and dopamine–glutamate interactions." International review of neurobiology 78 (2007): 69–108.

Jaiswal, Shashank. "Dynamic deep learning for automatic facial expression recognition and its application in diagnosis of ADHD & ASD." PhD diss., University of Nottingham, 2018.

Huang, Jie, Yanli Zhao, Wei Qu, Zhanxiao Tian, Yunlong Tan, Zhiren Wang, and Shuping Tan. "Automatic recognition of schizophrenia from facial videos using 3D convolutional neural network." Asian Journal of Psychiatry 77 (2022): 103263.

Chakraborty, Debsubhra, Zixu Yang, Yasir Tahir, Tomasz Maszczyk, Justin Dauwels, Nadia Thalmann, Jianmin Zheng et al. "Prediction of negative symptoms of schizophrenia from emotion related low-level speech signals." In 2018 IEEE International Conference on Acoustics, Speech and Signal Processing (ICASSP), pp. 6024–6028. IEEE, 2018.

Song, Yongning, and Yuji Hakoda. "Selective impairment of basic emotion recognition in people with autism: Discrimination thresholds for recognition of facial expressions of varying intensities." Journal of autism and developmental disorders 48 (2018): 1886–1894.

Bautista, Miguel Angel, Antonio Hernández-Vela, Sergio Escalera, Laura Igual, Oriol Pujol, Josep Moya, Verónica Violant, and María T. Anguera. "A gesture recognition system for detecting behavioral patterns of ADHD." IEEE transactions on cybernetics 46, no. 1 (2015): 136–147.

Lee, Ying-Han, Chen-Sen Ouyang, Yi-Hung Chiu, Ching-Tai Chiang, Rong-Ching Wu, Rei-Cheng Yang, and Lung-Chang Lin. "Early and objective evaluation of the therapeutic effects of ADHD medication through movement analysis using video recording pixel subtraction." International Journal of Environmental Research and Public Health 19, no. 6 (2022): 3163.

Lin, Bing-Jhang, Yi-Ting Lin, Chen-Chung Liu, Lue-En Lee, Chih-Yuan Chuang, An-Sheng Liu, Shu-Hui Hung, and Li-Chen Fu. "Mental status detection for schizophrenia patients via deep visual perception." IEEE Journal of Biomedical and Health Informatics 26, no. 11 (2022): 5704–5715.

Fusaro, Vincent A., Jena Daniels, Marlena Duda, Todd F. DeLuca, Olivia D'Angelo, Jenna Tamburello, James Maniscalco, and Dennis P. Wall. "The potential of accelerating early detection of autism through content analysis of YouTube videos." PLOS one 9, no. 4 (2014): e93533.

Oh, Shu Lih, V. Jahmunah, N. Arunkumar, Enas W. Abdulhay, Raj Gururajan, Nahrizul Adib, Edward J. Ciaccio, Kang Hao Cheong, and U. Rajendra Acharya. "A novel automated autism spectrum disorder detection system." Complex & Intelligent Systems 7, no. 5 (2021): 2399–2413.

Bohland, Jason W., Sara Saperstein, Francisco Pereira, Jérémy Rapin, and Leo Grady. "Network, anatomical, and non-imaging measures for the prediction of ADHD diagnosis in individual subjects." Frontiers in systems neuroscience 6 (2012): 78.

Tang, Yibin, Jia Sun, Chun Wang, Yuan Zhong, Aimin Jiang, Gang Liu, and Xiaofeng Liu. "ADHD classification using auto-encoding neural network and binary hypothesis testing." Artificial Intelligence in Medicine 123 (2022): 102209.

Öztoprak, Hüseyin, Mehmet Toycan, Yaşar Kemal Alp, Orhan Arıkan, Elvin Doğutepe, and Sirel Karakaş. "Machine-based classification of ADHD and nonADHD participants using time/frequency features of event-related neuroelectric activity." Clinical Neurophysiology 128, no. 12 (2017): 2400–2410.

Ahmadi, Amirmasoud, Mehrdad Kashefi, Hassan Shahrokhi, and Mohammad Ali Nazari. "Computer aided diagnosis system using deep convolutional neural networks for ADHD subtypes." Biomedical Signal Processing and Control 63 (2021): 102227.

Koh, Joel EW, Chui Ping Ooi, Nikki SJ Lim-Ashworth, Jahmunah Vicnesh, Hui Tian Tor, Oh Shu Lih, Ru-San Tan, U. Rajendra Acharya, and Daniel Shuen Sheng Fung. "Automated classification of attention deficit hyperactivity disorder and conduct disorder using entropy features with ECG signals." Computers in biology and medicine 140 (2022): 105120.

O'Mahony, Niamh, Blanca Florentino-Liano, Juan J. Carballo, Enrique Baca-García, and Antonio Artés Rodríguez. "Objective diagnosis of ADHD using IMUs." Medical engineering & physics 36, no. 7 (2014): 922–926.

Heller, Monika D., Kurt Roots, Sanjana Srivastava, Jennifer Schumann, Jaideep Srivastava, and T. Sigi Hale. "A machine learning-based analysis of game data for attention deficit hyperactivity disorder assessment." GAMES FOR HEALTH: Research, Development, and Clinical Applications 2, no. 5 (2013): 291–298.

Alam, Md Ashad, Hui-Yi Lin, Hong-Wen Deng, Vince D. Calhoun, and Yu-Ping Wang. "A kernel machine method for detecting higher order interactions in multimodal datasets: Application to schizophrenia." Journal of neuroscience methods 309 (2018): 161–174.

Li, Jicheng, Vuthea Chheang, Pinar Kullu, Eli Brignac, Zhang Guo, Kenneth E. Barner, Anjana Bhat, and Roghayeh Leila Barmaki Name. "MMASD: A Multimodal Dataset for Autism Intervention Analysis." arXiv preprint arXiv:2306.08243 (2023).

Ahmed, Zeyad AT, Theyazn HH Aldhyani, Mukti E. Jadhav, Mohammed Y. Alzahrani, Mohammad Eid Alzahrani, Maha M. Althobaiti, Fawaz Alassery, Ahmed Alshaflut, Nouf Matar Alzahrani, and Ali Mansour Al-Madani. "Facial features detection system to identify children with autism spectrum disorder: Deep learning models." Computational and Mathematical Methods in Medicine 2022 (2022).

Bishay, Mina, Petar Palasek, Stefan Priebe, and Ioannis Patras. "Schinet: Automatic estimation of symptoms of schizophrenia from facial behaviour analysis." IEEE Transactions on Affective Computing 12, no. 4 (2019): 949–961.

Chakraborty, Debsubhra, Zixu Yang, Yasir Tahir, Tomasz Maszczyk, Justin Dauwels, Nadia Thalmann, Jianmin Zheng et al. "Prediction of negative symptoms of schizophrenia from emotion related low-level speech signals." In 2018 IEEE International Conference on Acoustics, Speech and Signal Processing (ICASSP), pp. 6024–6028. IEEE, 2018.

Huang, Jie, Yanli Zhao, Wei Qu, Zhanxiao Tian, Yunlong Tan, Zhiren Wang, and Shuping Tan. "Automatic recognition of schizophrenia from facial videos using 3D convolutional neural network." Asian Journal of Psychiatry 77 (2022): 103263

Lee, Wonjun, Sanghyub Lee, Deokwon Lee, Kooksung Jun, Dong Hyun Ahn, and Mun Sang Kim. "Deep Learning-Based ADHD and ADHD-RISK Classification Technology through the Recognition of Children's Abnormal Behaviors during the Robot-Led ADHD Screening Game." *Sensors* 23, no. 1 (2022): 278.

Maniruzzaman, Md, Jungpil Shin, and Md Al Mehedi Hasan. "Predicting children with adhd using behavioral activity: A machine learning analysis." *Applied Sciences* 12, no. 5 (2022): 2737.

Raj, Suman, and Sarfaraz Masood. "Analysis and detection of autism spectrum disorder using machine learning techniques." Procedia Computer Science 167 (2020): 994–1004.

2

Blockchain Applications in Neurological Disorders and Oncology

Gençay Sevim

2.1 Introduction

Blockchain is a decentralized ledger technology that provides a reliable and functional environment for storing and sharing information (Centobelli et al. 2022). It enables two or more parties to securely share information between themselves or store and use information jointly (Centobelli et al. 2022). In this context, it has the potential to be used not only in the field of cryptocurrency but also in many fields. Especially with the integration of different technologies developing in this field into blockchain technology, its use is gradually expanding (Abou Jaoude and Saade 2019). For example, with the integration of smart contracts into blockchain technology, its usage areas have started to increase (Nofer et al. 2017). Blockchain technology supported by these contracts has taken over decentralized autonomous organizations (DAOs). The DAOs have enabled many processes in the blockchain to be automated (Wang et al. 2019).

Today, one is trying to use blockchain-based systems and pilot applications developed for many different areas (Panda et al. 2020). Especially some commercial institutions are trying to benefit from blockchain technology to provide a secure operating mechanism for their commercial transactions (Flore 2018). Also, many commercial and public institutions want to integrate blockchain technology into their systems for transactions, such as keeping official records in such a way that they cannot be manipulated and sharing them with electronic signatures. In addition, one works on creating a blockchain infrastructure to keep track of products or contracts in some areas, such as supply chain, insurance, and so on (Queiroz, Telles, and Bonilla 2020). Apart from these, the use of blockchain in healthcare has also been focused on recently (Ghosh et al. 2023; Haleem et al. 2021; McBee and Wilcox 2020). Before moving on to this topic, let's briefly talk about the basics of blockchain technology.

2.2 Fundamentals of Blockchain Technology

2.2.1 Its History

Blockchain technology, made popular thanks to the Bitcoin, is a technology that has been worked on before. Especially in the 1990s, a series of developments laid the foundations of

DOI: 10.1201/9781003450153-3

this technology. Firstly, Haber and Stornetta, who worked in the field of cryptography, created the first blockchain technology (Haber and Stornetta 1991; Bayer, Haber, and Stornetta 1993). Later, the idea that data in a network could be recorded and shared in an encrypted form led to the emergence of an electronic money idea (Aggarwal and Kumar 2021; Larrier 2021). After these developments, interest in cryptography and electronic money systems increased. In 2008, the crisis that broke out in the banking sector in the USA, firstly affecting the USA and indirectly affecting the world economy, led to discussion about the global banking system. An anonymous person (or people) known as Satoshi Nakamoto put forward a new electronic cash system based on blockchain technology (Nakamoto 2008). This new electronic cash system is known as Bitcoin. Today, the integration of blockchain technology both in the banking system and in different fields such as industry, health, and government institutions, continues the historical development of the blockchain.

2.2.2 How Does a Blockchain Work?

Blockchain structures can be classified in four ways: public, private, hybrid, and consortium. Public blockchains are structures in which anyone can join the network without permission and inspect the information on the network (Ramadoss 2022). Private blockchains have a similar structure to the public blockchain but only those with special permissions or those who belong to the specialized group can be included in the network (Ramadoss 2022). A hybrid blockchain structure is a mixture of public and private blockchain structures (Li et al. 2018). Finally, consortium blockchains can be roughly expressed as the combined state of more than one blockchain, and its predetermined nodes can be thought of as a kind of hybrid blockchain, as they form the basis of the functioning of this network by controlling the consensus mechanisms (Dib et al. 2018). In addition to these blockchain structures, there are also sidechains. One designs sidechains to add functionality or increase scalability to this chain without breaking the main blockchain (Singh et al. 2020). There are different blockchain structures; however, the mechanisms of operation generally work similarly. Some fundamental components of the blockchain should be well-known to understand its working principle better. Peer-to-Peer, Node, Hash Function, Nonce, and Cryptographic Proofs are the most basic structures of a blockchain mechanism. The harmonious operation of these structures ensures the smooth functioning of a blockchain (Zheng et al. 2018).

Peer-to-Peer (P2P) is a network protocol that allows multiple computers to communicate with each other without a central control. It provides a decentralized network, unlike the central servers we currently use (Pourebrahimi, Bertels, and Vassiliadis 2005; Fox 2001). As illustrated in Figure 2.1, (A) represents the central system connected to central servers, and (B) shows the decentralized network structure of the P2P network between peers. Computers connected to this decentralized network can directly share data with each other and provide data to each other thanks to some protocols (Fox 2001). The decentralized nature of this network ensures that the network operates securely in many ways.

The role of the P2P protocol in blockchain technology is very significant because the encrypted data is transmitted in a decentralized way and recorded in a controlled manner by the computers connected to the network, thanks to this protocol (Pourebrahimi, Bertels, and Vassiliadis 2005; Fox 2001).

Node refers to each computer or system connected to the network in the blockchain. Nodes are responsible for the verification, integrity, storage, and security of data on the blockchain. The tasks of each node can differ from each other (Elrom 2019). They also determine the degree of security of the blockchain, as they are also responsible for maintaining

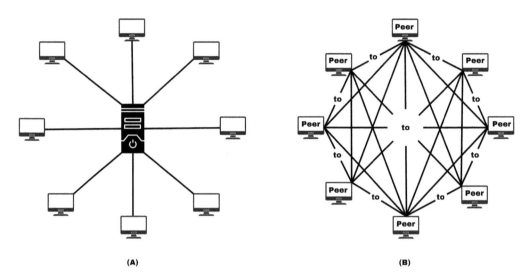

FIGURE 2.1
(A) Centralized structure (B) Decentralized Peer-to-Peer structure.

distributed copies of data. Therefore, the more nodes in the network, the stronger the security mechanism of the network can be (Elrom 2019).

Hash functions are mathematical algorithms that ensure the integrity and confidentiality of the data by converting the data to be added to the blockchain into values/codes (hash codes) in certain standards. The process of these algorithms is called hashing. With the process, data is encrypted and converted into an unpredictable format (Pierro 2017). Each algorithm produces hash codes in different formats with its unique structure. For example, Figure 2.2 shows the hash codes of this chapter's title created with different hash algorithms. One sees that even the lengths of the codes produced are different. Each of these algorithms transform the same data into the same codes and different data into different codes, making a unique encryption (Pierro 2017; Kammoun et al. 2020).

Number Only Used Once (Nonce) value is a random number generated during the hashing process in the blockchain. The block information, block number, and hash information of the previous block in each block are constant, but the nonce value is variable (Hazari and Mahmoud 2019).

Consensus mechanisms are algorithms that verify blocks in the blockchain to be added to the chain. The working mechanisms of each algorithm (Proof-of-Work, Proof-of-Stake, Delegated Proof of Stake, Proof of Capacity, etc.) used for a consensus process are different from each other (Aggarwal and Kumar 2021).

Smart contracts are transaction protocols that control, execute, and store many actions on the blockchain (Khan et al. 2021). They provide opportunities for automated operation to a blockchain, making many transactions on the blockchain easier. Also, they enable paper contracts to be issued without a central regulator and are securely stored as digital contracts on the network (Singh et al. 2020).

Briefly, P2P, Node, Hash, and Proof mechanisms working in harmony with each other and supported by smart contracts ensure the continuity, integrity, and security of a blockchain. These enormous components of blockchain technology have the potential to be able to solve problems in various fields. Therefore, one can study these technologies further and achieve their integration into different areas.

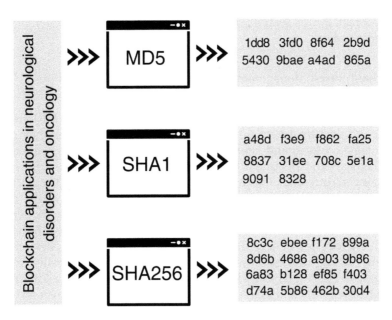

FIGURE 2.2
Different hash codes created with different hash algorithms of the chapter title, "Blockchain application in neurological disorders and oncology and oncology".

2.3 Blockchain Applications in Neurological Disorders and Oncology

After blockchain technology gained popularity with Bitcoin, studies on the integration of blockchain into the financial sector were focused on (Ali, Ally, and Dwivedi 2020), and this technology began to shape the financial sector over time (Chang et al. 2020). It has laid the foundations of a new era in this sector in many ways, such as transparency, security, fast information, verification, and storage of data. After blockchain technology proved itself in the financial sector, its potential for use in other sectors began to be discussed and examined (Hughes et al., 2019). One of these sectors is the health sector.

The worldwide healthcare industry still has many shortcomings, which can be developed (Kuo, Kim, and Ohno-Machado 2017). These shortcomings consist of many areas, such as the medical supply chain, patient record management, clinical trials, medical studies, pharmacological research, health care systems, health insurance, etc. Blockchain has the potential to offer solutions to many of these (Kuo, Kim, and Ohno-Machado 2017). When considering these, it is possible that the health sector will be affected in many ways, now and in the future. However, the integration of blockchain technology into the healthcare sector has brought about some concerns, and this has slowed down its development as well as not being accepted by the sector (Abu-Elezz et al. 2020; Esmaeilzadeh, 2022). However, over time, after these problems are solved, blockchain technology will be integrated into every field. Among these fields, oncology and neurology have priority because they still have several shortcomings and problems to be solved. Of these problems, understanding the mechanisms of some cancer and neurological diseases is critical for improving treatment methods. Also, the post-treatment processes of these diseases are one of the significant factors affecting the course of the diseases. Blockchain technology can offer effective solutions to such these shortcomings that need to be improved in this field. In this context, in this section, one will discuss potential blockchain applications in neurology and oncology.

2.3.1 Blockchain-Based Management of Electronic Health Record (EHR) and Health Information Exchange (HIE)

Health information exchange (HIE) and electronic health records (EHR) are vital for the pre-treatment and post-treatment processes of all diseases. However, they play a critical role for patients with cancer and neurological disorders because these patients have comprehensive diagnosis and treatment processes. For these processes, scientists and physicians specializing in different subjects make collaborative decisions. These processes need to be maintained effectively in terms of the course of the disease. However, current health systems have many deficiencies in the systems that provide this network between groups that will make collaborative decisions or between physicians who need to share data effectively. Also, many features such as data security, scalability, inclusiveness, and data standardization are missing in these systems (Zhang et al., 2018). Especially in recent years, with the increase in cyber-attacks on EHR, there has been a need for a scalable technology that can be shared securely and in a standard way, but that can also cover all health institutions (Luna et al. 2016). Due to its nature, a blockchain can easily overcome deficiencies in existing systems, such as scalability, security, inclusiveness, and standardization. With the distributed structure of the blockchain network, the data security of patients and HIE can be maintained and ensured effectively to certain standards (Gordon and Catalini 2018). In this way, scientists and physicians who will make vital decisions in neurology and oncology can easily share data and offer impactful solutions to the diagnosis and treatment of diseases. In accordance with this purpose, one has put forward different examples that ensure the safe storage and sharing of patient data. These examples and blockchain prototypes have stated that they can close the gaps in the health sector, such as data security and sharing (Barbaria et al., 2022; Buzachis et al. 2019; Ekblaw et al. 2016; Esmaeilzadeh and Mirzaei 2019; Gropper 2016; Murugan et al. 2020; Zhang et al. 2018). These studied blockchain technologies can effectively maintain interoperability and HIE in neurological and oncological diseases. This means an effective healthcare system for the treatment and care of patients. In addition, one has also proposed a blockchain framework for a blockchain-based healthcare system targeting oncology patients for this purpose (Dubovitskaya et al. 2017). The use of blockchain technology in healthcare not only makes interoperability effective but lays the foundations of a patient-centered healthcare system for patients with cancer and neurological disorders. The patient-centered healthcare system allows universal access to the records of patients with cancer and neurological diseases (Gordon and Catalini 2018; Hylock and Zeng 2019). This situation has brought out some problems, such as legal mechanisms, security problems, and patient privacy. However, it may be possible to solve these problems thanks to blockchain technology. There are some studies for this, which are still in development (Hylock and Zeng 2019; Wu and Du 2019).

Keeping these EHRs on the blockchain also makes global patient records accessible. Access to patient records is currently being done separately among some health institutions. However, these records will be accessible to all health institutions globally with the help of blockchain technology (Manion and Bizouati-Kennedy 2020). In short, blockchain has the potential to create a communication network that includes all healthcare institutions around the world. Thanks to blockchain-based healthcare, patients who change city, state, or country will be able to easily continue their treatment or control wherever they go.

The movement of patients with neurological and oncological diseases that require sensitive and long-term treatment will no longer be an obstacle to their treatment.

2.3.2 Blockchain-Based Management of Medical Supply Chain

Many institutions and organizations need a technological system to quickly access information about products and monitor and control some information. It has been realized that blockchain technology can meet this need. Therefore, some companies have worked on blockchain-based supply chain systems (Azzi, Chamoun, and Sokhn 2019; Kamath, 2018; Tan et al. 2018).

The potential for its use in the supply chain has opened a new field for blockchain technology: the medical supply chain. The integration of blockchain into the medical supply chain can make medical devices and supplies, even medicines, trackable (Nanda, Panda, and Dash 2023; Yue and Fu 2020). For example, a health organization purchasing a medical device can easily follow the transport conditions and status of the device. Also, the organization can check whether medical supplies that need to be transported under certain temperature conditions are, indeed, being transported under those conditions. This technology may also contribute to neurology and oncology. Surveillance and follow-up of anti-cancer drugs is of vital importance. If one does not provide proper anti-cancer drug supply-chain management, it may harm both patients and the environment (Ouasrhir, Rahhali, and Boukhatem 2019; Stocker et al., 2022; Fentie et al., 2023). It will be advantageous to have an auditable and traceable procurement process to confirm that the drugs are in applicable conditions for the patients and to prevent counterfeit drugs.

The blockchain-based medical supply chain can also have an economic impact. Such a supply chain can predict whether drugs have the potential to be reused because it provides the traceability of use in the cases of many expensive drugs. For this purpose, one has made some FDA-approved pilot applications that can provide more cost-effective use of highly expensive chemotherapeutics (Benniche 2019). These applications are aimed at being able to administer drugs left over from cancer patients undergoing treatment to other patients. If cancer patients do not need chemotherapeutics after a certain use or if the patient's condition results in death, some of the chemotherapeutics are usually wasted. One has used blockchain technology to prevent this and to offer treatment to more people. In this way, one followed up chemotherapeutics, and used the remaining drugs for different patients. One of these pilot applications is RemediChain (Benniche 2019). It was stated that thanks to the drugs donated to this practice, more patients were treated, and the economic waste based on drugs began to be reduced. As such practices develop and become widespread, more patients will be treated, and the waste of medicine will be prevented.

2.3.3 Blockchain-Based Medical Research and Pharmacological Studies

Blockchain technology allows information to be shared immutably and transparently, thanks to its decentralized network structure consisting of distributed nodes. Although this sharing is seen in the transactions of cryptocurrencies today, it is in a structure that can close an important gap in the scientific world. In the scientific world, many research groups work independently of each other, and for this reason, the data they produce cannot be tested effectively by different groups. Thanks to blockchain technology, scientists can share their scientific data and outputs over a network with each other (Lee and Yoon 2022). Therefore, one can easily control the accuracy of the produced data.

There is much research for new diagnostic and treatment methods in neurology and oncology. Multidisciplinary teams, usually consisting of people with different fields of expertise, such as physicians, physicists and biophysicists, biologists and molecular biologists, chemists, technologists, histologists, physiologists, pharmacists, biostatisticians, etc., conduct all research. It is backbreaking for such wide-ranging teams to come together on-site and share information. For this, they can connect online through some meeting applications. However, at this stage, a security problem arises. In many scientific studies, the confidentiality of data and information is significant until the research ends, and the results are published. Therefore, a more secure and effective system is needed. Blockchain technology has a structure that can meet this need. Thanks to its security, immutable, and transparency features, it can play a vital role in maintaining medical research effectively (Lee and Yoon 2022).

In addition, blockchain-based medical research has focused on pharmaceutical research. Especially, therapeutic agents and systems are still being developed for the treatment of cancer and neurodegenerative disorders. At this stage, it becomes difficult to find effective treatment methods due to the excessive costs of materials, difficulties in preclinical research and clinical studies, and deficiencies in evaluating the results (Clauson et al. 2022). Clinical trials and phase studies are among the most crucial stages of impactful drug development in pharmacological research because one examines the possible effects of the drug developed with these studies on human subjects. At this stage, one can make some mistakes or commit fraud while collecting data. This situation brings with it many problems (Hang et al. 2022). However, blockchain technology can overcome difficulties and deficiencies in pharmaceutical research and development. The use of blockchain technology can be beneficial, especially in studies conducted from preclinical research to phase 4. In this context blockchain-based pharmacology applications have been studied in recent years (Hang et al. 2022; Clauson et al. 2022). These studies are based on many stages that influence pharmaceutical research, such as clinical trial recruitment, obtaining patient consent, data collection and coordinating data, controlling manipulation of clinical trial data, and more (Benchoufi, Porcher, and Ravaud 2017; Nugent, Upton, and Cimpoesu 2016; Omar et al. 2020; Tith et al. 2020; Wong, Bhattacharya, and Butte 2019).

In conclusion, blockchain technology can increase the effectiveness and reliability of such pharmacological research. In addition, it can automate data sharing and storage. In this way, it can be ensured that therapeutic agents or systems to be used in cancer and neurodegenerative diseases can be evaluated and applied effectively. Also, one can eliminate false or fraudulent information about them.

2.3.4 Controllable IoMT-Based Medical Devices via Blockchain

With the development of technology, communication networks digitized in the form of the internet have played a leading role in the emerging concept of the Internet of Things (IoT). Objects used at home, used individually in daily life, or used in industry have started to communicate via the internet with each other. The synchronization and control of all objects connected to a network has become possible with the concept of the IoT (Khodadadi, Dastjerdi, and Buyya 2016). This situation has also revealed the potential of controlling medical objects by connecting to the internet and providing data communication with them. This has led to the emerging concept of the Internet of Medical

Things (IoMT) (Limaye and Adegbija 2018). The IoMT has provided the ability to check the patient's health data periodically and store it with various sensors and networked equipment.

With the inclusion of blockchain technology in this system, the IoMT, and medical devices have gained the potential to be used more effectively. Devices connected to the network have become reliably controlled and usable with blockchain technology. Therefore, it has enabled security in devices used for many diseases, including cancer and neurological disorders (Aileni and Suciu 2020). For example, when there is a malfunction in a medical device and the specialist in charge of the device is not aware of it, life-threatening consequences can occur. However, one can notice a problem occurring in a device connected to the blockchain network immediately, and thus one can respond to the problem quickly. An example of this is a pilot study conducted with university–industry cooperation in Scotland. In this pilot study, one instantly accessed information such as the status of the device, its location, and expert personnel information for each medical device (Clauson et al. 2018). As such blockchain-based medical supply chain networks develop and become widespread, the persons with permission will easily access information, such as which devices are operating effectively throughout the city and even the country, what medical devices are in a health institution, who is responsible for these devices, and what the usage status of the devices are. In this way, devices that are used for patients with cancer and neurodegenerative disorders and need to be constantly checked can be effectively monitored.

In addition, some cancers, such as, particularly, lung cancer, progress aggressively. The use of IoMT systems is crucial for the early diagnosis of these cancers. Integration of these systems with the blockchain can improve early diagnosis systems and change the prognostics for these cancers because lung cancer symptoms usually appear in the advanced stages of the disease. In particular, these technologies can provide early diagnosis of lung cancer by enhancing nodule prediction and malignancy level detection. For example, a study using artificial intelligence, IoT, and blockchain technology suggested that nodule prediction and malignancy level detection can be improved using lungscan images (Pawar et al. 2022). Like this study, another study showed that osteosarcomas can be detected with a blockchain and IoMT-supported deep learning–based detection method (Nasir et al. 2022). By this means, cancers can be diagnosed at an early stage and treated effectively.

In addition to these applications, as an outcome of IoT and blockchain technologies, the metaverse-based healthcare system can contribute to the pre-treatment and post-treatment processes of patients with cancer and neurological diseases. Metaverse technology emerged thanks to the integration of IoT components such as virtual reality (VR), augmented reality (AR), and mixed reality with blockchain technology. One can briefly express metaverse as a blockchain-based virtual environment accessed through visual and audio IoT components (Zeng et al. 2022). Studies on its use in the health sector are still ongoing. It is being developed as an educational platform in medicine or a practice platform that will allow intern students to gain experience (Sandrone 2022). Moreover, the blockchain-based metaverse can reduce the heavy care burden of cancer patients and patients with neurological diseases. To effectively maintain the care of these patients, appropriate care can be provided via the metaverse using IoMT systems where instant health data is received and analyzed. It can even play a crucial role in the treatment and post-treatment processes of cancer and neurological disorders by making many contributions to telemedicine, which is becoming increasingly widespread today (Zeng et al. 2022; Yang et al. 2022).

2.3.5 Blockchain-Based Genomic Research

Blockchain technology can also be used for processing, storing, and sharing genomic data in cancer and neurological disorders research. Since cancer is a disease caused by genomic changes (Weber 2002; Chin, Andersen, and Futreal 2011) and some neurological disorders may be based on genomic changes (Han et al. 2014; Simón-Sánchez and Singleton 2008), genomic research may lead to the development of new and effective treatments and even personalized treatment methods for cancer and neurological disorders. Processing genomic data in genomic studies can cause excessive computational load. One needs innovative technologies to overcome this load more effectively and to store genomic data more securely. At that point, blockchain technology will be able to help eliminate or alleviate many of these problems (Ozercan et al. 2018; Alghazwi et al. 2022; Dedeturk, Soran, and Bakir-Gungor 2021).

2.4 Conclusion

The potential of blockchain technology in cancer and neurologic diseases is currently limited. However, considering the features of blockchain technology and the innovations it brings, its integration into these areas is inevitable. Although there are few blockchain-based studies in these areas, as blockchain technology is better understood and adopted, studies will increase over time. In fact, this technology is not limited to oncology and neurology. Blockchain technology in the entire healthcare industry is still in its infancy. Accelerating this stage will ensure that the integration of this technology into the health sector will be faster. Rapid integration is a situation that is predicted to provide advantages to the health sector in many ways. However, there are some crucial challenges at this stage. One can address these challenges from various aspects. Firstly, the lack of acceptance of blockchain technology is one of the biggest obstacles. The fact that it is a new technology and most people in the healthcare industry do not know about it raises doubts about its integration into this sector. In addition, the lack of standards and regulations about the usage of blockchain technology in the health sector can also trigger doubts. This situation leads to slowness in blockchain research and integration.

Another obstacle that may affect the applicability of blockchain to the health sector is the complex nature of health data. Although one makes some standards and classifications in health data, complex and irregular medical data can make the integration of blockchain technology difficult because one should create a blockchain structure with 3-D data flow rather than 1-D or 2-D data flow.

With the elimination of many obstacles like these, one will use blockchain technology in many areas in the future. Just as people have gotten used to and embraced the internet in the present, they will also get used to and embrace blockchain technology in the future.

Acknowledgements

I would like to express my heartfelt thanks to my wife, Betül Sevim, who assisted in the design of the figures, evaluated the first draft of chapter, and helped me see the deficiencies.

References

Abou Jaoude, Joe, and Raafat George Saade. 2019. 'Blockchain Applications–Usage in Different Domains'. *IEEE Access* 7: 45360–81.

Abu-Elezz, Israa, Asma Hassan, Anjanarani Nazeemudeen, Mowafa Househ, and Alaa Abd-Alrazaq. 2020. 'The Benefits and Threats of Blockchain Technology in Healthcare: A Scoping Review'. *International Journal of Medical Informatics* 142: 104246.

Aggarwal, Shubhani, and Neeraj Kumar. 2021. 'Cryptographic Consensus Mechanisms'. *Advances in Computers* 121: 211–26. Elsevier.

Aileni, Raluca Maria, and George Suciu. 2020. 'IoMT: A Blockchain Perspective'. In Mohammad Ayoub Khan, Mohammad Tabrez Quasim, Fahad Algarni, Abdullah Alharthi (eds) *Decentralised Internet of Things: A Blockchain Perspective*, 199–215, Springer, Cham.

Alghazwi, Mohammed, Fatih Turkmen, Joeri Van Der Velde, and Dimka Karastoyanova. 2022. 'Blockchain for Genomics: A Systematic Literature Review'. *Distributed Ledger Technologies: Research and Practice* 1 (2): 1–28.

Ali, Omar, Mustafa Ally, and Yogesh Dwivedi. 2020. 'The State of Play of Blockchain Technology in the Financial Services Sector: A Systematic Literature Review'. *International Journal of Information Management* 54: 102199.

Azzi, Rita, Rima Kilany Chamoun, and Maria Sokhn. 2019. 'The Power of a Blockchain-Based Supply Chain'. *Computers & Industrial Engineering* 135: 582–92.

Barbaria, Sabri, Marco Casassa Mont, Essam Ghadafi, Halima Mahjoubi Machraoui, and Hanene Boussi Rahmouni. 2022. 'Leveraging Patient Information Sharing Using Blockchain-Based Distributed Networks'. *IEEE Access* 10: 106334–51.

Bayer, Dave, Stuart Haber, and W Scott Stornetta. 1993. 'Improving the Efficiency and Reliability of Digital Time-Stamping'. In Renato Capocelli, Alfredo De Santis, Ugo Vaccaro (eds) *Sequences II: Methods in Communication, Security, and Computer Science*, 329–34. Springer, Verlag New York.

Benchoufi, Mehdi, Raphael Porcher, and Philippe Ravaud. 2017. 'Blockchain Protocols in Clinical Trials: Transparency and Traceability of Consent'. *F1000Research* 6, 1–66.

Benniche, Saffya. 2019. 'Using Blockchain Technology to Recycle Cancer Drugs'. *The Lancet Oncology* 20 (6): e300.

Buzachis, Alina, Antonio Celesti, Maria Fazio, and Massimo Villari. 2019. 'On the Design of a Blockchain-as-a-Service-Based Health Information Exchange (BaaS-HIE) System for Patient Monitoring'. In *2019 IEEE Symposium on Computers and Communications (ISCC)*, 1–6. IEEE.

Centobelli, Piera, Roberto Cerchione, Pasquale Del Vecchio, Eugenio Oropallo, and Giustina Secundo. 2022. 'Blockchain Technology for Bridging Trust, Traceability and Transparency in Circular Supply Chain'. *Information & Management* 59 (7): 103508.

Chang, Victor, Patricia Baudier, Hui Zhang, Qianwen Xu, Jingqi Zhang, and Mitra Arami. 2020. 'How Blockchain Can Impact Financial Services–The Overview, Challenges and Recommendations from Expert Interviewees'. *Technological Forecasting and Social Change* 158: 120166.

Chin, Lynda, Jannik N. Andersen, and P. Andrew Futreal. 2011. 'Cancer Genomics: From Discovery Science to Personalized Medicine'. *Nature Medicine* 17 (3): 297–303.

Clauson, Kevin A., Elizabeth A. Breeden, Cameron Davidson, and Timothy K. Mackey. 2018. 'Leveraging Blockchain Technology to Enhance Supply Chain Management in Healthcare: An Exploration of Challenges and Opportunities in the Health Supply Chain'. *Blockchain in Healthcare Today*, 1–12.

Clauson, Kevin A., Rachel D. Crouch, Elizabeth A. Breeden, and Nicole Salata. 2022. 'Blockchain in Pharmaceutical Research and the Pharmaceutical Value Chain'. In Wendy Charles (ed) *Blockchain in Life Sciences*, 25–52. Springer, Singapore.

Dedeturk, Beyhan Adanur, Ahmet Soran, and Burcu Bakir-Gungor. 2021. 'Blockchain for Genomics and Healthcare: A Literature Review, Current Status, Classification and Open Issues'. *PeerJ* 9: e12130.

Dib, Omar, Kei-Leo Brousmiche, Antoine Durand, Eric Thea, and Elyes Ben Hamida. 2018. 'Consortium Blockchains: Overview, Applications and Challenges'. *International Journal On Advances in Telecommunications* 11 (1): 51–64.

Dubovitskaya, Alevtina, Zhigang Xu, Samuel Ryu, Michael Schumacher, and Fusheng Wang. 2017. 'Secure and Trustable Electronic Medical Records Sharing Using Blockchain'. In *AMIA Annual Symposium Proceedings* 2017: 650. American Medical Informatics Association.

Ekblaw, Ariel, Asaph Azaria, John D. Halamka, and Andrew Lippman. 2016. 'A Case Study for Blockchain in Healthcare:"MedRec" Prototype for Electronic Health Records and Medical Research Data'. In *Proceedings of IEEE Open & Big Data Conference* 13: 13.

Elrom, Elad. 2019. 'Blockchain Nodes'. In *The Blockchain Developer: A Practical Guide for Designing, Implementing, Publishing, Testing, and Securing Distributed Blockchain-Based Projects*, edited by Elad Elrom, 31–72. Berkeley, CA: Apress. https://doi.org/10.1007/978-1-4842-4847-8_2.

Esmaeilzadeh, Pouyan. 2022. 'Benefits and Concerns Associated with Blockchain-Based Health Information Exchange (HIE): A Qualitative Study from Physicians' Perspectives'. *BMC Medical Informatics and Decision Making* 22 (1): 80.

Esmaeilzadeh, Pouyan, and Tala Mirzaei. 2019. 'The Potential of Blockchain Technology for Health Information Exchange: Experimental Study from Patients' Perspectives'. *Journal of Medical Internet Research* 21 (6): e14184.

Fentie, Atalay Mulu, Zelalem Tilahun Mekonen, Zelalem Gizachew, Mahlet Hailemariam, Stephen M. Clark, Jaime Richardson, and Benyam Muluneh. 2023. 'Chemotherapy Supply Chain Management, Safe-Handling and Disposal in Ethiopia: The Case of Tikur Anbessa Specialized Hospital'. *Pediatric Hematology and Oncology* 40 (3): 258–66.

Flore, Massimo. 2018. 'How Blockchain-Based Technology Is Disrupting Migrants' Remittances: A Preliminary Assessment'. Luxembourg: EUR 29492.

Fox, Geoffrey. 2001. 'Peer-to-Peer Networks'. *Computing in Science & Engineering* 3 (3): 75–77.

Ghosh, Pranto Kumar, Arindom Chakraborty, Mehedi Hasan, Khalid Rashid, and Abdul Hasib Siddique. 2023. 'Blockchain Application in Healthcare Systems: A Review'. *Systems* 11 (1): 38.

Gordon, William J., and Christian Catalini. 2018. 'Blockchain Technology for Healthcare: Facilitating the Transition to Patient-Driven Interoperability'. *Computational and Structural Biotechnology Journal* 16: 224–30.

Gropper, Adrian. 2016. 'Powering the Physician-Patient Relationship with HIE of One Blockchain Health IT'. In *ONC/NIST Use of Blockchain for Healthcare and Research Workshop*. Gaithersburg, Maryland: ONC/NIST. Vol. 212.

Haber, Stuart, and W. Scott Stornetta. 1991. *How to Time-Stamp a Digital Document*. In: Menezes, A.J., Vanstone, S.A. (eds) *Advances in Cryptology-CRYPTO' 90. CRYPTO 1990. Lecture Notes in Computer Science*, vol 537, Springer, Berlin, Heidelberg.

Haleem, Abid, Mohd Javaid, Ravi Pratap Singh, Rajiv Suman, and Shanay Rab. 2021. 'Blockchain Technology Applications in Healthcare: An Overview'. *International Journal of Intelligent Networks* 2: 130–39.

Han, Guangchun, Jiya Sun, Jiajia Wang, Zhouxian Bai, Fuhai Song, and Hongxing Lei. 2014. 'Genomics in Neurological Disorders'. *Genomics, Proteomics & Bioinformatics* 12 (4): 156–63.

Hang, Lei, Chun Chen, Linchao Zhang, and Jun Yang. 2022. 'Blockchain for Applications of Clinical Trials: Taxonomy, Challenges, and Future Directions'. *IET Communications* 16 (20): 2371–93.

Hazari, S. S., and Q. H. Mahmoud. 2019. 'A Parallel Proof of Work to Improve Transaction Speed and Scalability in Blockchain Systems'. In *2019 IEEE 9th Annual Computing and Communication Workshop and Conference (CCWC)*, 916–21. https://doi.org/10.1109/CCWC.2019.8666535.

Hughes, Alex, Andrew Park, Jan Kietzmann, and Chris Archer-Brown. 2019. 'Beyond Bitcoin: What Blockchain and Distributed Ledger Technologies Mean for Firms'. *Business Horizons* 62 (3): 273–81.

Hylock, Ray Hales, and Xiaoming Zeng. 2019. 'A Blockchain Framework for Patient-Centered Health Records and Exchange (HealthChain): Evaluation and Proof-of-Concept Study'. *Journal of Medical Internet Research* 21 (8): e13592.

Kamath, Reshma. 2018. 'Food Traceability on Blockchain: Walmart's Pork and Mango Pilots with IBM'. *The Journal of the British Blockchain Association* 1 (1), 47–53.

Kammoun, M., M. Elleuchi, M. Abid, and M. S. BenSaleh. 2020. 'FPGA-Based Implementation of the SHA-256 Hash Algorithm'. In *2020 IEEE International Conference on Design & Test of Integrated Micro & Nano-Systems (DTS)*, 1–6. https://doi.org/10.1109/DTS48731.2020.9196134.

Khan, Shafaq Naheed, Faiza Loukil, Chirine Ghedira-Guegan, Elhadj Benkhelifa, and Anoud Bani-Hani. 2021. 'Blockchain Smart Contracts: Applications, Challenges, and Future Trends'. *Peer-to-Peer Networking and Applications* 14: 2901–25.

Khodadadi, F., A. V. Dastjerdi, and R. Buyya. 2016. 'Chapter 1 - Internet of Things: An Overview'. In *Internet of Things*, edited by Rajkumar Buyya and Amir Vahid Dastjerdi, 3–27. Morgan Kaufmann. https://doi.org/10.1016/B978-0-12-805395-9.00001-0.

Kuo, Tsung-Ting, Hyeon-Eui Kim, and Lucila Ohno-Machado. 2017. 'Blockchain Distributed Ledger Technologies for Biomedical and Health Care Applications'. *Journal of the American Medical Informatics Association* 24 (6): 1211–20.

Larrier, John H. 2021. 'A Brief History of Blockchain'. In Darrell Wayne Gunter (ed) *Transforming Scholarly Publishing With Blockchain Technologies and AI*, 85–100, IGI Global, Hershey.

Lee, Eunhee, and Yongik Yoon. 2022. 'Trusted Information Project Platform Based on Blockchain for Sharing Strategy'. *Journal of Ambient Intelligence and Humanized Computing*: 13, 1575–1585.

Li, Zhijie, Haoyan Wu, Brian King, Zina Ben Miled, John Wassick, and Jeffrey Tazelaar. 2018. 'A Hybrid Blockchain Ledger for Supply Chain Visibility'. In *2018 17th International Symposium on Parallel and Distributed Computing (ISPDC)*, 118–25. IEEE.

Limaye, Ankur, and Tosiron Adegbija. 2018. 'HERMIT: A Benchmark Suite for the Internet of Medical Things'. *IEEE Internet of Things Journal* 5 (5): 4212–22.

Luna, Raul, Emily Rhine, Matthew Myhra, Ross Sullivan, and Clemens Scott Kruse. 2016. 'Cyber Threats to Health Information Systems: A Systematic Review'. *Technology and Health Care* 24 (1): 1–9.

Manion, Sean T., and Yaël Bizouati-Kennedy. 2020. *Blockchain for Medical Research: Accelerating Trust in Healthcare*. CRC Press, New York.

McBee, Morgan P., and Chad Wilcox. 2020. 'Blockchain Technology: Principles and Applications in Medical Imaging'. *Journal of Digital Imaging* 33: 726–34.

Murugan, A., Tushar Chechare, B. Muruganantham, and S. Ganesh Kumar. 2020. 'Healthcare Information Exchange Using Blockchain Technology'. *International Journal of Electrical and Computer Engineering* 10 (1): 421.

Nakamoto, Satoshi. 2008. 'Bitcoin: A Peer-to-Peer Electronic Cash System'. Available at SSRN 3440802.

Nanda, Saroj Kumar, Sandeep Kumar Panda, and Madhabananda Dash. 2023. 'Medical Supply Chain Integrated with Blockchain and IoT to Track the Logistics of Medical Products'. *Multimedia Tools and Applications*: 82, 32917–32939 .

Nasir, Muhammad Umar, Safiullah Khan, Shahid Mehmood, Muhammad Adnan Khan, Atta-ur Rahman, and Seong Oun Hwang. 2022. 'IoMT-Based Osteosarcoma Cancer Detection in Histopathology Images Using Transfer Learning Empowered with Blockchain, Fog Computing, and Edge Computing'. *Sensors* 22 (14). https://doi.org/10.3390/s22145444.

Nofer, Michael, Peter Gomber, Oliver Hinz, and Dirk Schiereck. 2017. 'Blockchain'. *Business & Information Systems Engineering* 59: 183–87.

Nugent, Timothy, David Upton, and Mihai Cimpoesu. 2016. 'Improving Data Transparency in Clinical Trials Using Blockchain Smart Contracts'. *F1000Research* 5, 1–7.

Omar, Ilhaam A., Raja Jayaraman, Khaled Salah, Mecit Can Emre Simsekler, Ibrar Yaqoob, and Samer Ellahham. 2020. 'Ensuring Protocol Compliance and Data Transparency in Clinical Trials Using Blockchain Smart Contracts'. *BMC Medical Research Methodology* 20: 1–17.

Ouasrhir, Abdelali, Rabie Rahhali, and Noureddine Boukhatem. 2019. 'Chemotherapy Supply Chain Safety: Current Data from Public Oncology Centers in Morocco'. *European Journal of Oncology Pharmacy* 2 (3). https://journals.lww.com/ejop/fulltext/2019/09000/chemotherapy_supply _chain_safety__current_data.3.aspx.

Ozercan, Halil Ibrahim, Atalay Mert Ileri, Erman Ayday, and Can Alkan. 2018. 'Realizing the Potential of Blockchain Technologies in Genomics'. *Genome Research* 28 (9): 1255–63.

Panda, Sandeep Kumar, Ahmed A. Elngar, Valentina Emilia Balas, and Mohammed Kayed. 2020. *Bitcoin and Blockchain: History and Current Applications*. CRC Press.

Pawar, A. B., M. A. Jawale, P. William, G. S. Chhabra, Dhananjay S. Rakshe, Sachin K. Korde, and Nikhil Marriwala. 2022. 'Implementation of Blockchain Technology Using Extended CNN for Lung Cancer Prediction'. *Measurement: Sensors* 24: 100530. https://doi.org/10.1016/j.measen .2022.100530.

Pierro, M. Di. 2017. 'What Is the Blockchain?' *Computing in Science & Engineering* 19 (5): 92–95. https://doi.org/10.1109/MCSE.2017.3421554.

Pourebrahimi, B., K. Bertels, and S. Vassiliadis. 2005. 'A Survey of Peer-to-Peer Networks'. In *Proceedings of the 16th Annual Workshop on Circuits, Systems and Signal Processing*, 570–77.

Queiroz, Maciel M., Renato Telles, and Silvia H. Bonilla. 2020. 'Blockchain and Supply Chain Management Integration: A Systematic Review of the Literature'. *Supply Chain Management: An International Journal* 25 (2): 241–54.

Ramadoss, R. 2022. 'Blockchain Technology: An Overview'. *IEEE Potentials* 41 (6): 6–12. https://doi .org/10.1109/MPOT.2022.3208395.

Sandrone, Stefano. 2022. 'Medical Education in the Metaverse'. *Nature Medicine* 28 (12): 2456–57.

Simón-Sánchez, Javier, and Andrew Singleton. 2008. 'Genome-Wide Association Studies in Neurological Disorders'. *The Lancet Neurology* 7 (11): 1067–72.

Singh, Amritraj, Reza M. Parizi, Qi Zhang, Kim-Kwang Raymond Choo, and Ali Dehghantanha. 2020. 'Blockchain Smart Contracts Formalization: Approaches and Challenges to Address Vulnerabilities'. *Computers & Security* 88: 101654.

Stocker, Kurtis J., Andrew Tiemann, Kelly M. Brunk, Bemnat Agegnehu, Kaitlyn Buhlinger, Lindsey Amerine, Megan C. Roberts, Jacqueline E. McLaughlin, Stephen M. Clark, and Robert Rose. 2022. 'Processes and Perceptions of Chemotherapy Supply Chain in Ethiopia: A Mixed-Method Study'. *Journal of Oncology Pharmacy Practice*: 10781552221134254.

Tan, Bowen, Jiaqi Yan, Si Chen, and Xingchen Liu. 2018. 'The Impact of Blockchain on Food Supply Chain: The Case of Walmart'. In *Smart Blockchain: First International Conference, SmartBlock 2018, Tokyo, Japan, December 10–12, 2018, Proceedings 1*, 167–77. Springer.

Tith, Dara, Joong-Sun Lee, Hiroyuki Suzuki, WMAB Wijesundara, Naoko Taira, Takashi Obi, and Nagaaki Ohyama. 2020. 'Patient Consent Management by a Purpose-Based Consent Model for Electronic Health Record Based on Blockchain Technology'. *Healthcare Informatics Research* 26 (4): 265–73.

Wang, Shuai, Wenwen Ding, Juanjuan Li, Yong Yuan, Liwei Ouyang, and Fei-Yue Wang. 2019. 'Decentralized Autonomous Organizations: Concept, Model, and Applications'. *IEEE Transactions on Computational Social Systems* 6 (5): 870–78.

Weber, Barbara L. 2002. 'Cancer Genomics'. *Cancer Cell* 1 (1): 37–47.

Wong, Daniel R., Sanchita Bhattacharya, and Atul J. Butte. 2019. 'Prototype of Running Clinical Trials in an Untrustworthy Environment Using Blockchain'. *Nature Communications* 10 (1): 917.

Wu, Sihua, and Jiang Du. 2019. 'Electronic Medical Record Security Sharing Model Based on Blockchain'. In *Proceedings of the 3rd International Conference on Cryptography, Security and Privacy*, 13–17.

Yang, Dawei, Jian Zhou, Rongchang Chen, Yuanlin Song, Zhenju Song, Xiaoju Zhang, Qi Wang, et al. 2022. 'Expert Consensus on the Metaverse in Medicine'. *Clinical EHealth* 5: 1–9. https://doi .org/10.1016/j.ceh.2022.02.001.

Yaqoob, Ibrar, Khaled Salah, Raja Jayaraman, and Yousof Al-Hammadi. 2021. 'Blockchain for Healthcare Data Management: Opportunities, Challenges, and Future Recommendations'. *Neural Computing and Applications*: 34, 11475–11490.

Yue, Yaoming, and Xueliang Fu. 2020. 'Research on Medical Equipment Supply Chain Management Method Based on Blockchain Technology'. In *2020 International Conference on Service Science (ICSS)*, 143–48. IEEE.

Zeng, Yingchun, Linghui Zeng, Chong Zhang, and Andy S. K. Cheng. 2022. 'The Metaverse in Cancer Care: Applications and Challenges'. *Asia-Pacific Journal of Oncology Nursing* 9 (12), 100111.

Zhang, Peng, Jules White, Douglas C. Schmidt, Gunther Lenz, and S. Trent Rosenbloom. 2018. 'FHIRChain: Applying Blockchain to Securely and Scalably Share Clinical Data'. *Computational and Structural Biotechnology Journal* 16: 267–78.

Zheng, Zibin, Shaoan Xie, Hong-Ning Dai, Xiangping Chen, and Huaimin Wang. 2018. 'Blockchain Challenges and Opportunities: A Survey'. *International Journal of Web and Grid Services* 14 (4): 352–75.

3

Deep Scattering Wavelet Network and Marine Predators Algorithm-Based Stuttering Disfluency Detection

Roohum Jegan, Bhakti Kaushal, Gajanan K. Birajdar, and Mukesh D. Patil

3.1 Introduction

Speech is a vital and powerful gift given to human beings. The ability to express our thoughts, feelings, and emotions by moving lips, jaw, tongue, and teeth to produce meaningful sounds is called articulation of speech. It is an important tool to communicate and share ideas with each other [1]. Speech development is a crucial factor in a child's learning and development. Stuttering, stammering, or disfluency in speech is a speech disorder. More than 3 million individuals suffer from speech disorders in the USA [2]. It affects individuals of all ages, but mostly, it is present in children between the ages of 2 and 6 during a child's speech development years.

For a few weeks to some years' time, approximately 5 to 10% of children do stutter to some extent in their lives [2]. Boys suffer from speech disfluency two to three times more compared to girls, and with age, the gender difference increases, and the ratio becomes three to four times more. As children mature with age, most of them stop stuttering and speak normally. Speech disfluency persists in approximately 25% of children, and it becomes a lifelong disorder. However, approximately 75% of children recover from it and start speaking normally [2].

A person suffering from speech disorder repeats sounds or words or interrupts a speech with prolonged silence, also called blocks. A person who stammers has the ability to think and knows what to communicate but is unable to make a normal flow of speech. These interruptions may go along with rapid blinking of eyes, trembling of lips, or legs [1]. A child with speech difficulties can have poor concentration and attention. They have miserable social skills, and hence, they are difficult to understand by others. It affects an individual badly with their interpersonal relationships and quality of life. It also impacts a person negatively with such job opportunities where communicating with others is key. A person's stuttering symptoms may become severe when they are speaking in public, in a group, or during a telephone conversation, and it reduces when they are practicing alone or simultaneously performing with others.

Earlier, speech disfluency was believed to occur due to psychogenesis attributed to behavioral disturbances or emotional trauma, but that is rare. The real cause of stuttering is yet to be unraveled. It is categorized into two types, i.e., developmental and neurogenic. Developmental stuttering occurs in children during the learning phase of speech and

DOI: 10.1201/9781003450153-4

language. It occurs when there is a difference in a child's verbal demands and their ability to speak. In 2010, researchers identified that genetic factors may also contribute to developmental stuttering. Neurogenic stuttering may occur after a brain injury, head trauma, or a stroke. Due to this, the brain has difficulty coordinating with different regions of the brain involved in producing clear and fluent speaking [1].

The diagnosis of speech disfluency is carried out by a health professional known as a speech-language pathologist. They are trained for testing and treating individuals with speech disorders. By understanding the individual's case history and stuttering behavior, the speech-language pathologist evaluates the individual based on their speaking abilities and the impact it will have on their life. By considering the above factors, they try to determine whether the individual will outgrow their stuttering behavior or continue to suffer from this speech disorder [1]. A child may suffer lifelong if speech disfluency is not detected in a timely manner. Early treatment can help a child outgrow this problem, and they can speak in a fluent manner confidently. Hence, speech classification plays an important role for speech-language pathologists to determine the treatment, and they can plan therapy accordingly.

In this chapter, a stuttering disfluency disorder detection algorithm has been proposed that makes use of a deep scattering wavelet network, a marine predator optimization algorithm, and a KNN classifier for classifying stuttering events (repetition or prolongation) of speech signals. An open-access dataset of speech disfluency recordings, the UCLASS database [3], is used in this work. In the initial stage, the audio recordings were acquired from the database, and they were applied to the scattering wavelet network (SWN) for feature extraction. The high-dimension features are extracted from ScatNet, and they are further reduced using biologically inspired marine predator techniques for optimization. The redundant features are discarded, and the most discriminative features are selected and given to the KNN classifier for the detection of stuttering events.

The main contributions of this chapter are:

1. Robust and efficient feature extraction technique based on deep scattering wavelet network (ScatNet) resulting in improved stuttering dysfluency detection accuracy. The multiple-layer fixed-weight network of ScatNet is employed to extract deformation and translation invariant local features.

2. Feature selection using a marine predator optimization algorithm which is designed to efficiently search through solution spaces resulting in the low dimensional feature vector.

The rest of the chapter is organized as follows: Section 2 surveys the literature, section 3 presents the proposed algorithm, Section 4 explains the feature extraction, feature selection, and classification methods used in this algorithm, Section 5 illustrates and discusses the experimental results, and Section 6 concludes the chapter.

3.2 Literature Survey

This section helps in presenting the various techniques used for speech disfluency detection and classification using different datasets, feature extraction and selection methods, and classifiers [4–11].

Ai et al. [12] suggested a speech disfluency detection method for recognition of stuttering events (prolongation and repetition). A total of 39 speech samples in the English language, with 2 female and 36 male speech samples, were acquired from the UCLASS database. The two speech parameterization methods, i.e., Mel-frequency cepstrum coefficients (MFCC) and linear prediction cepstrum coefficients (LPCC), were used for feature extraction, and KNN and linear discriminant analysis (LDA) classifiers were used. An accuracy of 94.51% was achieved using the combination of LPCC and KNN.

Garg et al. [13] developed a database and recognition system for multiple speech disfluencies in the Indian English language. They used two feature sets, i.e., a combination of log Mel filterbank features with fundamental frequency computed for each frame and MFCC features for extraction from the recordings acquired from the database. The method turned out to be better performing when a random forest classifier was used with MFCC features, and an accuracy of 89.61% was obtained.

To detect multiple speech disfluencies, Mehrotra et al. [14] proposed a pre-linguistic automatic syllabification method that utilizes acoustic and prosody features. They acquired the audio recordings from two databases, namely, UCLASS and IIITH-IED databases, to classify the stuttering events into four types, i.e., prolongation, filled pause (interjection), word repetition, and part-word repetition. The baseline MFCC features were used for feature extraction to get acoustic representation by using BiLSTM, and they are concatenated with prosody features. The detection accuracy of 88.75% and 91.24% was obtained for the UCLASS and IIITH-IED database, respectively.

Jouaiti and Kerstin [15] used the biological texture model of sound texture perception for multi-class classification of speech signals into fluent interjections, word-repetitions (word rep), prolongations, sound repetitions (sound rep), and blocks. They acquired data from two datasets, i.e., FluencyBank and UCLASS databases. They used McDermott and Simoncelli's proposed model for feature extraction and the post-hoc Conover–Iman test for feature selection. Finally, Random Forest and support vector machine (SVM) classifiers were used for multi-label classification on these two datasets.

Jouaiti and Kerstin [16] proposed a real-time application for disfluency in speech classification. They utilized MFCC and phoneme probabilities for feature extraction. These features are used as input to train a BiLSTM network for the classification of four types of disfluencies. The three datasets used to acquire the speech signals were UCLASS, FluencyBank, and SEP-28K datasets. The highest accuracy of 94.3% and 98% was achieved when MFCC and phoneme features were combined for binary and 5-class classification, respectively.

Jegan and Jayagowri [17] suggested MFCC, filter bank energy (FBE), and textural features based on disfluency binary classification for stuttering events, repetition, and prolongation. The Gray-level run length matrix (GLRLM) and gray-level co-occurrence matrix (GLCM) were employed as textural descriptors for feature extraction. To choose the most relevant features, the Laplacian score-based feature selection technique was used. The extreme learning machine (ELM) was utilized as a classifier. The suggested method was evaluated using the UCLASS database, and the accuracy obtained was 96.36%.

Al-Banna et al. [18] proposed an atrous convolutional neural network (CNN)–based stuttering detection method for helping speech-language pathologists. They employed log Mel spectrograms for extracting features and a 2D-CNN for learning temporal and spectral features. They evaluated their model on two datasets, namely, UCLASS and FluencyBank databases, and the F1-score of 52% and 44% was achieved, respectively.

Al-Banna et al. [19] used 13 cepstral coefficients and eight different classifiers to detect stuttering disfluency. Firstly, they used a pre-emphasis filter, and then they applied the short-time Fourier transform (STFT) to the filtered signal. Finally, the Mel-frequency cepstrum coefficients (MFCC) were obtained by applying discrete cosine transform (DCT) and decorrelating filter bank coefficients. The best performance was achieved using a random forest classifier with an accuracy of 50.3% and 50.35% against the two datasets, FluencyBank and SEP-28K, respectively.

Sheikh et al. [20] proposed an advanced stuttering detection technique that utilizes MFCC, pitch and phoneme features, and multi-contextual (MC) StutterNet. They used three datasets, namely, SEP-28K, FluencyBank, and LibriStutter, to acquire data. For the selection of relevant features, Adam optimizer was employed, and a combination of ResNet and BiLSTM and ConvLSTM network were used. The F1 score of 91% was obtained with MC StutterNet against the LibriStutter dataset.

To detect speech disfluency in the Indian Telugu language, Devi et al. [21] suggested a machine learning algorithm that is integrated with a user interface. They utilized 39 acoustic-based MFCC features and four classifiers, i.e., random forest, decision tree, naive Bayes, and logistic regression. They developed a self-made database with the help of the user-interface and the highest accuracy of 86.97% was achieved through random forest.

Kourkounakis et al. [22] proposed FluentNet, a deep learning-based speech disfluency detection algorithm. They employed STFT spectrograms of audio signals as input, and these input features were provided to Squeeze and Excitation (SE-ResNet) and BiLSTM to learn spectral features and temporal features, respectively. The data was acquired from UCLASS and LibriStutter datasets, and an average accuracy of 91.75% and 86.70% was achieved with this model, respectively. Table 3.1 provides the literature review of all the existing methods for speech disfluency algorithms.

3.3 Proposed Scattering Wavelet Network-Based Stuttering Disfluency Detection Algorithm

A stuttering disfluency detection method based on scattering wavelet network features and the marine predator optimization algorithm is presented in this chapter. Two types of dysfluencies, (1) prolongation and (2) word repetition, are detected specifically in this work. The proposed framework of the stuttering disfluency event detection algorithm is shown in Figure 3.1.

The UCLASS database [3] is utilized to acquire stuttered speech audio recordings for performing the experimental evaluation. As depicted as the first block in the proposed framework, as shown in Figure 3.1, prolongation and word repetition samples are extracted from the UCLASS recordings. The dataset comprises 43 speakers recorded using 107 audio files with different time durations. Twenty-three audio samples were selected to generate prolongation and repetition of stuttering events.

Scattering wavelet network features are extracted from these prolongation and repetition audio samples collected from the UCLASS database. Scattering features by varying sample length and scattering order are extracted for the classification task. As the scattering order increases, the generated feature vector dimension increases dramatically.

In order to reduce the dimensionality of the feature vector and to select the most discriminating feature subset, a nature-inspired marine predator optimization algorithm-based feature selection technique is employed. The marine predator optimization produces an optimized feature set, removing redundant and less important features from the input.

TABLE 3.1

The Existing Methods for Speech Disfluency Algorithm against their Databases, Different Feature Extraction, Selection and Classification Techniques, and Accuracy/F1 Score Obtained

Authors	Feature Extraction	Feature Selection	Classifier	Database	Accuracy
Ai et al. [12]	MFCC & LPCC	–	KNN & LDA	UCLASS	94.51%
Garg et al. [13]	log Mel-filterbank features & MFCC	–	Random Forest	IIITH-IED Dataset	89.61%
Mehrotra et al. [14]	Acoustic and prosody features	–	DNN	UCLASS & IIITH-IED	88.75% & 91.24%
Jouaiti & Kerstin [15]	biological texture representation for sound texture perception	post-hoc Conover–Iman test	Random Forest (RF) & SVM	FluencyBank & UCLASS	96.16% & 94.29%
Jouaiti & Kerstin [16]	MFCC and phoneme probabilities	–	BiLSTM	UCLASS, FluencyBank & SEP-28K	94.3%
Jegan & Jayagowri [17]	MFCC, FBE, GLCM & GLRLM	Laplacian score	Extreme learning machine (ELM)	UCLASS	96.36%
Al-Banna et al. [18]	Log Mel spectrogram	–	2D atrous CNN	UCLASS & FluencyBank	(F1 score) 52% & 44%
Al-Banna et al. [19]	STFT, Mel spectrogram, MFCC	–	Random Forest	FluencyBank & SEP-28K	50.3% & 50.35%
Sheikh et al. [20]	MFCC, pitch and phoneme features	Adam optimizer	ResNet+BiLSTM & ConvLSTM	SEP-28K, FluencyBank & Simulated LibriStutter	91% (F1 score)
Devi et al. [21]	MFCC	–	Random forest	Self-made	86.97%
Kourkounakis et al. [22]	STFT spectrograms	–	SE-ResNet+ BiLSTM	UCLASS & LibriStutter	91.75% & 86.70%

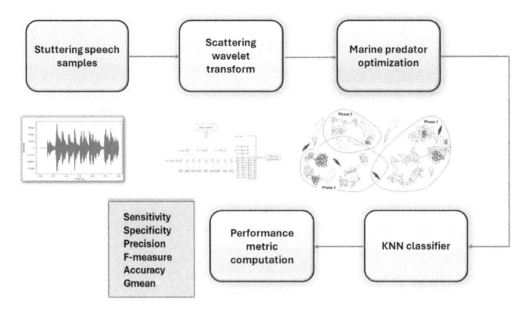

FIGURE 3.1
The proposed framework for scattering wavelet network-based stuttering disfluency detection algorithm.

This optimal feature subset is fed to the K-nearest neighbor classification algorithm; 80% of the randomly selected features are used as a training set and the remaining for testing the trained model. The KNN classification model detects a test sample as prolongation or word repetition. Finally, the experimental results are evaluated using (1) sensitivity, (2) specificity, (3) precision, (4) F-measure, (5) gmean, and (6) average detection accuracy.

3.4 Feature Extraction and Feature Selection

3.4.1 Scattering Wavelet Network (ScatNet)

A novel scattering wavelet network (ScatNet) introduced by Mallat [23] is proposed for speech disfluency feature extraction. As the signal representations produced by them are stable to deformations, they are useful in a lot of texture classifications. ScatNet helps in extracting translation invariant local features. The important properties of ScatNet are that they help in the preservation of signal energy and retention of higher-order information. The group invariant scattering is used to make a multi-layer fixed-weight network that is a product of nonlinear and non-commuting operators, and each one of them is employed to calculate the modulus of the wavelet transform. The main advantage is that it doesn't require any training to set the hyperparameters, i.e., number of deep layers, number of filters, size of hidden layers, etc.

Let the input signal be denoted by A(v), where $v \in R^2$. For making a scattering wavelet transform, let a Gaussian lowpass filter with scaling factor J [24] be given by

$$\phi_J(v) = 2^{-2J} \phi\left(2^{-J}v\right) \tag{4.1}$$

Let ψ_λ be the mother wavelet with dilation and rotation versions and $\lambda = (\theta, j)$ where θ is the orientation, and 2^j are the dyadic scales where $j = (1,2, 3, \ldots, J)$. Wavelet transform is used to retain high-frequency and low-frequency components of the signal. Here, we need to retain the translation invariance features, and they are not preserved up to the maximum value, 2^J, but up to 2^j. Hence, to solve this problem, the modulus operator is convolved with ϕ_J. The scattering wavelet transform [24] is defined by,

$$\left| Wf(x) \right| = \left\{ f(x) \cdot \phi_J, \left| f(x) \cdot \psi_\lambda \right| \right\}_\lambda \tag{4.2}$$

The zeroth layer of the ScatNet [24] is given by,

$$S_0 f(x) = f(x) \cdot \phi_J \tag{4.3}$$

The first average component and second non-linear component are translation invariant up to the scale of 2^J and 2^j, respectively. The second non-linear component is also built translation invariant up to the scale of 2^J by averaging to get the second layer of ScatNet or first-order scattering coefficients [24] given by

$$S_1 f(x, \lambda_1) = \left| f(x) \cdot \psi_{\lambda_1} \right| \cdot \phi_J \tag{4.4}$$

Similarly, the second-order scattering coefficients [24] are given by

$$S_2 f(x, \lambda_1, \lambda_2) = \left\| f(x) \cdot \psi_{\lambda_1} \right| \cdot \psi_{\lambda_2} \right| \cdot \phi_J \tag{4.5}$$

Similarly, the m-order order scattering coefficients [24] are given by

$$S_m f(x, \lambda_1, \lambda_2, \ldots, \lambda_m) = \left\| \left| f(x) \cdot \psi_{\lambda_1} \right| \cdot \psi_{\lambda_2} \right| \cdots \psi_{\lambda_m} \right| \cdot \phi_J \tag{4.6}$$

ScatNet can be built using any type of real or complex wavelet. In this chapter, we have employed the Morlet wavelet, i.e., a variant of the Gabor wavelet. The Morlet wavelets are produced by subtracting the Gaussian function from the Gabor wavelet by making its mean zero. The ScatNet employed in this work is made for a second level or order scattering coefficients, i.e., m = 0,1,2 with three scales and eight orientations, i.e., J=2 and L=8, respectively. Therefore, $\lambda = (\theta, j)$ ranges from λ_1 to λ_{16}.

3.4.2 Marine Predator Algorithm

Recently, the focus of the artificial intelligence research communities has increasingly shifted towards the realm of optimization. This shift has been driven by the remarkable effectiveness of optimization in addressing complex optimization problem scenarios. Traditional deterministic approaches often struggle to effectively handle complex optimization problems within a reasonable polynomial timeframe, as indicated by prior research [25]. These optimization problems can be classified according to the inherent characteristics of the variables within the search space, encompassing continuous, discrete, binary, permutation, and structural categories. Metaheuristic-based algorithms represent a class of highly effective optimization techniques designed to address a diverse spectrum of optimization challenges through a generic optimization framework. These algorithms are categorized according to their initial solution count, falling into the groups of local search-based and population-based methodologies [26, 27].

The Marine Predator Algorithm is a computational optimization technique inspired by the hunting behaviors and strategies of marine predators in the ocean ecosystem [28]. This algorithm mimics the way marine predators search for prey and adapt their movements based on environmental cues. In the Marine Predator Algorithm, a population of potential solutions (representing candidate solutions to an optimization problem) is evolved over several iterations. The algorithm introduces the concepts of "prey" and "predators" to guide the search process. Prey represents potential solutions, and predators simulate the actions of marine predators in hunting for prey.

The initiation of the Marine Predator Algorithm involves utilizing information within the search space to create the initial set of solutions for the first generation. The subsequent step entails assigning the top-performing predator (referred to as the Elite matrix) and the prey (denoted as U). Subsequently, the solutions undergo modification through three distinct phases, using the attributes inherent to the MPA methodology. The initial phase depends on the velocity ratio existing between the prey and the predator. Meanwhile, the subsequent two phases evaluate the rates of unit and low velocity.

In the first phase, i.e., the exploration phase (high-velocity ratio), during the initial one-third of the iterations, the agent explores the search space. The prey initiates its search for food while the predator carefully observes its movements. As a result, the high-velocity ratio becomes a prominent characteristic of this phase. In phase two, i.e., unit velocity ratio, following the identification of the optimal position, the subsequent stage is the exploitation phase. Nonetheless, there exists an intermediary transmission phase between exploitation and exploration, executed during the second third of the iterations. During this phase, the velocities of both the prey and predator are the same. Furthermore, the movement patterns of the prey and predator correspond to the Lévy flight and Brownian motion, respectively.

During stage three, i.e., the low-velocity ratio (exploitation stage) phase, the focus shifts to exploitation, where the predator accelerates its movement to catch up with the prey. This phase takes place during the final third of the iterations, during which the solutions adjust their positions through the utilization of the Lévy flight movement pattern. In the next step, eddy formation and fish aggregating devices' effect (FADS) are analyzed. The final step is marine memory, in which marine predators possess the remarkable capacity to remember locations of abundant food sources, aiding them in quickly capturing optimal solutions and avoiding local optima. The pseudo-code of the marine predator algorithm is shown in Algorithm 1.

Generate initial population of search agents (Prey) $i = 1,...,$N
While termination criteria are not met
Compute the fitness, build the Elite matrix and accomplish memory saving
      If Iterat < Max_Iterat/3
          Update prey using equation below,
          $\overrightarrow{Prey_i} = \overrightarrow{Prey_i} + P\,R\!\uparrow \otimes \overrightarrow{Stepsize_i}$
      Else if Max_Iterat/3 < Iterat < 2 *Max_Iterat/3
          Update prey position for initial half of the population ($i = 1,...,$n/2)
          $\overrightarrow{Prey_i} = \overrightarrow{Prey_i} + P\,R\!\uparrow \otimes \overrightarrow{Stepsize_i}$
          For the remaining half of the populations ($i = n$ /2,...,n), update the pray as mentioned below
          $\overrightarrow{Prey_i} = \overrightarrow{Elite_i} + P\,CF\!\uparrow \otimes \overrightarrow{Stepsize_i}$

Else if Iterat > 2 ∗Max_Iterat/3
        Update prey based using
End (if)
        Perform memory saving and Elite update
        Applying FADs effect and update
End **while**

Algorithm 1: Pseudo code of marine predator algorithm.

3.5 Experimental Results and Discussions

This chapter presents stuttering disfluency event detection into prolongation or repletion technique using scattering wavelet network feature extraction and marine predator feature selection algorithm. The scattering wavelet employs wavelet filters and low pass filter averaging to produce desired features from input speech samples. In this section, the database details, experimental settings, and results are presented. The experimental evaluations are produced on the UCLASS database. The UCLASS database consists of monologs, readings, and conversation recordings, mostly with school-age subjects. In the monolog category, there are 139 audio recordings with 43 different speakers.

The UCLASS database has two releases, and this study utilized recording from Release One to extract scattering features and stuttering detection. The database selected has speech recordings from ages 8 to 18 years with stuttering and various dysfluency. Scattering wavelet features are extracted from 25 speech recordings from the Release One database based on the available transcriptions. The timestamp for each recording is used to extract prolongation and repletion stuttering events [12, 17].

K-Nearest Neighbors (KNN) is a supervised machine learning algorithm used for classification and regression tasks. It is a simple and intuitive algorithm that can be used for both binary and multiclass classification problems. KNN is a non-parametric and instance-based algorithm. K is a hyperparameter that represents the number of nearest neighbors to consider when making a prediction. We need to choose an appropriate value for K, which can impact the performance of the classifier. A smaller K makes the model more sensitive to noise, while a larger K can smooth out the decision boundary but may not capture local patterns effectively. Once the distances are calculated, the algorithm selects the K data points (neighbors) from the training set that are closest to the new data point. For classification tasks, KNN uses a majority voting mechanism to determine the class label of the new data point. It counts the number of neighbors in each class among the K nearest neighbors and assigns the class label that has the most votes as the predicted class for the new data point.

Scattering wavelet transform is applied to these two types of stuttering events to extract the features. For the feature extraction, a 1-D wavelet filter bank with an averaging scale of 1024, 2048, and 4096 samples is utilized. Four types of scattering levels, zeroth, first, second, and third-order scattering, are applied to extract deformation-invariant local features. As prolongation and repletion events are different, different scattering coefficients are produced in both cases.

Figure 3.2 depicts the scattering wavelet coefficient spectrogram of two types of stuttering samples. The figure shows prolongation and repetition speech samples from the

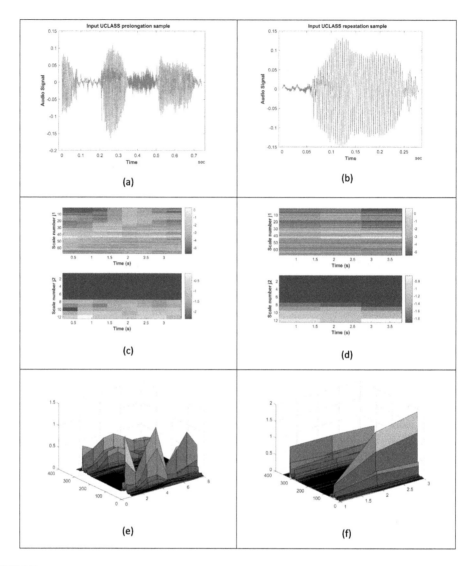

FIGURE 3.2
Scattering wavelet coefficient spectrogram of stuttering samples. (a) prolongation UCLASS sample (b) repetition speech sample (c) spectrogram of prolongation sample (d) spectrogram of repetition sample (e) framewise scattering wavelet coefficient distribution of prolongation sample (f) framewise scattering wavelet coefficient distribution of repetition sample.

UCLASS database with corresponding spectrogram representation. The figure also illustrates the framewise scattering wavelet coefficient distribution of these samples. As is evident from these illustrations, the scattering wavelet coefficient distribution and representations are different for prolongation and prepetition stuttering events.

During the feature extraction step, scattering features by varying sample length and scattering order are extracted for the classification task. As the scattering order increases, the generated feature vector dimension increases dramatically. In order to reduce the dimensionality of the feature vector and to choose the most discriminating feature subset, a nature-inspired marine predator optimization algorithm-based feature selection technique is employed; 80% of randomly selected spectrogram images are employed to obtain training features from deep learning models, and the remaining 20% for testing features.

The marine predator optimization algorithm effectively furnishes the most discriminating optimized feature subset, thereby improving the detection accuracy. The number of solutions and the maximum number of iteration counts are set as 10 and 170 in marine predator optimization settings. Fish aggregating devices (FDA) are selected as 0.2, with the constant p=0.5. These FDA and p values are selected after analyzing the effect on the detection rate. K (number of nearest neighbors) is set to 5 in the KNN classifier. The proposed stuttering dysfluency detection technique in implemented on a computer with i-5 processor running at 2.444GHz using 16GB of RAM running Windows 10. The performance metric presented in this section are average of 10 trials.

The fitness function in the marine predator optimization is opted as an error rate of the KNN classifier. Various performance metrics are employed for evaluating the proposed algorithm performance: gmean, sensitivity, precision, specificity, accuracy, and F1-measure, and are defined in the equations (5.1) to (5.6).

$$Sensitivity = \frac{TPos}{FNeg + TPos} \tag{5.1}$$

$$Specificity = \frac{TNeg}{FPos + TNeg} \tag{5.2}$$

$$Accuracy = \frac{TPos + TNeg}{FNeg + Tros + FPos + TNeg} \tag{5.3}$$

$$Precision = \frac{TPos}{FPos + TPos} \tag{5.4}$$

$$F1 - score = \frac{2 \times TPos}{2 \times TPos \, FPos + FNeg} \tag{5.5}$$

$$gmean = \sqrt{Specificity \times Sensitivity} \tag{5.6}$$

The first set of experimental results is presented without applying the marine predator feature selection algorithm. Tables 3.2 to 3.3 show accuracy, sensitivity, specificity, precision, F1-score, and gmean with a sample size of 1024, 2048, and 4096 without applying the marine predator optimization technique for two and three levels, respectively. It can be seen from Tables 3.2 to 3.3 that both levels (levels 2 and 3) attained a similar average detection rate of 90.48%.

It is also observed that in the case of three-level scattering wavelet features, the sensitivity and F-measure parameter values are improved as opposed to second-level features. The number of samples also affects the algorithm performance. The highest metric values are obtained in the case of 4096 samples as compared to 1024 and 2048, effectively extracting deformation and translation invariant local features from the stuttering speech samples, resulting in an improved detection rate.

TABLE 3.2

Performance Measures Obtained Using Various Scattering Wavelet Sample Size Features with Two Level Decomposition without Feature Selection

Samples	Accuracy	Sensitivity	Specificity	Precision	F-Measure	Gmean
1024	80.95	83.33	77.78	83.33	83.33	80.51
2048	85.71	83.33	88.89	90.91	86.96	86.07
4096	90.48	91.67	88.89	91.67	91.67	90.27

TABLE 3.3

Accuracy, Sensitivity, Specificity, Precision, F1-Score, and Gmean Values Derived from Three-level Scattering Wavelet with a Sample Size of 1024, 2048, and 4096 without Applying Marine Predator Optimization Technique

Samples	Accuracy	Sensitivity	Specificity	Precision	F-Measure	Gmean
1024	80.95	83.33	77.78	83.33	83.33	80.51
2048	85.71	83.33	88.89	90.91	86.96	86.07
4096	90.48	100	77.78	84.62	92.31	88.19

TABLE 3.4

Performance Measures Obtained Using Various Scattering Wavelet Sample Size Features with Two Level Decomposition with Marine Predator Feature Selection

Samples	Accuracy	Sensitivity	Specificity	Precision	F-Measure	Gmean
1024	85.71	91.67	77.78	84.62	88.00	84.44
2048	90.48	83.33	100	100	90.91	91.29
4096	95.24	91.67	100	100	95.65	95.74

TABLE 3.5

Accuracy, Sensitivity, Specificity, Precision, F1-Score, and Gmean Values Derived from Three-level Scattering Wavelet with a Sample Size of 1024, 2048, and 4096 after Applying Marine Predator Optimization Technique

Samples	Accuracy	Sensitivity	Specificity	Precision	F-Measure	Gmean
1024	85.71	91.67	77.78	84.62	88.00	84.44
2048	90.48	91.67	88.89	91.67	91.67	90.27
4096	95.24	100	88.89	92.31	96.00	94.28

In the next step, experimental results are obtained after applying a marine predator optimization algorithm for feature selection. Tables 3.4 to 3.5 show different performance measures obtained with different sample sizes and manta ray optimization-based feature selection using two and three-level scattering features. In all sample sizes and scattering levels, the detection accuracy and other parameters are notably improved. Similar to the first set of experiments, both levels attained a similar detection accuracy of 95.24% at a sample size of 4096.

As evident from these experimental results, the marine predator optimization algorithm improves the sensitivity, accuracy, precision, F1-score, and Gmean parameter values in addition to the reduction of the feature vector. F1-Measue and Gmean are reported as 96%

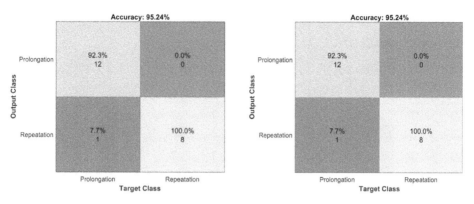

FIGURE 3.3
Confusion matrix: Left-side image depicts scattering level two and right-side image shows level three confusion matrix obtained with marine predator optimization algorithm.

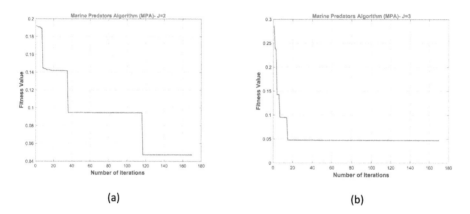

(a)   (b)

FIGURE 3.4
Fitness value vs. a number of iterations for marine predator optimization for (a) second-order feature extraction and (b) third-order feature extraction.

and 95.74% at levels 3 and 2, respectively. Figure 3.3 shows the confusion matrix obtained using two and three-level scattering wavelet features.

3.6 Marine Predator Optimization-based Feature Selection Analysis

As stated earlier, the proposed algorithm employs a marine predator optimization algorithm for feature selection. The most relevant and discriminating features from the input feature pool are chosen using marine predator optimization. The detection error rate of the KNN classification model is used as a fitness function. The fitness value is evaluated for each iteration for selecting the important feature subset. Figures 3.4 (a) and (b) depict fitness value vs. number of iterations for manta ray optimization using second and third-order scattering wavelet coefficients.

The Fish Aggregating Devices (FADs) and the constant P play a crucial role and have a major impact on marine predator behavior. The optimum selection of these parameters

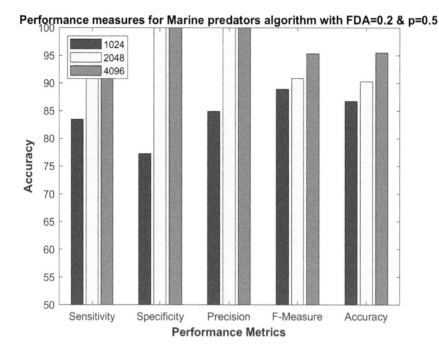

FIGURE 3.5
Sensitivity, specificity, precision, F-measure, and average accuracy when marine predator optimization FDA =0.2 and P=0.5.

affects the detection accuracy and other related parameter values. The effect of FDA and P on this performance metric is also analyzed in this work. Figures 3.5 to 3.10 show sensitivity, specificity, precision, F-measure, and average accuracy for three-level scattering wavelet features. The FDA is varied in the range of 0.2, 0.4, 0.6, and 1.2, whereas P values are selected as 0.5 and 0.7 to obtain these experimental evaluations. It is observed that the FDA of 0.2 at P at 0.5 attains the highest detection rate as compared to 0.4 and 1.2. Accordingly, experiment results are presented using these parameter values. Receiver operating plots with AUC are displayed in Figures 3.5 to 3.11, with and without applying marine predator optimization-based feature selection.

The proposed wavelet scattering features and marine predator optimization-based feature selection algorithm are compared with recent stuttering disfluency detection techniques in Table 3.6. For a fair comparison, existing algorithms that employed the UCLASS database for experimental evaluation are considered. As is evident from Table 3.6, the proposed scattering wavelet-based features outperform existing approaches in terms of detection accuracy. As seen in [6, 29, 31], MFCC is the most popular choice for feature selection, whereas the proposed approach utilizes scattering wavelet transform features for the detection task.

3.7 Conclusion

Stuttering event detection is a complex task that demands various disciplines, such as speech processing, pathology, signal processing, and machine learning. This study

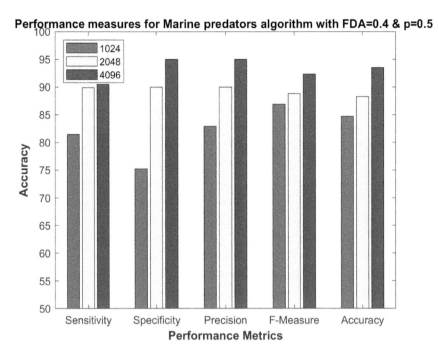

FIGURE 3.6
Various performance measures when marine predator optimization threshold FDA = 0.4 and P=0.5.

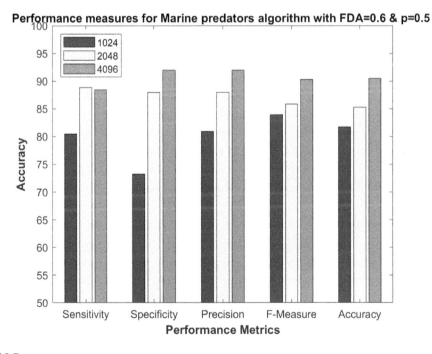

FIGURE 3.7
Sensitivity, specificity, precision, F-measure, and average accuracy when marine predator optimization FDA =0.6 and P=0.5.

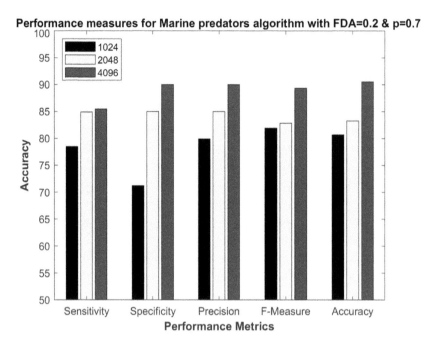

FIGURE 3.8
Various performance measures when marine predator optimization threshold FDA = 0.2 and P=0.7.

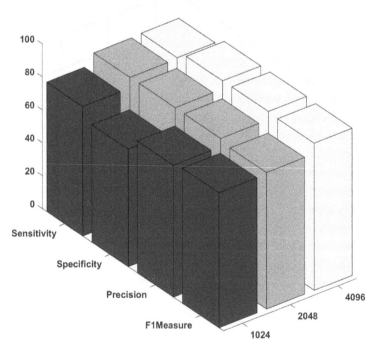

FIGURE 3.9
Sensitivity, specificity, precision, F-measure, and average accuracy when marine predator optimization FDA = 1.2 and P=0.5.

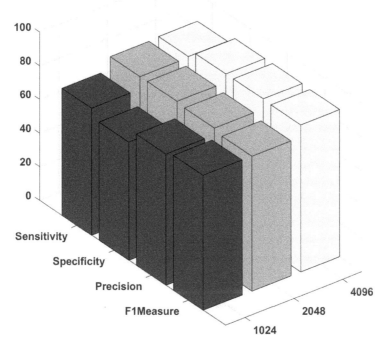

FIGURE 3.10
Various performance measures when marine predator optimization threshold FDA = 1.2 and P=0.7.

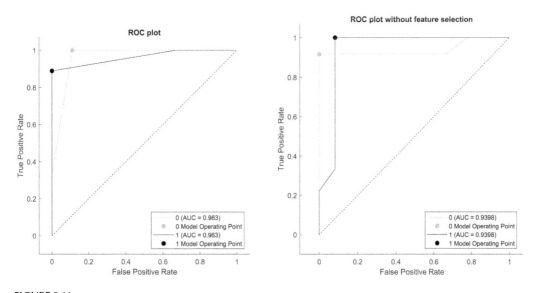

FIGURE 3.11
Receiver operating plots with AUC with and without applying marine predator optimization-based feature selection.

TABLE 3.6

Comparison of the Proposed Stuttering Disfluency Detection Algorithm with Existing Techniques

Algorithm	Technique/Features	Database	Classifier	Average Accuracy
[6]	MFCC	UCLASS	SVM	90%
[29]	MFCC	UCLASS	DTW	86%
[22]	Spectrogram features	UCLASS	CNN	84.10%
[30]	Spectrogram features	UCLASS	CNN	91.75%
[31]	MFCC	UCLASS	GMM	94.98%
Proposed	Scattering wavelet network features with 4096 samples	UCLASS	KNN	95.24%

presented word repetition and prolongation stuttering event classification based on scattering wavelet network translation and deformation invariant local features. Further, the most prominent feature subset is identified using the marine predator optimization feature selection algorithm. Experimental results in terms of various performance parameters are evaluated using the KNN classifier. Additional analysis is also performed to verify the effect of the marine predator feature selection algorithm. The most widely and publicly available UCLASS database is employed for the assessment of the proposed technique. The highest detection accuracy of 95.24% is attained by the proposed scattering wavelet features and marine predator feature selection. The experimental evaluation revealed that higher-order scattering wavelet features slightly outperform in most situations, such as sample sizes of 1024, 2048, and 4096. Moreover, a higher sample size resulted in improved detection accuracy, which has the ability to capture prominent details from repetition and prolongation of stuttering disfluencies sample.

References

1. National institute on deafness and other communication disorders. Stuttering. [cited 2023 August 24] Available from: https://www.nidcd.nih.gov/health/stuttering
2. National institute on deafness and other communication disorders. Stuttering. [cited 2023 August 24] Available from: https://www.nidcd.nih.gov/health/statistics/quick-statistics-voice -speech-language
3. Howell, Peter, Stephen Davis, and Jon Bartrip. "The university college london archive of stuttered speech (uclass)." *Journal of Speech, Language, and Hearing Research* 52, no 2 (2009) 556–569.
4. Waghmare, Swapnil D., Ratnadeep R. Deshmukh, Pukhraj P. Shrishrimal, Vishal B. Waghmare, Ganesh B. Janvale, and Babasaheb Sonawane. "A comparative study of recognition technique used for development of automatic stuttered speech Dysfluency recognition system." *Indian Journal of Science and Technology* 10, no. 21 (2017): 1–14.
5. Sheikh, Shakeel A., Md Sahidullah, Fabrice Hirsch, and Slim Ouni. "Machine learning for stuttering identification: Review, challenges and future directions." *Neurocomputing* 514, (2022) 385–402.
6. Banerjee, Nilanjan, Samarjeet Borah, and Nilambar Sethi. "Intelligent stuttering speech recognition: A succinct review." *Multimedia Tools and Applications* 81, no. 17 (2022): 24145–24166.
7. Villegas B., Flores K. M., José Acuña K., Pacheco-Barrios K., and Elias D. "A Novel Stuttering Disfluency Classification System Based on Respiratory Biosignals," 2019 41st Annual International Conference of the IEEE Engineering in Medicine and Biology Society (EMBC), Berlin, Germany, pp. 4660–4663. 2019.

8. Bayerl, Sebastian P., Maurice Gerczuk, Anton Batliner, Christian Bergler, Shahin Amiriparian, Björn Schuller, Elmar Nöth, and Korbinian Riedhammer. "Classification of stuttering–The ComParE challenge and beyond." *Computer Speech & Language* 81 (2023): 101519.

9. Sharma, Nitin Mohan, Vikas Kumar, Prasant Kumar Mahapatra, and Vaibhav Gandhi. "Comparative analysis of various feature extraction techniques for classification of speech disfluencies." *Speech Communication* 150 (2023): 23–31.

10. Kaushal, Bhakti, Smitha Raveendran, Mukesh D. Patil, and Gajanan K. Birajdar. "Spectrogram image textural descriptors for lung sound classification." In *Machine Learning and Deep Learning in Efficacy Improvement of Healthcare Systems*. CRC Press (2022): 109–136.

11. Mistry, Yogita D., Gajanan K. Birajdar, and Archana M. Khodke. "Time-frequency visual representation and texture features for audio applications: A comprehensive review, recent trends, and challenges." *Multimedia Tools and Applications* 82 (2023): 36143–3617735.

12. Ai, Ooi Chia, M. Hariharan, Sazali Yaacob, and Lim Sin Chee. "Classification of speech dysfluencies with MFCC and LPCC features." *Expert Systems with Applications* 39, no. 2 (2012): 2157–2165.

13. Garg, Sparsh, Utkarsh Mehrotra, Gurugubelli Krishna, and Anil Kumar Vuppala. "Towards a database for detection of multiple speech disfluencies in Indian English." In 2021 National Conference on Communications (NCC), pp. 1–6. IEEE, 2021.

14. Mehrotra, Utkarsh, Sparsh Garg, Gurugubelli Krishna, and Anil Kumar Vuppala. "Detecting multiple disfluencies from speech using pre-linguistic automatic syllabification with acoustic and prosody features." In 2021 Asia-Pacific Signal and Information Processing Association Annual Summit and Conference (APSIPA ASC), pp. 761–768. IEEE, 2021.

15. Jouaiti, Melanie, and Kerstin Dautenhahn. "Dysfluency classification in speech using a biological sound perception model." In 2022 9th International Conference on Soft Computing & Machine Intelligence (ISCMI), pp. 173–177. IEEE, 2022.

16. Jouaiti, Melanie, and Kerstin Dautenhahn. "Dysfluency classification in stuttered speech using deep learning for real-time applications." In ICASSP 2022-2022 IEEE International Conference on Acoustics, Speech and Signal Processing (ICASSP), pp. 6482–6486. IEEE, 2022.

17. Jegan, Roohum, and R. Jayagowri. "MFCC and texture descriptors based stuttering dysfluencies classification using extreme learning machine." *International Journal of Advanced Computer Science and Applications* 13, no. 8 (2022). 612–619.

18. Al-Banna, Abedal-Kareem, Eran Edirisinghe, and Hui Fang. "Stuttering detection using atrous convolutional neural networks." In 2022 13th International Conference on Information and Communication Systems (ICICS), pp. 252–256. IEEE, 2022.

19. Al-Banna, Abedal-Kareem, Eran Edirisinghe, Hui Fang, and Wael Hadi. "Stuttering disfluency detection using machine learning approaches." *Journal of Information & Knowledge Management* 21, no. 2 (2022): 2250020.

20. Sheikh, Shakeel A., Md Sahidullah, Fabrice Hirsch, and Slim Ouni. "Advancing stuttering detection via data augmentation, class-balanced loss and multi-contextual deep learning." *IEEE Journal of Biomedical and Health Informatics* 27, 5 (2023). 2553–2564.

21. Devi, P. Sunitha, Sarvagna Gudlavalleti, Ramyasri Lakka, Rithika Kuchanpally, and Sai Sonali Dudekula. "Comparison of machine learning algorithms for detection of stuttering in speech." *Advances in Computational Sciences and Technology* 16, no. 1 (2023): 45–53.

22. Kourkounakis, Tedd, Amirhossein Hajavi, and Ali Etemad. "FluentNet: end-to-end detection of speech disfluency with deep learning." arXiv preprint arXiv:2009.11394 (2020).

23. Mallat, Stéphane. "Group invariant scattering." *Communications on Pure and Applied Mathematics* 65, no. 10 (2012): 1331–1398.

24. Birajdar, Parmeshwar, Meet Haria, Sagar G. Sangodkar, and Vikram Gadre. "Unconstrained ear recognition using deep scattering wavelet network." In 2019 IEEE Bombay Section Signature Conference (IBSSC), pp. 1–6. IEEE, 2019.

25. Chong, Edwin K. P., and Stanisław H. Żak. *An Introduction to Optimization*. Vol. 75. John Wiley & Sons, 2013.

26. Al-Betar, Mohammed Azmi, Mohammed A. Awadallah, Sharif Naser Makhadmeh, Zaid Abdi Alkareem Alyasseri, Ghazi Al-Naymat, and Seyedali Mirjalili. "Marine predators algorithm: A review." *Archives of Computational Methods in Engineering* 30, (2023): 1–31.

27. Mugemanyi, Sylvère, Zhaoyang Qu, François Xavier Rugema, Yunchang Dong, Lei Wang, Christophe Bananeza, Arcade Nshimiyimana, and Emmanuel Mutabazi. "Marine predators algorithm: A comprehensive review." *Machine Learning with Applications* 12 (2023): 100471.

28. Faramarzi, Afshin, Mohammad Heidarinejad, Seyedali Mirjalili, and Amir H. Gandomi. "Marine Predators Algorithm: A nature-inspired metaheuristic." *Expert Systems with Applications* 152 (2020): 113377.

29. Girish, M., R. Anil, A. Ahmed, and M. Hithaish Kumar. "Word repetition analysis in stuttered speech using MFCC and dynamic time warping." In National Conference on Communication and Image Processing TJIT, Bangalore, 2017.

30. Kourkounakis, Tedd, Amirhossein Hajavi, and Ali Etemad. "Detecting multiple speech disfluencies using a deep residual network with bidirectional long short-term memory." In ICASSP 2020-2020 IEEE International Conference on Acoustics, Speech and Signal Processing (ICASSP), pp. 6089–6093. IEEE, 2020.

31. Mahesha, P., and D. S. Vinod. "LP-Hillbert transform based MFCC for effective discrimination of stuttering dysfluencies." In 2017 International Conference on Wireless Communications, Signal Processing and Networking (WiSPNET), pp. 2561–2565. IEEE, 2017.

4

AI in Neurological Disorders: A Systematic Review

Shashwati Mishra and Gobinda Chandra Panda

4.1 Introduction

Every day, a substantial volume of medical data is generated, necessitating the arduous process of analysing these data. Multiple methodologies are employed to analyse such data for the sake of disease detection and therapy. Recent breakthroughs in the field of analysis have seen the utilisation of machine learning algorithms, image processing, and Artificial Intelligence (AI) approaches to enhance the quality of manual analysis of medical data. Additionally, this automated method expedites the analysis process in comparison to the traditional approach.

Machine learning techniques can be employed for the identification of many neurological disorders, such as dementia, multiple sclerosis, schizophrenia, Alzheimer's disease, cancer, and other infectious and degenerative ailments. Numerous scientific endeavours have been conducted to ascertain and categorise the anatomical components of the brain [1]. The identification of both good and diseased structures is crucial in order to facilitate surgical planning, diagnosis, therapy, and analysis at different phases of medical intervention. The diagnostic and treatment processes in machine learning encompass several stages, including data preparation, feature extraction, and feature selection. These early procedures are undertaken to enhance the algorithm's performance [2].

The paramount significance of health is seen in all living organisms. Advancements in technology have facilitated the development of novel diagnostic and therapeutic approaches for a wide range of ailments. The utilisation of imaging and image processing techniques, like ultrasound, MRI, X-ray, and CT scan has facilitated the examination of tissue and organ structures within the human body. These techniques enable the observation of their functionality and the detection of any abnormalities present in various body sections. Currently, medical imaging plays a crucial role in the healthcare industry and significantly impacts the process of diagnosing and treating various diseases. Medical imaging techniques are employed to obtain a comprehensive visualisation of the internal anatomical structures of the human body. These visualisations serve as a valuable resource for medical practitioners in identifying deviations from normalcy, detecting abnormalities, and facilitating the treatment of various disorders. The analysis of the extensive collection of biomedical data is a significant challenge for healthcare practitioners. Numerous research efforts have been undertaken to enhance the speed, efficiency, and accuracy of the methodologies employed in addressing this issue [3].

DOI: 10.1201/9781003450153-5

4.1.1 Objective of the Work

The objective of this work is to discuss:

- The diverse components and applications of artificial intelligence (AI).
- The utilisation of AI in the field of healthcare.
- The factors contributing to the development of neurological illnesses.
- The implementation of AI in the prognosis and treatment of neurological disorders.

4.1.2 Organisation of the Chapter

Section 4.2 provides an introductory overview of Artificial Intelligence (AI) and its constituent components. The utilisation of Artificial Intelligence (AI) principles has practical applications across several domains, as elaborated in section 4.3. This section additionally includes a diagram illustrating the applications of artificial devices in the field of healthcare, as well as a subsection dedicated to discussing medical image file formats. Section 4.4 provides an in-depth analysis of the causes, symptoms, and types of neurological illnesses. In Section 4.5, an examination is conducted on the application of Artificial Intelligence (AI) methodologies in addressing a range of concerns pertaining to neurological illnesses. This is subsequently followed by a section dedicated to the conclusion and the potential possibilities for future research in this domain.

4.2 Artificial Intelligence Techniques

Artificial Intelligence (AI) encompasses a range of approaches and procedures that are employed in the creation of intelligent computers capable of cognitive processes such as reasoning, retention of information, analysis, inference, and learning. These machines has the ability to address a multitude of difficulties, assist individuals, provide expert-like guidance, alleviate job burdens, and execute tasks with enhanced speed and accuracy. The concept of Artificial Intelligence (AI) was initially proposed by John McCarthy, an esteemed American computer scientist, in the year 1956 [4, 5]. The process of digitisation has resulted in an expansion of data volume.

Furthermore, there have been suggestions for employing advanced methodologies to effectively manage and process large quantities of data. Artificial intelligence approaches have been widely applied across diverse domains, including but not limited to education, healthcare, finance, the production sector, and industry. Artificial Intelligence (AI) approaches are employed to facilitate decision-making processes and automate a wide range of activities. The steady development of technology utilised for the analysis of medical data has resulted in a reduction of the burden placed on healthcare workers in the realm of disease diagnosis. Artificial Intelligence (AI) has been employed in the management of many neurological illnesses through the utilisation of smart gadgets. AI-enabled smart devices have the potential to mitigate the occurrence of diseases, monitor the health state of patients, and aid medical personnel in detecting diseases with enhanced accuracy and efficiency [6].

The artificial neural network is composed of several units distributed across various layers, including the input layer, hidden layer(s), and output layer. The output from one layer

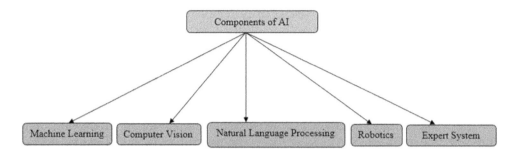

FIGURE 4.1
Components of AI

is sent as input to subsequent layers, with several nodes present in each layer of the neural network. Recent breakthroughs in artificial neural networks include convolutional neural networks, deep neural networks, recurrent neural networks, and graph neural networks.

Figure 4.1 illustrates the key components of Artificial Intelligence (AI), namely machine learning, natural language processing, computer vision, robotics, and expert systems. Machine learning algorithms are employed for the purpose of constructing diverse models capable of generating predictions based on input data. In the field of machine learning, a model is developed by utilising a set of training data. This model is subsequently employed to classify and predict outcomes by applying test data. Machine learning approaches can be categorised into three main types: supervised learning, unsupervised learning, and reinforcement learning. The data provided as input to the model is classified into two categories: training data and test data. Supervised learning refers to the process of training a model using labelled data, while unsupervised learning pertains to the training of a model using unlabelled data. Reinforcement learning techniques are employed to enhance outcomes based on feedback obtained through interactions with the environment.

Computer vision techniques are employed in order to comprehend and evaluate visual information. In the field of medical science, these techniques hold significant importance in the analysis of medical image information for the purpose of diagnosis and treatment. Natural Language Processing (NLP) techniques are employed to facilitate the interaction between computers and human beings, enabling machines to comprehend and interpret human language. It is crucial to facilitate the functionality of machines as human assistants, enabling them to comprehend the emotions and sentiments of individuals. A combination of diverse technologies is employed to develop robots that have the ability to aid medical practitioners in surgical procedures, oversee patients' health data, and manage patients' medication.

Expert systems utilise historical knowledge stored in their knowledge base and employ reasoning procedures to make conclusions similar to those made by human beings. In the field of healthcare, these systems have the potential to provide recommendations to healthcare practitioners based on the analysis of patient records. Expert systems offer recommendations to medical practitioners, aiding them in the process of disease diagnosis. Expert systems provide guidance and recommendations to both physicians and patients regarding treatment options. A complete investigation was conducted on the use of expert systems in the field of medical science for the purpose of disease diagnosis [7].

Image segmentation techniques are employed in the identification of neurological, neurodegenerative illnesses, and infections through the analysis of MRI, CT scan, and X-ray images. Machine learning, as a subfield of artificial intelligence, facilitates the process by which computers acquire knowledge through the utilisation of examples, analysis, and experiential data [8]. In their study, Raghavendra et al. provided a comprehensive compilation of machine learning–driven Computer-Aided Design (CAD) systems utilised in the detection of several neurological illnesses, including Parkinson's disease, Alzheimer's disease, epilepsy, multiple sclerosis, and ischemic brain stroke. The authors of the study proposed a machine learning–based Computer-Aided Design (CAD) system that consists of five stages: signal transformation, feature extraction, dimensionality reduction, optimal feature selection/ranking, and classification. The use of convolutional neural networks, deep neural networks, and recurrent neural networks in the diagnosis of neurological illnesses was the subject of their discussion [9].

4.3 Applications of AI

Artificial Intelligence draws upon principles and theories from diverse academic fields, including computation, mathematics/logic, psychology/cognitive science, philosophy, biology/neuroscience. AI techniques have applications in a wide range of fields like processing of natural languages, game playing, speech recognition, designing decision support systems, classification, prediction, object detection, object tracking, designing intelligent control devices, self-driven vehicles, recommender systems, social media data analysis, processing an image for analysis. Artificial Intelligence (AI) techniques are utilised for the purpose of analysing data and images acquired from spacecraft in order to enhance our understanding of the universe and make predictions regarding future changes in its various components. Intelligent systems are employed within the travel business to provide assistance to individuals in various aspects, such as the selection of hotels and restaurants, determining optimal travel routes, and facilitating the buying of travel tickets. The principles of artificial intelligence are also employed in the development of intelligent robots that possess the ability to engage in cognitive processes, communication, behaviour, and decision-making akin to those of human beings.

Artificial Intelligence (AI) encompasses a variety of methodologies aimed at analysing complex datasets in order to recognise correlations within the data. The utilisation of Artificial Intelligence (AI) ideas enables the attainment of more precise and quick examination of pathological and medical information. This process aids in the discovery and treatment of diseases, as well as providing support during and after surgical procedures. The classification and prediction of diseases involve the evaluation of the internal structure of organs, cells, and tissues, as well as the communication between these components. Artificial Intelligence (AI) technologies play a crucial role in supporting and facilitating surgical procedures, as well as aiding in the formulation of post-surgical care plans and future therapy recommendations. Artificial intelligence techniques are also utilised to provide support to individuals such as older citizens and individuals with disabilities. Intelligent procedures are utilised to periodically examine the well-being of individuals, while simultaneously documenting their test outcomes and health advancements. Artificial Intelligence (AI) is being utilised in the field of drug discovery. Figure 4.2 depicts the diverse applications of artificial intelligence (AI) across multiple domains, whereas Figure 4.3 specifically illustrates its implementation in the healthcare sector.

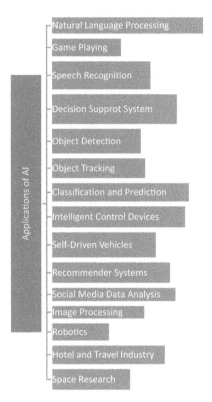

FIGURE 4.2
Applications of AI in various fields

4.3.1 Medical Image File Formats

Images also have a significant effect in the prognostication of a patient's health status. Images are captured using different types of imaging techniques like X-ray, ultrasound, MRI (Magnetic Resonance Imaging) and CT (Computed Tomography) scans. These images facilitate the examination of the anatomical composition of the human body, enable the observation and analysis of the functioning of internal organs, aid in the identification of aberrant tissues, and assist in the detection of disease-affected regions within the body, among other purposes.

Medical imaging use many file formats like Analyze, Nifti (Neuroimaging Informatics Technology Initiative), Minc, and Dicom (Digital Imaging and Communications in Medicine). Larobina and Murino discussed these file formats along with an analysis of their characteristics [10].

4.3.2 Measures of Brain Activity

The process of obtaining information about the structures and activities of the brain can be carried out in a variety of different ways. Functional magnetic resonance imaging, also known as fMRI, magnetoencephalography, also known as MEG, and electroencephalography, also known as EEG, are the three measurements that are utilised the most regularly and most commonly. The electroencephalogram (EEG) is the method that is both the most flexible and the most cost-effective option. Functional magnetic resonance imaging (fMRI)

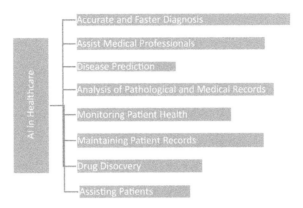

FIGURE 4.3
AI in healthcare

is a neuroimaging technique that assesses brain function through the detection of alterations in blood flow that are linked to neural activity. Magnetoencephalography (MEG)
is a non-invasive neuroimaging technique that detects and records the magnetic fields
produced by cerebral activity. The utilisation of electroencephalography (EEG) involves
the quantification of electrical activity produced by the diverse cortical layers within the
human brain.

4.4 Neurological Disorders and their Types

Neurological diseases exert an enormous impact on the brain, spinal cord, and overall nervous system within the human body. Biochemical, electrical, or structural abnormalities of
brain, nerves, and spinal cord lead to neurological disorders. The neurological disorders
may be congenital, acute onset, or developmental in nature [11].

The prevalence of chronic neurological disorders has experienced a notable rise due
to the growth of the population and the ageing process, despite a decrease in mortality rates associated with stroke and other communicable diseases. Neurological problems
have a significant impact on an individual's motor skills, cognitive abilities, and communication capabilities. The presence of biochemical, structural, and electrical anomalies
within bodily systems can result in impaired coordination across various organs. This
phenomenon has been implicated in the cause of autism, neuromuscular diseases, epilepsy, brain tumors, Alzheimer's disease, Parkinson's disease, and various other conditions. Neurological problems can arise from various factors, such as infection, brain or
nerve injury, spinal cord injury, vitamin shortage, and genetic abnormalities. Certain individuals may experience neurological issues from birth, while others may develop similar
problems later in life as a result of hormonal fluctuations, environmental influences, or
unforeseen circumstances. The nervous system is impacted in all instances, subsequently
exerting influence on other bodily organs. Neurological problems can arise from a variety
of factors, as illustrated in Figure 4.4.

Neurological illnesses are characterised by a range of general symptoms, such as
paralysis, muscle weakness, pain, seizures, impaired consciousness, and compromised

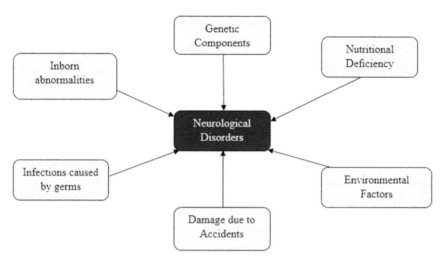

FIGURE 4.4
Causes of neurological disorders

coordination [12]. More than 600 diseases like multiple sclerosis, Alzheimer's disease, Parkinson's disease, epilepsy, dementia, stroke, brain tumour, headache, traumatic brain injuries, and neuroinfections are caused due to underlying issues within the neurological system. Viral, bacterial, fungal, and parasitic illnesses exert a comprehensive impact on the entire nervous system [12–17]. Neurological disorder is one form of brain-related disorder that affects the movement, speaking, and learning abilities of individuals [18]. Some neurological conditions result in permanent and others in temporary disability. Compared to all other human disorders, neurological and neuropsychiatric disorders are the leading cause of disability [19]. The manual identification of these illnesses through the examination of medical records is a challenging task. Computer-Aided Design (CAD) systems have been developed to aid medical practitioners in the evaluation of medical records. These systems involve a series of phases, including pre-processing, feature extraction, and classification. The primary objectives of these systems are to enhance the accuracy of diagnoses, ensure consistency in diagnoses, and expedite the analysis process. CAD systems that are both efficient and cost-effective have the potential to serve as decision support systems for medical professionals in the field of diagnosing and treating neurological disorders. Following the preprocessing of the input medical data, the retrieved features are utilised as input for the classifier with the aim of performing classification [20].

4.5 AI in the Prediction of Neurological Disorders

Segato et al. conducted a comprehensive examination on the application of artificial intelligence techniques for diagnosis and treatment of diverse brain diseases [21]. AI techniques have been applied in various domains of healthcare, such as medical decision support systems [22], medical image segmentation and classification [23], screening for diabetic retinopathy [24], predicting diabetes [25], cardiovascular medicine [26], diagnosing strokes [27], providing behavioural and mental health care [28], conducting neuroscience research [29], psychoradiology [30], managing healthcare data [31], designing clinical trials [32], clinical genomics [33] and many more. Artificial Intelligence (AI) has the potential to assist radiologists and physicians by facilitating the management of challenging and time-consuming tasks, such as the identification and categorisation of anomalies [34]. The human mind possesses inherent limitations regarding its capacity to process information during a given time frame. Artificial Intelligence (AI) methodologies can be applied for the identification and diagnosis of neurological disorders, as well as for the detection of neurotransmitters [35]. Table 4.1 reviews and summarises recent AI applications in the detection, diagnosis, classification, and prediction of neurological disorders.

A vocational problem-solving training programme based on artificial intelligent virtual reality was designed for people with traumatic brain injuries. The effectiveness of this approach is proved to be better in enhancing the employment opportunities of people having traumatic brain injury than the conventional psycho-educational approach [36]. Farrugia et al. [37] examined the use of intelligent computing tools like rule- based expert systems, fuzzy logic, genetic algorithms, and neural networks for diagnosis in medical science. A smartphone application has been proposed for the purpose of analysing, diagnosing, and treating hydrocephalus [37]. AI has also been applied for the detection and segmentation of abnormal tissues considering brain MRI images. The initial step of the proposed study involves the extraction of features from the brain images. These extracted features are then utilised as input for a neuro-fuzzy classifier, which is responsible for the classification process. The classifier is responsible for distinguishing between abnormal and normal images. The region growing method is applied to segment the abnormal tissues such as tumour and atrophy [38]. Verbal frequency tests were carried out to assess the cognitive psychological and neuro-psychological disorders. A computer-aided diagnosis tool was designed using the concepts from semantic reasoning and artificial intelligence. Semantic pattern analysis was performed to interpret the verbal frequency tests [39].

A fuzzy rule–based expert system was devised for the purpose of diagnosing multiple sclerosis. A person's identity, signs, and symptoms were considered for making decisions. A direct approach is used to build the knowledge base and a forward chaining method is applied for inference [40]. In order to address the challenges associated with early detection, cost, and time requirements in the diagnosis of epilepsy, Fergus et al. [41] developed a supervised machine learning technique for the classification of epileptic seizure and non-seizure records [41]. Artificial neural networks, machine learning techniques, Naïve Bayes (NB), k-Nearest Neighbour (k-NN), and Support Vector Machines (SVM) were applied for classifying trichotillomania (TTM) and Obsessive-Compulsive Disorder (OCD) patients. It was observed that the performance of SVM is best among all the tested techniques. So, to enhance feature selection efficiency while minimising the number of iterations, the researchers integrated the Support Vector Machines (SVM) algorithm with the Improved Ant Colony Optimization (IACO) technique [42].

Erguzel et al. [43] used Particle Swarm Optimization (PSO) for selecting the features and artificial neural network to train the classification model. Their proposed approach differentiates the bipolar disorders from unipolar disorders [43]. Artificial intelligence was also applied to design a decision support system for dyscalculia [44]. A deep learning–based reliable technique was proposed to detect Alzheimer's disease and its early stage, which is mild cognitive impairment [45]. IBM Watson was used to detect additional RNA-binding proteins altered in an Amyotrophic Lateral Sclerosis (ALS) which is a neurodegenerative disease [46]. Vashistha et al [47] discussed different techniques that uses AI for quicker,

TABLE 4.1

Summary of works on survey on neurological disorders

Author (s) with Year of Publication	Disease under Study	Dataset	Method(s) Used	Aim of the Study	Remarks
Man, D. W. K., Poon, W. S., & Lam, C. (2013) [36]	Traumatic brain injury	Forty participants with mild or moderate brain injury were randomly chosen	Virtual reality (VR)–based vocational problem-solving skill training programme	Enhancing employment opportunities of people having traumatic brain injury	Comparisons of problem-solving skills using Wisconsin Card Sorting Test, the Tower of London Test, and the Vocational Cognitive Rating Scale
Farrugia, A., Al-Jumeily, D., Al-Jumaily, M., Hussain, A., & Lamb, D. (2013) [37]	Hydrocephalus which causes headaches	Patients' information is gathered utilising a mobile app.	–	Proposed a mobile application for the analysis, diagnosis, and treatment of hydrocephalus	Acts as an expert system, reviews the headache cases of hydrocephalus patients, aids in decision-making
Bhanumurthy, M. Y., & Anne, K. (2014) [38]	Brain tumour	Brain web images	Features extracted includes entropy, energy, homogeneity, correlation, and contrast. Neuro-fuzzy classifier is applied on the extracted features for classification and region-growing approach is used for segmenting the abnormal tissues	Detection and segmentation of abnormal tissues such as tumour and atrophy from MRI images of brain	False Positive Ratio, False Negative Ratio, sensitivity, specificity, and accuracy are calculated for the segmentation result
Sukumar, S. R. et al. (2014) [39]	Neurological disorders	de-identified dataset of verbal fluency tests of 75 participants	Ten semantic features were considered and k-nearest neighbour method applied for classification	Verbal frequency tests to assess neuropsychological disorders and its semantic pattern analysis	–
Ghahazi, M. A. et al. (2014) [40]	Multiple sclerosis	–	Direct approach is applied to design knowledge base, forward chaining is employed for inference, fuzzy results are obtained using Mamdani inference method	Diagnosis of multiple sclerosis	Identity of the person, symptoms are considered for decision-making

(Continued)

TABLE 4.1 (CONTINUED)

Summary of works on survey on neurological disorders

Author (s) with Year of Publication	Disease under Study	Dataset	Method(s) Used	Aim of the Study	Remarks
Fergus, P. et al. (2015) [41]	Epilepsy	Open dataset containing 342 records	Supervised machine learning method, k-class nearest neighbour classifier	Automatic detection of epileptic seizure	Sensitivity and specificity calculated
Erguzel, T. T. et al. (2015) [42]	Trichotillomania (TTM), obsessive–compulsive disorder (OCD)	Quantitative EEG (QEEG) cordance values with 19 electrodes from 10 brain regions in 4 frequency bands	SVM combined with improved ant colony optimization (IACO) approach	Classification of trichotillomania (TTM) and obsessive–compulsive disorder (OCD)	Machine learning techniques, artificial neural networks, support vector machine, k-nearest neighbour and Naïve Bayes were used to classify TTM and OCD patients and it was observed that the performance of SVM is better than others
Erguzel, T. T. et al. (2016) [43]	Unipolar and bipolar disorder		Particle swarm optimization (PSO) algorithm for feature selection and ANN for training	Classification of unipolar and bipolar depressive disorders	
Ferraz, F. et al. (2016) [44]	Dyscalculia	Android app disMAT	The computational framework is constructed on top of a logic programming methodology for knowledge representation and reasoning, grounded on a case-based approach to computing, that allows for the handling of incomplete, unknown, or even self-contradictory information	Decision support system for the analysis of dyscalculia	Sensitivity, specificity, positive predictive value (PPV), and negative predictive value (NPV), receiver operating characteristic (ROC) curve

(Continued)

TABLE 4.1 (CONTINUED)

Summary of works on survey on neurological disorders

Author (s) with Year of Publication	Disease under Study	Dataset	Method(s) Used	Aim of the Study	Remarks
Farooq, A. et al. (2017) [45]	Alzheimer's disease and mild cognitive impairment	MRI data taken from Alzheimer's disease neuroimaging initiative (ADNI)	Deep learning	Diagnosis of Alzheimer's disease and mild cognitive impairment	Three distinct data subsets are utilised, which include binary, unbalanced multiclass, and balanced multiclass datasets
Al Nahian et al. (2020) [48]	Neurological disorder	Data collected using IoT sensors and camera device	Used concepts from IoT, artificial intelligence and big data analytics	Develop an emotion-aware fall-monitoring framework for aged people having neurological disorder	Applied a cognitive engine, an AI-enabled emotion detection module, and a fall-detection module on a remote cloud server that keeps the accumulated data
Ćosić, K. et al. (2020) [49]	Mental health disorders	Official hospital archives and clinical records	Statistical analysis, supervised and unsupervised machine learning techniques	Predicting mental health disorders of health care workers due to COVID-19 pandemic	–
Chen, T. et al. (2020) [50]	Autism spectrum disorder	Four datasets from the second edition of the Autism Brain Imaging Data Exchange, including the ETH Zürich (ETH), NYU Langone Medical Center: Sample 1, Oregon Health and Science University, and Stanford University (SU) sites	Histogram of oriented gradients (HOG) for feature extraction, Naïve Bayes approach to identify the predictive ASD-related brain regions based on classification contributions of each HOG feature	Diagnosing and evaluating autism spectrum disorder	
Sabzevari, F. et al. (2023) [55]	Autism	Survey data gathered from 87 children diagnosed with autism spectrum disorders (ASD)	CBCL (child behaviour checklist) and neuro-fuzzy approach	Studying the impact of COVID-19 restrictions and speech therapy on autistic children	Used a fully connected adaptive neuro-fuzzy inference system which takes type and duration of treatments as input and T-score is calculated

more accurate, and less expensive diagnosis of various neurodegenerative problems [47]. IoT and big data analytics concepts were combined with AI techniques to develop an emotion-aware fall-monitoring framework to recognise the emotions of elderly people, predict the conditions of their health, and fall-monitoring in real time. In an emergency, a predefined caregiver receives an alert message and a mobile clinic or smart ambulance will reach at the address of the aged person [48]. Ćosić et al. [49] studied the mental health of health workers affected by COVID-19 and proposed a method to predict their mental health disorders due to the pandemic [49]. A study was carried out for the diagnosis and evaluation of Autism Spectrum Disorder (ASD) on the basis of structural patterns of brain [50]. AI techniques were also applied for brain MRI image classification [51], detecting structural and functional optic nerve head abnormalities and ocular movement disorders in neuro-ophthalmology [52], diagnosis of dementia disorders of old age people [53], and diagnosis and treatment of motor neuron diseases [54]. Sabzevari et al. [55] studied the impact of restrictions during COVID-19 and speech treatment methods in lockdowns on autistic children using a neuro-fuzzy approach [55].

4.6 Conclusion and Future Scope

Intelligent approaches have a wide range of applications across several domains, including the field of medical science. This chapter provides an overview of the applications of artificial intelligence techniques in the detection, diagnosis, classification, and prediction of neurological illnesses. Intelligent methodologies are also employed for the examination of medical images, such as brain MRI scans, in order to identify any deviations or irregularities within the brain. Various environmental circumstances, such as the constraints imposed during the COVID-19 pandemic, have an impact on individuals' mental well-being and overall way of life. Artificial Intelligence (AI) methodologies are additionally employed to provide support for individuals afflicted with neurological diseases. Expert systems utilise patient records to perform analysis and employ the knowledge base to facilitate clinical decision-making. Computer-based detection strategies have been found to exhibit superior performance in terms of speed, cost-effectiveness, and accuracy when compared to manual approaches. Academic researchers are currently engaged in the pursuit of developing intelligent devices with the aim of providing assistance and alleviating the burdens experienced by individuals.

In contrast to human decision-making processes, decisions made by artificial gadgets are mostly grounded in observations and remain unaffected by emotional factors. These technologies possess the ability to make impartial judgements and exhibit extended operational endurance without experiencing fatigue or boredom. These machines also exhibit superior speed and efficiency compared to their human creators. Notwithstanding these advancements, the integration of Artificial Intelligence (AI) in the healthcare sector is still in its nascent phase and requires substantial further research and development. Scientists are currently engaged in the pursuit of creating gadgets that possess inherent creativity, the capacity to effectively address novel challenges, and the ability to employ independent reasoning when confronted with unforeseen circumstances. Improper utilisation of AI devices has the potential to result in extensive devastation, while their suitable application can prove to be highly advantageous for society.

References

1. Balafar, M. A., Ramli, A. R., Saripan, M. I., & Mashohor, S. (2010). Review of brain MRI image segmentation methods. *Artificial Intelligence Review, 33,* 261–274.
2. Gudigar, A., Raghavendra, U., Hegde, A., Kalyani, M., Ciaccio, E. J., & Acharya, U. R. (2020). Brain pathology identification using computer aided diagnostic tool: A systematic review. *Computer Methods and Programs in Biomedicine, 187,* 105205.
3. Lima, A. A., Mridha, M. F., Das, S. C., Kabir, M. M., Islam, M. R., & Watanobe, Y. (2022). A comprehensive survey on the detection, classification, and challenges of neurological disorders. *Biology, 11*(3), 469.
4. Cukier, K. (2019). Ready for robots: How to think about the future of AI. *Foreign Affairs, 98,* 192.
5. Myers, A. (2011). Stanford's John McCarthy, seminal figure of artificial intelligence, dies at 84. Stanford Report. Retrieved July 14, 2019, https://news.stanford.edu/news/2011/october/john-mccarthy-obit-102511.html
6. Patel, U. K., Anwar, A., Saleem, S., Malik, P., Rasul, B., Patel, K., & Arumaithurai, K. (2021). Artificial intelligence as an emerging technology in the current care of neurological disorders. *Journal of Neurology, 268,* 1623–1642.
7. Singla, J., Grover, D., & Bhandari, A. (2014). Medical expert systems for diagnosis of various diseases. *International Journal of Computer Applications, 93*(7). 36–43.
8. Mitchell, T. M. et al. (1997). *Machine Learning.* McGraw-Hill.
9. Raghavendra, U., Acharya, U. R., & Adeli, H. (2020). Artificial intelligence techniques for automated diagnosis of neurological disorders. *European Neurology, 82*(1–3), 41–64.
10. Larobina, M., & Murino, L. (2014). Medical image file formats. *Journal of Digital Imaging, 27,* 200–206.
11. Chandra, J., Rangaswamy, M., Banerjee, B., Prajapati, A., Akhtar, Z., Sakauye, K., & Joseph, A. (2022). Applications of artificial intelligence to neurological disorders: Current technologies and open problems. In *Augmenting Neurological Disorder Prediction and Rehabilitation Using Artificial Intelligence* (pp. 243–272). Academic Press.
12. World Health Organization. World Health Organization, 27-02-2017. Retrieved December 12, 2018, from https://www.who.int/mediacentre/news/releases/2007/pr04/e/
13. Acharya, U. R., Hagiwara, Y., & Adeli, H. (2018). Automated seizure prediction. *Epilepsy & Behavior, 88,* 251–261.
14. Bairy, G. M., Lih, O. S., Hagiwara, Y., Puthankattil, S. D., Faust, O., Niranjan, U. C., & Acharya, U. R. (2017). Automated diagnosis of depression electroencephalograph signals using linear prediction coding and higher order spectra features. *Journal of Medical Imaging and Health Informatics, 7*(8), 1857–1862.
15. Bhat, S., Acharya, U. R., Adeli, H., Bairy, G. M., & Adeli, A. (2014). Autism: Cause factors, early diagnosis and therapies. *Reviews in the Neurosciences, 25*(6), 841–850.
16. Bhat, S., Acharya, U. R., Adeli, H., Bairy, G. M., & Adeli, A. (2014). Automated diagnosis of autism: In search of a mathematical marker. *Reviews in the Neurosciences, 25*(6), 851–861.
17. Sridhar, C., Bhat, S., Acharya, U. R., Adeli, H., & Bairy, G. M. (2017). Diagnosis of attention deficit hyperactivity disorder using imaging and signal processing techniques. *Computers in Biology and Medicine, 88,* 93–99.
18. Kennedy, D. P., & Adolphs, R. (2012). The social brain in psychiatric and neurological disorders. *Trends in Cognitive Sciences, 16*(11), 559–572.
19. Gautam, R., & Sharma, M. (2020). Prevalence and diagnosis of neurological disorders using different deep learning techniques: A meta-analysis. *Journal of Medical Systems, 44*(2), 49.
20. Siuly, S., & Zhang, Y. (2016). Medical big data: Neurological diseases diagnosis through medical data analysis. *Data Science and Engineering, 1,* 54–64.
21. Segato, A., Marzullo, A., Calimeri, F., & De Momi, E. (2020). Artificial intelligence for brain diseases: A systematic review. *APL Bioengineering, 4*(4). 1–35.

22. Aljaaf, A. J., Al-Jumeily, D., Hussain, A. J., Fergus, P., Al-Jumaily, M., & Abdel-Aziz, K. (2015, July). Toward an optimal use of artificial intelligence techniques within a clinical decision support system. In *2015 Science and Information Conference (SAI)* (pp. 548–554). IEEE.

23. Aljaaf, A. J., Al-Jumeily, D., Hussain, A. J., Fergus, P., Al-Jumaily, M., & Abdel-Aziz, K. (2015, July). Toward an optimal use of artificial intelligence techniques within a clinical decision support system. In *2015 Science and Information Conference (SAI)* (pp. 548–554). IEEE.

24. Wong, T. Y., & Bressler, N. M. (2016). Artificial intelligence with deep learning technology looks into diabetic retinopathy screening. *JAMA, 316*(22), 2366–2367.

25. Samira, K., & Ahmad, J. (2016). A new artificial intelligence method for prediction of diabetes type 2. *Bulletin de la Société Royale des Sciences de Liège, 85*, 376–91.

26. Krittanawong, C., Zhang, H., Wang, Z., Aydar, M., & Kitai, T. (2017). Artificial intelligence in precision cardiovascular medicine. *Journal of the American College of Cardiology, 69*(21), 2657–2664.

27. Abedi, V., Khan, A., Chaudhary, D., Misra, D., Avula, V., Mathrawala, D., ... Zand, R. (2020). Using artificial intelligence for improving stroke diagnosis in emergency departments: A practical framework. *Therapeutic Advances in Neurological Disorders, 13*, 1756286420938962.

28. Luxton, D. D. (2016). An introduction to artificial intelligence in behavioral and mental health care. In David D. Luxton *Artificial Intelligence in Behavioral and Mental Health Care* (pp. 1–26). Academic Press.

29. Gonzalez, R. T., Riascos, J. A., & Barone, D. A. (2017). How artificial intelligence is supporting neuroscience research: A discussion about foundations, methods and applications. In *Computational Neuroscience: First Latin American Workshop, LAWCN 2017, Porto Alegre, Brazil, November 22–24, 2017, Proceedings* (pp. 63–77). Springer International Publishing.

30. Li, F., Sun, H., Biswal, B. B., Sweeney, J. A., & Gong, Q. (2021). Artificial intelligence applications in psychoradiology. *Psychoradiology, 1*(2), 94–107.

31. Gupta, N. S., & Kumar, P. (2023). Perspective of artificial intelligence in healthcare data management: A journey towards precision medicine. *Computers in Biology and Medicine, 162*, 107051.

32. Harrer, S., Shah, P., Antony, B., & Hu, J. (2019). Artificial intelligence for clinical trial design. *Trends in Pharmacological Sciences, 40*(8), 577–591.

33. Dias, R., & Torkamani, A. (2019). Artificial intelligence in clinical and genomic diagnostics. *Genome Medicine, 11*(1), 1–12.

34. Hainc, N., Federau, C., Stieltjes, B., Blatow, M., Bink, A., & Stippich, C. (2017). The bright, artificial intelligence-augmented future of neuroimaging reading. *Frontiers in Neurology, 8*, 489.

35. Gopinath, N. (2023). Artificial intelligence and neuroscience: An update on fascinating relationships. *Process Biochemistry, 125*, 113–120.

36. Man, D. W. K., Poon, W. S., & Lam, C. (2013). The effectiveness of artificial intelligent 3-D virtual reality vocational problem-solving training in enhancing employment opportunities for people with traumatic brain injury. *Brain Injury, 27*(9), 1016–1025.

37. Farrugia, A., Al-Jumeily, D., Al-Jumaily, M., Hussain, A., & Lamb, D. (2013, December). Medical diagnosis: Are artificial intelligence systems able to diagnose the underlying causes of specific headaches?. In *2013 Sixth International Conference on Developments in eSystems Engineering* (pp. 376–382). IEEE.

38. Bhanumurthy, M. Y., & Anne, K. (2014, December). An automated detection and segmentation of tumor in brain MRI using artificial intelligence. In *2014 IEEE International Conference on Computational Intelligence and Computing Research* (pp. 1–6). IEEE.

39. Sukumar, S. R., Ainsworth, K. C., & Brown, T. C. (2014, May). Semantic pattern analysis for verbal fluency based assessment of neurological disorders. In *Proceedings of the 2014 Biomedical Sciences and Engineering Conference* (pp. 1–4). IEEE.

40. Ghahazi, M. A., Zarandi, M. F., Harirchian, M. H., & Damirchi-Darasi, S. R. (2014, June). Fuzzy rule based expert system for diagnosis of multiple sclerosis. In *2014 IEEE Conference on Norbert Wiener in the 21st Century (21CW)* (pp. 1–5). IEEE.

41. Fergus, P., Hignett, D., Hussain, A., Al-Jumeily, D., & Abdel-Aziz, K. (2015). Automatic epileptic seizure detection using scalp EEG and advanced artificial intelligence techniques. *BioMed Research International, 2015*, 1–17.

42. Erguzel, T. T., Ozekes, S., Sayar, G. H., Tan, O., & Tarhan, N. (2015). A hybrid artificial intelligence method to classify trichotillomania and obsessive compulsive disorder. *Neurocomputing*, *161*, 220–228.
43. Erguzel, T. T., Sayar, G. H., & Tarhan, N. (2016). Artificial intelligence approach to classify unipolar and bipolar depressive disorders. *Neural Computing and Applications*, *27*(6), 1607–1616.
44. Ferraz, F., Vicente, H., Costa, A., & Neves, J. (2016). Analysis of dyscalculia evidences through artificial intelligence systems. *Journal of Software Networking*, 53–78, River Publishers.
45. Farooq, A., Anwar, S., Awais, M., & Alnowami, M. (2017, September). Artificial intelligence based smart diagnosis of Alzheimer's disease and mild cognitive impairment. In *2017 International Smart Cities Conference (ISC2)* (pp. 1–4). IEEE.
46. Bakkar, N., Kovalik, T., Lorenzini, I., Spangler, S., Lacoste, A., Sponaugle, K., ... Bowser, R. (2018). Artificial intelligence in neurodegenerative disease research: Use of IBM Watson to identify additional RNA-binding proteins altered in amyotrophic lateral sclerosis. *Acta Neuropathologica*, *135*, 227–247.
47. Vashistha, R., Yadav, D., Chhabra, D., & Shukla, P. (2019). Artificial intelligence integration for neurodegenerative disorders. In *Leveraging Biomedical and Healthcare Data* (pp. 77–89). Academic Press.
48. Al Nahian, M. J., Ghosh, T., Uddin, M. N., Islam, M. M., Mahmud, M., & Kaiser, M. S. (2020, September). Towards artificial intelligence driven emotion aware fall monitoring framework suitable for elderly people with neurological disorder. In *International Conference on Brain Informatics* (pp. 275–286). Springer International Publishing.
49. Ćosić, K., Popović, S., Šarlija, M., Kesedžić, I., & Jovanovic, T. (2020). Artificial intelligence in prediction of mental health disorders induced by the COVID-19 pandemic among health care workers. *Croatian Medical Journal*, *61*(3), 279.
50. Chen, T., Chen, Y., Yuan, M., Gerstein, M., Li, T., Liang, H., ... Lu, L. (2020). The development of a practical artificial intelligence tool for diagnosing and evaluating autism spectrum disorder: Multicenter study. *JMIR Medical Informatics*, *8*(5), e15767.
51. Zhang, Z., Li, G., Xu, Y., & Tang, X. (2021). Application of artificial intelligence in the MRI classification task of human brain neurological and psychiatric diseases: A scoping review. *Diagnostics*, *11*(8), 1402.
52. Leong, Y. Y., Vasseneix, C., Finkelstein, M. T., Milea, D., & Najjar, R. P. (2022). Artificial intelligence meets neuro-ophthalmology. *The Asia-Pacific Journal of Ophthalmology*, *11*(2), 111–125.
53. Battineni, G., Chintalapudi, N., Hossain, M. A., Losco, G., Ruocco, C., Sagaro, G. G., ... Amenta, F. (2022). Artificial intelligence models in the diagnosis of adult-onset dementia disorders: A review. *Bioengineering*, *9*(8), 370.
54. Lopez-Bernal, D., Balderas, D., Ponce, P., Rojas, M., & Molina, A. (2023). Implications of artificial intelligence algorithms in the diagnosis and treatment of motor neuron diseases—A review. *Life*, *13*(4), 1031.
55. Sabzevari, F., Amelirad, O., Moradi, Z., & Habibi, M. (2023). Artificial intelligence evaluation of COVID-19 restrictions and speech therapy effects on the autistic children's behavior. *Scientific Reports*, *13*(1), 4312.

5

Malformation Risk Prediction with Machine Learning Modelling for Pregnant Women with Epilepsy

Tessy Mathew, Jesna Mohan, Jisha John, P. L. Deepa, and Sanjeev V. Thomas

5.1 Introduction

There are approximately 50 million individuals affected by epilepsy, with a significant portion of them, roughly a quarter, being women of reproductive age. Most women with epilepsy (WWE) require the continuous use of antiseizure medicines (ASM) during pregnancy to prevent seizures. Extensive data from large prospective pregnancy registries and meta-analyses have established that infants exposed to ASMs in the womb face an elevated risk of major congenital malformations (MCM). It's important to note that the relative risk of MCM associated with ASMs varies significantly among different drugs, with the highest risk linked to valproate and the lowest with lamotrigine [5–6]. Furthermore, there's evidence indicating a dose-dependent increase in MCM risk for several ASMs. For WWE on polytherapy with multiple ASMs, the interaction between these drugs introduces added complexity.

Additionally, various other factors can influence the risk of MCM for WWE. Changes in blood levels of folate induced by ASMs and its crucial role in embryogenesis have been linked to neural tube defects associated with ASM use [1]. Surprisingly, folate supplementation does not appear to reduce the risk of MCM in WWE, despite its effectiveness in reducing such risks in studies involving the general population. The impact of generalized seizures during pregnancy on the risk of MCM remains somewhat unclear, but it may lead to cesarean-section deliveries. There have been isolated cases of adverse fetal effects following tonic-clonic seizures during pregnancy [10]. Socioeconomic factors, nutritional status, and other environmental variables are known to have an impact on pregnancy outcomes and the occurrence of MCM.

The relationship between biological and environmental factors and their combined impact on fetal outcomes and MCM is intricate and resists straightforward association studies. Machine learning (ML) techniques are now gaining prominence in developing algorithms and models for clinical decision-making. These models typically rely on extensive real-world datasets and have the capacity to create models without preconceived hypotheses. They can effectively incorporate multiple parameters and address issues related to imbalances when the outcome of interest is rare.

In this study, our objective was to harness ML techniques to construct a robust model capable of predicting the risk of MCM in WWE. We placed particular emphasis on maternal

DOI: 10.1201/9781003450153-6

characteristics, ASM usage, and other environmental factors during the periconceptional period. Furthermore, we aimed to develop a model that could offer insights into how the risk of MCM may vary across different ASM therapies and dosages.

5.2 Materials and Methods

The Kerala Registry of Epilepsy and Pregnancy was established to investigate the maternal and fetal outcomes of women with epilepsy (WWE). Between 1998 and 2020, this registry enrolled over 3,000 women. The protocol and the outcomes related to malformations in this registry were previously published [2].

Pregnancies were categorized as having or not having major congenital malformations (MCM) [3] based on antenatal and postnatal assessments. The highest dosage of antiseizure medication (ASM) used at any point during the first trimester was considered the exposure level. Confounding factors examined included the use of folic acid [16], the maternal epilepsy syndrome, and the educational background of both parents [9].

The educational and occupational status of the woman and her husband were rated on a scale from 1 to 6, with the combined score of the couple representing the education and occupation score for the pregnancy. The registry obtained approval from the institutional ethics committee (Approval no: SCTIEC/17/2003, dated 13 June 2003), and written informed consent was obtained from all participants.

5.3 Dataset and Framework of MCM Prediction

All pertinent data were obtained from the primary registry records and underwent anonymization, where any identifying information was substituted with randomly generated values. For the purpose of the study, only anonymized data was used. The schematic representation of the method proposed for predicting malformations is provided in Figure 5.1.

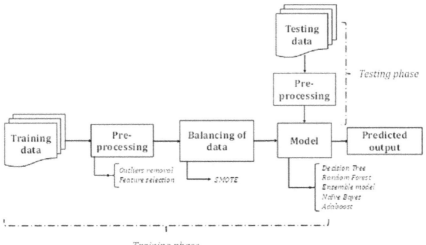

FIGURE 5.1
Framework of MCM prediction.

TABLE 5.1

Table Showing Different Features

Features	Details
Age	Age at the time of registration
Education/occupation	Sum of the scores for education and occupation for the parents (WWE and husband)
Eclassgroup	Epilepsy classification(generalized, focal, or unclassified)
PBTM1Max	Phenobarbitone highest dose (mg) used in the first trimester
LTGTM1Max	Lamotrigine highest dose (mg) used in the first trimester
CLZTM1Max	Clonazepam highest dose (mg) used in the first trimester
PHTTM1Max	Phenytoin highest dose (mg) used in the first trimester
CLBTM1Max	Clobazam highest dose (mg) used in the first trimester
CBZTM1Max	Carbamazepine highest dose (mg) used in the first trimester
VPATM1Max	Valproate highest dose (mg) used in the first trimester
TPMTM1Max	Topiramate highest dose (mg) used in the first trimester
LEVTM1Max	Levetiracetam highest dose (mg) used in the first trimester
OXCTM1Max	Oxcarbazepine highest dose (mg) used in the first trimester
TSMPPAv	Count of all types of seizures during the pre-pregnancy month
GTMPPAv#	Count of Generalized tonic-clonic seizures during the pre-pregnancy month
FAPPMax	The highest dose of folic acid (mg) in pre-pregnancy month

includes secondary generalized (bilateral tonic-clonic seizures) also

This framework comprises four key stages: pre-processing, data balancing, training the machine learning model, and ultimately, validating and testing the trained model.

5.4 Pre-processing and Balancing the Data

The pre-processing phase involved two main steps: the removal of outliers and the selection of pertinent features. The features associated with major congenital malformations (MCM) [3] were designated as the primary classifiers (outcome measure), while all other features were considered as potential predictors for subsequent processing, as illustrated in Table 5.1.

To identify the most significant features, we applied various feature selection algorithms [13], including those based on Information Gain, Gain Ratio, Gini, ANOVA, Chi-square, ReliefF, and Fast Correlation-based Filter (FCBF).

Data imbalance can significantly impact classifier performance. To address this issue, we employed Synthetic Oversampling Technique (SMOTE) [14] to rebalance the data, achieving a 1:1 ratio.

5.5 Machine Learning Models and Experimental Analysis

5.5.1 Logistic Regression

This a predictive method used to model the relationship between one or more independent variables (represented as $x1$ and $x2$) and a binary dependent variable (represented as Y). The logistic regression model calculates coefficients (β 0, β 1, and β 2) based on the given data to establish a linear relationship that predicts the probability of a positive or negative outcome.

In mathematical terms, the logistic regression model is represented as:

$$(p \: / \: (1-p)) = \beta\,0 + \beta\,1x1 + \beta\,2x2 \tag{1}$$

Here, p represents the probability of the positive outcome, while the values of β 0, β 1, and β 2 are determined from the data and are essential for predicting the classification into positive and negative classes.

5.5.2 Naïve Bayes Classifier (NBC)

This is a classification technique based on conditional probabilities of events. It offers the advantage of learning from limited information, even when information about specific features is missing. In the context of NBC, let $F = (f1, f2, ..., fn)$ be the input vector, and C1 and C2 represent two possible outcomes or classes.

Naïve Bayes classifies based on conditional probabilities as follows:

$$(Ci \mid F) = ((X \mid Ci) * (Ci)) \: / \: (F) \tag{2}$$

Where:

(Ci) represents the prior probability of class Ci.

$(X \mid Ci)$ represents the conditional probability of the input vector F given class Ci.

The overall probability $(Ci \mid F)$ is used to classify an instance into one of the classes (C1 or C2) based on the highest probability.

Additionally, the total probability (F) is calculated as a combination of class-specific conditional probabilities for each feature fi.

5.5.3 Decision Tree

This is a type of classification model represented as a tree structure. It consists of internal nodes, branches, and leaves, where each internal node represents a feature from the dataset, branches denote decisions or conditions, and leaves represent the final outcomes or classifications. Decision Trees are learned from labeled training data. The tree-building process involves iteratively selecting the best feature to split the data until a predefined stopping condition is met. It is widely used in classification and regression tasks.

5.5.4 Adaboost

Adaboost is short for adaptive boosting, is an ensemble learning technique that combines multiple weak classifiers to create a strong classifier. It is primarily used for binary classification problems. Adaboost assigns weights to training instances, and in each iteration, it focuses on the misclassified instances, thus improving the model's overall performance. The final prediction is a weighted combination of the individual classifier predictions, resulting in an accurate and robust model.

5.5.5 Random Forest (RF)

This is another ensemble learning model that builds a collection of decision trees during the training process. It works by selecting a random subset of samples from the training data and building decision trees using these samples. At each node in each tree, feature selection is carried out based on criteria such as the GINI index or Information Gain. RF combines the results from multiple decision trees to make a final prediction. It's known for its robustness and is particularly effective in handling complex datasets.

5.5.6 Stacking

Known as stacked generalization, stacking is a meta-ensemble model that combines the predictions of various base models, including Logistic Regression, Naïve Bayes, Decision Tree, Adaboost, and Random Forest, as considered in this study. Stacking involves training multiple base models, and then a meta-model is trained to learn how to best combine the predictions of these base models. This approach leverages the strengths of different models to improve predictive performance. Stacking is useful when you want to create a highly accurate and adaptable model by combining the expertise of various machine learning techniques.

In our study, we employed the stacking ensemble model as the ultimate machine learning model, which integrated the predictive capabilities of several base models, including Logistic Regression, Naïve Bayes, Decision Tree, Adaboost, and Random Forest. This ensemble model was subjected to rigorous testing and evaluation using a dataset that was randomly partitioned into separate training and testing subsets. The data-splitting process involved various proportions, with the dataset being divided into training and testing subsets in the following ratios: 60% for training and 40% for testing, 70% for training and 30% for testing, and 80% for training and 20% for testing. These different ratios allowed us to assess how the model's performance varied under various training/testing scenarios.

To comprehensively evaluate the model's performance, we applied both cross-validation and leave-one-out techniques. Cross-validation is a technique that involves dividing the dataset into subsets for training and testing multiple times to ensure robust model assessment. Leave-one-out is a specific form of cross-validation where each data point is used as a test set exactly once. By employing these rigorous testing and evaluation methods, we aimed to provide a thorough analysis of the ensemble model's performance and its ability to make accurate predictions across different training and testing scenarios. This approach allowed us to assess the model's generalizability and reliability in real-world applications.

5.6 Performance Metrics

The performance of the models was assessed on the metrics: area under the curve (AUC), classification accuracy (CA), recall (R), precision (P), and F1 score. Precision (P) measures the fraction of relevant positive instances among the retrieved positive instances. Recall (R) measures the fraction of relevant positive instances among the actual positive instances. F1- score is the harmonic mean of precision and recall. It was further evaluated with a confusion matrix that tabulates the true positive and negatives against the false positive and negatives. The models were analyzed using both cross-validation and leave-one-out techniques.

5.7 Results

There were 148 infants with MCM in this data set of 2328 completed pregnancies (2066 live births). The characteristics of the class with MCM and without MCM are given in Table 5.2.

There were 117 features in the dataset for each case that broadly fell into parental demographic characteristics (n=12), maternal epilepsy syndrome and seizure characteristics (n=18), details of the ASM usage during pregnancy (n=73), and the details of the MCM (n=14). All the features were ranked based on the feature selection algorithms, and we identified 16 highest ranked features for further analysis and generation of the MCM prediction model as given in Table 5.3. This dataset was imbalanced as only 148 cases (6.87%) of the 2328 pregnancies had MCM. We balanced the dataset by SMOTE before generating the models that attempted the best classification (prediction of MCM).

We used different techniques viz. Decision Tree (DT), Random Forest (RF), Naïve Bayes (NB), Logistic Regression (LR), AdaBoost (AB), and Stack model to the reliability of the model, and the results obtained are as shown in Tables 5.4 and 5.5.

The evaluation metrics of the model increased steadily as the proportion of training data increased from 60–40% to 70–30% and 80–20%. The results show that the ensemble classifier outperformed other classifiers considered in the study with an accuracy of 93.63% when cross-validation is done using 80/20 ratio. The results of the leave-one-out test is given in Table 5.5.

TABLE 5.2

Distribution of Features among Class with MCM and Class without MCM

Features	No Malformation, Mean (Standard Deviation)	Malformation Present, Mean (Standard Deviation)
N – Total number of instances	2066	148
Age years mean (SD)	26.12 (4.43)	25.79 (3.99)
Epilepsy classification (Eclassgrp)		
generalized epilepsy	793	60
focal epilepsy	941	63
others	73	4
ASM exposure mg/ day	Mean (SD)	Mean (SD)
PBTM1Max	85.93 (47.81)	109.44 (53.86)
LTGTM1Max	196.69 (132.22)	75
CLZTM1Max	1.48 (1.36)	3.08 (2.50)
PHTTM1Max	224.93 (81.35)	230 (67.61)
CLBTM1Max	13.84 (7.12	13.02 (7.45)
CBZTM1Max	621.24 (287.96)	720.75 (308.44)
VPATM1Max	540.51 (266.54)	719.02 (324.43)
TPMTM1Max	162.07 (94.87)	121.43 (68.36)
LEVTM1Max	1253.72 (591.17)	1113.64 (551.86)
OXCTM1Max	879.44 (380.31)	825 (474.34)
Seizure count in pre-pregnancy month	Mean (SD)	Mean (SD)
TSMPPAv	3.24 (5.70)	4.09 (7.15)
GTMPPAv#	2.07 (2.43)	5 (9.80)
FAPPMax	5 (0.78)	5.06 (0.55)

Includes secondary generalized (bilateral) tonic-clonic seizures also

TABLE 5.3

Scores Obtained Using Different Ranking Algorithms

Features	Info Gain	Gain Ratio	GINI	ANOVA	$\chi2$	ReliefF	FCBF
VPATM1Max	0.009	0.009	0.002	29.305	49.047	0.020	0.014
TPMTM1Max	0.003	0.024	0.001	3.254	15.865	0.002	0.014
LTGTM1Max	0.003	0.009	0.000	3.695	9.703	0.006	0.008
PBTM1Max	0.002	0.003	0.000	4.894	6.161	0.007	0.000
PRMTM1Max	0.002	0.051	0.001	7.788	15.478	0.000	0.011
LACTM1Max	0.002	0.109	0.001	7.763	18.047	0.000	0.010
CBZTM1Max	0.001	0.001	0.000	1.071	0.977	0.023	0.000
FATM1AV	0.001	0.001	0.000	1.814	0.609	0.034	0.000
Combined	0.001	0.001	0.000	1.298	1.860	0.050	0.000
CLZTM1Max	0.001	0.004	0.000	0.580	0.195	0.000	0.000
Age	0.001	0.000	0.000	0.805	0.126	0.019	0.000
GTMPPAv	0.001	0.003	0.000	4.146	0.014	0.000	0.000
LEVTM1Max	0.000	0.001	0.000	0.054	0.162	0.006	0.000
Eclassgrp	0.000	0.000	0.000	0.973	0.392	0.030	0.000
TSMTM1AV	0.000	0.000	0.000	0.071	0.111	0.000	0.000
GTMTM1AV	0.000	0.000	0.000	0.797	0.788	0.000	0.000
TSMPPAV	0.000	0.000	0.000	0.905	1.193	0.001	0.000
CLBTM1Max	0.000	0.000	0.000	0.042	0.302	0.024	0.000
PHTTM1Max	0.000	0.000	0.000	0.000	0.003	0.023	0.000
NTZTM1Max	0.000	0.008	0.000	0.105	0.215	0.000	0.000
ACTTM1Max	0.000	0.009	0.000	0.143	0.143	0.000	0.000
PRLTM1Max	0.000	0.008	0.000	0.072	0.072	0.000	0.000
DZPTM1Max	0.000	0.008	0.000	0.072	0.072	0.000	0.000
OXCTM1Max	0.000	0.000	0.000	0.179	0.087	0.030	0.000

The confusion matrices of all the classifiers are compared as shown in Figure 5.2.

5.8 Discussion

We conducted a study that holds a distinctive focus on the applicability of machine learning (ML) models to a comprehensive dataset concerning pregnancy outcomes in women with epilepsy (WWE). The approach encompassed a systematic methodology with several critical steps, including data pre-processing, data balancing, and model creation. To enhance efficiency and reduce generalization error, we initiated a feature selection process to pinpoint the most relevant features. Real-world datasets often exhibit imbalances, as observed in our study, where a mere 6.5% of cases exhibited positive outcomes (indicating the presence of major congenital malformations). Applying ML techniques to such imbalanced data, without balancing, results in lower accuracy, as we observed. In our dataset, the count of cases with major congenital malformations surpassed those without. This dataset imbalance led to a tendency for the model to predict negative outcomes. Consequently, the false positive rate was high, which we successfully mitigated through the application of data balancing techniques. We compared two balancing techniques, SMOTE and ADASYN [15], and SMOTE emerged as the more effective choice for our dataset.

TABLE 5.4

Comparison of the Results of Cross-Validation by Different Techniques for Original and SMOTE Data

Cross-Validation	Models	AUC (%)		CA (%)		F1 (%)		P (%)		R (%)	
		Original	SMOTE	Original	SMOTE	Original	SMOTE	Original	SMOTE	Original	SMOTE
60–40	DT	50.6	89.44	91.84	88.36	89.73	88.36	88.04	88.42	91.84	88.36
	RF	56.33	97.06	92.77	92.42	89.95	92.42	87.74	92.45	92.77	92.45
	NB	55.5	89.09	92.95	89.09	90.28	83.41	88.94	84.74	92.95	83.41
	LR	55.99	62.5	93.24	56.85	90.09	56.59	87.47	57.03	93.24	56.85
	AB	53.14	95.2	90.25	91.8	88.98	91.8	87.82	91.84	90.25	91.8
	Stack	56.4	97.49	93.34	93.31	90.13	93.31	87.13	93.34	93.34	93.31
70–30	DT	49.2	90.35	91.86	89.27	89.75	89.26	88.02	89.38	91.86	89.27
	RF	55.87	97.02	92.74	92.48	89.95	92.48	87.61	92.49	92.74	92.48
	NB	55.57	88.88	93.18	83.37	90.39	83.2	89.38	84.93	93.18	83.37
	LR	57.04	61.95	93.31	56.69	90.15	56.36	87.2	56.89	93.31	56.69
	AB	53.47	95.69	90.45	92.67	89.12	92.67	87.92	92.7	9.45	92.67
	Stack	56.8	97.54	93.4	93.52	90.2	93.52	87.2	93.54	93.4	93.52
80–20	DT	51.72	90.13	91.79	88.91	89.66	88.91	88.01	88.95	91.79	88.91
	RF	56.22	97.41	92.56	92.85	89.76	92.85	87.59	92.86	92.56	92.85
	NB	54.5	89.19	93.13	83.78	90.1	83.62	89.25	85.17	93.13	83.78
	LR	54.7	62.99	93.14	57.56	89.92	57.27	86.91	57.77	93.14	57.56
	AB	52.49	95.15	90.88	92.39	89.16	92.39	87.65	92.4	90.88	92.39
	Stack	53.8	97.53	93.32	93.63	90.09	93.63	87.08	93.64	93.32	93.63

AUC-Area Under the curve, CA- Classifier Accuracy, F1- f1 Score, P- Precision, R-Recall

TABLE 5.5

Comparison of Result of Cross-Validation by Leave-One-Out for Original and SMOTE Data

Leave-One-Out Models	AUC (%)		CA (%)		F1(%)		P(%)		R(%)	
	Original	SMOTE	Original	SMOTE	Original	SMOTE	Original	SMOTE	Original	SMOTE
DT	54.25	91	92.32	90.6	90.51	90.6	89.41	90.6	92.32	90.6
RF	56.14	97.8	92.86	94.2	89.94	94.2	87.64	94.3	92.86	94.2
NB	54.19	89.2	93.32	83.5	90.26	83.3	90.49	85	93.32	83.5
LR	55.37	62.4	93.22	56.9	90.04	56.6	87.07	57.2	93.22	56.9
AB	51.51	96.8	90.65	94.1	89.04	94.1	87.58	94.2	90.65	94.1
Stack	56.25	97.54	93.32	93.52	90.09	93.52	87.08	93.54	93.32	93.52

AUC – Area under the curve, CA – Classifier accuracy, F1– f1 score, P – Precision, R – Recall

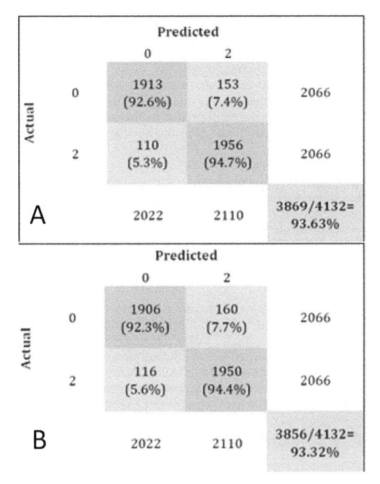

FIGURE 5.2
Confusion matrices of stack model using SMOTE data (a) cross-validation by 80–20% technique and (b) leave-one-out technique.

Although the target feature (major congenital malformations) is binary (with or without malformations), we employed probabilistic models to account for the inherent uncertainty in predictions. This approach allowed our model to generate malformation predictions with varying certainties, ranging from 0 to 100. The certainty of a malformation prediction could fluctuate based on changes in feature values. For example, the certainty of malformation in a patient undergoing valproate (VPA) therapy might increase with higher dosages and decrease with low-dose monotherapy.

To comprehensively assess the model's performance, we applied cross-validation and leave-one-out techniques, experimenting with different training and testing proportions (e.g., 60–40, 70–30, and 80–20). The results indicated that ensemble models outperformed individual models, showcasing the value of combining multiple weak classifiers. Ensemble models leverage the statistical properties of their constituent members, thereby reducing the variance associated with individual errors.

Our primary objective was to evaluate the feasibility and utility of six ML-based models for predicting malformation occurrences in newborns. The results demonstrated that all models exhibited moderate to excellent discrimination and were well-trained. While Logistic Regression is a commonly used method in the medical domain due to its interpretability and simplicity, the ML methods we adopted in this study provided more accurate predictions than the conventional Logistic Regression model. This superiority arises from the complexity of the relationship between features and outcomes, which ML models can capture more effectively. Unlike regression models, ML models like Random Forest do not assume a linear relationship between predictors and outcomes. Instead, they employ ensemble learning, leveraging multiple decision trees and providing superior feature selection capabilities.

Prediction models offer a myriad of potential applications in both research and practical contexts. They can effectively model the risk of major congenital malformations associated with various antiseizure medications (ASMs) and dosages. Moreover, these models are highly adaptable and customizable to accommodate varying needs across different regions. Machine learning algorithms, as artificial intelligence tools [11–12], can autonomously train on datasets from diverse geographic and practice environments, facilitating the generation of tailored reports. Healthcare providers can utilize these models to communicate the risk of major congenital malformations under different treatment protocols to women planning pregnancies.

Our study's strengths lie in its extensive sample size, precise parental demographic data, well-defined epilepsy classification, reliable information on ASM usage and folic acid intake, and comprehensive screening for major congenital malformations [7–8]. However, certain limitations must be acknowledged. We did not verify family histories of malformations or the economic backgrounds of WWE. Additionally, other potential confounding factors, such as exposure to environmental pollutants, smoking habits, and maternal obesity or metabolic syndromes, were not ascertained. Nevertheless, our use of multivariate analyses among pregnant WWE has helped ensure that the comparison groups exhibit similar lifestyles, thereby minimizing the risk of bias.

5.9 Future Scope

Exposure to antiseizure medications (ASMs) during pregnancy amplifies the risk of major congenital malformations (MCM). However, predicting the likelihood of MCM is a formidable task, given the multitude of known and unknown factors that may influence outcomes alongside ASM exposure. The ensemble of machine learning (ML) techniques applied in this study has demonstrated reasonable accuracy in predicting malformations. Yet, for this model to gain wider acceptance and applicability, further validation on independent datasets is essential.

The study's findings open doors to several potential avenues for future research and development

5.9.1 Validation and Generalization

As indicated, the ML-based model's performance should be validated on diverse, independent datasets to ensure its generalizability and robustness. This step is critical to establish the model's reliability across various clinical settings.

5.9.2 Refinement and Enhancement

Ongoing efforts to refine and enhance the ML model can improve its predictive accuracy. This could involve incorporating additional relevant features or optimizing the model's parameters.

5.9.3 Personalized Medicine

Future research may focus on tailoring ASM prescriptions during pregnancy to minimize MCM risks for individual patients. This could involve developing personalized prediction models that consider a patient's specific medical history and ASM usage.

5.9.4 Real-Time Risk Assessment

The development of real-time risk assessment tools that provide immediate feedback to healthcare providers and pregnant women could be beneficial. Such tools could offer dynamic risk assessments as ASM dosages or other factors change.

5.9.5 Patient Education and Counseling

The research findings could inform patient education and counseling strategies. Women with epilepsy (WWE) can be provided with more precise information about the potential risks and benefits of ASM usage during pregnancy, aiding them in making informed decisions.

5.9.6 Longitudinal Studies

Long-term studies tracking the health and development of children born to WWE with ASM exposure could shed light on the actual incidence of MCM and the long-term consequences [4].

5.9.7 International Collaboration

Collaborative efforts across different regions and countries could help gather a more extensive dataset, improving the model's accuracy and reliability in diverse global settings.

5.10 Conclusion

In conclusion, the study highlights the potential of ML techniques to predict MCM risks in pregnancies among WWE. Further research and validation are vital steps to bring these models into practical clinical use, ultimately benefiting both healthcare providers and expectant mothers in making informed decisions regarding ASM usage during pregnancy.

References

1. Epilepsy [Internet]. [cited 2021]. Available from: https://www.who.int/news-room/fact-sheets/detail/epilepsy

2. Thomas SV, Jose M, Divakaran S, Sankara Sarma P. Malformation risk of antiepileptic drug exposure during pregnancy in women with epilepsy: Results from a pregnancy registry in South India. *Epilepsia*. 2017/01/14 ed. 2017; 58(2):274–81.

3. Tomson T, Battino D, Bonizzoni E, Craig J, Lindhout D, Perucca E, et al. Comparative risk of major congenital malformations with eight different antiepileptic drugs: a prospective cohort study of the EURAP registry. *Lancet Neurol*. 2018/04/24 ed. 2018; 17(6):530–8.

4. Weston J, Bromley R, Jackson CF, Adab N, Clayton-Smith J, Greenhalgh J, et al. Monotherapy treatment of epilepsy in pregnancy: Congenital malformation outcomes in the child. *Cochrane Database Syst Rev*. 2016/11/08 ed. 2016; 11(11):Cd010224.

5. Veroniki AA, Cogo E, Rios P, Straus SE, Finkelstein Y, Kealey R, et al. Comparative safety of anti-epileptic drugs during pregnancy: A systematic review and network meta-analysis of congenital malformations and prenatal outcomes. *BMC Med*. 2017/05/06 ed. 2017; 15(1):95.

6. Keni RR, Jose M, Sarma PS, Thomas SV. Teratogenicity of antiepileptic dual therapy: Dose-dependent, drug-specific, or both? *Neurology*. 2018; 90(9):e790–6.

7. US Preventive Services Task Force, Bibbins-Domingo K, Grossman DC, Curry SJ, Davidson KW, Epling JW, et al. Folic acid supplementation for the prevention of neural tube defects: US preventive services task force recommendation statement. *JAMA*. 2017; 317(2):183–9.

8. Morrow JI, Hunt SJ, Russell AJ, Smithson WH, Parsons L, Robertson I, et al. Folic acid use and major congenital malformations in offspring of women with epilepsy: a prospective study from the UK Epilepsy and Pregnancy Register. *J Neurol Neurosurg Psychiatry*. 2008/11/04 ed. 2009; 80(5):506–11.

9. Melikova S, Bagirova H, Magalov S. The impact of maternal epilepsy on delivery and neonatal outcomes. *Childs Nerv Syst*. 2020; 36(4):775–82.

10. Congenital anomalies [Internet]. [cited 2021]. Available from: https://www.who.int/news -room/fact-sheets/detail/congenital-anomalies

11. Giordano C, Brennan M, Mohamed B, Rashidi P, Modave F, Tighe P. Accessing Artificial intelligence for clinical decision-making. *Front Digit Health* [Internet]. 2021 [cited 2021]; 3. Available from: https://www.frontiersin.org/articles/10.3389/fdgth.2021.645232/full

12. Shortliffe EH, Sepúlveda MJ. Clinical decision support in the era of artificial intelligence. *JAMA*. 2018; 320(21):2199–200.

13. Dittman D, Khoshgoftaar T, Wald R, Napolitano A. Similarity analysis of feature ranking techniques on imbalanced DNA microarray datasets. IEEE International Conference on Bioinformatics and Biomedicine, pp. 398–402, 2012.

14. Blagus R, Lusa L. SMOTE for high-dimensional class-imbalanced data. *BMC Bioinformatics*. 2013; 14:106.

15. He H, Bai Y, Garcia EA, Li S. ADASYN: Adaptive synthetic sampling approach for imbalanced learning. International Joint Conference on Neural Networks (IJCNN 2008).

16. Hernández-Díaz S, Werler MM, Walker AM, Mitchell AA. Neural tube defects in relation to use of folic acid antagonists during pregnancy. *Am J Epidemiol*. 2001/06/01 ed. 2001; 153(10):961–8.

6

The Computational Techniques in Mutational Disease Prediction: A Comprehensive and Comparative Review

Lopamudra Das, Aruna Tripathy, Sarita Nanda, and J. K. Das

6.1 Introduction

Digital signal processing approaches have been playing a vital role in genomic sequence analysis with considerable success. These include filtering, windowing, pattern analysis, and several soft-computing approaches to resolve various gene-related issues. The issue of mutational disease prediction is accomplished by detecting exon location in DNA sequences. This further takes advantage of the remarkable property exhibited by the coding regions, known as Period-3 property, or triple-base periodicity (TBP), which is not revealed by the non-coding regions (intron) of DNA. The implementation details and extensive performance analysis of the techniques are presented with the help of evaluation parameters. It requires a minimal amount of cost, time, effort, and, obviously, a noninvasive method of engineering technique applications to reveal biological issues. Consequently, signal processing is becoming significantly important in molecular biology. In this work, both protein and nucleotide biological sequences are analyzed. Proteins are made of amino acids which depict the exact role of protein. In fact, the DNA character string determines protein functions as the arrangement of nucleotides in the DNA decides the corresponding amino acid. DNA carries all the hereditary information in terms of A, C, T, and G (Watson & Crick, 1953). Each cell has a similar arrangement and is unique for an organism. A disorder in this regular array leads to various genetic diseases. Computational techniques are more significant than laboratory analysis regarding this purpose. Proteins, on the other hand, are urbanized from amino acids, driving almost all the biological processes in a living organism. The amino-acid sequence primarily determines the biological functions of proteins within them.

The main contributions of this work are:

- This chapter focuses on various efficient signal processing techniques used for proteomic and genomics study including transform, window, and adaptive filter-based approaches.
- This chapter also explores the sequence for accurate identification of exon location which in turn facilitates the detection of genetic disorders, leading to discrimination between disease genes and healthy genes.
- These efficient signal processing techniques are extended for their application in predicting mutational diseases like Huntington's disease (HD, breast cancer, etc.)

DOI: 10.1201/9781003450153-7

6.1.1 Biological Character Sequence

The genomic signals to be analyzed are collected from the available open access databases in FASTA format. Web addresses for some resources commonly used are given in Section 6.7, before References.

6.1.2 Numerical Representation

To be processed using DSP tools, the input biological character string is required to be represented in numerical values (i.e. time-domain signals), known as mapping. Once a time-domain signal corresponding to the character sequence is achieved, the signal processing methods can be easily implemented on it. Literature says (Lopamudra Das et al., 2021) the mapping schemes have impact on exon location problems. So a detailed study has been carried out for a suitable mapping scheme. Scores of research have been accomplished on numeric encoding schemes and the merits and demerits of each method have been investigated carefully. The study on mappings for nucleotides and amino acids gives an idea of the input signal. The findings are expected to be very helpful to readers and to researchers working in this field.

6.1.3 Exon Detection in DNA

Accurate location of exon in genomes is very important for understanding life processes. A brief study on protein coding region (exon) detection in DNA has been accomplished during the literature survey. A mixture of merits and demerits of various detection methods have been analyzed. A brief discussion has been provided for reference. DNA consists of genes as well as intergenic space, from which genes are again divided as exons and introns. The coding region is the core of the gene and is denoted by the coding sequence (CDS) that contains the nucleotides translated in the protein amino acids (Rao & Swamy, 2008). There is one start codon (ATG) that begins the protein-coding part (exon) and three stop codons (TAA/TAG/TGA) at termination of translation. Intron and exon regions lie between start and stop codons. All genes begin with the exon having a variable number of introns within them that alternate with the exon. The splicing mechanisms recognize the intron boundaries in the exon-intron junctions. Splicing this non-coding part, the CDS part is acquired and any interruption in this causes genetic confusion or health disorder in living beings. Coding sequences exhibit a period-3 property which states a strong peak is obtained at frequency $f = 1/3$ in the power spectrum of the exon and is missing in introns. It is a quite reliable property and widely used as a superior measure for coding to extend DSP techniques.

6.1.4 The Purpose of Exon Detection in DNA

From the DNA sequence, the intron locations are spliced out for mRNA as these are the noncoding (NC) regions. The coding part is analyzed for the mutation and is responsible for the issues related to disease detection. Ideal exon detection methods can locate the exon positions perfectly without the prior knowledge of its location in a DNA sequence (Marhon & Kremer, 2016). Splicing the introns from the sequence, and the accurate coding part for mRNA, can be extracted for further analysis. Important biological problems such as identifying exons, hotspots, and proteins in genes, hereditary disease detection, pathogenic CpG islands, and many more are contingent on the determination of the ideal gene prototype in DNA sequences. Therefore, it has become a tough assignment for computational biologists to detect the position of exons accurately in eukaryote genomes. Because of the complex composition and background noise in sequence, the triple base periodicity property of exons has been implemented as a pointer of exon detection. Numerous techniques based on the spectral characteristics, Fourier spectral content, digital filtering, and correlation of structure of nucleotide sequences have previously been applied for the same.

6.1.5 Mutation

Before splitting, a cell repeats its DNA and sometimes makes mistakes; mainly one or more nucleotide base is detached or is added. Frequently this process of alteration of the position of nucleotides from its original position is termed as mutation. The mutation results in confusion in the interpretation of the codons for amino acid and leads to health disorders in living beings; it also gives rise to genetic disorders in organisms (Tsonis et al., 1991). Although there are billions of nucleotides in an organism's DNA, alteration in any single pair causes theatrical compositional malfunctions. Cancer cells increase and divide, riotously creating malicious tumours in body parts.

6.1.6 Types of Mutations

Various types of mutations and diseases associated with them are described in Clancy (2008). Generally, the following types of mutations are notable as given below:

1. Substitution
2. Insertion
3. Deletion
4. Translocation
5. Copy number alterations

Substitution, insertion, and deletion involve changing a nucleotide with any other nucleotide and addition or deletion of nucleotides in a gene sequence correspondingly. In translocation, a region from one chromosome is abnormally linked to another chromosome that results in leukaemia. The copy number alteration is considered to be duplication.

6.1.7 The Mutational Disease

Even though genes encompass 33.4% of the human genome genes, only 3.66% of it includes exon regions (Sterne-Weiler & Sanford, 2014). Introns cover the rest of the area, unscrambling adjoining exons. To figure out mRNA that encodes an uninterrupted string of codons, the NC parts are spliced out and the exons are put together. Aberrant mRNA splicing is identified to be the principal reason for most diseases. Research on mutated disease genes like breast cancer, Huntington's disease, cystic fibrosis, ataxia telangiectasia, etc. has confirmed that mutations interrupt the exonic splicing resulting in anomalous mRNA. Tri-nucleotide repeat expansion genes, transcribed from RNAs, also induce disease. For example, human diseases like X-linked spinal and bulbar muscular atrophy, Huntington disease, type-1 spinocerebellar ataxia, dentatorubral pallidoluysian atrophy, as well as Machado–Joseph disease are the result of an undue number of codon recurrences in their DNA. All these genes contain a region of CAG repetition.

6.1.8 Mutational Disease Analysis

Since a disease occurs because of mutation, the gene sequence is to be tested for its mutation. This gives rise to a disturbing nucleotide sequence and the codons related to amino acid are misinterpreted and hence the protein coding region (exon) responsible for producing amino acids behaves differently and causes diseases. Figure 6.1 represents one example of such a type, where there is repeated addition of CAG in the DNA sequence resulting in HD.

6.1.9 The Mutational Disease Prediction

The literature says much work has been done for mutational disease prediction based on microarray data. But here an effort has been made to present a review grouping together work based on preprocessing, i.e. mapping the biological sequence into a numeric domain before applying any analysis to it. Since disorder in normal sequencing of nucleotides in the protein coding region causes mutation, the main reason for various diseases and for hereditary disease prediction, mutational analysis is considered. In 2011, Barman et al. (2011) used signals representation based on weak and strong hydrogen bonding and discrete Fourier transform (DFT) was applied to the mapped DNA sequences. Then, power spectral density (PSD) was calculated and IIR Butterworth approximation was designed to restrain the noise from the spectrum; the mean amplitude and the mean frequency for various sequences were discovered. From the results, cancer was detected based on PSD. Since more energy is absorbed by the cancerous cells in comparison to the healthy genes, sharp peaks were obtained in the spectrum of a cancer sequence. In 2013, Ghosh and Barman (2013) used electron-ion interaction pseudo potential (EIIP) to map an amino acid sequence and computed DFT with principal component analysis (PCA) to predict prostate cancer. In 2014, Das et al. (2014) also used the amino acid EIIP values and obtained DFT for the healthy, the cancer reference, and the target gene. Mean and variances were calculated. The probability density function of each gene was found using the Gaussian

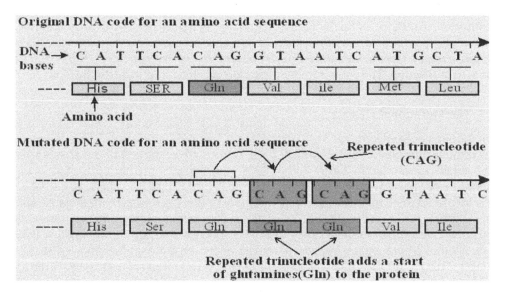

FIGURE 6.1
Mutation in DNA code for mutational disease (Huntington's disease).

distribution function. Then, Bayesian fusion on μ and σ was applied to obtain the fused probability density function. Bayesian fusion is used as a predictor. From the results, when the target gene was healthy and fused using Bayesian fusion, a positive peak was given while the target gene (cancer) gave a single negative peak. This feature was used to differentiate cancerous from healthy genes.

6.2 Literature Survey

This section provides a comprehensive and systematic survey on the literatures relevant to this topic. In 2014, Inbamalar and Siva Kumar (2014) proposed a method based on the entropy of the mapped DNA sequence (Ekštein & Pavelka, 2004). To evaluate their method, evaluation metrics parameters were compared with the previous methods. From the results, the method gave better evaluation metrics parameters. In 2014, T. Roy et al. (2014) designed an electrical network model based on the physicochemical properties of amino acid that predicts cancer and healthy cells. In 2015, Jindal et al. (2015) introduced modified wavelet transform (MWT) on the Voss-mapped DNA sequences with the help of the optimized coefficients obtained from the glow swarm optimization (GSO) algorithm, and the thresholding process was applied to diagnose cancer. In 2017, J. Das (Joyshri Das & Barman, 2017) used entropy estimation and mutual information methods along with hydropathic index (HI) values of mapping for amino acids. Identification of healthy and cancerous *Homo sapiens* genes is done by Rayleigh distribution of gene entropy. In 2016, T. Thiali, et al. in Gayathri (2017) applied wavelet transform to EIIP mapped sequence to detect cancer cells based upon the mean and standard deviation ratio. In 2018, S.S. Roy (S. S. Roy & Barman, n.d.) used functional link artificial neural network (FLANN)-based least mean square (LMS) algorithm on EIIP mapped sequences to differentiate between cancer and normal cells and the prediction is based on mean square error. Almost all the work of disease prediction, the respective findings, and signal processing techniques discussed above have been briefed in Table 6.1, which may assist future researchers.

6.2.1 Evaluation Parameters

Estimating the performance of a technique is carried out by some evaluation parameters:
Sensitivity(Sn):
The fraction of coding nucleotides correctly acknowledged as coding, given as (1).

$$Sn = \frac{TP}{TP + FN} \tag{1}$$

Specificity(Sp):
The fraction of NC nucleotides correctly acknowledged as NC, given as (2).

$$Sp = \frac{TP}{TP + FP} \tag{2}$$

Mathew correlation coefficient (CC) is given by (3).

$$CC = \frac{TP*TN\text{-}FN*FP}{\sqrt{TP+FN*TN+FP*TP+FP*TN+FN}} \tag{3}$$

TABLE 6.1

Application of Biological Sequence Analysis in Disease Prediction

Sl. No.	References	Methods	Findings
1	(Qiu et al., 2007)	Review of cancer prediction methods	Cancer detection
2	(Ismaeel & Ablahad, 2013)	Feedforward back-propagation neural network technique	Breast cancer prediction
3	(Meher & Rath, n.d.)	2-bit binary map, IIR anti-notch filter	Duchene muscular dystrophy (DMD) disease gene detection
4	(Zhou et al., 2009)	Voss mapping with AR-PSD sliding window-based SNR estimation.	Tandem repeat in the genome
5	(Soni & Shakya, 2016)	EIIP mapped Kaiser for exon and C-G binary mapping with Lab VIEW	Identification of CPG island
6	(T Roy et al., 2014)	Electrical network model of an amino acid chain designed	Cancer prediction
7	(Sharma et al., 2015)	Adaptive S.T with complex mapping	Huntington's disease, Frederick's ataxia
8	(Sharma et al., 2017)	Adaptive S-transform, with Kaiser window, LMS	Detection of tandem repeats in DNA sequences
9	(A Ghosh & Barman, 2013)	Amino acid EIIP mapped input DFT with the PCA technique	Differentiating prostate cancer from normal cells
10	(S. S. Roy & Barman, n.d.)	FLANN-based adaptive filter with LMS algorithm on EIIP mapped sequences	Differentiate between cancer and normal cells
11	(Barman et al., 2011)	Voss mapping, DFT, IIR Butterworth filter	Prediction of cancer cells
12	(Adetiba & Olugbara, 2015)	Voss mapping, ANN, SVM	Lung cancer prediction
13	(Gayathri, 2017)	EIIP mapping, wavelet transform	Cancer and non-cancer discrimination
14	(Naseem et al., 2017)	ASCII code, Goertzel algorithm	Ebola virus gene prediction
15	(Saini & Dewan, 2016)	DNA walks, DWT	Comparison of MTB
16	(Jindal et al., 2015)	MWT for transforming the DNA sequences with optimized co-efficient using the GSO algorithm	Identification of cancer cells
17	(Tanusree Roy & Barman, 2016)	Peak, gain analysis and shape of Nyquist curve	Cancer classification
18	(A Ghosh & Barman, 2013)	Amino acid EIIP mapping, DFT, PCA	Prediction of prostate cancer
19	(Rao & Swamy, 2008)	Nucleotides and amino acid EIIP mapped CWT using the modified Morlet wavelet	Cystic-fibrosis gene identification, hotspot detection
20	(Antara Ghosh & Barman, 2016)	Euclidean distance measurement PCA method	Gene identification
21	(J Das & Barman, 2014)	EIIP Amino acid mapping, DFT, Bayesian fusion technique	Screen out cancer gene from the healthy gene
22	(Meng et al., 2013)	Amino-acid complex mapping, WT	Survey on wavelet techniques for cancer
23	(Joyshri Das & Barman, 2017)	Amino acid HI mapping, Rayleigh distribution of entropy estimation	Classification of cancer genes
24	(Chakraborty & Gupta, 2016)	EIIP mapping, DWT	Cancer identification
25	(Kakumani et al., 2012)	Voss mapping and SONF	Identification of CpG
26	(Barman et al., 2011)	Voss-map, DFT, IIR Butter-worth filter	Prediction of cancer

Where, TP (True-Positive), TN (True-Negative), FP (False-Positive), and FN (False Negative)
Accuracy (AC) is given by (4)

$$Accuracy = \frac{S_\partial + S_p}{2} \tag{4}$$

Discrimination measure (DM)
The DM is given by (5); for DM > 1 each exons is well detected and for DM < 1 at least one of the exons is not detected.

$$DM = \frac{Lowest\ peak\ amplitude\ in\ Coding\ region}{Highest\ peak\ amplitude\ in\ noncoding\ region} \tag{5}$$

Receiver Operating Characteristics (ROC)
For ROC S_n is plotted against Sp.The closer the curve to 1 more is the AUC (Area under Curve) and better is the technique .
Geometric mean (gm):
It is an overall classifier and is given by (6)

$$gm = \sqrt{S_n \times S_p} \tag{6}$$

Signal to noise ratio (SNR)
More the SNR implies superior performance and is given as (7).

$$SNR\ \frac{mean(\mu)}{standard\ deviation(\sigma)} \tag{7}$$

6.3 Computational Techniques in Mutational Disease Prediction

6.3.1 FLANN-Based Levenberg Marquardt Adaptive Algorithm in Discrimination of Diseased and Healthy Gene

Here, the adaptive filter technique is implemented for HD prediction. It is well known that cancer is caused due to alteration in the DNA sequence (Lopamudra Das, Nanda, et al., 2020). The diseased gene is recognized precisely by finding this change. FLANN is used to detect the diseased gene sequence which expands the input patterns by nonlinear basis functions and reduces the computational complexity. Tracking the non-stationary behaviour of the signal is accomplished by the LM algorithm that results in faster convergence speed and better noise reduction. The diseased (mutated) genes detection is based on how much they are dissimilar to a healthy one, i.e., mean square error (MSE). Coefficients of the adaptive filter are modified to reduce the MSE. The input nucleotide sequences are mapped by EIIP techniques and are used for training and testing by exploiting the particle swarm optimization (PSO)–based Levenberg–Marquardt algorithm as elucidated in Figure 6.2.

The x(k) is the unknown input, which is expanded using non-linear functions (Patra et al., 1999). The w(k) is the weight vector. The PSO leads faster convergence. The method provides improved evaluation parameters. Thus, a combined approach discriminates the

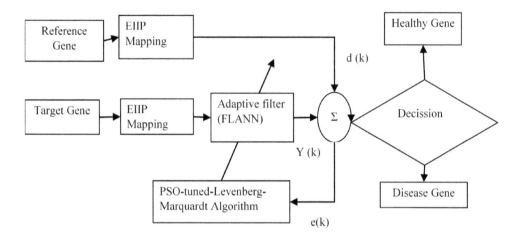

FIGURE 6.2
Block diagram of the FLANN-based Levenberg–Marquardt adaptive method for disease assessment (Lopamudra Das, Nanda, et al., 2020).

disease genes more accurately and with faster speed. The approach has been compared with the existing technologies and tested on benchmark datasets to prove its efficacy.

6.3.2 A Hybrid Deep-Learning Approach for COVID–19 Detection Based on Genomic Image Processing Techniques

This technique is an automated detection of the COVID-19 mutational disease. Molecular techniques and medical imaging have been implemented for this purpose; still, these have limitations. To overcome the limitations of the techniques, the whole and partial genome sequences of human coronavirus (HCoV) diseases is studied(Hammad et al., 2023). This is a hybrid approach based on genomic image processing techniques to detect the disease rapidly and effectively. This method translates the genome sequences of HCoVs into gray-scale images exploiting a genomic frequency chaos game representation image mapping. The pre-trained convolution neural network, AlexNet technique, is implemented to extract deep features from these images. Removing the redundant ones, most significant features were obtained. This is done by using the ReliefF and least absolute shrinkage and selection operator (LASSO) algorithms. The two classifiers used are decision trees and k-nearest neighbours (KNN). Extracting deep features using the KNN classifier has resulted in the best hybrid approach. The hybrid deep learning method detected COVID-19, among other HCoV diseases, with good accuracy.

6.3.3 Comprehensive Evaluation of Computational Methods for Predicting Cancer Driver Genes

Identification of driver genes is effectively improved using optimal methods. This work overcomes the limitation related to assessment of the performance levels of network-, function-, and frequency-based approaches. Here, eight benchmark datasets are used for eight network-based, one function-based, and three frequency-based algorithms. Eight performance criteria were evaluated and compared using these datasets(Shi et al., 2022). The best overall performance is observed by frequency-based driver MAPS and network-based

HotNet2 methods. The network-based algorithms superseded the function- and the frequency-based approaches. The evaluation parameters were low for most approaches. To correctly distinguish driver and non-driver genes, these algorithms require stringent cutoffs. In the Cancer Driver Catalogue (http://159.226.67.237/sun/cancer_driver/) the gene scores were united and predicted by the former software programs. This resource delivers important direction for cancer researchers using an optimal tool.

6.3.4 An Adaptive Neural Network Model for Predicting Breast Cancer Disease in Mapped Nucleotide Sequences

This work is an ANN technique to predict breast cancer in numerically encoded DNA. The expansion of DNA input samples is based on adaptive exponential FLANN (Lopamudra Das et al., 2023). The concept that the disease genes encompasses more randomness than the healthier ones has been considered. The integral square error (ISE) factor is used to carry out this discrimination. For faster convergence and reduced computational complexity the least mean square/fourth (LMS/F) algorithm is used. The method is compared with the existing ones. Within the first 50 iterations, almost all the test genes were discriminated appropriately. However, this AE-FLANN–based LMS/F method was also validated using 10-fold cross-validation. This work also incorporates a unique case of candidate genes, i.e. sporadic BC, and the approach exhibits satisfactory performance. A schematic diagram to indicated this method is shown in Figure 6.3 along with an adaptive FLAN structure in Figure 6.4.

This work involves an adaptive structure AEFLANN modelled by LMS/F algorithm. Moreover, applying an appropriate learning rule, the filter weights are iteratively updated. The input sequence (unknown) is X(k), expanded in a span of n-dimensional depiction space (Patra et al., 1999). The parameter b(k) and weight vector w(k) is adapted iterationwise. For 'y(k)'is the filter response of 'x(k)'and 'x(k)' is the target input (unknown gene), 'd(k)' is the reference signal (desired known input), 'e(k)' is the error vector. Lastly, the output 'y(k)' attains 'd(k)'. The AEFLANN weights are updated by learning algorithm. The LMS/F algorithm used. The ISE value for the disease gene (healthy gene as reference) is found to be more and less than healthy ones. Thus, to predict the category of the gene, this method discriminates well at a faster rate and with a very small number of iterations.

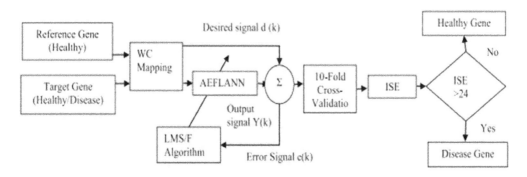

FIGURE 6.3
Block diagram of the adaptive neural network model for predicting breast cancer disease (Lopamudra Das et al., 2023).

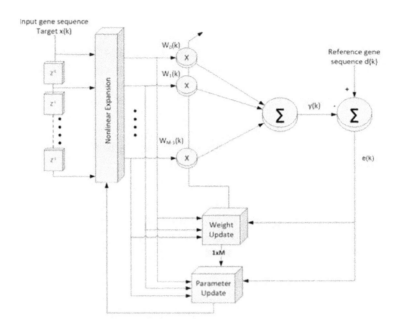

FIGURE 6.4
Adaptive structure representing the input samples expanded by AEFLANN method.

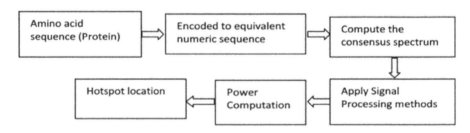

FIGURE 6.5
Hotspot detection in protein (Lopamudra Das et al., 2022).

6.3.5 Signal Processing Approaches for Encoded Protein Sequences in Gynaecological Cancer Hotspot Prediction: A Review

This work includes a comprehensive analysis of the existing techniques for revelation of hotspot regions in genomic sequences (L. Das et al., 2022). The hotspot mutation of TP53 is a frequent genetic modification concentrated on exons 5 to 9. The hotspot mutation in the case of endometrial carcinoma (EC) is stated in exon 9 and exon 13 of the sequence. For hotspot location, this work focuses on a patient's genetic profile and, in turn, a prediction of cancer. It provides a concise technical review on gynaecological cancer hotspot prediction issues. The EIIP encoded sequences established the spectrum that demonstrates characteristic frequency (cf), a distinctive dominant frequency of the functional group. The product of the DFTs of encoded protein sequences of a particular functional group is the consensus spectrum. The cf is superseding in an encoded protein sequence region, is a hotspot, and is located by tracking the potency of cf down the duration of a protein sequence. A block diagram of hotspot location detection in protein is shown in Figure 6.5. The figure is the step-wise procedure of signal processing methods to get consensus spectrum. The approaches applied for this purpose are machine learning methods, for example neural network, KNN, unsupervised learning methods, principle component analysis (PCA), whale optimization algorithm (WOA) with mixed kernel function (MKF)-based support vector machine (SVM); a deep learning, constrained convolutional neural network (SC–CNN) method was used. These methods are updated by researchers. To predict hotspot location, the next step is the power calculation.

Mutation focuses on a specific location called hotspots. They replicate the structural and functional features of genetic sequences. The abnormal interactions are the foundation of critical cancer. The hotspots subsidize the binding energy in protein–protein interactions (PPI).The identification of hotspots provides a source to discover molecular medicines. The oncogenes' cf and functional active sites are determined by the Fourier transform and CWT.

6.3.6 Modified Gabor Wavelet Transform in Prediction of Cancerous Genes

In this work, the modified Gabor wavelet transform (MGWT) has been utilized with a geometric mapping technique to discriminate cancerous and non-cancerous genes. This technique is independent of the window-length strategy and is exploited to acquire the spectral components in the signal correctly with less complexity. Some benchmark datasets are tested and the results predicted reliability of the method. The steps in this work are depicted in Figure 6.6. The visual representation of the result is depicted in scalogram and corresponding PSD plots are given in Figure 6.7, which shows a clear comparison between cancer and healthy genes. Modified Gabor wavelet technique is noise resistant and is adaptive to the length of the gene sequence. The method correctly differentiates

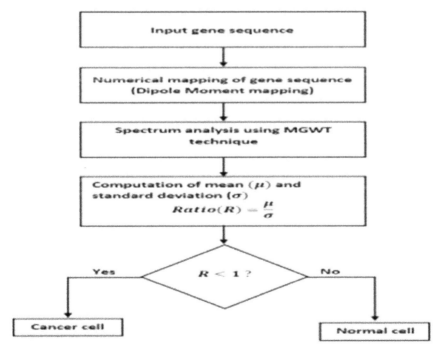

FIGURE 6.6
Steps used in modified Gabor wavelet transform for prediction of cancerous genes (L. Das et al., 2019.)

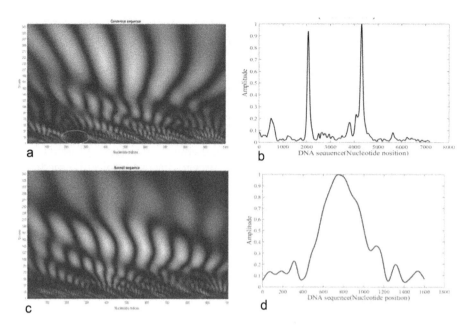

FIGURE 6.7
Scalogram and PSD plots comparison between cancer and healthy gene (L. Das et al., 2019); (a) Scalogram plot of breast cancer gene sequence (AF012108.1), (b) Figure 2PSD plot of sequence AF012108.1 (breast cancer), (c) scalogram plot of healthy gene sequence (AF007546.1), (d) psd plot of healthy sequence AF007981.1.

normal and cancer cells non-invasively without any biological experiments and without using any costly equipment.

6.4 Case Study and Discussion

6.4.1 Goat Dataset

This has been collected and the correct coding region has been detected using signal processing approach, e.g. identification of coding regions of Goat (Accession number X01913) sequence having length 2275 bp by using the FAGWT method (Lopamudra Das, Das, et al., 2020). Regions at positions of 471–562, 689–911, and 1754–1879 were identified. The dotted areas indicate the corresponding relative physical position of the true coding regions as depicted in Figure 6.8.

6.4.2 The Computational Techniques

The computational techniques are applied for the prediction of cancerous and healthy gene, and a comparative analysis between two types reveals that the Accession number AF008216 (a-exon at location 4453-5157 bp) and another gene with accession number NM_012403 (b-exon at location 1-705 bp) has a picky spectrum. In contrast, the non-cancer cells have psd smooth with accession number AF186607.1 (a-exon location 1210-1301 bp and AF083883 (b- exon-at 1210-1301 bp).

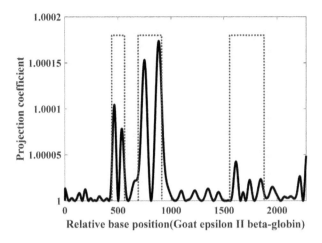

FIGURE 6.8
Goat exon location detection.

6.5 Conclusions

This chapter presents the conclusions gained from research work as well as future research directions. Predicting genetic disease without the help of any biological experiments has turned out to be a demanding topic for the present researchers. An attempt has been made in this regard to predict the diseased gene, distinguishing it from normal healthy ones. Although the microarray technique has been widely used in the past, this mapped sequence-based method has many advantages over it for perfect prediction accuracy. It facilitates correct splicing to get perfect CDS for mRNA in applications like disease detection, organism classification, mutation, and many more. The literature review is the collection of work carried out by different researchers, which is based on the application of biological sequence analysis in mutational disease prediction. This review will help researchers working on gene prediction by providing a complete overview of the signal processing tools utilized in this chapter. It also included performance evaluation parameters that have been used throughout to measure the efficacy of a method. The computational evaluations and the visual representations on the spectrum plot show the effectiveness of the methods. The subsequent section of this chapter deals with the mutational disease detection problem. The PSD plots are differentiated by peaky and non-peaky output. The scalogram plots give a clear vision of the difference. This method assures preliminary detection and prediction of genetic abnormalities of genes. The spliced CDS (also known as mRNA) of an unknown gene is tested, taking the known gene sequence as the reference, and the MSE value is calculated between the reference (known healthy) and unknown (healthy/disease) input sequence. Since the diseased gene is more random, MSE between healthy and diseased genes is more compared to MSE between healthy and healthy genes. Also, the convergence speed is less in the case of a diseased gene. Considering these factors, the distinction is accomplished. The adaptive filter has been applied in noise cancellation, system identification, signal prediction, etc., but here it could successfully identify the disease genes as they show divergent nature compared to healthy ones. The weaknesses of the chapter are that, according to current literature review, the noncoding regions also contain important information which is yet to be explored. The authors of this work are trying to extend the work for hotspot prediction in mutation disease analysis. For proper analysis and validation of signal processing approaches sufficient real-time data needed to be obtained from cancer hospitals and certified by doctors. The method is applied for the first time in the bioinformatics field for mutation detection to distinguish between healthy and disease genes and gives a satisfactory result.

6.6 Future Aspects of the Work

- An attempt towards the analysis of the NC part in DNA may be taken where some information may be concealed to help the research work further.
- In future, different advanced algorithms may be incorporated to get more accuracy and efficiency in predicting disease genes. The effectiveness of the algorithm can further be enhanced by identifying the stage of the disease.
- An interesting problem is to build an adequate algorithm that can automatically discover any disease by investigating the DNA sequence pattern. Since the CDS gives information about all the activities, there must be a particular pattern causing a specific disease. If that can be detected, almost all the problems of medical science can be solved. Therefore, a robust signal processing method may be designed, so that the mutation pattern may be analyzed perfectly with minimized computational cost to solve this problem.
- Current COVID-19 is a mutational disease. Rigorous research based on CDS can successfully detect the correct disease pattern. Subsequently, the best medication can be designed to cure it. This may be a great help to protect mankind by abolishing this disease. Since perfect and faithful disease identification has not yet been achieved, wrong treatment is leading to lots of deaths, so this notion may be a great help to society.

6.7 Open Access Database

Available open-access databases which are used for the analysis of the techniques to prepare the thesis are as follows:

- NCBI: National Centre for Biotechnology Information, www.ncbi.nlm.nih.gov
- The EMBL Nucleotide Sequence Database www.ebi.ac.uk/embl.htm
- DDBJ: DNA Data Bank of Japan, www.ddbj.nig.ac.jp
- Swiss-Port Protein Knowledgebase is the Swiss Institute of Bioinformatics (SIB) Available: http://us.expasy.org/sprot/
- Protein Data Bank (PDB), Research Collaborators for Structural Bioinformatics (RCSB). Available: http://www.rcsb.org/pdb

References

Adetiba, E., & Olugbara, O. O. (2015). Lung cancer prediction using neural network ensemble with histogram of oriented gradient genomic features. *The Scientific World Journal*, Vol 2015. pp. 1-17, Article ID 786013

Barman, S., Roy, M., Biswas, S., & Saha, S. (2011). Prediction of cancer cell using digital signal processing. *Annals of the Faculty of Engineering Hunedoara*, 9(3), 91.

Chakraborty, S., & Gupta, V. (2016). Dwt based cancer identification using EIIP. *Computational Intelligence & Communication Technology (CICT), 2016 Second International Conference On*, 718–723.

Clancy, S. (2008). *Genetic Mutation | Learn Science at Scitable*. Genetic Mutation. Nature Education.

Das, J., & Barman, S. (2014). Bayesian fusion in cancer gene prediction. *International Journal of Computer Applications*, 1, 5–10.

Das, J., & Barman, S. (2017). DSP based entropy estimation for identification and classification of Homo sapiens cancer genes. *Microsystem Technologies*, 23(9), 4145–4154.

Das, L., Das, J. K., Mohapatra, S., & Nanda, S. (2021). DNA numerical encoding schemes for exon prediction: A recent history. *Nucleosides, Nucleotides & Nucleic Acids*, 40(100), 985–1017.

Das, L., Das, J. K., & Nanda, S. (2020). Detection of exon location in eukaryotic DNA using a fuzzy adaptive Gabor wavelet transform. *Genomics*, 112(6), 4406–4416.

Das, L., Das, J. K., Nanda, S., & Nanda, S. (2023). An adaptive neural network model for predicting breast cancer disease in mapped nucleotide sequences. *Iranian Journal of Science and Technology, Transactions of Electrical Engineering*, 47(4) 1569–,1582.

Das, L., Kumar, A., Das, J. K., & Nanda, S. (2019). Modified gabor wavelet transform in prediction of cancerous genes. *International Journal of Engineering and Advanced Technology*, 9(1). https://doi.org/10.35940/ijeat.A9417.109119

Das, L., Nanda, S., & Das, J. K. (2020). Hereditary disease prediction in eukaryotic DNA: An adaptive signal processing approach. *Nucleosides, Nucleotides & Nucleic Acids*, 39(8), 1179–1199.

Das, L., Nanda, S., Nayak, B., & Nanda, S. (2022). Signal processing approaches for encoded protein sequences in gynecological cancer hotspot prediction: A review. In *International Conference on Metaheuristics in Software Engineering and its Application 2022 Feb 24* (pp. 232–246). Cham: Springer International Publishing.

Ekštein, K., & Pavelka, T. (2004). Entropy and entropy-based features in signal processing. *Proceedings of PhD Workshop Systems & Control*.

Gayathri, T. T. (2017). *Analysis of Genomic Sequences for Prediction of Cancerous Cells using Wavelet Technique*. International Research Journal of Engineering and Technology (IRJET). 4(4):1071–7,

Ghosh, A., & Barman, S. (2013). Prediction of prostate cancer cells based on principal component analysis technique. *Procedia Technology*, 10, 37–44.

Ghosh, A., & Barman, S. (2016). Application of Euclidean distance measurement and principal component analysis for gene identification. *Gene*, 583(2), 112–120.

Hammad, M. S., Ghoneim, V. F., Mabrouk, M. S., & Al-Atabany, W. I. (2023). A hybrid deep learning approach for COVID-19 detection based on genomic image processing techniques. *Scientific Reports*, 13(1), 4003.

Inbamalar, T. M., & Sivakumar, R. 2014. An efficient approach for cancer prediction using genomic signal processing. *International Review on Computers and Software (IRECOS)*. 9(3), 585–591.

Ismaeel, A. G., & Ablahad, A. A. (2013). Novel method for mutational disease prediction using bioinformatics techniques and backpropagation algorithm. *ArXiv Preprint ArXiv:1303.0539*.

Jindal, R., Banerji, B., & Grover, D. (2015). Prediction and identification of cancerous cells using genomic signal processing. *The International Journal of Research in Engineering, IT and Social Sciences*, 5, 14–26.

Kakumani, R., Ahmad, O., & Devabhaktuni, V. (2012). Identification of CpG islands in DNA sequences using statistically optimal null filters. *EURASIP Journal on Bioinformatics and Systems Biology*, 2012(1), 12.

Marhon, S. A., & Kremer, S. C. (2016). Prediction of protein coding regions using a wide-range wavelet window method. *IEEE/ACM Transactions on Computational Biology and Bioinformatics (TCBB)*, 13(4), 742–753.

Meher, J. K., & Rath, A. K. (2014). *Detection of Mutation-Hotspots and Exon-Deletions using Digital Signal Processing in Duchenne Muscular Dystrophy (DMD) Gene*, IOSR Journal of Dental and Medical Sciences 13, 34–39.

Meng, T., Soliman, A. T., Shyu, M.-L., Yang, Y., Chen, S.-C., Iyengar, S. S., Yordy, J. S., & Iyengar, P. (2013). Wavelet analysis in current cancer genome research: A survey. *IEEE/ACM Transactions on Computational Biology and Bioinformatics*, 10(6), 1442–14359.

Naseem, M. T., Britto, K. R. A., Jaber, M. M., Chandrasekar, M., Balaji, V. S., Rajkumar, G., Narasimhan, K., & Elamaran, V. (2017). *Preprocessing and Signal Processing Techniques on Genomic Data Sequences*, . Biomedical Research; 28 (22): 10205–10209

Patra, J. C., Pal, R. N., Chatterji, B. N., & Panda, G. (1999). Identification of nonlinear dynamic systems using functional link artificial neural networks. *IEEE Transactions on Systems, Man, and Cybernetics, Part B (Cybernetics)*, 29(2), 254–262.

Qiu, P., Wang, Z. J., & Liu, K. J. R. (2007). Genomic processing for cancer classification and prediction-Abroad review of the recent advances in model-based genomoric and proteomic signal processing for cancer detection. *IEEE Signal Processing Magazine*, 24(1), 100–110.

Rao, K. D., & Swamy, M. N. S. (2008). Analysis of genomics and proteomics using DSP techniques. *IEEE Transactions on Circuits and Systems I: Regular Papers*, 55(1), 370–378.

Roy, S. S., & Barman, S. (2021). A non-invasive cancer gene detection technique using FLANN based adaptive filter. *Microsystem Technologies*,27)(2) 463–478.

Roy, T., Das, S., & Barman, S. (2014). Electrical network modeling of amino acid string and its application in cancer cell prediction. In *Intelligent Computing, Networking, and Informatics*Advances in Intelligent Systems and Computing 243,DOI: 10.1007/978-81-322-1665-0_28, (pp. 293–301). Springer. India

Roy, T., & Barman, S. (2016). Modeling of cancer classifier to predict site of origin. *IEEE Transactions on Nanobioscience*, 15(5), 481–487.

Saini, S., & Dewan, L. (2016). Application of discrete wavelet transform for analysis of genomic sequences of Mycobacterium tuberculosis. *SpringerPlus*, 5(1), 64.

Sharma, S. D., Saxena, R., & Sharma, S. N. (2015). Identification of microsatellites in DNA using adaptive S-transform. *IEEE Journal of Biomedical and Health Informatics*, 19(3), 1097–1105.

Sharma, S. D., Saxena, R., & Sharma, S. N. (2017). Tandem repeats detection in DNA sequences using Kaiser window based adaptive S-transform. *Bio-Algorithms and Med-Systems*, 13(3), 167–173.

Shi, X., Teng, H., Shi, L., Bi, W., Wei, W., Mao, F., & Sun, Z. (2022). Comprehensive evaluation of computational methods for predicting cancer driver genes. *Briefings in Bioinformatics*, 23(2), bbab548.

Soni, S., & Shakya, D. K. (2016). *Identification of CPG Island in DNA Sequence using Labview*. International Conference on Signal Processing (ICSP 2016). **DOI https://doi.org/10.1049/cp.2016.1462**

Sterne-Weiler, T., & Sanford, J. R. (2014). Exon identity crisis: Disease-causing mutations that disrupt the splicing code. *Genome Biology*, 15(1), 1–8.

Tsonis, A. A., Elsner, J. B., & Tsonis, P. A. (1991). Periodicity in DNA coding sequences: Implications in gene evolution. *Journal of Theoretical Biology*, 151(3), 323–331.

Watson, J. D., & Crick, F. H. C. (1953). Genetical implications of the structure of deoxyribonucleic acid. *Nature*, 171(4361), 964–967.

Zhou, H., Du, L., & Yan, H. (2009). Detection of tandem repeats in DNA sequences based on parametric spectral estimation. *IEEE Transactions on Information Technology in Biomedicine*, 13(5), 747–755.

7

Comparative Analysis of U-Net and DeepLab for Accurate Brain MRI Segmentation

Soumya Ranjan Mahanta and Mrutyunjaya Panda

7.1 Introduction

The precise segmentation of brain structures from MRI scans is crucial for diverse medical applications such as diagnosis, treatment planning, and the monitoring of neurological disorders. Within the brain, tumors represent abnormal cell growth, which can manifest as either benign or malignant. These tumors arise when cells within the brain begin to multiply uncontrollably, forming a mass or lump. The exact cause of brain tumors is often not clear, but certain factors are believed to contribute to their development. These factors may include genetic predispositions, exposure to certain environmental toxins, or radiation.

Brain tumors have a profound impact on human health. Depending on factors such as size, location, and whether they are benign or malignant, these tumors can exert pressure on surrounding brain tissues, resulting in a variety of neurological symptoms. Common effects include cognitive impairments, such as difficulty with concentration and memory, as well as neurological symptoms like headaches, seizures, changes in personality, and impaired motor functions. In severe cases, brain tumors can pose life-threatening risks.

Understanding the causes and effects of brain tumors is crucial for early detection and effective treatment. As the field of medical imaging advances, particularly through technologies like MRI, along with tools such as deep learning models, there is a notable enhancement in the ability to achieve precise and automated segmentation of brain MRI. This study specifically examines and contrasts the efficacy of two widely used deep learning models, U-Net and DeepLab, in the precise segmentation of brain MRI images, employing the TensorFlow framework. This advancement contributes to improved diagnosis and treatment planning for individuals affected by brain tumors, thereby mitigating the impact of these conditions on human health.

Accurately segmenting brain structures poses challenges due to intricate anatomical variations, image noise, and the requirement for precise boundary delineation. Both U-Net and DeepLab have demonstrated exceptional capabilities in overcoming these challenges and achieving state-of-the-art performance in tasks related to medical image segmentation.

U-Net is recognized for its fully convolutional encoder–decoder architecture [1], allowing the model to comprehend both global and local features. The encoder path captures high-level contextual information, while the decoder path allows precise localization of structures by upsampling the feature maps. This architecture has demonstrated excellent

DOI: 10.1201/9781003450153-8

performance in various segmentation tasks and is particularly suitable for pixel-level labeling.

DeepLab, in contrast [2], utilizes atrous convolutions and the atrous spatial pyramid pooling module for capturing multi-scale contextual information. This approach empowers the model to effectively manage variations in the size and shape of brain structures, resulting in heightened segmentation accuracy. DeepLab models have demonstrated remarkable performance in semantic segmentation tasks and have gained widespread adoption in medical image analysis.

To assess the performance of both U-Net and DeepLab models [3], experiments were executed on a diverse brain MRI dataset. This dataset comprises a range of brain images along with corresponding ground truth segmentations. The models underwent training and optimization using the Adam optimizer, incorporating early stopping to prevent overfitting. Performance evaluation employed metrics such as binary cross-entropy loss and the Dice coefficient, measuring the overlap between predicted and ground truth segmentations.

The comparative analysis centered on various facets. Initially, an examination of training loss and metrics was conducted to evaluate the models' convergence and generalization capabilities. Subsequently, the training time required for each model was compared to glean insights into their computational efficiency [4]. Additionally, the analysis involved scrutinizing Dice coefficient scores obtained from testing to assess the segmentation accuracy of each model. Furthermore, a qualitative analysis was performed on image results by comparing predicted masks generated by each model with ground truth masks, providing a nuanced understanding of the models' proficiency in accurately delineating brain structures.

The findings of this research enrich the expanding realm of medical image analysis knowledge, offering valuable insights for both researchers and practitioners engaged in brain MRI segmentation. Through a meticulous comparison of U-Net and DeepLab models [5], the aim is to guide the selection of the most suitable model for specific segmentation tasks [24–29], considering factors such as accuracy, efficiency, and computational requirements.

Accurate brain MRI segmentation has significant implications for improving diagnosis, treatment planning, and patient care in neurological disorders [23]. The advancements made in advanced deep learning models, exemplified by U-Net and DeepLab, sets the stage for continued enhancements in automated medical image analysis [6]. This progress promises to elevate the precision and efficiency of brain-structure segmentation in clinical applications.

The research in this study lacks specificity in specifying model versions such as U-Net, DeepLab Series, nnU-Net, and PSPNet. Future research should explore how these specific model versions influence performance. Moreover, there is a research gap due to the absence of detailed performance benchmarking, requiring evaluations on metrics like accuracy, sensitivity, specificity, and computational efficiency. Understanding how these models, designed for various tasks, adapt to segmenting low-grade gliomas is essential, indicating a need for research in task-specific adaptations [31]. This study falls short in exploring the influence of model complexity, especially in comparing intricate architectures like DeepLab V3+ with simpler models like U-Net for glioma segmentation. The potential of transfer learning across different models is unexplored, necessitating investigation into the effectiveness of pre-trained models on general segmentation tasks for glioma segmentation. The issue of class imbalance in glioma segmentation is mentioned but not thoroughly addressed, demanding research to understand how different segmentation models handle class imbalance in this specific application. Addressing these gaps will enhance our understanding of how semantic segmentation models perform in associating imaging features with genomic subtypes in low-grade gliomas.

The subsequent sections of this chapter are structured as follows: Section 7.2 delves into related work, followed by an exploration of the dataset in Section 7.3. Section 7.4 focuses on models, while Section 7.5 provides an in-depth explanation of each phase of the experimental analysis process. The limitations are outlined in Section 7.6, leading to the conclusion with future scope of the research in Section 7.7.

7.2 Related Work

Zhao et al. (2018) presented ICNet [7], a real-time semantic segmentation model tailored for high-resolution images. Through the incorporation of a multi-scale feature fusion strategy and a cascade refinement module, ICNet demonstrated its effectiveness in real-time semantic segmentation tasks, showcasing potential applications in the field of medical imaging.

Hu et al. (2018) introduced Squeeze-and-Excitation Networks [8], an innovative approach that integrates channel-wise feature recalibration into convolutional neural networks (CNNs). This novel mechanism allows for adaptive emphasis on informative features, thereby improving the performance of segmentation models. Their contributions have noteworthy implications for medical image segmentation, including the analysis of brain MRI data.

Isensee et al. (2018) introduced nnU-Net [9], a versatile framework built upon the widely used U-Net architecture. With a cascaded structure involving iterative training and testing phases, nnU-Net autonomously adjusts to diverse datasets and segmentation tasks. This framework has demonstrated leading-edge performance across various medical imaging challenges, underscoring its efficacy in the domain.

Zhao et al. (2017) proposed the Pyramid Scene Parsing Network (PSPNet) [10], initially designed for comprehending scenes in natural images. Employing a pyramid pooling module to capture contextual information at multiple scales, this model has influenced advancements in medical image segmentation, including applications in segmenting brain MRI data.

Çiçek et al. (2016) introduced the 3D U-Net architecture [11], a specialized variant of the U-Net model tailored for dense volumetric segmentation with sparse annotation. This adaptation facilitates precise segmentation of anatomical structures in 3D medical images [32], particularly evident in applications such as brain MRI scans. Due to its proficiency in capturing spatial information, the 3D U-Net architecture has become widely adopted in the realm of brain MRI segmentation.

Nair and Hinton (2010) pioneered the use of Rectified Linear Units (ReLU) [12] as an activation function, enhancing the performance of restricted Boltzmann machines. The adoption of ReLU activation extends to CNNs, proving beneficial in various medical image segmentation tasks, including the segmentation of brain MRI data.

Moeskops et al. (2016) proposed an automated segmentation approach for MR brain images [13], leveraging a convolutional neural network (CNN). This CNN architecture learns to segment brain structures without explicit reliance on handcrafted features or prior knowledge, highlighting the effectiveness of deep learning methodologies in the analysis of brain MRI data.

Havaei et al. (2017) pioneered the development of deep neural networks tailored explicitly for brain-tumor segmentation. Their research underscored the potential of deep learning models in precisely delineating brain tumors [14], offering crucial implications for applications in clinical decision support systems and treatment planning.

Yosinski et al. (2014) explored the transferability of features within deep neural networks [15], emphasizing the prospect of harnessing pre-trained models for tasks related to medical image segmentation. This study provides insights into the transfer learning capabilities of deep learning models, particularly in the context of medical imaging applications.

Litjens et al. (2017) conducted an extensive survey on the application of deep learning in the analysis of medical images [16], covering a variety of approaches, architectures, and applications. Their survey spans various medical imaging modalities, highlighting the substantial impact of deep learning techniques in the medical field. Zhou et al. (2019) introduced UNet++ [17], a nested U-Net architecture that incorporates skip connections and dense skip pathways to capture hierarchical features, thereby enhancing segmentation accuracy. This study highlights the capability of nested architectures in medical image segmentation, encompassing the examination of brain MRI data.

7.3 Brain MRI Segmentation Dataset

The "Brain MRI Segmentation" dataset available on Kaggle consists of brain MRI images [18] and manually segmented masks for abnormality detection using FLAIR imaging. Obtained from 110 individuals in The Cancer Genome Atlas (TCGA) collection of lower-grade gliomas, this dataset comprises MRI scans accompanied by genomic cluster information. Each MRI image is paired with a corresponding manual segmentation mask that highlights abnormal areas detected through FLAIR imaging. This labeled dataset [19, 20] is valuable for medical imaging researchers and practitioners, facilitating the training and evaluation of algorithms and models focused on brain abnormality segmentation. Figure 7.1 showcases the image visualizations derived from this dataset, providing critical

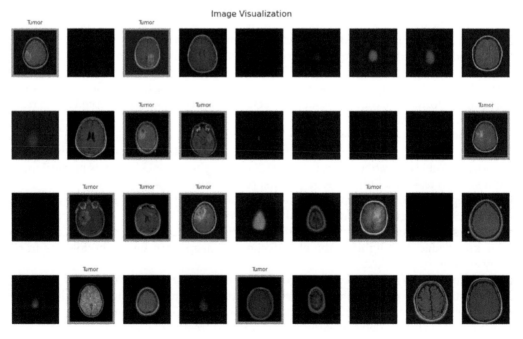

FIGURE 7.1
Image visualization as per the dataset.

insights into the morphological characteristics of brain abnormalities. By exploring the relationship between MRI findings, genomic data, and lower-grade glioma, this dataset can contribute to advancements in understanding and treating brain tumors. It supports the development of automated segmentation algorithms, aids in performance assessment, and has the potential to assist in clinical diagnosis and management of brain abnormalities

7.4 Experimental Models

This section discusses the proposed models used for our experimental analysis.

7.4.1 U-Net

The U-Net model stands as a prevalent architecture for image segmentation assignments [21], especially in the realm of medical imaging. It incorporates both an encoder and a decoder. The encoder is responsible for feature extraction using convolutional layers and down-sampling through max-pooling. The bottleneck layer further reduces dimensions while preserving information. The decoder uses transpose convolutional layers for upsampling and integrates skip connections to retain both high- and low-level features. The model produces a segmentation mask using a 1×1 convolutional layer with sigmoid activation. U-Net excels in capturing local and global features, making it effective for accurate segmentation, especially in medical imaging applications.

7.4.2 DeepLab

DeepLab is a series of deep learning models known for their accurate semantic image segmentation [22]. They utilize atrous convolutions to capture fine-grained details without losing spatial resolution. DeepLab V1 introduced atrous convolutions, V2 added Atrous Spatial Pyramid Pooling (ASPP), V3 incorporated image-level features, and V3+ included skip connections. These models excel at capturing local and global contextual information, and improving segmentation accuracy. DeepLab has been widely used for object recognition and scene parsing, making significant contributions to the field of computer vision.

7.5 Explanation of Each Phase of the Experiment Analysis Process

The experimental flow of the proposed research is presented in Figure 7.2.

From Figure 7.2, it can be observed that the initial phase of the workflow encompasses essential preparatory steps. This begins with the incorporation of requisite libraries and models, establishing the foundation for subsequent actions. Moving onward, the attention shifts to dataset procurement. Within this phase, there is a pivotal emphasis on collecting

FIGURE 7.2
Methodological framework: integrating libraries, models, and dataset insights for image segmentation.

metadata and undergoing an exploratory analysis. This preliminary exploration is instrumental in informing the subsequent stage: a thorough process of data preprocessing. These preprocessing procedures are designed to ensure the dataset's quality and readiness, laying the groundwork for the subsequent and intricate phase of image segmentation.

Semantic segmentation analysis methodology by exploration of both U-Net and the DeepLab model series is presented in Figure 7.3. In this, specialized helper functions are

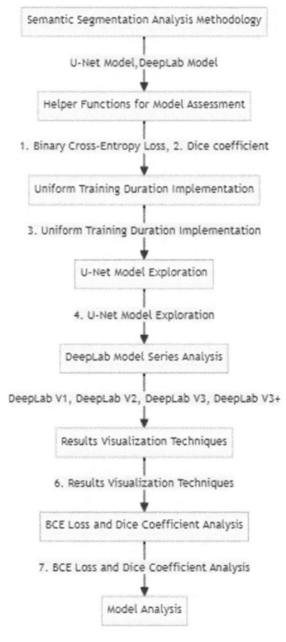

FIGURE 7.3
Flow diagram of the Semantic Segmentation Analysis Methodology.

considered for model assessment, covering binary cross-entropy loss and Dice coefficient calculations. Further, a uniform training duration implementation ensures consistent and fair model evaluation. The in-depth analysis of the proposed U-Net model, and the complete DeepLab model series, comprising DeepLab V1, V2, V3, and V3+ are performed through visualization techniques and by using BCE loss and Dice coefficient metrics. The final phase involves an overarching model analysis, offering a holistic view of the semantic segmentation models under scrutiny.

7.5.1 Helper Function

The helper functions defined in the code serve specific purposes for loss and metrics calculations in the segmentation model. The BCE_loss function is designed for computing the binary cross-entropy loss, quantifying the dissimilarity between predicted and true labels in binary classification tasks. This function leverages the binary_cross-entropy functionality from the Keras library. For the dice_coef function, it calculates the Dice coefficient, a metric assessing the overlap between two sets. By determining the intersection and sums of predicted and true labels, it gauges the similarity. The formula used is (2 * intersection + 1) / (sum of true labels + sum of predicted labels + 1). The function bce_dice_loss combines both the binary cross-entropy loss and the Dice loss by summing them. This composite loss function is designed to strike a balance between achieving accurate segmentation and ensuring spatial overlap.This composite loss function helps balance accurate segmentation with spatial overlap.

7.5.1.1 *BCE_loss (Binary Cross-Entropy Loss)*

y_true: This represents the true binary labels, which can take values of 0 or 1 in binary classification tasks. y_pred: Refers to the predicted probabilities of the positive class, falling within the range of 0 to 1.

The binary cross-entropy loss is mathematically defined as:

$$bce\_loss(y\_true, y\_pred) = \sum_{i=0}^{N}(y\_true.\log(y\_pred)$$

$$+(1-y\_true).\log(1-y\_pred))\frac{-b \pm \sqrt{b^2 - 4ac}}{2a}$$

Here, N represents the total number of samples in the dataset.

7.5.1.2 *dice_coef (Dice coefficient*

$$dice\_coef(y\_true, y\_pred) = \frac{2.\sum_{i=1}^{N}(y\_true.y\_pred) + 1}{\sum_{i=1}^{N}(y\_true) + \sum_{i=1}^{N}(y\_pred) + 1}$$

7.5.2 Uniform Training Duration

For consistency, all models U-Net, DeepLab V1, DeepLab V2, DeepLab V3, and DeepLab V3+, were trained for precisely 100 epochs. This standardized training duration facilitated an impartial assessment of their performance and convergence patterns. The consistent epoch count enabled an accurate evaluation of their learning capabilities, providing insights into their segmentation efficacy and potential areas for improvement.

7.5.3 U-Net Model

The U-Net architecture is widely acclaimed for its efficacy in image segmentation tasks, adept at capturing both local and global features efficiently.

Figure 7.4 explains the application of the U-Net model for the tasks of skull stripping and segmentation. Utilizing the Keras functional API, the model incorporates key components, encompasses several crucial components as outlined below:

a. Input: This module accepts MRI images as inputs, assuming dimensions of (IMG_HEIGHT, IMG_WIDTH, IMG_CHANNELS).

b. Encoder: This section features convolutional layers incorporating Rectified Linear Unit (ReLU) activation. It's responsible for capturing and extracting features from the input images. Max pooling layers facilitate downsampling, reducing spatial dimensions while retaining critical features.

c. Bottleneck: Operating as the central element of the U-Net, the bottleneck typically incorporates convolutional layers. It further reduces spatial dimensions while preserving vital information.

d. Decoder: In this segment, transpose convolutional layers (Conv2DTranspose) facilitate upsampling. This functionality allows the model to regain spatial details that might have been lost in the encoding phase. Additionally, the incorporation of skip connections involves concatenating feature maps from corresponding encoder layers, enabling the model to preserve both high-level and low-level features.

e. Output: The final output is generated through a 1×1 convolutional layer utilizing a sigmoid activation function. This produces a segmentation mask for each input image.

7.5.3.1 Model Compilation

Compilation of the U-Net model involves the utilization of the Adam optimizer, a widely adopted optimizer for training deep learning models. The chosen loss function is BCE_dice_loss, a composite function that merges binary cross-entropy loss and the Dice loss. This amalgamation is designed to optimize both precise segmentation and spatial overlap. Additionally, the model is configured to monitor the Dice coefficient as a performance metric throughout the training process.

7.5.3.2 Callbacks

Two crucial callbacks are integrated into the training pipeline to enhance its efficiency and facilitate model monitoring as follows:

• Early stopping: Implemented to curb over-fitting and expedite training, this callback meticulously assesses the validation loss. If no improvement is observed over a predetermined number of epochs (defined by the patience parameter), the training process is halted.

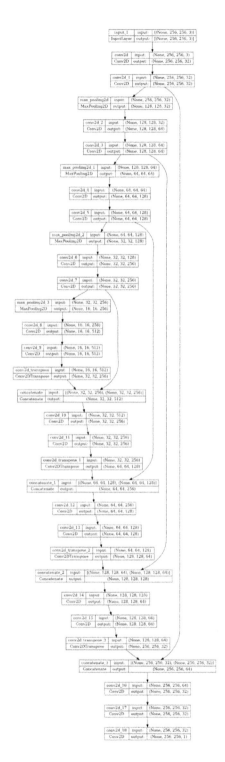

FIGURE 7.4
Proposed U-Net architecture.

- Model checkpoint: This function plays a pivotal role in preserving the model with the optimal performance based on the validation loss. By saving the best-performing model, determined during training, it ensures that this optimal configuration can be reinstated for subsequent use.

7.5.3.3 Training Process

The U-Net model is trained using the fit function, which takes the training data (X_train and Y_train) and iterates over a specified number of epochs. Throughout the training phase, a validation split of 1/9 is implemented, allocating one-ninth of the training data for continuous evaluation. After each epoch, the model undergoes assessment on this reserved validation set to gauge its evolving performance.

7.5.3.4 Evaluation

Post-training, the model's effectiveness is appraised by evaluating its performance on the designated test data (X_test and Y_test) using the evaluate function. The model computes BCE loss and Dice coefficient scores on the test data, providing a quantitative assessment of its performance. Lower BCE loss indicates better agreement between the predicted and true labels, while a higher Dice coefficient suggests a greater overlap between the predicted and true labels.

7.5.3.5 Results

The evaluation step outputs the binary cross-entropy (BCE) loss and Dice coefficient scores [30], providing a quantitative assessment of the model's performance on the test data. Additionally, the time taken for the entire U-Net experiment is recorded using the start_time and end_time variables, offering an indication of the experiment's duration.

7.5.4 DeepLab V1

The experiment analysis process for the different DeepLab versions can be divided into the following phases.

7.5.4.1 Model Architecture

In Figure 7.5, the DeepLab architecture, employed for segmentation, demonstrates the utilization of a modified U-Net architecture. The model comprises an encoder with convolutional and max-pooling layers for feature extraction, followed by atrous (dilated) convolutions with varying rates to achieve multi-scale feature representation. The model then performs a concatenation of the atrous layers and a decoder with convolutional transpose layers for upsampling. The final output is generated by a sigmoid activation function.

7.5.4.2 Model Compiling

For the DeepLab V1 model, the compilation involves the utilization of the Adam optimizer, with the defined bce_dice_loss as the chosen loss function and the dice_coef metric for evaluation.

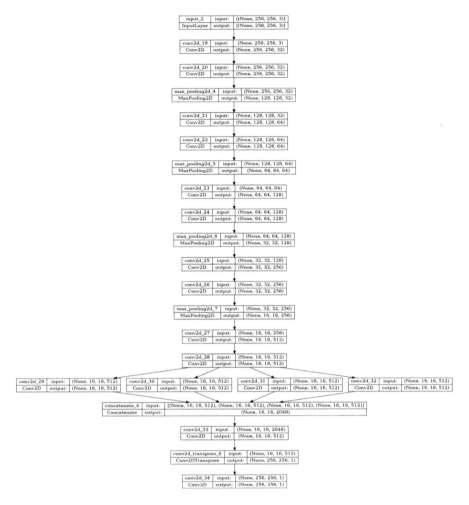

FIGURE 7.5
Proposed DeepLab model architecture.

Callbacks: Much like the training procedure for the U-Net model, the DeepLab V1 model's training process incorporates the establishment of early stopping and model checkpoint callbacks.

Training: The model is trained on the designated training data (X_train and Y_train) using the fit function, incorporating a validation split of 1/9 for monitoring its performance.

Evaluation: After the training phase, the performance of the trained DeepLab V1 model is assessed on the separate test data (X_test and Y_test) using the evaluate function. The calculated BCE loss and Dice coefficient scores are then printed for further analysis.

7.5.5 DeepLab V2

7.5.5.1 Model Architecture

The DeepLab V2 model follows a similar architecture to DeepLab V1 but incorporates an additional Atrous Spatial Pyramid Pooling (ASPP) module. The ASPP module conducts convolutional operations with varied atrous rates and then merges the resulting outputs. The remaining components of the model architecture are consistent with those of DeepLab V1.

7.5.5.2 Model Compiling, Callbacks, Training, and Evaluation

These steps are similar to DeepLab V1, using the appropriate model, compiling, callbacks, training, and evaluation functions for DeepLab V2.

7.5.6 DeepLab V3

7.5.6.1 Model Architecture

The DeepLab V3 model introduces improvements over DeepLab V2, specifically in the ASPP module. In addition to the convolutional operations with different atrous rates, DeepLab V3 adds an image-level feature module. Global average pooling is utilized to extract image-level features, which undergo further processing through convolutional layers prior to upsampling.Subsequently, the ASPP module and image-level features are combined through concatenation before being transmitted to the decoder.

7.5.6.2 Model Compiling, Callbacks, Training, and Evaluation

These steps are similar to the previous models, using the appropriate model, compiling, callbacks, training, and evaluation functions for DeepLab V3.

7.5.7 DeepLab V3+

7.5.7.1 Model Architecture

The DeepLab V3+ model further enhances the DeepLab V3 architecture by incorporating the concept of skip connections.In the decoder, connections are established between the upsampled output from the ASPP module and the corresponding low-level features from the encoder. This incorporation aids in preserving and leveraging low-level spatial information during the upsampling process.

7.5.7.2 Model Compiling, Callbacks, Training, and Evaluation

These steps are similar to the previous models, using the appropriate model, compiling, callbacks, training, and evaluation functions for DeepLab V3+.

In each instance, the model is compiled using the Adam optimizer and the specified loss function (bce_dice_loss), with the Dice coefficient monitored as a metric. The models undergo training with the fit function, incorporating the designated batch size, number of epochs, and validation split. Post-training, the models are evaluated on the test data, and the BCE loss and Dice coefficient scores are printed. Finally, the models are deleted to free up memory.

Table 7.1 provides a comprehensive summary of binary cross-entropy (BCE) loss values for various segmentation models, providing insights into their performance. The BCE loss serves as a measure of

concordance between predicted and actual labels, shedding light on the model's accuracy in aligning its segmentations with the ground truth data. These BCE loss values

TABLE 7.1

BCE Loss across Different Models

Sl no.	Model	BCE Loss
1	U-Net	0.5261
2	DeepLab V1	0.1984
3	DeepLab V2	0.2127
4	DeepLab V3	0.2231
5	DeepLab V3+	0.3431

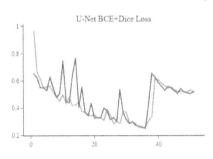
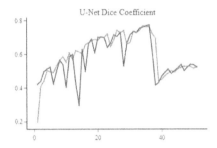

FIGURE 7.6
Visualization of the training loss and metrics (BCE loss and Dice coefficient) for U-Net.

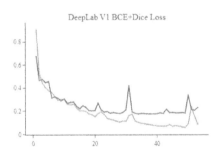
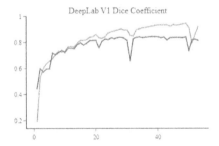

FIGURE 7.7
Visualization of the training loss and metrics (BCE loss and Dice coefficient) for DeepLab V1.

provide a quantitative assessment of how well each model's predicted segmentations align with the actual data. Lower BCE loss values indicate better agreement. This table serves as a crucial tool for evaluating and comparing the models' performance and can guide the selection of the most suitable model for specific segmentation tasks.

7.5.8 Training Loss and Metrics

In this section, a comprehensive visualization of the training loss and metrics (BCE loss and Dice coefficient) for each model, including U-Net (Figure 7.6), DeepLab V1 (Figure 7.7), DeepLab V2 (Figure 7.8), DeepLab V3 (Figure 7.9), and DeepLab V3+ (Figure 7.10), is presented using subplots. Several iterations over the history of each model are taken to

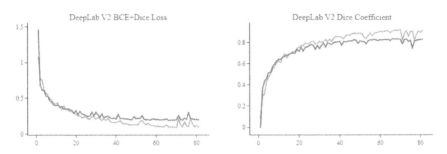

FIGURE 7.8
Visualization of the training loss and metrics (BCE loss and Dice coefficient) for DeepLab V2.

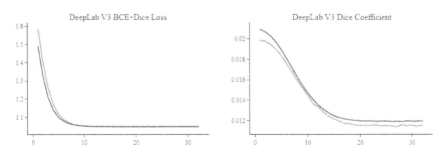

FIGURE 7.9
Visualization of the training loss and metrics (BCE loss and Dice coefficient) for DeepLab V3.

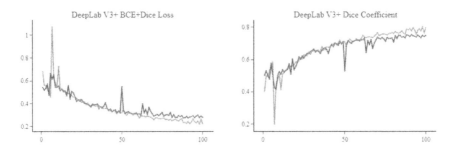

FIGURE 7.10
Visualization of the training loss and metrics (BCE loss and Dice coefficient) for DeepLab V3+.

extract the loss and metric values. The left column of plots displays the loss values, encompassing both training loss and validation loss, providing insights into the model's convergence and generalization. Simultaneously, the right column showcases the Dice coefficient values, including training Dice coefficient and validation Dice coefficient, offering a comprehensive view of the model's segmentation accuracy and performance throughout training. These visualizations serve as valuable tools for assessing the training progress and performance of each model.

7.5.9 Training Time

This section presents the training time for each model (U-Net, DeepLab V1, DeepLab V2, DeepLab V3, and DeepLab V3+). A bar chart is created, wherein the y-axis signifies the models and the x-axis denotes the training time in seconds. The models are arranged in order of decreasing training time, from the longest to the shortest. Simultaneously, Table 7.2 is presented as a tool for contrasting the training durations among different models. This table provides valuable insights into the computational efficiency of each model, helping researchers understand the time required for training and potentially aiding in model selection based on training time constraints. The training time can be a critical factor when considering the practicality of deploying these models in various applications. Additionally, Figure 7.11 presents a bar chart illustrating the training times across the various models. This visual representation facilitates a straightforward comparison of training times among various models.

7.5.10 Testing Metrics

In this section, the testing metrics, specifically the Dice coefficient, for each model (U-Net, DeepLab V1, DeepLab V2, DeepLab V3, DeepLab V3+), are presented. Table 7.3 offers a comprehensive comparison of Dice coefficient values across different models, providing a detailed assessment of their segmentation accuracy. The Dice coefficient serves as a metric to gauge the similarity or overlap between predicted and true segmentation masks, ranging from 0 (no overlap) to 1 (perfect overlap). Additionally, a bar chart is generated, where the y-axis represents the models, and the x-axis represents the corresponding Dice

TABLE 7.2

Comparative Analysis of the Training Times for Different Models

Sl no.	Model	Time
1	DeepLab V1	3409.664319
2	DeepLab V2	2411.709603
3	U-Net	2391.769868
4	DeepLab V3+	2148.098355
5	DeepLab V3	1615.335104

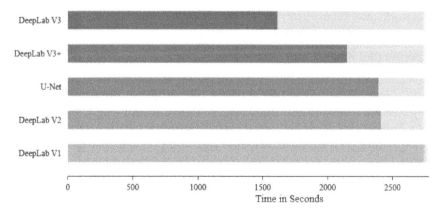

FIGURE 7.11
Comparison of training times across different models.

TABLE 7.3

Comparison of the Dice Coefficient across Different Models

Sl no.	Model	dice_coef
1	U-Net	0.498783
2	DeepLab V3+	0.691064
3	DeepLab V3	0.800540
4	DeepLab V2	0.815100
5	DeepLab V1	0.833213

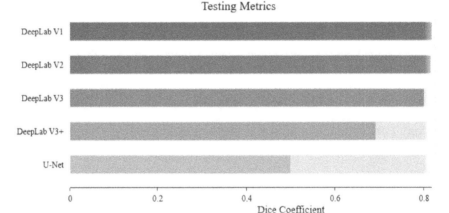

FIGURE 7.12
Comparison of the Dice coefficient across different models.

coefficient values. The models are arranged in ascending order based on their Dice coefficient scores. These Dice coefficient values provide a quantitative measure of how well each model performed in terms of accurately segmenting the brain structures in the MRI images. Higher Dice coefficients indicate more accurate segmentations. This table is crucial for evaluating and comparing the models' performance and can guide the selection of the most suitable model for specific segmentation tasks. In Figure 7.12, a bar chart specifically illustrates the Dice coefficient for a given model. This chart offers a means to evaluate the model's segmentation accuracy performance.

7.5.11 Experimental Results and Discussion

This section presents the outcomes of the image segmentation for each model in Figure 7.12, providing a visual representation of the segmentation outcomes across different models. The segmentation results are organized as a grid of subplots. Every row in the grid represents a distinct sample image, while each column corresponds to a different segmentation model. Within each subplot, various critical components are depicted:

1. Original MRI Image: The leftmost part of each subplot shows the original MRI brain image. This is the input image that the model processes for segmentation.
2. Original Mask: Next to the original MRI image, there is the original mask. This mask represents the true segmentation of the brain structures within the MRI image. It serves as the reference for evaluating how well the models are performing.

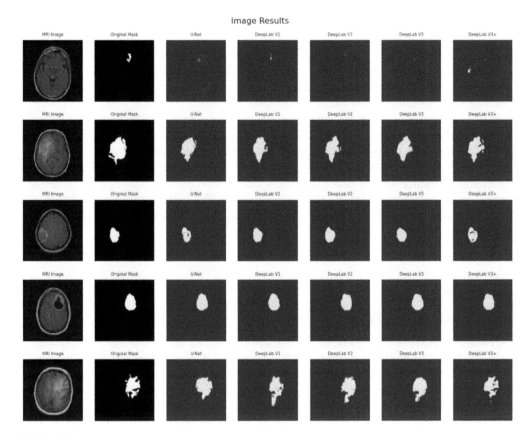

FIGURE 7.13
Comparison of image segmentation across different models.

3. Predicted Mask: On the right side of each subplot is the predicted mask. This mask is generated by the segmentation model being evaluated. It shows the model's effort to recognize and delineate the structures of the brain within the MRI image.

By comparing the original mask (ground truth) with the predicted mask generated by each model, viewers can visually assess how accurate the segmentation results are. This visual representation aids in comprehending the performance of each model on real-world image data. Thus, Figure 7.13 provides a side-by-side visual evaluation of the segmentation outcomes generated by different models on various MRI images, offering insights into their performance and accuracy in delineating brain structures.

7.6 Limitations

Primarily, this study lacks an exploration of the transfer learning potential across different semantic segmentation models. The absence of discussion on whether pre-trained models on general segmentation tasks effectively transfer to the specific task of glioma segmentation or if task-specific pre-training yields superior results represents a notable limitation. Additionally, this study does not thoroughly address the robustness of the models to variations in imaging conditions, such as differences in MRI machines and acquisition parameters. The extent to which the models can generalize to diverse datasets and imaging conditions remains unexplored, limiting the understanding of their performance in real-world scenarios. Furthermore, this study does not delve into ensemble approaches that combine predictions from multiple segmentation models. The potential enhancement in segmentation accuracy through ensemble methods is an area left unexplored. Lastly, while this study acknowledges the common challenge of class imbalance in medical imaging, particularly in the context of glioma segmentation, it does not provide a detailed exploration of how different segmentation models handle this challenge. A more in-depth exploration into the strategies employed by various models to address class imbalance would enhance our understanding of their limitations in practical real-world applications.

7.7 Conclusions and Future Scope

This chapter conducts an extensive assessment of various segmentation models, encompassing U-Net, DeepLab V1, DeepLab V2, DeepLab V3, and DeepLab V3+. Through an extensive analysis of critical factors such as training progress, performance metrics, training times, and image segmentation outcomes, a nuanced understanding of each model's capabilities was gained.

The examination began with an exploration of BCE loss values, revealing distinct performance ranges. U-Net and DeepLab V3+ occupied the performance extremes, while DeepLab V1, DeepLab V2, and DeepLab V3 showcased intermediate levels of proficiency. The analysis then delved into training loss and Dice coefficients across various epochs, highlighting the models' convergence dynamics. The consistent reduction in training loss, accompanied by improved Dice coefficients, indicated the models' progressive ability to capture and integrate intricate segmentation features.

Leveraging the Dice coefficient as a metric, a thorough evaluation was conducted on the testing dataset. Notably, DeepLab V3 emerged as the leading performer, boasting a remarkable Dice coefficient of 0.800540. Close behind were DeepLab V2 with a score of 0.815100 and DeepLab V1 with 0.833213. DeepLab V3+ also demonstrated robust performance, achieving a Dice coefficient of 0.691064, while U-Net secured a respectable score of 0.498783.

Moreover, the study delved into the critical aspect of training times, revealing an intriguing trade-off between computational efficiency and segmentation accuracy. Surprisingly, despite its significantly shorter training time (1615.335104 seconds), DeepLab V3 achieved noteworthy segmentation accuracy. On the contrary, DeepLab V1 required the longest training time (3409.664319 seconds), pointing towards a potential compromise between its high accuracy and the training duration.

The findings bear valuable implications for both researchers and practitioners engaged in medical image analysis. Depending on specific application needs, whether emphasizing precision or computational efficiency, the optimal choice among DeepLab V3, DeepLab V2, or DeepLab V1 can be determined. This choice can be further tailored based on available computational resources. Notably, U-Net, with its simpler design and shorter training time, remains a practical choice for scenarios that seek a balance between simplicity and acceptable performance.

In essence, this comprehensive evaluation not only underscores the effectiveness of DeepLab V3, DeepLab V2, and DeepLab V1 in brain MRI segmentation but also empowers decision-making. Researchers and practitioners can confidently select the most suitable model according to their specific needs, whether prioritizing high accuracy, computational efficiency, or striking a balance. Through a thoughtful evaluation of the interplay between segmentation accuracy, training time, and computational efficiency, decision-makers can make informed choices for real-world applications in neurological disorder analysis, diagnosis, and treatment planning.

The visually intuitive depiction of training progress, segmentation performance, and image outcomes adds significant value to this study's contributions in the domain of medical image analysis.

The thorough evaluation of diverse segmentation models such as U-Net, DeepLab V1, V2, V3, and V3+ in brain MRI segmentation has illuminated several paths for future advancement. One avenue involves hybrid models that leverage the strengths of these architectures, potentially yielding even higher accuracy. Attention mechanisms could enhance focus on critical features, improving performance in complex cases. Investigating transfer learning might enhance generalization to new datasets with limited samples. As medical data is inherently noisy, robustness-enhancing techniques are vital. Lastly, ensuring model interpretability is key for clinical deployment, warranting further research to explain decisions and establish trust.

References

1. Ronneberger, O., Fischer, P., & Brox, T. (2015). U-net: Convolutional networks for biomedical image segmentation. In *Medical Image Computing and Computer-Assisted Intervention–MICCAI 2015: 18th International Conference*, Munich, Germany, October 5–9, 2015, Proceedings, Part III 18 (pp. 234–241). Springer International Publishing.
2. Chen, L. C., Papandreou, G., Kokkinos, I., Murphy, K., & Yuille, A. L. (2017). Deeplab: Semantic image segmentation with deep convolutional nets, atrous convolution, and fully connected CRFs. *IEEE Transactions on Pattern Analysis and Machine Intelligence*, 40(4), 834–848.
3. de Gelder, B., & Solanas, M. P. (2021). A computational neuroethology perspective on body and expression perception. *Trends in Cognitive Sciences*, 25(9), 744–756.
4. Singha, A., Thakur, R. S., & Patel, T. (2021). Deep learning applications in medical image analysis. In Sujata Dash, Subhendu Kumar Pani, S. Balamurugan, Ajith Abraham (eds), *Biomedical Data Mining for Information Retrieval: Methodologies, Techniques and Applications* (pp. 293–350). John Wiley & Sons DOI:10.1002/9781119711278.ch11, Book
5. Zhao, Y., Huang, Z., Che, H., Xie, F., Liu, M., Wang, M., & Sun, D. (2023). Segmentation of brain tissues from MRI images using multitask fuzzy clustering algorithm. *Journal of Neuroimaging*, 31(3), 423–430. https://doi.org/10.1111/jon.12779.
6. Ben Yedder, H., Cardoen, B., & Hamarneh, G. (2021). Deep learning for biomedical image reconstruction: A survey. *Artificial Intelligence Review*, 54, 215–251.
7. Zhao, H., Qi, X., Shen, X., Shi, J., & Jia, J. (2018). Icnet for real-time semantic segmentation on high-resolution images. In *Proceedings of the European Conference on Computer Vision (ECCV)* (pp. 405–420).
8. Hu, J., Shen, L., & Sun, G. (2018). Squeeze-and-excitation networks. In *Proceedings of the IEEE Conference on Computer Vision and Pattern Recognition* (pp. 7132–7141).

9. Isensee, F., Petersen, J., Klein, A., Zimmerer, D., Jaeger, P. F., Kohl, S., ... Maier-Hein, K. H. (2018). nnU-net: Self-adapting framework for u-net-based medical image segmentation. arXiv preprint arXiv:1809.10486.

10. Zhao, H., Shi, J., Qi, X., Wang, X., & Jia, J. (2017). Pyramid scene parsing network. In *Proceedings of the IEEE Conference on Computer Vision and Pattern Recognition* (pp. 2881–2890).

11. Çiçek, Ö., Abdulkadir, A., Lienkamp, S. S., Brox, T., & Ronneberger, O. (2016). 3D U-Net: Learning dense volumetric segmentation from sparse annotation. In *Medical Image Computing and Computer-Assisted Intervention–MICCAI 2016: 19th International Conference*, Athens, Greece, October 17–21, 2016, Proceedings, Part II 19 (pp. 424–432). Springer International Publishing.

12. Nair, V., & Hinton, G. E. (2010). Rectified linear units improve restricted boltzmann machines. In *Proceedings of the 27th International Conference on Machine Learning (ICML-10)* (pp. 807–814).

13. Moeskops, P., Viergever, M. A., Mendrik, A. M., De Vries, L. S., Benders, M. J., & Išgum, I. (2016). Automatic segmentation of MR brain images with a convolutional neural network. *IEEE Transactions on Medical Imaging*, 35(5), 1252–1261.

14. Havaei, M., Davy, A., Warde-Farley, D., Biard, A., Courville, A., Bengio, Y., ... Larochelle, H. (2017). Brain tumor segmentation with deep neural networks. *Medical Image Analysis*, 35, 18–31.

15. Yosinski, J., Clune, J., Bengio, Y., & Lipson, H. (2014). How transferable are features in deep neural networks?. *Advances in Neural Information Processing Systems*, 27. 3320–3328. Dec. 2014. https://doi.org/10.48550/arXiv.1411.1792

16. Litjens, G., Kooi, T., Bejnordi, B. E., Setio, A. A. A., Ciompi, F., Ghafoorian, M., ... Sánchez, C. I. (2017). A survey on deep learning in medical image analysis. *Medical Image Analysis*, 42, 60–88.

17. Zhou, Z., Rahman Siddiquee, M. M., Tajbakhsh, N., & Liang, J. (2018). Unet++: A nested u-net architecture for medical image segmentation. In *Deep Learning in Medical Image Analysis and Multimodal Learning for Clinical Decision Support: 4th International Workshop, DLMIA 2018, and 8th International Workshop, ML-CDS 2018, Held in Conjunction with MICCAI 2018*, Granada, September 20, 2018, Proceedings 4 (pp. 3–11). Springer International Publishing.

18. Brain MRI Segmentation Dataset. https://www.kaggle.com/datasets/mateuszbuda/lgg-mri-segmentation.

19. Buda, M., Saha, A., & Mazurowski, M. A. (2019). Association of genomic subtypes of lower-grade gliomas with shape features automatically extracted by a deep learning algorithm. *Computers in Biology and Medicine*, 109, 218–225.

20. Mazurowski, M. A., Clark, K., Czarnek, N. M., Shamsesfandabadi, P., Peters, K. B., & Saha, A. (2017). Radiogenomics of lower-grade glioma: Algorithmically-assessed tumor shape is associated with tumor genomic subtypes and patient outcomes in a multi-institutional study with The Cancer Genome Atlas data. *Journal of Neuro-Oncology*, 133, 27–35.

21. Yousef, R., Khan, S., Gupta, G., Siddiqui, T., Albahlal, B. M., Alajlan, S. A., & Haq, M. A. (2023). U-Net-based models towards optimal MR brain image segmentation. *Diagnostics*, 13(9), 1624.

22. Lee, B., Yamanakkanavar, N., & Choi, J. Y. (2020). Automatic segmentation of brain MRI using a novel patch-wise U-net deep architecture. *Plos One*, 15(8), e0236493.

23. Wright, R., Kyriakopoulou, V., Ledig, C., Rutherford, M. A., Hajnal, J. V., Rueckert, D., & Aljabar, P. (2014). Automatic quantification of normal cortical folding patterns from fetal brain MRI. *Neuroimage*, 91, 21–32. https://doi.org/10.1016/j.neuroimage.2014.01.034

24. Moeskops, P., Benders, M. J., Kersbergen, K. J., Groenendaal, F., de Vries, L. S., Viergever, M. A., & Išgum, I. (2015). Development of cortical morphology evaluated with longitudinal MR brain images of preterm infants. *PloS One*, 10(7), e0131552.

25. Fischl, B., Salat, D. H., Busa, E., Albert, M., Dieterich, M., Haselgrove, C., ... Dale, A. M. (2002). Whole brain segmentation: Automated labeling of neuroanatomical structures in the human brain. *Neuron*, 33(3), 341–355.

26. Prastawa, M., Gilmore, J. H., Lin, W., & Gerig, G. (2005). Automatic segmentation of MR images of the developing newborn brain. *Medical Image Analysis*, 9(5), 457–466.

27. Xue, H., Srinivasan, L., Jiang, S., Rutherford, M., Edwards, A. D., Rueckert, D., & Hajnal, J. V. (2007). Automatic segmentation and reconstruction of the cortex from neonatal MRI. *Neuroimage*, 38(3), 461–477.

28. Gui, L., Lisowski, R., Faundez, T., Hüppi, P. S., Lazeyras, F., & Kocher, M. (2012). Morphology-driven automatic segmentation of MR images of the neonatal brain. *Medical Image Analysis*, 16(8), 1565–1579.
29. Marcus, D. S., Wang, T. H., Parker, J., Csernansky, J. G., Morris, J. C., & Buckner, R. L. (2007). Open Access Series of Imaging Studies (OASIS): Cross-sectional MRI data in young, middle aged, nondemented, and demented older adults. *Journal of Cognitive Neuroscience*, 19(9), 1498–1507.
30. Roth, H. R., Farag, A., Lu, L., Turkbey, E. B., & Summers, R. M. (2015, March). Deep convolutional networks for pancreas segmentation in CT imaging. In *Medical Imaging 2015: Image Processing* (Vol. 9413, pp. 378–385). SPIE.
31. Likar, B., Viergever, M. A., & Pernus, F. (2001). Retrospective correction of MR intensity inhomogeneity by information minimization. *IEEE Transactions on Medical Imaging*, 20(12), 1398–1410.
32. Rodriguez-Carranza, C. E., Mukherjee, P., Vigneron, D., Barkovich, J., & Studholme, C. (2008). A framework for in vivo quantification of regional brain folding in premature neonates. *Neuroimage*, 41(2), 462–478.

8

A Comprehensive Review on Depression Detection Based on Text from Social Media Posts

Vankayala Tejaswini, Bibhudatta Sahoo, and Korra Sathya Babu

8.1 Introduction

The state of mental health describes a person well-being, which includes mental state, behavioral patterns, and social involvement. It dramatically impacts an individual's thoughts, feelings, and cognitive behavior. Furthermore, it affects interpersonal interactions, the management of stress, and the processes involved in making decisions. The maintenance of mental well-being is crucial throughout all stages of human life. It is vital to take necessary actions or seek professional support when psychological well-being is adversely affected by a traumatic incident or experience at any point in our lives. Mental diseases exhibit a significant incidence across diverse countries on a global scale [1].

The global recognition of mental health as a significant concern can be attributed to various factors, such as inadequate awareness and comprehension of mental health, unstable financial situations, inadequate access to healthcare professionals, and high expenses associated with mental health services. The number of cases of depression, stress, and anxiety has experienced a substantial increase in modern culture. Teenagers are more prone to developing depressive symptoms due to low self-esteem, excessive self-criticism, and a sense of powerlessness in the face of stressful situations [2].

Major depressive disorder (MDD) is a debilitating illness distinguished by mood fluctuations, decreasing interest and pleasure in everyday tasks, disrupted sleep and eating patterns, reduced energy levels, and mental retardation or hyperactivity. According to the WHO, depression is a significant contributor to illness and disability on a global scale, affecting around 4.4% of the adult population annually [3]. Depression significantly impedes patients' ability to function and imposes financial burdens on the public health system, resulting in increased death rates, suicide rates, the severity of medical conditions, and the prevalence of alcohol and illicit drug use [4–7].

Traditional clinical examinations commonly rely on historical self-reports, where patients provide descriptions of their symptoms and personal experiences over the preceding weeks. Growing data suggests that these measurements may not fully consider MDD circumstances, such as changing symptoms or mood over time [8, 9]. It has been found that patients diagnosed with depression tend to modify the content of their stories when prompted to take part in a critical remembering of past events [10, 11]. They frequently interpret negative information more strongly [12] or commonly see their symptoms as more severe [13]. Empirical evidence has demonstrated that approximately

DOI: 10.1201/9781003450153-9

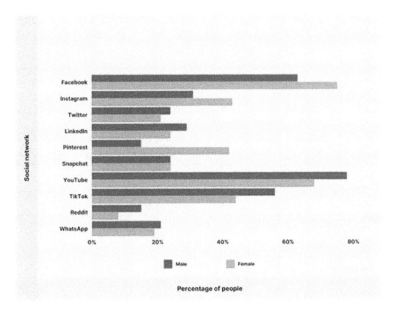

FIGURE 8.1
The gender distribution of social media audiences worldwide. https://th.bing.com/th/id/OIP.mmZeE8ZBIzm
djBwDKbT21gHaFo?pid=ImgDet&w=474&h=360&rs=1

70% of people with depression cannot access sufficient treatment or achieve full clinical
recovery [14]. Kazdin and Blase [15] argue that technological advancements hold promise in offering innovative channels for the transmission of evidence-based psychiatric
treatment.

Regardless of a person's location, social media platforms can encourage interpersonal interactions [16]. The utilization of social networking sites is undergoing a consistent increase, as illustrated in Figure 8.1. The social media networks Facebook, X
(formerly and colloquially known, and referred to in this chapter, as Twitter), Reddit,
and Instagram have experienced substantial growth in popularity throughout several
emerging nations. Furthermore, these platforms will allow individuals to effectively
articulate their perspectives, emotions, aspirations, achievements, and other relevant
aspects [17].

Text messaging has emerged as a novel approach to enhance healthcare and public
health, owing to recent progressions in telecoms and information technology [18]. The
field of health research related to text messaging had significant global growth after the
initial publication of a study on health text messaging in 2002. Nevertheless, the field of
study is in its nascent phase of advancement and establishment [19–21]. Currently, social
networking platforms are being used to identify and discern those who may be experiencing symptoms of depression.

8.1.1 Objectives and Research Questions

The objective of the comprehensive review is to detect depression through text from social
media platforms. This includes systematically analyzing existing studies and literature
to gain a deep understanding on the state-of-the-art methods, techniques, and challenges
related to detecting depression from textual data. The review aims to provide insights

and identify gaps in current knowledge to develop more effective solutions for detecting depression systems.

Research Question 1 :	Which social networks were explored in the identification of depressive mood disorders?
Research Question 2 :	What are the various textual data sources available using social media platforms to detect signs of depression?
Research Question 3 :	What are the challenges in doing text-based approach for depression detection?
Research Question 4 :	What is the most effective text-based approach for early depression detection?

8.2 Searching Strategies

8.2.1 Search Source

This study aimed to aggregate pertinent data from diverse social media websites to facilitate the detection of depression. A comprehensive search strategy was devised to accomplish the systematic review. Reputable academic databases such as PubMed, Google Scholar, IEEE Xplore, and ACM Digital Library gather a wide range of sources, including peer-reviewed articles, conference papers, and relevant reports, which are primary sources for gathering scholarly articles and studies.

8.2.2 Search Terms

The search strings were employed to encompass pivotal themes related to the research objective. Specifically, a combination of keywords such as "Machine Learning," "Deep Learning," or "Artificial Intelligence," "Depression," "major depressive disorder," AND "social media," "Text," or "Mental health" were used. Moreover, the search extended beyond academic databases to include diverse social media platforms. Using platform-specific search functions, content related to depression, its expressions, and discussions were directly mined from sources like Twitter, Facebook, Reddit, and other applicable platforms. This augmented approach allowed us to access real-time conversations, posts, and comments that pertained to individuals' experiences with depression.

8.2.3 Dataset Extraction

The dataset utilized in our research has been meticulously assembled from various reputable sources, including prominent academic platforms such as Google Scholar, IEEE Xplore, ACM Digital Library, and more. Drawing from a rich pool of scholarly literature, our approach to dataset extraction was guided by targeted keywords—specifically, "Twitter," "Reddit," and "Facebook." These keywords served as the compass guiding us through the expansive sea of information, enabling us to pinpoint datasets that are directly pertinent to these renowned social networking platforms. We ensured a comprehensive and well-rounded collection process by leveraging the vast repositories of knowledge available on these platforms. Each source contributes to the diversity and depth of our dataset, encompassing a broad spectrum of insights, trends, and observations related to user behavior, interactions, and discussions on these digital platforms.

8.3 Related Work

The widespread adoption of social networking platforms, like Facebook, Twitter, and Reddit, has generated an increased enthusiasm for leveraging these platforms to identify signs of depression [22]. The emergence of a significant number of real-time posts has occurred due to the integration of social networks into contemporary life. As a result, there have been efforts to investigate the mental well-being of individuals, precisely their emotions and depression, through the analysis of textual data obtained from these platforms.

It can be argued that language represents many facets of human thinking, feeling, belief, conduct, and identity. As a result, the increased availability of extensive textual data has led to inquiries on utilizing natural language processing (NLP) to identify depression and perform emotional analysis. Examples of this phenomenon can be found in research projects that analyze sentences taken from social media platforms to find word similarities [23] or classify sentences based on topics related to depression. Several studies [24] described a close association between depression and activity level concerning the exhibition of depressed symptoms. Furthermore, there have been attempts to create lexicons that can assist in the recognition and diagnosis of specific symptoms [25]. Furthermore, efforts have been made to take advantage of social networks to distinguish between suicidal ideation and depression [26].

Correctly diagnosing depression depends on the efficacy of communication between healthcare providers and patients. In contemporary times, significant technological advancements have facilitated the investigation of ML and DL methodologies in depression detection. The strategies, as mentioned earlier, have been implemented in several applications within the field of medicine [27].

8.3.1 Application of Twitter Data in Mental Health with Different Approaches

Twitter is a widely accessible network for messaging that enables the distribution of content created by users through tweets, retweets, and active engagement with posts. In 2019, Twitter reported a significant number of active users, over 330 million, who engaged with the network monthly. These users collectively produced approximately 500 million tweets, spanning a wide range of topics.

Deshpande et al. [28] successfully diagnose depression in people using emotional artificial intelligence approaches. Natural language processing methodologies and sentiment analysis algorithms are employed to facilitate the detection and recognition of depressive symptoms by studying tweets. The data is initially acquired from the Twitter site. Various pre-processing techniques are applied to keep the data in a more suitable form. The findings suggest that the multinomial naïve Bayes approach has shown superior effectiveness to the SVM strategy.

Biradar et al. [29] utilized a corpus of tweets as a primary data source for knowledge retrieval. The Senti Strength sentiment assessment tool is employed to generate the data. The tweets are subsequently categorized into two categories, depressive and non-depressive, employing a backpropagation neural network model. Subsequently, the sentiment analysis technique is executed, assigning a sentiment score to each tweet.

A variety of machine-learning approaches were used by Ramalingam et al. [30] to analyze depression. The current study examines how temporal perception works in depressed individuals, focusing on the filtering and categorization processes. Time-perceptron analysis examines how a person's use of social media influences their anxiety levels by measuring how much time they spend on various sites. Syntax and semantic analysis techniques are applied to examine multiple social media posts to recognize and decipher the user's emotional state. The application of machine-learning methodologies allows for identifying emotional and cognitive states, mainly related to suicidal or non-suicidal inclinations, through analyzing an individual's Twitter posts. Moreover, this methodology enables the detection of depression across several age cohorts.

Rajaraman et al. [31] utilized TF-IDF predictions to detect tweets showing depression. The data acquisition procedure encompasses the collection of a dataset from the social media platform Twitter. After that, the data that has undergone pre-processing is exposed to word embedding methodologies, which encompass the conversion of words into numerical vectors. The data is utilized for training and evaluating the models, classifying tweets into two distinct categories: standard and depressive. Their work suggests long short-term memory (LSTM)-RNN exhibits the highest level of precision in detecting sadness by analyzing tweets collected from the social media site Twitter.

The presence of depression in Twitter users was determined by Razak et al. [32] Vader Sentiment Analysis and two Machine Learning and deep learning approaches NB and CNN, are used in the system. The system's output is a percentage of positive and negative tweets from the users' accounts on Twitter platform and the followers they have.

The research undertaken by Shetty et al. [33] employs machine-learning classifiers to analyze a Twitter dataset to determine depression in individuals. The procedure can be divided into two discrete steps. In the preliminary stage, sentiment analysis is utilized to examine an individual's Twitter tweets in order to forecast binary categories, explicitly determining whether the individual is undergoing depression or not. A comparison is made between the outcomes of classifiers employing LSTM and convolutional neural network (CNN) architectures.

Wonkoblap et al. [34] aimed to construct a prediction model capable of identifying Twitter users with depression and promptly recognizing textual information related to mental health subjects. The dataset was obtained from Twitter by utilizing a regular expression or a continuous stream of real-time tweets. The dataset consists of 3,682 people, among whom 1,983 individuals self-identified as experiencing depression, whereas 1,699 individuals indicated that they did not experience depression. The use of bidirectional long short-term memory (BLSTM) was proposed by Mathur et al. [35] as a means of early detection of depression through the analysis of past tweets from users on the Twitter platform.

Mehra et al. [36] successfully retrieved raw data from Twitter by employing tokenization, stopping word removal, and eliminating repeated characters. The researchers employed the SentiStrength tool to identify tweets exhibiting negative sentiment. Orabi et al. [37] introduced a neural approach that utilizes a CNN and recurrent neural network (RNN) for the purpose of detecting depression. Tamblin et al. [38] investigated many expressions of depression as observed in a real-life textual platform, specifically Twitter. The authors analyzed the content of tweets that utilized the hashtag "#depressionsucks" to explore the topics spoken by users that were pertinent to their experiences with depression. A total of 169 distinct tweets were gathered over a duration of four weeks using the n-capture tool. The study conducted by Khafaga et al.[39] employs a unique approach called the MDHAN to categorize depression data.

Choudhury et al. [40] proposed an intelligent model to diagnose depression by analyzing the data obtained through the Twitter platform. Vioules et al. [41] describe a method that includes the measurement of highly suggestable indicators regarding suicidal intentions. Two discrete classifications of behavioral traits have been defined: user-driven and post-driven. The post's content is evaluated using a text score, which includes important data related to an individual's current state of mind and psychological welfare. The material's categorization is accomplished using two distinct approaches, specifically natural language processing (NLP) and a distress classifier. The research results indicate that the NLP text-scoring approach effectively detects tweets that pertain to mental health concerns, thereby improving the current framework around suicidal ideation.

The study conducted by Shahreen et al. [42] centered on analyzing Twitter data through machine-learning techniques and neural networks. Three types of weight optimizers were employed in the context of neural networks. The researchers expressed their interest in acquiring the unique identification number of a tweet, known as the Tweet ID, as well as the textual content of the Tweet, referred to as the Tweet Text. The SVM achieved a classification accuracy of 95.2%, while the neural networks achieved a higher accuracy of 97.6%.

Jashinsky et al. [43] analyzed to identify the risk variables associated with suicide on the social media platform Twitter. The tweet dataset was subjected to a refinement process wherein sarcastic tweets were eliminated, and afterward, an analysis was conducted on the subset of tweets that were geographic. A comparative analysis was conducted between suicide-related tweets and the official national data on suicide rates. Significant progress has been made in the acquisition of data about mental disorders associated with depression.

Yazdavar et al. [44] employed a statistical model to assess the relationship between the length of symptoms and their manifestation on Twitter among individuals with depression. The user did not provide any text to rewrite. Various techniques were employed on the Twitter data in the study of Gupta et al. [45]. The dataset is obtained in two variations, namely balanced and imbalanced, with a specific focus on the technical examination of oversampling techniques. The findings indicate that the LSTM classification model has marked good performance compared to the other baseline models in detecting depression.

8.3.2 Application of Facebook Data in Mental Health with Different Approaches

Facebook is the most popular social media platform that enables users to share content, connect with others, and engage in online communities. In 2019, Facebook reported a substantial user base of more than 2.4 billion monthly active users. These users collectively contributed to creating around 90 million posts across various formats. Moreover, the platform witnessed remarkable user engagement, with over 120 billion reactions.

The study conducted by Islam et al. [46] suggests ML techniques to detect indicators of depression among individuals who actively use social media platforms, particularly Facebook. This research investigates three discrete classifications of elements, and the findings suggest that decision trees have a greater degree of precision in categorizing remark characteristics when compared to alternative machine-learning techniques.

The research by Islam et al. [47] seeks to diagnose depression by employing the k-nearest neighbors (KNN) classification approach. The procedure entails retrieving data from Facebook comments on social media platforms, with a specific emphasis on categorizing emotions. NCapture is a software utility that is employed for the aim of collecting data. The comments in this tool are classified into two unique categories: comments that exhibit signs of depression (designated as "1") and comments that do not exhibit signs of sadness (designated as "0"). Among the various classifiers based on the KNN algorithm, it has been concluded that the coarse KNN classifier has superior performance.

Noureen et al. [48] examined different classifiers to identify psychotic behaviors shown by individuals. The process of data collection was conducted through the Facebook API. The posts underwent pre-processing procedures, and the findings indicate that no singular method can be considered a definitive standard for classifying user psychotic conduct. Different machine-learning techniques can be employed and applied with appropriate validation to enhance accuracy and achieve improved outcomes.

Eichstaedt et al. [49] obtained a dataset of the Facebook statuses of 683 individuals seeking medical attention at an urban emergency department. Out of the total 1sample, 114 individuals were diagnosed with depression. Primarily utilizing the linguistic patterns observed prior to the initial recording of a depression diagnosis, the researchers could reasonably identify individuals suffering from depression (AUC = 0.69). It was determined that the ability to forecast future depression states was feasible up to three months prior to its initial documentation.

Wu et al. [50] employed Word2vec to acquire word embeddings. Subsequently, these word vectors were utilized as input for LSTM in order to make predictions on depression based on content posted on Facebook. In a recent study conducted by [51], it was discovered that there were explicit references to depression among adolescents. The Facebook postings exhibited characteristics of depression, such as a higher frequency of references to depressed symptoms. Additionally, these posts displayed an increased prevalence of cognitive distortions and a greater expression of negative attitudes towards individuals within the social sphere.

8.3.3 Application of Reddit Data in Mental Health with Different Approaches

Reddit is a publicly accessible platform that facilitates disseminating user-generated content through publishing, commenting, and voting on entries. In 2019, Reddit's social media platform boasted a substantial user base of over 430 million individuals who actively engaged with the platform monthly. Together, these users contributed to creating around 199 million posts, spanning over 130,000 active groups. Additionally, the platform witnessed a staggering amount of user-generated content in the form of 1.7 billion comments and an impressive 32 billion upvotes.

The research undertaken by Tadesse et al. [52] investigates the analysis of user-generated content on the online platform Reddit to predict occurrences of depression. The researchers utilized natural language processing (NLP) methodologies and executed an SVM classifier in order to forecast occurrences of depression and non-depression. TrifanAlina et al. [53] introduced a rule-based estimator that uses a TF-IDF weighting technique to detect sorrow in the Reddit social media site, using bag-of-words features.

Yates et al. [54] presented a comprehensive Reddit dataset comprising individuals who self-reported experiencing depression alongside a control group of users exhibiting similar characteristics. Initial findings about its categorization accompanied the publication of the dataset. As mentioned earlier, the research used precise temporal intervals that correspond to the date of diagnosis to demonstrate the dynamic nature of this particular diagnostic process [55].

Cohan et al. [56] recently made available a new dataset from Reddit. In their study, the authors examined patterns of extended self-diagnoses by comparing depressive synonyms with a particular emphasis on nine distinct mental health illnesses. Shing et al. [57] recently described a notable instance where suicide-risk assessment was conducted using Reddit posts in conjunction with professional expertise. According to Boettcher et al. [58], a significant proportion of studies, roughly two-thirds, utilized language derived from Reddit as the primary source for predictive classifications of depression and anxiety.

Naseem et al. [59] reconceptualized the task of identifying depression by framing it as an ordinal classification problem, employing a system that categorized depression into four distinct levels of severity. The researchers presented a novel deep neural network architecture to address the classification issue.

Ren et al. [60] extracted positive and negative phrases. These words were then subjected to two distinct BiLSTM layers, followed by attention layers. The dataset from Reddit comprises 1,293 posts indicating symptoms of depression and 549 posts classified as standard.

Urban et al. [61] conducted an empirical study wherein various classifiers were evaluated using Reddit data. Linguistic-based models were constructed to examine various diseases. Each of the three had distinct explanatory variables. It has been determined that depression poses the most significant challenge in terms of classification. Another notable finding is that posts that are too old do not contribute to the accurate classification of mental health issues.

DQingCong et al. [62] directed their attention towards resolving the issue arising from data volatility inside the realm of the physical world. The Reddit dataset was utilized to detect the feeling of depression. This dataset consisted of 9,000 individuals who self-identified as having been diagnosed with depression, along with a control group of 100,000 matched candidates. The researchers employed the X-ABiLSTM model as the basis for their investigation. The authors [63] and [64] examined Reddit focused on depression, anxiety, stress, and happiness. A notable benefit of this platform is that these communities, referred to as subreddits, employ a slightly more formal and structured mode of English sentence construction for communication purposes. These phrases facilitate the advancement of scientific research in text analysis to reduce the laboriousness of content pre-processing. Table 8.1 illustrates the literature review on social media text with different models.

8.3.4 Challenges

The difficulty mentioned in the chosen recordings is displayed in Table 8.2. The fact that not every publication discussed the challenges faced during the research procedure demonstrates that ethical issues are the most frequently raised worries. This addresses every concern relating to data accessibility and privacy protection. Data about mental health and diseases are classified as sensitive, despite the fact that the majority of the data utilized is made public on social networking sites. After more observation, it appears that many of the problems listed in Table 8.2 are connected. According to record number 26, for instance, it is challenging to determine whether the Twitter user is actually depressed due to ethical considerations. As a result, APIs are used to acquire data, which may not yield a representative sample.

8.4 Methodology

Detecting depression from social media posts has emerged as an essential application of data analysis techniques. One intriguing avenue involves harnessing the power of social media posts for this purpose. By analyzing the textual content from these online expressions, it has been observed that signs of depression can be discerned.

The core process of this analysis entails two fundamental steps. Firstly, an extensive collection of social media data, encompassing posts and tweets from various platforms, serves as the dataset for examination. Given the unstructured nature of this textual data, a preliminary text pre-processing phase becomes essential. This stage involves applying techniques such as removing stopwords to eliminate commonly occurring but contextually

TABLE 8.1

Literature Review from the Years 2017 to 2024 [65–79]

Author	Year	Dataset Sources	Methods	Pros	Cons
Shen et al. [65]	2017	Twitter	MDL, MSNL, WDL, NB	MDL accuracy is high	Focused on user confession
Hassan et al. [66]	2017	Twitter	SVM, NB, ME	SVM accuracy is high	There is no clear explanation of the data
Chen et al. [67]	2018	Survey and WeChat	LSTM	Shortens the screening time and reduces the doctor–patient communication costs	Conducted on single classifier
Burdisso et al. [68]	2019	Reddit	SS3, KNN, LR, SVM, NB	SS3 is best	Time-consuming
Alsagri and Mourad [69]	2020	Twitter	SVM, NB, DT	SVM gives high accuracy	Cannot avoid over-fit data
Kim et al. [70]	2020	Reddit	CNN, XGBoost	CNN accuracy is high	Limited scope
Shah et al. [71]	2020	Reddit	BiLSTM	Used different word embedding techniques	Executed only single classifier
Shreya Ghosh and Tarique Anwar [72]	2021	Twitter	SVM, DNN, GRU AND LSTM	LSTM	They have not taken benchmark dataset
Chiong et al. [73]	2021	Twitter, Facebook, Reddit	LR, LSVM, RD, MLP, DT	Random forestgot balanced accuracy for two datasets	IT was not clearly in results
Mali et al. [74]	2021	Kaggle	RT, SVM, Neural Network, Bay Net, RF, XG Boost, C5.0	C5.0	Less data
Prakash et al. [75]	2021	Twitter	SVM, RF	SVM	Only two algorithms are compared
Amna Amanat et al. [76]	2022	Twitter	LSTM, RNN	The proposed model got high accuracy	Testing data is significantly less. Future suggestions include creating a hybrid recurrent neural network to study the behavior of depressed people with large datasets
Tejaswini et al. [77]	2024	Reddit, kaggle	FCL(fastText, CNN, LSTM)	Achieved high accuracy	It can be implemented in other platforms
Ghosh et al. [78]	2023	Facebook, Twitter, and YouTube	BiLSTM, CNN	To predict mental health condition	They have used their own dataset from social media API
Kabir et al. [79]	2023	Twitter	BERT and DistilBERT	The accuracy of DistilBERT is high	The data is collected from COVID-19 data

MDL: minimum description length; MSNL: multiple social network learning; WDL: weighted deep learning; NB: naïve Bayes; SVM: support vector machine; LSTM: long short-term memory; SS3: a text classification method; DT: decision tree; KNN: k-nearest neighbor; CNN: convolutional neural network; LR: linear regression; RNN: recurrent neural network.

TABLE 8.2

Difficulties in Text-Based Depression Detection

Challenge	Reference
Not possible to check the accuracy of the data	26,65,66,67
Lack of sample characteristics in the data	26,65,66,71
Ethical concerns	26,23,65
Stigma and/or lack of awareness	23
Oversimplification	23
Temporal dynamics	40
Data Imbalance	54,65,77,79

insignificant words, stemming from reducing words to their base forms, and lemmatization to simplify word variations further. The subsequent stages involve the utilization of advanced ML and DL techniques, enabling the algorithm to discern patterns and correlations indicative of depressive tendencies. The ultimate evaluation of the model's performance depends on deploying performance metrics, foremost among them accuracy. This metric quantifies the model's ability to classify individuals as either depressed or not accurately.

In summary, the approach to detect depression through the analysis of social networks comprises stages of data collection, text pre-processing, ML and DL application, and performance evaluation. This method demonstrates the potential of leveraging unconventional data sources and cutting-edge analytical techniques to address critical mental health challenges.

8.4.1 Data Collection

Having conducted an exhaustive exploration across various sources, we worked a meticulous screening process to curate a robust dataset for our study. Initially, 356 articles were identified and subjected to rigorous evaluation based on their titles and abstracts. This initial scrutiny enabled us to distill our selection into 156 articles, which showed promising relevance to our research objectives.

Undeterred by the considerable volume of material, a subsequent refinement was undertaken—a more focused analysis that further distilled our collection. After this meticulous second pass, a refined corpus of 58 publications emerged. These selected publications seamlessly aligned with our comprehensive prerequisites and research criteria, as shown in Figure 8.2.

8.4.2 Text-Based Approaches for Early Depression Detection

Table 8.3 records the methods that are used when taking a text-based approach to depression detection. The most popular methods used in the set of selected articles are the usage of classifiers in deep learning approaches and word embeddings in fast Text.

8.4.3 Performance Measures

Performance measures are commonly used to assess the effectiveness of depression detection models and systems. Depending on the specific context and goals of the early detection system, certain measures may be more important than others, as shown in Table 8.4.

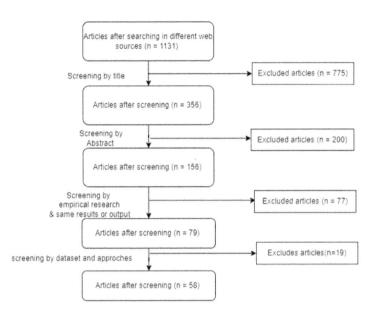

FIGURE 8.2
The detailed screening procedure.

TABLE 8.3

Methods Used for Text-Based Depression Detection

Method	Study identifiers
SVM, and naïve Bayes classifier	22,28,32,42,52,66,69,75
Machine classification	23,46,48,73
C5.0 classifier	74
K-nearest neighbors (KNN)	47
Back propagation neural network model	29
CNN	33,37,70
LSTM	31,45,50,72
BI-LSTM	35,60,62,71
Deep learning hybrid models	76,77,78,79

- True positive (TP): Number of depressed individuals correctly identified as depressed.
- False positive (FP): Number of non-depressed individuals incorrectly identified as depressed.
- True negative (TN): Number of non-depressed individuals correctly identified as non-depressed.
- False negative (FN): Number of depressed individuals incorrectly identified as non-depressed.

8.4.4 BERT Classification

The twitter text dataset related to depression obtained from the Kaggle repository contains twitter tweets. Among these, only 643 are taken to conduct a random experiment, of which

TABLE 8.4

Performance Measure

Performance Measure	Formula
Accuracy	$\dfrac{\left(TP + TN\right)}{\left(TP + TN + FP + FN\right)}$
Precision	$\dfrac{TP}{\left(TP + FP\right)}$
Recall	$\dfrac{TP}{\left(TP + FN\right)}$
F1 Score	$\dfrac{2*\left(precision*Recall\right)}{\left(Precision + Recall\right)}$

429 are from depressed Tweets (1)and 214 are from non-depressed Tweets (0). The data is pre-processed to remove stop words and converted it to lowercase. The Bert tokenizer is applied to tokenize the input data. Sample Tweets from each category are displayed below.

Content	Label
i be sick of make things worse i be sick of be hurt i be sick of cry myself to sleep i be sick of hat everything i be sick of fake a smile i be sick of feel this way i be sick of let people down i be sick of be me	1
live with depression and anxiety no motivation to leave your bed dread leave your house not be able to go out unable to make new friends be paranoid or restless mentally hurt zone out a lot ignore people not be yourself	1
i love tactical stuff like this on twitter you just earn a new fan	0
i meet for the first time and we do a pod together at his office in austini think this one have some gems in it	0

8.5 Conclusion

Depression, a rapidly emerging epidemic, affects individuals across diverse social strata, ethnic backgrounds, and nationalities with notable frequency. Identifying individuals who require mental health therapy poses a significant challenge, primarily stemming from the inherent nature of isolation. Textual analysis in disease diagnosis has promise due to its non-invasive nature, allowing for continual monitoring and regulation.

The prevalence of social media has led to the emergence of specific indicators within textual content shared on popular platforms such as Twitter, Facebook, and Reddit. The texts mentioned above can be analyzed to ascertain whether the writing style aligns with a pattern indicative of depression. Natural language processing(NLP) is a branch of artificial intelligence (AI) that endows machines with the capacity to comprehend and analyze human language, surpassing mere reading capabilities.

NLP techniques are suitable methods to pre-process the text data and make the data suitable for further analysis. Machine learning (ML) and deep learning (DL) techniques are employed to identify depression. ML algorithms require feature extraction and need to be better suited for massive datasets. Consequently, deep learning algorithms are utilized more frequently in this domain. Deep learning algorithms are the best way to predict depressed individuals from the processed text. The present work is limited to the social network platforms Twitter, Facebook, and Reddit. In the future, the study on detecting depression using other platforms such as Instagram and others can be explored.

References

1. Denecke, K., Vaaheesan, S., &Arulnathan, A. (2020). A mental health chatbot for regulating emotions (SERMO)-concept and usability test. *IEEE Transactions on Emerging Topics in Computing, 9*(3), 1170–1182.
2. Church, D., De Asis, M. A., &Brooks, A. J. (2012). Brief group intervention using emotional freedom techniques for depression in college students: A randomized controlled trial. *Depression Research and Treatment, ,*2012, 7 Article ID 257172, 2012.
3. World Health Organization. (2017). *Other common mental disorders: Global health estimates.* Geneva: World Health Organization, 24.
4. Katon, W., &Ciechanowski, P. (2002). Impact of major depression on chronic medical illness. *Journal of Psychosomatic Research, 53*(4), 859–863.
5. Simon, G. E. (2003). Social and economic burden of mood disorders. *Biological Psychiatry, 54*(3), 208–215.
6. Sullivan, L. E., Fiellin, D. A., &O'Connor, P. G. (2005). The prevalence and impact of alcohol problems in major depression: A systematic review. *The American Journal of Medicine, 118*(4), 330–341.
7. Swendsen, J. D., &Merikangas, K. R. (2000). The comorbidity of depression and substance use disorders. *Clinical Psychology Review, 20*(2), 173–189.
8. McConville, C., &Cooper, C. (1996). Mood variability and the intensity of depressive states. *Current Psychology, 14*, 329–338.
9. Peeters, F., Berkhof, J., Delespaul, P., Rottenberg, J., &Nicolson, N. A. (2006). Diurnal mood variation in major depressive disorder. *Emotion, 6*(3), 383.
10. Ben-Zeev, D., Young, M. A., &Madsen, J. W. (2009). Retrospective recall of affect in clinically depressed individuals and controls. *Cognition and Emotion, 23*(5), 1021–1040.
11. Colombo, D., Fernández-Álvarez, J., Patané, A., Semonella, M., Kwiatkowska, M., García-Palacios, A., ... Botella, C. (2019). Current state and future directions of technology-based ecological momentary assessment and intervention for major depressive disorder: A systematic review. *Journal of Clinical Medicine, 8*(4), 465.
12. Möller, H. J., &Von Zerssen, D. (1995). Self-rating procedures in the evaluation of antidepressants: Review of the literature and results of our studies. *Psychopathology, 28*(6), 291–306.
13. Gotlib, I. H., &Joormann, J. (2010). Cognition and depression: Current status and future directions. *Annual Review of Clinical Psychology, 6*, 285–312.
14. Henderson, C., Evans-Lacko, S., &Thornicroft, G. (2013). Mental illness stigma, help seeking, and public health programs. *American Journal of Public Health, 103*(5), 777–780.
15. Kazdin, A. E., &Blase, S. L. (2011). Rebooting psychotherapy research and practice to reduce the burden of mental illness. *Perspectives on Psychological Science, 6*(1), 21–37.
16. Halfin, A. (2007). Depression: The benefits of early and appropriate treatment. *American Journal of Managed Care, 13*(4), S92.

17. Picardi, A., Lega, I., Tarsitani, L., Caredda, M., Matteucci, G., Zerella, M. P., ... SET-DEP Group. (2016). A randomised controlled trial of the effectiveness of a program for early detection and treatment of depression in primary care. *Journal of Affective Disorders, 198*, 96–101.
18. Donker, T., Petrie, K., Proudfoot, J., Clarke, J., Birch, M. R., &Christensen, H. (2013). Smartphones for smarter delivery of mental health programs: A systematic review. *Journal of Medical Internet Research, 15*(11), e2791.
19. Hall, A. K., Cole-Lewis, H., &Bernhardt, J. M. (2015). Mobile text messaging for health: A systematic review of reviews. *Annual Review of Public Health, 36*, 393–415.
20. Head, K. J., Noar, S. M., Iannarino, N. T., &Harrington, N. G. (2013). Efficacy of text messaging-based interventions for health promotion: A meta-analysis. *Social Science & Medicine, 97*, 41–48.
21. Ryu, S. (2012). Book review: mHealth: New horizons for health through mobile technologies: Based on the findings of the second global survey on eHealth (global observatory for eHealth series, volume 3). *Healthcare Informatics Research, 18*(3), 231–233.
22. Aldarwish, M. M., &Ahmad, H. F. (2017, March). Predicting depression levels using social media posts. In *2017 IEEE 13th International Symposium on Autonomous Decentralized System (ISADS)* (pp. 277–280). IEEE.
23. Chancellor, S., Baumer, E. P. S., &Choudhury, M. D. (2019). Who is the "Human" in human-centered machine learning: The case of predicting mental health from social media. In *Proceedings of ACM human-computer interaction* (pp. 1–32).
24. Schwartz, H. A., &Ungar, L. H. (2015). Data-driven content analysis of social media: A systematic overview of automated methods. *The ANNALS of the American Academy of Political and Social Science, 659*(1), 78–94.
25. Yazdavar, A. H., Al-Olimat, H. S., Ebrahimi, M., Bajaj, G., Banerjee, T., Thirunarayan, K., ... Sheth, A. (2017, July). Semi-supervised approach to monitoring clinical depressive symptoms in social media. In *Proceedings of the 2017 IEEE/ACM international conference on advances in social networks analysis and mining 2017* (pp. 1191–1198).
26. O'dea, B., Wan, S., Batterham, P. J., Calear, A. L., Paris, C., &Christensen, H. (2015). Detecting suicidality on Twitter. *Internet Interventions, 2*(2), 183–188.
27. Li, X., Zhang, X., Zhu, J., Mao, W., Sun, S., Wang, Z., ... Hu, B. (2019). Depression recognition using machine learning methods with different feature generation strategies. *Artificial Intelligence in Medicine, 99*, 101696.
28. Deshpande, M., &Rao, V. (2017, December). Depression detection using emotion artificial intelligence. In *2017 international conference on intelligent sustainable systems (ICISS)* (pp. 858–862). IEEE.
29. Biradar, A., &Totad, S. G. (2018, December). Detecting depression in social media posts using machine learning. In *International conference on recent trends in image processing and pattern recognition* (pp. 716–725). Singapore: Springer Singapore.
30. Ramalingam, D., Sharma, V., &Zar, P. (2019). Study of depression analysis using machine learning techniques. *International Journal of Innovative Technology and Exploring Engineering, 8*(7C2), 187–191.
31. Rajaraman, P. V., Nath, A., Akshaya, P. R., &Bhuja, G. C. (2020). Depression detection of tweets and a comparative test. *International Journal of Engineering Research, 9*(3), 422–425
32. Razak, C. S. A., Zulkarnain, M. A., Hamid, S. H. A. Anuar, N. B., Jali, M. Z., & Meon, H. (2020). Tweep: a system development to detect depression in twitter posts. In *Computational Science and Technology: 6th ICCST 2019, Kota Kinabalu, Malaysia, 29-30 August 2019* (pp. 543–552). Springer Singapore.
33. Shetty, N. P., Muniyal, B., Anand, A., Kumar, S., &Prabhu, S. (2020). Predicting depression using deep learning and ensemble algorithms on raw twitter data. *International Journal of Electrical and Computer Engineering, 10*(4), 3751.
34. Wongkoblap, A., Vadillo, M., &Curcin, V. (2021). Depression detection of Twitter posters using deep learning with anaphora resolution: Algorithm development and validation. *JMIR Mental Health. 1*(8), (pp. 1–17).
35. Mathur, P., Sawhney, R., Chopra, S., Leekha, M., &Ratn Shah, R. (2020). Utilizing temporal psycholinguistic cues for suicidal intent estimation. In *Advances in information retrieval: 42nd*

European conference on IR research, ECIR 2020, Lisbon, Portugal, April 14–17, 2020, Proceedings, Part II 42 (pp. 265–271). Springer International Publishing.

36. Mehra, R., Bedi, M. K., Singh, G., Arora, R., Bala, T., &Saxena, S. (2017, July). Sentimental analysis using fuzzy and naive bayes. In *2017 International Conference on Computing Methodologies and Communication (ICCMC)* (pp. 945–950). IEEE.

37. Orabi, A. H., Buddhitha, P., Orabi, M. H., &Inkpen, D. (2018, June). Deep learning for depression detection of twitter users. In *Proceedings of the fifth workshop on computational linguistics and clinical psychology: From keyboard to clinic* (pp. 88–97).

38. Tambling, R. R., D'Aniello-Heyda, C., &Hynes, K. C. (2023). Manifestations of depression on social media: A content analysis of Twitter posts. *Journal of Technology in Behavioral Science*, 8, 1–10,2023

39. Khafaga, D. S., Auvdaiappan, M., Deepa, K., Abouhawwash, M., &Karim, F. K. (2023). Deep learning for depression detection using Twitter data. *Intelligent Automation and Soft Computing*, 36(2), 1301–1313.

40. De Choudhury, M., Gamon, M., Counts, S., &Horvitz, E. (2013). Predicting depression via social media. In *Proceedings of the international AAAI conference on web and social media* (Vol. 7, No. 1, pp. 128–137).

41. Vioules, M. J., Moulahi, B., Azé, J., &Bringay, S. (2018). Detection of suicide-related posts in Twitter data streams. *IBM Journal of Research and Development*, 62(1), 7–1.

42. Shahreen, N., Subhani, M., &Rahman, M. M. (2018, September). Suicidal trend analysis of twitter using machine learning and neural network. In *2018 International Conference on Bangla Speech and Language Processing (ICBSLP)* (pp. 1–5). IEEE.

43. Jashinsky, J., Burton, S. H., Hanson, C. L., West, J., Giraud-Carrier, C., Barnes, M. D., &Argyle, T. (2014), Tracking suicide risk factors through Twitter in the US. *Crisis*. 35(1), (pp. 1–9).

44. Yazdavar, A. H., Al-Olimat, H. S., Ebrahimi, M., Bajaj, G., Banerjee, T., Thirunarayan, K., ... Sheth, A. (2017, July). Semi-supervised approach to monitoring clinical depressive symptoms in social media. In *Proceedings of the 2017 IEEE/ACM international conference on advances in social networks analysis and mining 2017* (pp. 1191–1198).

45. Gupta, S., Goel, L., Singh, A., Prasad, A., &Ullah, M. A. (2022). Psychological analysis for depression detection from social networking sites. *Computational Intelligence and Neuroscience*, 2022, 1–14.

46. Islam, M. R., Kabir, M. A., Ahmed, A., Kamal, A. R. M., Wang, H., &Ulhaq, A. (2018). Depression detection from social network data using machine learning techniques. *Health Information Science and Systems*, 6, 1–12.

47. Islam, M. R., Kamal, A. R. M., Sultana, N., Islam, R., &Moni, M. A. (2018, February). Detecting depression using k-nearest neighbors (knn) classification technique. In *2018 International Conference on Computer, Communication, Chemical, Material and Electronic Engineering (IC4ME2)* (pp. 1–4). IEEE.

48. Noureen, A., Qamar, U., &Ali, M. (2017, July). Semantic analysis of social media and associated psychotic behavior. In *2017 13th International Conference on Natural Computation, Fuzzy Systems and Knowledge Discovery (ICNC-FSKD)* (pp. 1621–1630). IEEE.

49. Eichstaedt, J. C., Smith, R. J., Merchant, R. M., Ungar, L. H., Crutchley, P., Preoţiuc-Pietro, D., ... Schwartz, H. A. (2018). Facebook language predicts depression in medical records. *Proceedings of the National Academy of Sciences*, 115(44), 11203–11208.

50. Wu, M. Y., Shen, C. Y., Wang, E. T., &Chen, A. L. (2020). A deep architecture for depression detection using posting, behavior, and living environment data. *Journal of Intelligent Information Systems*, 54, 225–244.

51. Ophir, Y., Asterhan, C. S., &Schwarz, B. B. (2017). Unfolding the notes from the walls: Adolescents' depression manifestations on Facebook. *Computers in Human Behavior*, 72, 96–107.

52. Tadesse, M. M., Lin, H., Xu, B., &Yang, L. (2019). Detection of depression-related posts in reddit social media forum. *IEEE Access*, 7, 44883–44893.

53. Trifan, A., Antunes, R., Matos, S., &Oliveira, J. L. (2020, April). Understanding depression from psycholinguistic patterns in social media texts. In *European conference on information retrieval* (pp. 402–409). Cham: Springer International Publishing.

54. Yates, A., Cohan, A., &Goharian, N. (2017). Depression and self-harm risk assessment in online forums. *arXiv preprint arXiv:1709.01848*.

55. MacAvaney, S., Desmet, B., Cohan, A., Soldaini, L., Yates, A., Zirikly, A., &Goharian, N. (2018). Rsdd-time: Temporal annotation of self-reported mental health diagnoses. *arXiv preprint arXiv:1806.07916*.

56. Cohan, A., Desmet, B., Yates, A., Soldaini, L., MacAvaney, S., &Goharian, N. (2018). SMHD: A large-scale resource for exploring online language usage for multiple mental health conditions. *arXiv preprint arXiv:1806.05258*.

57. Shing, H. C., Nair, S., Zirikly, A., Friedenberg, M., Daumé III, H., &Resnik, P. (2018, June). Expert, crowdsourced, and machine assessment of suicide risk via online postings. In *Proceedings of the fifth workshop on computational linguistics and clinical psychology: From keyboard to clinic* (pp. 25–36).

58. Boettcher, N. (2021). Studies of depression and anxiety using reddit as a data source: Scoping review. *JMIR Mental Health*, 8(11), e29487.

59. Naseem, U., Dunn, A. G., Kim, J., &Khushi, M. (2022, April). Early identification of depression severity levels on reddit using ordinal classification. In *Proceedings of the ACM web conference 2022* (pp. 2563–2572).

60. Ren, L., Lin, H., Xu, B., Zhang, S., Yang, L., &Sun, S. (2021). Depression detection on reddit with an emotion-based attention network: Algorithm development and validation. *JMIR Medical Informatics*, 9(7), e28754.

61. Uban, A. S., Chulvi, B., &Rosso, P. (2021). An emotion and cognitive based analysis of mental health disorders from social media data. *Future Generation Computer Systems*, 124, 480–494.

62. Cong, Q., Feng, Z., Li, F., Xiang, Y., Rao, G., &Tao, C. (2018, December). XA-BiLSTM: A deep learning approach for depression detection in imbalanced data. In *2018 IEEE international conference on bioinformatics and biomedicine (BIBM)* (pp. 1624–1627). IEEE.

63. Leiva, V., &Freire, A. (2017). Towards suicide prevention: Early detection of depression on social media. In *Internet science: 4th international conference, INSCI 2017*, Thessaloniki, Greece, November 22–24, 2017, Proceedings 4 (pp. 428–436). Springer International Publishing.

64. Park, A., &Conway, M. (2018). Harnessing reddit to understand the written-communication challenges experienced by individuals with mental health disorders: Analysis of texts from mental health communities. *Journal of Medical Internet Research*, 20(4), e8219.

65. Shen, G., Jia, J., Nie, L., Feng, F., Zhang, C., Hu, T., ... Zhu, W. (2017, August). Depression detection via harvesting social media: A multimodal dictionary learning solution. In *IJCAI* (pp. 3838–3844).

66. Hassan, A. U., Hussain, J., Hussain, M., Sadiq, M., &Lee, S. (2017, October). Sentiment analysis of social networking sites (SNS) data using machine learning approach for the measurement of depression. In *2017 international conference on Information and Communication Technology Convergence (ICTC)* (pp. 138–140). IEEE.

67. Chen, Y., Zhou, B., Zhang, W., Gong, W., &Sun, G. (2018, June). Sentiment analysis based on deep learning and its application in screening for perinatal depression. In *2018 IEEE Third International Conference on Data Science in Cyberspace (DSC)* (pp. 451–456). IEEE.

68. Burdisso, S. G., Errecalde, M., &Montes-y-Gómez, M. (2019). A text classification framework for simple and effective early depression detection over social media streams. *Expert Systems with Applications*, 133, 182–197.

69. AlSagri, H. S., &Ykhlef, M. (2020). Machine learning-based approach for depression detection in twitter using content and activity features. *IEICE Transactions on Information and Systems*, 103(8), 1825–1832.

70. Kim, J., Lee, J., Park, E., &Han, J. (2020). A deep learning model for detecting mental illness from user content on social media. *Scientific Reports*, 10(1), 11846.

71. Shah, F. M., Ahmed, F., Joy, S. K. S., Ahmed, S., Sadek, S., Shil, R., &Kabir, M. H. (2020, June). Early depression detection from social network using deep learning techniques. In *2020 IEEE Region 10 Symposium (TENSYMP)* (pp. 823–826). IEEE.

72. Ghosh, S., &Anwar, T. (2021). Depression intensity estimation via social media: A deep learning approach. *IEEE Transactions on Computational Social Systems*, 8(6), 1465–1474.

73. Chiong, R., Budhi, G. S., Dhakal, S., &Chiong, F. (2021). A textual-based featuring approach for depression detection using machine learning classifiers and social media texts. *Computers in Biology and Medicine, 135,* 104499.

74. Mali, D., Kumawat, K., Kumawat, G., Chakrabarti, P., Poddar, S., Chakrabarti, T., ... Nami, M. (2021). A machine learning technique to analyze depressive disorders.

75. Prakash, A., Agarwal, K., Shekhar, S., Mutreja, T., &Chakraborty, P. S. (2021, March). An ensemble learning approach for the detection of depression and mental illness over twitter data. In *2021 8th International Conference on Computing for Sustainable Global Development (INDIACom)* (pp. 565–570). IEEE.

76. Amanat, A., Rizwan, M., Javed, A. R., Abdelhaq, M., Alsaqour, R., Pandya, S., &Uddin, M. (2022). Deep learning for depression detection from textual data. *Electronics, 11*(5), 676.

77. Tejaswini, V., Babu, K. S., &Sahoo, B. (2024). Depression detection from social media text analysis using natural language processing techniques and hybrid deep learning model. *ACM Transactions on Asian and Low-Resource Language Information Processing. 23*(1), 1–20.

78. Ghosh, T., Al Banna, M. H., Al Nahian, M. J., Uddin, M. N., Kaiser, M. S., &Mahmud, M. (2023). An attention-based hybrid architecture with explainability for depressive social media text detection in Bangla. *Expert Systems with Applications, 213,* 119007.

79. Kabir, M., Ahmed, T., Hasan, M. B., Laskar, M. T. R., Joarder, T. K., Mahmud, H., &Hasan, K. (2023). DEPTWEET: A typology for social media texts to detect depression severities. *Computers in Human Behavior, 139,* 107503.

Part 2

Oncology

9

Artificial Intelligence in Radiation Oncology

Ashwani Kumar Aggarwal

9.1 Introduction

Radiation oncology stands at the forefront of the battle against cancer, employing radiation therapy to target and eradicate malignant tumors while preserving healthy tissues. Historically, treatment planning and image analysis in radiation oncology have relied heavily on manual processes, subject to inter-observer variability and time-consuming procedures. However, in recent years, the integration of artificial intelligence (AI) has catalyzed a transformative revolution in the field, offering unprecedented opportunities to enhance patient care and treatment outcomes [1]. The advent of AI in radiation oncology has introduced a plethora of sophisticated algorithms and techniques that harness the power of machine learning and deep neural networks. These AI-driven innovations have the potential to significantly impact various facets of radiation therapy, ranging from treatment planning and image analysis to outcome prediction and adaptive therapy. AI's role in treatment planning cannot be overstated. Traditionally, radiation therapy treatment planning necessitated the laborious and meticulous manual contouring of organs and tumor volumes. This process demanded extensive expertise and consumed valuable clinical time. However, AI-powered automated segmentation algorithms have emerged as a game-changer, accelerating the contouring process while ensuring precise delineation of target volumes and organs at risk. By reducing human error and enhancing consistency, AI streamlines treatment planning workflows, ultimately leading to improved treatment quality and efficiency [2]. Moreover, AI has demonstrated remarkable capabilities in dose optimization. In radiation therapy, achieving the delicate balance between delivering sufficient radiation to destroy tumor cells while sparing healthy tissues is paramount. AI models, utilizing complex optimization algorithms, can analyze patient-specific data, tumor characteristics, and anatomical constraints to derive optimal radiation dose distributions [3]. As a result, radiation oncologists can confidently administer treatments with improved efficacy and minimal toxicity, further enhancing patient outcomes and quality of life. The integration of AI in image analysis has ushered in a new era of precision medicine. Radiomics, a rapidly evolving field, leverages AI algorithms to extract quantitative information from medical images, generating an extensive array of radiomic features. These features encompass tumor shape, texture, and intensity variations, among others, providing valuable insights into tumor heterogeneity and response to treatment [4]. AI-powered radiomic analyses can offer radiation oncologists a deeper understanding of tumor biology, enabling the development of personalized treatment strategies tailored to each patient's unique characteristics [5].

TABLE 9.1

Literature Review

Bibault, J.-E., Giraud, P., & Burgun, A. (2016). Big data and machine learning in radiation oncology: state of the art and future prospects. *Cancer Letters, 382*(1), 110–117.	The role of AI techniques in radiation oncology is discussed.
Bitterman, D. S., Miller, T. A., Mak, R. H., & Savova, G. K. (2021). Clinical natural language processing for radiation oncology: a review and practical primer. *International Journal of Radiation Oncology* Biology* Physics, 110*(3), 641–655.	A review on the AI methods used in radiation oncology
Cilla, S., & Barajas, J. E. V. (2022). Automation and artificial intelligence in radiation oncology. *Frontiers in Oncology, 12*, 1038834.	The automation techniques used in radiation oncology are discussed.
Cohen, E. B., & Gordon, I. K. (2022). First, do no harm. Ethical and legal issues of artificial intelligence and machine learning in veterinary radiology and radiation oncology. *Veterinary Radiology & Ultrasound, 63*, 840–850.	The ethical considerations of using AI techniques in radiation oncology are discussed.

Furthermore, deep learning techniques have proven indispensable in image classification tasks, distinguishing between benign and malignant tumors with remarkable accuracy. By swiftly and accurately identifying cancerous lesions, AI-powered image analysis expedites diagnosis and treatment planning, expediting the initiation of timely therapies for patients in need. Beyond the realms of treatment planning and image analysis, AI holds immense promise in outcome prediction [6]. The amalgamation of vast amounts of patient data, including clinical records, imaging data, and genetic profiles, enables AI algorithms to develop predictive models that forecast treatment outcomes and patient responses. By identifying potential risks or opportunities for favorable outcomes, AI empowers radiation oncologists to tailor treatment plans based on individual patient needs, leading to more personalized and effective treatments [7]. Perhaps one of the most revolutionary applications of AI in radiation oncology lies in adaptive therapy. Traditionally, radiation treatment plans were designed based on static anatomical images acquired during the initial stages of treatment [8]. However, as cancer is a dynamic disease, changes in tumor size, shape, and location may occur during the course of treatment. AI-driven online adaptive radiotherapy addresses this challenge by continuously monitoring and analyzing real-time imaging data, allowing for dynamic adjustments in radiation dose and treatment volumes. This adaptive approach ensures that treatments remain optimal and precise, maximizing the therapeutic effect while minimizing damage to healthy tissues [9]. As the utilization of AI in radiation oncology continues to gain momentum, it is crucial to recognize and address the challenges and opportunities that come with these advancements. Data privacy and security are paramount concerns, as AI necessitates access to extensive patient data for training and validation [10]. Strict adherence to regulatory guidelines and ethical considerations is essential to ensure that patient safety and confidentiality are upheld throughout the process [11]. The related work is put in the tabular form as given in Table 9.1.

9.2 AI in Treatment Planning

Treatment planning is a cornerstone of radiation oncology, determining the most effective approach to deliver radiation therapy while safeguarding surrounding healthy tissues [12].

Traditionally, treatment planning has been a labor-intensive process, involving manual contouring of target volumes and organs at risk based on medical imaging, clinical expertise, and treatment protocols [13]. However, with the advent of artificial intelligence (AI), this critical aspect of radiation therapy has undergone a profound transformation, leveraging advanced algorithms to streamline and enhance the treatment planning process [14]. One of the primary challenges in treatment planning is the time-consuming and subjective nature of manual contouring. Human variability in contouring can lead to discrepancies in dose distribution and ultimately impact treatment outcomes [15]. AI-powered automated segmentation addresses this challenge by utilizing machine learning algorithms, such as deep learning and image processing techniques, to accurately delineate target volumes and critical structures from medical imaging data. Deep neural networks, a subset of AI algorithms, have emerged as a potent tool in automating segmentation tasks [16]. By training on large datasets of annotated medical images, these networks can learn intricate spatial relationships and patterns, enabling them to accurately segment organs and tumors on new patient images. The adoption of AI-driven segmentation not only reduces the burden on radiation oncologists but also significantly improves contouring consistency and precision. As a result, the accuracy of treatment planning increases, leading to enhanced target coverage and reduced radiation exposure to surrounding healthy tissues [17]. In addition to automated segmentation, AI plays a crucial role in radiation dose optimization. Determining the optimal radiation dose distribution is a complex and multi-dimensional problem, influenced by various factors, such as tumor size, location, and sensitivity to radiation, as well as the proximity of critical organs [18]. AI-driven dose-optimization algorithms employ mathematical optimization techniques and machine learning to analyze these factors and generate optimal radiation plans tailored to individual patients [19].

The deep learning methods are subset of machine learning methods, and the machine learning methods are subset of artificial intelligence methods as shown in Figure 9.1. Machine learning models can be trained on historical treatment plans, outcomes, and patient characteristics to derive patterns and correlations that influence treatment success. By understanding the relationship between various dosimetric parameters and treatment outcomes, AI can assist radiation oncologists in designing customized treatment plans that maximize tumor control while minimizing the risk of adverse effects [20]. These AI-driven optimizations lead

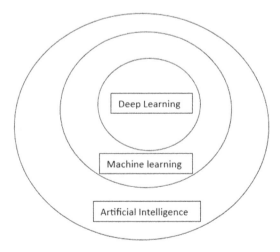

FIGURE 9.1
Deep learning vs Machine learning.

to more effective treatments, reduced treatment times, and improved patient experiences. Furthermore, AI augments the process of plan evaluation by automatically assessing the quality of generated radiation treatment plans [21]. Quality assurance of radiation therapy plans is critical to ensure adherence to clinical protocols and safety guidelines. AI algorithms, trained on a diverse set of high-quality treatment plans, can be used to evaluate and verify new treatment plans, flagging potential dosimetric deviations or inconsistencies [22]. This automated plan evaluation process streamlines plan approval and enhances the overall quality of radiation therapy delivery [23]. AI also plays a pivotal role in the development of knowledge-based treatment planning systems. These systems utilize vast databases of historical treatment plans and outcomes to build models of best practices [24]. By referencing this knowledge base, radiation oncologists can rapidly generate high-quality treatment plans with minimal manual intervention. The integration of AI in knowledge-based treatment planning not only expedites plan creation but also empowers clinicians with evidence-based decision support, fostering a culture of continuous improvement in radiation therapy [25]. Moreover, AI-driven treatment planning enables the exploration of novel treatment techniques and delivery modalities. With the increasing availability of advanced treatment technologies, such as intensity-modulated radiation therapy (IMRT), volumetric modulated arc therapy (VMAT), and proton therapy, the complexity of treatment planning has grown significantly [26]. AI algorithms can be employed to optimize these sophisticated delivery techniques, ensuring that they are utilized efficiently and effectively for each patient's specific case [27]. While AI in treatment planning has witnessed remarkable progress, challenges remain in terms of model interpretability, validation, and generalizability [28]. The black-box nature of deep learning algorithms can make it challenging to understand the reasoning behind specific treatment plan recommendations, limiting their acceptance in clinical practice. Efforts to develop interpretable AI models and establish validation frameworks are ongoing to build confidence in AI-driven treatment planning systems [29].

9.3 AI in Image Analysis

AI in image analysis is transforming the field of medical imaging, including radiation oncology, by enabling automated and precise extraction of valuable information from medical images [30]. Advanced deep learning algorithms, such as convolutional neural networks (CNNs), excel at identifying intricate patterns and features in images, leading to improved diagnostic accuracy and treatment planning [31]. AI-driven radiomics leverages the power of quantitative image analysis to uncover hidden patterns and biomarkers, offering insights into tumor behavior, treatment response, and patient prognosis. The integration of AI in image analysis streamlines the interpretation of complex imaging data, empowering clinicians with efficient decision support and personalized treatment recommendations [32]. Through continuous research and validation, AI in image analysis holds the promise of revolutionizing medical imaging practices, ultimately enhancing patient care and outcomes [33].

9.3.1 Radiomics

Radiomics is a rapidly evolving field within radiation oncology that capitalizes on the power of AI and advanced image-analysis techniques to extract a wealth of quantitative data from medical images. While traditional imaging focuses on visual interpretation, radiomics delves into the hidden complexities of images, uncovering subtle patterns and features that may hold valuable insights into a patient's disease state, treatment response, and overall prognosis [34]. The foundation of radiomics lies in the extraction of a vast array of quantitative features, known as radiomic features, from medical images. These features encompass a wide range of information, including statistical properties, texture patterns, shape characteristics, and intensity distributions within the region of interest [35]. The process of radiomic feature extraction is highly data-driven and requires standardized segmentation of tumor and surrounding regions to ensure consistency and reproducibility. AI plays a pivotal role in the radiomics workflow by automating the extraction of radiomic features, thus reducing the burden of manual effort and ensuring higher precision and reproducibility [36]. Deep learning models, such as convolutional neural networks (CNNs), have demonstrated remarkable success in identifying intricate patterns within images, making them well-suited for radiomic feature extraction. These models learn from large datasets of annotated medical images, enabling them to recognize subtle features that may not be apparent to the human eye. Once radiomic features are extracted, the subsequent step involves mining and analyzing this data to identify clinically relevant patterns and correlations. AI-driven radiomic analysis aims to identify robust biomarkers and imaging signatures that can serve as indicators of tumor aggressiveness, treatment response, and overall patient prognosis. For example, certain texture features extracted from a tumor's texture map may indicate the presence of intratumoral heterogeneity, which has been associated with more aggressive tumor behavior and poorer treatment outcomes. In clinical practice, radiomics holds the potential to impact various aspects of radiation therapy. One significant application is the prediction of treatment response. By correlating radiomic features extracted from pre-treatment imaging with subsequent treatment outcomes, AI models can be developed to predict a patient's response to radiation therapy. These predictive models can aid radiation oncologists in identifying patients who may benefit from alternative treatment approaches or additional interventions, ultimately leading to more personalized and effective treatment strategies. Radiomics can also play a pivotal role in the assessment of tumor recurrence and progression during the follow-up phase of treatment. By analyzing sequential imaging data, AI algorithms can detect subtle changes in radiomic features over time, providing early indications of treatment failure or tumor recurrence. This early detection allows for prompt intervention and adaptive treatment planning, potentially improving patient outcomes [37]. Another promising application of radiomics is its integration with genomic data, giving rise to the emerging field of radiogenomics. Radiogenomics seeks to establish connections between radiomic features and underlying genetic or molecular characteristics of tumors. By combining radiomic and genomic data, AI-powered radiogenomic models can unravel unique tumor profiles, aiding in the identification of potential therapeutic targets and guiding the selection of personalized treatment regimens. While radiomics holds immense promise, several challenges must be addressed for its successful translation into routine clinical practice. One significant challenge is the standardization and harmonization of radiomic feature extraction protocols. Variability in imaging equipment, acquisition parameters, and image preprocessing can introduce biases and impact the reproducibility of radiomic analyses. Collaborative efforts, such as the image biomarker standardization initiative (IBSI), aim to establish standardized protocols to address these challenges and promote the adoption of radiomics in multicenter studies and clinical trials [38].

9.3.2 Deep Learning for Image Classification

Deep learning has emerged as a transformative technology in medical image analysis, particularly in the field of radiation oncology. With its ability to automatically learn complex patterns and features from data, deep learning algorithms have revolutionized image classification tasks, enabling accurate and efficient differentiation between benign and malignant tumors from medical imaging data. Traditionally, image classification in radiation oncology required meticulous visual inspection by radiation oncologists and radiologists [39]. While these experts possess invaluable clinical experience, the process can be time-consuming, subject to inter-observer variability, and may not scale well with the increasing volume of medical imaging data. This is where deep learning steps in, offering a data-driven, automated approach to image classification that significantly enhances efficiency and consistency. Deep learning algorithms, specifically convolutional neural networks (CNNs), have demonstrated unparalleled success in a wide range of image classification tasks, including identifying tumors and distinguishing them from normal tissues. CNNs excel at learning hierarchical representations of images, starting from low-level features, such as edges and textures, and progressively capturing higher-level features, such as tumor boundaries and spatial relationships. The ability of CNNs to learn complex features from vast amounts of labeled training data enables them to generalize well to unseen images, making them ideal for medical image classification. Training a CNN for medical image classification involves feeding it a large dataset of annotated images, with labels indicating whether the image represents a benign or malignant tumor. The network then iteratively learns from this data, adjusting its internal parameters to optimize its ability to correctly classify tumors. This process, known as training, involves forward and backward passes of data through the network, with the objective of minimizing the classification error. Once trained, the deep learning model can be used to classify new, unseen medical images. The model takes in an image as input, processes it through its layers, and produces a probability score or a categorical label representing the likelihood of the image belonging to a specific class (e.g., benign or malignant). The output can be further thresholded to make a binary classification decision, aiding radiation oncologists in identifying the presence of tumors and making treatment decisions based on the classification results. The integration of deep learning for image classification in radiation oncology has several practical applications. One primary use case is in the detection and diagnosis of tumors from medical imaging data. By rapidly and accurately identifying tumors, deep learning algorithms facilitate timely diagnoses and treatment planning. Early detection of malignancies is crucial for initiating appropriate therapies at the earliest stage, potentially improving patient outcomes and survival rates. Moreover, deep learning models can assist radiation oncologists in assessing treatment response during the course of therapy. By analyzing sequential imaging data, the model can detect changes in tumor size, shape, and density, providing valuable information on the effectiveness of the ongoing treatment. Early identification of treatment response allows radiation oncologists to adapt treatment plans as needed, ensuring that patients receive the most effective therapy throughout their treatment journey [40]. Deep learning for image classification can also aid in tumor subtyping and characterization. By analyzing the distinctive features of different tumor subtypes, deep learning models can categorize tumors into specific subgroups, each with unique biological and clinical characteristics. This information can guide treatment decisions, enabling personalized therapies that target the specific molecular and genetic features of each tumor subtype. However, there are several challenges that must be addressed to ensure the successful integration of deep learning for image classification in clinical practice. One significant challenge is the requirement for large, high-quality, and diverse datasets for training robust deep learning models. Annotated medical imaging datasets with sufficient representation of different tumor types and clinical scenarios are essential to enable the model to generalize well across various patient populations. Another important consideration is the need for model interpretability and transparency. Deep learning models are often perceived as black boxes due to their complex architectures and numerous parameters. Efforts to develop interpretable deep learning models and visualization techniques are ongoing to enhance the trust and acceptance of these models in clinical decision-making.

9.4 AI in Outcome Prediction

AI in outcome prediction is a game-changer in the field of radiation oncology, enabling accurate and data-driven prognostication of treatment outcomes for cancer patients. Through the analysis of diverse patient data, including clinical characteristics, genetic profiles, and imaging features, AI algorithms can identify relevant predictive factors associated with treatment response and overall prognosis. This valuable information empowers radiation oncologists to make informed decisions about personalized treatment strategies, optimizing therapeutic efficacy and patient quality of life. As AI technologies continue to evolve, the integration of outcome prediction models into routine clinical practice promises to revolutionize cancer care, providing patients and clinicians with valuable insights to guide treatment decisions and improve long-term treatment outcomes [41].

9.4.1 Predictive Models

The use of artificial intelligence (AI) in developing predictive models has revolutionized the field of radiation oncology, offering the potential to forecast treatment outcomes and patient responses based on a combination of clinical, imaging, and genetic data. Predictive models in radiation oncology aim to provide radiation oncologists with valuable insights into the likely effectiveness of a proposed treatment plan, allowing for personalized and optimized therapy strategies. The foundation of predictive models lies in the integration of diverse patient data, including clinical characteristics, treatment parameters, imaging features, and genetic profiles. This multidimensional approach enables AI algorithms to capture the complexity and heterogeneity of cancer and its response to radiation therapy. Leveraging machine learning techniques, such as decision trees, support vector machines, random forests, or more sophisticated deep learning models, these algorithms learn patterns and correlations from historical patient data [42]. The training of predictive models necessitates access to large and diverse datasets, comprising patients with varying tumor types, stages, and treatment regimens. This data-driven approach allows the AI model to identify relevant features and biomarkers associated with treatment outcomes, facilitating the identification of factors that contribute to treatment success or failure. As the model trains, it learns to generalize from the dataset, enabling it to make accurate predictions on new, unseen patient data. One of the key applications of predictive models is the ability to estimate treatment response before the initiation of radiation therapy. By inputting patient-specific data into the AI model, radiation oncologists can obtain predictions on the likelihood of tumor control, potential side effects, and overall treatment success. Such insights allow for informed shared decision-making between clinicians and patients, enabling the tailoring of treatment plans to individual patient needs and preferences. Furthermore, predictive models can aid in the identification of patients who may benefit from alternative treatment approaches or additional interventions. For example, patients predicted to have a lower likelihood of achieving complete tumor control with standard radiation therapy may be considered for combination treatments, including systemic therapies or novel radiation techniques. Conversely, patients with a high predicted treatment response may be candidates for less aggressive treatment strategies, potentially reducing treatment-related toxicities. Moreover, predictive models can be utilized for treatment-plan optimization and exploration of treatment scenarios. By simulating various treatment scenarios and predicting their potential outcomes, AI models can assist radiation oncologists in selecting the most effective and personalized treatment plan for each patient. This approach ensures that the treatment plan is tailored to the patient's unique characteristics, optimizing therapeutic efficacy while minimizing potential risks. The integration of genomic and radiomic data with clinical features further enriches predictive models, giving rise to the emerging field of radiogenomics. Radiogenomic models aim to identify associations between specific imaging features and underlying genetic or molecular characteristics of tumors. By fusing radiomic and genomic data, AI-driven radiogenomic models can unveil unique tumor profiles and identify potential therapeutic targets. This information guides personalized treatment selection and fosters precision oncology, where therapy is tailored based on the individual genetic makeup of each patient's tumor [43].

9.4.2 Treatment Response Monitoring

In the realm of radiation oncology, monitoring a patient's response to treatment is crucial for making timely and informed decisions to optimize therapeutic outcomes. The conventional approach to treatment response assessment involves periodic imaging and clinical evaluations, which may not always capture the dynamic changes occurring within the tumor during the course of radiation therapy. However, with the integration of artificial intelligence (AI), treatment response monitoring has witnessed a paradigm shift, enabling real-time and data-driven assessment of a patient's response to radiation treatment. AI-driven treatment response monitoring leverages advanced image analysis algorithms and machine learning techniques to continuously analyze sequential imaging data acquired during the course of radiation therapy. By comparing these subsequent images with the pre-treatment baseline, AI models can detect subtle changes in tumor size, shape, and density, providing valuable insights into treatment efficacy and tumor behavior. One of the significant advantages of AI-driven treatment response monitoring is the ability to detect early signs of treatment success or failure, enabling timely intervention and adaptive therapy planning. The real-time feedback from AI algorithms empowers radiation oncologists to make informed decisions about modifying treatment plans to optimize tumor control while minimizing the risk of normal tissue toxicity. This adaptability is particularly valuable in managing tumors that demonstrate aggressive growth patterns or unexpected responses to radiation therapy [44]. Deep learning models have demonstrated exceptional capabilities in analyzing sequential medical images and predicting treatment response. These models can be trained on large datasets of paired pre- and post-treatment images, enabling them to learn the subtle changes indicative of treatment response. The integration of longitudinal imaging data with other patient-specific information, such as tumor biology and dosimetric data, further enhances the accuracy and robustness of treatment response prediction. Furthermore, AI-driven treatment response monitoring allows for the identification of patients who may require additional treatments or interventions. Patients who exhibit a poor response to initial radiation therapy can be identified early in the treatment process, prompting a timely reassessment of their treatment plan. This may involve the addition of systemic therapies, changes in radiation fractionation schedules, or the exploration of alternative radiation modalities, such as stereotactic body radiation therapy (SBRT) or proton therapy, to enhance tumor control. In addition to aiding clinical decision-making, AI-driven treatment response monitoring contributes to the accumulation of valuable real-world data for research purposes. The analysis of longitudinal imaging data from diverse patient populations facilitates the identification of patterns and predictive biomarkers associated with treatment outcomes. This knowledge fosters the development of new predictive models and radiomic signatures that can further enhance treatment response prediction and individualized therapy planning. Despite its numerous advantages, AI-driven treatment response monitoring also faces challenges and considerations. The integration of AI technologies into clinical workflows requires careful validation and rigorous testing to ensure the accuracy and safety of the algorithms. Validation studies should include diverse patient populations and various treatment scenarios to assess the generalizability of AI models in different clinical settings. Moreover, the implementation of AI-driven treatment response monitoring necessitates seamless integration with existing electronic health record (EHR) systems and imaging platforms. Interoperability and data exchange standards are essential to enable the smooth flow of information between AI algorithms and clinical workflows, ensuring that AI-driven insights are readily available to radiation oncologists during patient care. Another critical aspect is the ethical use of AI in treatment response monitoring. Ensuring patient privacy, data security, and informed consent are essential considerations in AI implementation. Radiation oncologists must be mindful of patient autonomy and be transparent in communicating the role of AI in treatment decision-making to foster patient trust and confidence in the technology.

9.5 AI in Adaptive Therapy

AI in adaptive therapy is revolutionizing the landscape of radiation oncology by enabling real-time treatment modifications based on dynamic changes in tumor response and patient anatomy. Through continuous analysis of imaging data and treatment outcomes, AI algorithms can predict treatment response and identify patterns indicative of tumor growth or regression. This proactive approach allows radiation oncologists to adapt treatment plans promptly, optimizing therapeutic efficacy and minimizing radiation exposure to healthy tissues. The integration of AI in adaptive therapy holds immense promise in tailoring cancer treatments to each patient's unique characteristics, ultimately leading to improved treatment outcomes and enhanced patient quality of life.

9.5.1 Online Adaptive Radiotherapy

Online adaptive radiotherapy, also known as real-time adaptive radiotherapy, is an innovative approach that harnesses the power of artificial intelligence (AI) to continuously monitor and adapt radiation treatment plans during the course of therapy. Unlike traditional radiation therapy, where treatment plans are based on pre-treatment imaging and remain fixed throughout the treatment course, online adaptive radiotherapy integrates real-time imaging data to dynamically modify treatment plans as the tumor and surrounding anatomy change. The core principle of online adaptive radiotherapy is to account for intra-fractional and inter-fractional changes in tumor size, shape, and position, as well as variations in surrounding normal tissues. These changes can be due to factors such as patient setup variations, organ motion, and tumor response to treatment [45]. By continuously assessing these changes through real-time imaging, AI algorithms can make timely and precise adjustments to radiation delivery, ensuring that the therapeutic dose precisely targets the tumor while sparing healthy tissues. The process of online adaptive radiotherapy typically involves integrating high-quality imaging technologies, such as cone-beam computed tomography (CBCT) or magnetic resonance imaging (MRI), into the treatment delivery system. During treatment sessions, periodic imaging scans are acquired to visualize the tumor and surrounding anatomy. These images are then automatically registered to the initial treatment planning images or reference images using AI-based image registration algorithms. The registration process aligns the target volume and organs at risk with their corresponding locations on the planning images. After image registration, AI algorithms analyze the differences between the acquired images and the reference images, providing valuable information on changes in tumor position, size, and shape. These changes are then used to dynamically adjust the radiation beam delivery parameters, such as beam angles, field sizes, and dose distributions, to match the real-time tumor position and anatomy. The potential benefits of online adaptive radiotherapy are significant. By adapting treatment plans based on real-time imaging, the risk of underdosing the tumor due to setup errors or organ motion is minimized. Additionally, the potential for overexposing healthy tissues is reduced, enhancing the sparing of critical organs and reducing the likelihood of treatment-related side effects. Online adaptive radiotherapy is particularly advantageous in the treatment of tumors located in mobile organs, such as the lung, liver, or prostate, where organ motion can significantly affect treatment accuracy. By continuously accounting for organ motion and tumor changes, online adaptive radiotherapy ensures that the radiation beam accurately targets the tumor, even as it moves within the body during treatment. Moreover, online adaptive radiotherapy has the potential to improve treatment outcomes for patients with rapidly responding tumors or those experiencing changes in tumor size and shape during the treatment course. The adaptability of treatment plans allows radiation oncologists to deliver optimal doses to evolving tumor volumes, enhancing tumor control and potentially improving long-term patient survival. AI plays a critical role in enabling real-time decision-making in online adaptive radiotherapy. Deep learning algorithms and AI-based decision support systems analyze the real-time imaging data and quickly generate updated treatment plans. The ability of AI models to process large volumes of imaging data rapidly is paramount for the success of online adaptive radiotherapy, where quick and accurate adjustments are essential to maintain treatment efficacy. Ethical considerations surrounding the use of AI in online adaptive radiotherapy are also important. Patient privacy and data security must be safeguarded, as real-time imaging involves the acquisition and processing of sensitive medical information. Ensuring informed consent and transparent communication about the use of AI technologies in treatment decision-making is essential to foster patient trust and engagement.

9.5.2 Response-Driven Personalization

Treatment plan optimization is a fundamental aspect of radiation oncology, aiming to devise radiation therapy plans that maximize tumor control while minimizing radiation exposure to healthy tissues. The complexity of treatment planning arises from the need to strike a delicate balance between delivering an effective radiation dose to eradicate tumor cells and minimizing the risk of radiation-related side effects. Artificial intelligence (AI) has emerged as a powerful tool in treatment plan optimization, offering sophisticated algorithms and machine learning techniques that analyze patient-specific data to generate personalized and optimal radiation therapy plans. AI-driven treatment plan optimization begins with the collection of patient-specific data, including tumor characteristics, anatomical information, dose constraints, and clinical objectives. This data is then utilized to formulate an optimization problem, seeking an optimal radiation dose distribution that fulfills treatment objectives while adhering to safety constraints. The complexity of this optimization problem arises from the large number of variables, including beam angles, beam weights, and fluence profiles, that must be determined to achieve a high-quality treatment plan. Traditionally, treatment plan optimization has relied on manual trial-and-error methods, with radiation oncologists iteratively adjusting treatment parameters until an acceptable plan is achieved [46]. However, AI-driven optimization streamlines this process by automating the search for optimal treatment plans in a more efficient and data-driven manner. AI algorithms, such as genetic algorithms, simulated annealing, or deep reinforcement learning, iteratively explore the solution space to identify the best combination of treatment parameters that meet clinical objectives. Deep learning models, such as convolutional neural networks (CNNs) or generative adversarial networks (GANs), have demonstrated exceptional capabilities in treatment plan optimization. These models can learn from large datasets of high-quality treatment plans and clinical outcomes to uncover complex relationships between treatment parameters and plan quality. Once trained, the AI model can rapidly generate high-quality treatment plans for new patients, delivering personalized and effective treatments tailored to each patient's unique characteristics. AI-driven treatment plan optimization offers several advantages over traditional methods. The automation of the optimization process saves valuable time for radiation oncologists and medical physicists, allowing them to focus on other critical aspects of patient care. Moreover, AI models can explore a broader range of possible treatment plans and assess their quality more efficiently, potentially identifying optimal plans that may have been missed in traditional manual approaches. Furthermore, AI-driven treatment plan optimization can address the challenge of plan quality consistency across different radiation centers. Standardizing the treatment planning process using AI models can help ensure that all patients receive high-quality and evidence-based treatments, regardless of their treatment facility. This approach fosters a culture of continuous improvement in radiation therapy and contributes to the development of best practices in treatment planning. Another exciting application of AI in treatment plan optimization is the integration of radiomic data into the optimization process. Radiomics, as discussed earlier, involves the extraction of quantitative information from medical images. By incorporating radiomic features into the treatment optimization process, AI models can consider tumor heterogeneity and biological characteristics in addition to anatomical constraints, potentially leading to more personalized and effective treatment plans. However, there are challenges and considerations in the implementation of AI-driven treatment plan optimization. The need for high-quality training data and validation datasets is critical to ensure the accuracy and generalizability of AI models. Collaborative efforts among radiation oncology centers and data-sharing initiatives are essential to create diverse and representative datasets that encompass different tumor types and clinical scenarios.

9.6 Challenges and Opportunities

As artificial intelligence (AI) continues to shape the landscape of radiation oncology, several challenges and opportunities emerge on the path towards its broader integration and adoption. Addressing these challenges and leveraging the full potential of AI will pave the way for the future of AI-driven radiation oncology, benefiting patients, clinicians, and researchers alike.

9.6.1 Data Quality and Diversity

One of the foremost challenges in AI-driven radiation oncology is the availability of high-quality and diverse datasets. AI models heavily rely on annotated data for training and validation. Ensuring the accuracy and representativeness of these datasets is essential to develop robust and generalizable AI models [47]. Collaborative efforts among institutions and data-sharing initiatives can facilitate the creation of large and diverse datasets, encompassing a wide range of tumor types, treatment modalities, and patient characteristics.

9.6.2 Interpretability and Explainability

The black-box nature of some AI algorithms, particularly deep learning models, poses a significant challenge in the field of radiation oncology. Interpretability and explainability are essential to gain trust and acceptance among radiation oncologists and patients. Efforts to develop interpretable AI models that provide clear explanations for their predictions are crucial to enhance the transparency of AI-driven decision-making.

9.6.3 Validation and Regulatory Approval

The successful translation of AI technologies into clinical practice requires rigorous validation and regulatory approval. AI-driven tools must undergo extensive testing and validation to demonstrate their safety, efficacy, and reliability. Regulatory bodies, such as the Food and Drug Administration (FDA) and other international health authorities, play a critical role in ensuring the appropriate and responsible use of AI in radiation oncology.

9.6.4 Integration into Clinical Workflow

Seamless integration of AI technologies into existing clinical workflows is vital for successful adoption. Radiation oncologists and medical physicists must be able to access AI-driven tools and insights within their treatment planning and decision-making processes. Ensuring interoperability with electronic health record (EHR) systems and treatment planning software is essential to facilitate the efficient utilization of AI in routine clinical care [48].

9.6.5 Ethical Considerations

The ethical use of AI in radiation oncology demands careful attention to patient privacy, data security, and informed consent. Radiation oncologists must be transparent in communicating the role of AI in treatment decision-making and ensure that patients fully understand the implications of using AI-driven technologies. Data anonymization and secure data storage are essential to protect patient confidentiality.

9.6.6 Collaborative Research and Education

Promoting collaboration among radiation oncologists, medical physicists, AI researchers, and industry partners is essential to advance the field of AI-driven radiation oncology. Collaborative research efforts can lead to the development of innovative AI applications and the creation of shared resources, such as benchmark datasets and validation frameworks [49]. Additionally, continuous education and training programs are critical to equip radiation oncologists with the skills and knowledge needed to effectively integrate and utilize AI technologies in clinical practice.

9.6.7 Bias and Fairness

AI models are susceptible to biases present in training data, which can lead to unequal treatment recommendations for different patient populations. Efforts to identify and mitigate bias in AI algorithms are essential to ensure equitable and fair treatment recommendations for all patients. Careful attention to the representation of diverse patient populations in training data is critical to address potential biases.

9.7 Conclusion

The integration of artificial intelligence into radiation oncology presents a wealth of opportunities for improved patient care, precision treatments, and optimized outcomes. As the field continues to evolve, close collaboration between radiation oncologists, AI researchers, and regulatory bodies will be crucial in realizing the full potential of AI technologies while upholding patient safety and ethical considerations. The future of AI in radiation oncology promises to be transformative, revolutionizing the way we combat cancer and enhancing the quality of life for patients worldwide.

References

1. Bibault, J.-E., Giraud, P., & Burgun, A. (2016). Big data and machine learning in radiation oncology: State of the art and future prospects. *Cancer Letters*, 382(1), 110–117.
2. Bitterman, D. S., Miller, T. A., Mak, R. H., & Savova, G. K. (2021). Clinical natural language processing for radiation oncology: A review and practical primer. *International Journal of Radiation Oncology* Biology* Physics*, 110(3), 641–655.
3. Brouwer, C. L., Dinkla, A. M., Vandewinckele, L., Crijns, W., Claessens, M., Verellen, D., & van Elmpt, W. (2020). Machine learning applications in radiation oncology: Current use and needs to support clinical implementation. *Physics and Imaging in Radiation Oncology*, 16, 144–148.
4. Chauhan, S., Singh, M., & Aggarwal, A. K. (2023). Investigative analysis of different mutation on diversity-driven multi-parent evolutionary algorithm and its application in area coverage optimization of WSN. *Soft Computing*, 27, 9565–9591.

5. Chopra, J., Kumar, A., Aggarwal, A. K., & Marwaha, A. (2016). Biometric system security issues and challenges. Second International Conference on Innovative Trends in Electronics Engineering (ICITEE2).

6. Cilla, S., & Barajas, J. E. V. (2022). Automation and artificial intelligence in radiation oncology. *Frontiers in Oncology*, 12, 1038834.

7. Cohen, E. B., & Gordon, I. K. (2022). First, do no harm. Ethical and legal issues of artificial intelligence and machine learning in veterinary radiology and radiation oncology. *Veterinary Radiology & Ultrasound*, 63, 840–850.

8. Cuccia, F., Carruba, G., & Ferrera, G. (2022). What we talk about when we talk about artificial intelligence in radiation oncology. In *Journal of Personalized Medicine* (Vol. 12, Issue 11, p. 1834). MDPI.

9. Deig, C. R., Kanwar, A., & Thompson, R. F. (2019). Artificial intelligence in radiation oncology. *Hematology/Oncology Clinics*, 33(6), 1095–1104.

10. El Naqa, I. (2021). Prospective clinical deployment of machine learning in radiation oncology. *Nature Reviews Clinical Oncology*, 18(10), 605–606.

11. El Naqa, I., Brock, K., Yu, Y., Langen, K., & Klein, E. E. (2018). On the fuzziness of machine learning, neural networks, and artificial intelligence in radiation oncology. *International Journal of Radiation Oncology, Biology, Physics*, 100(1), 1–4.

12. Feng, M., Valdes, G., Dixit, N., & Solberg, T. D. (2018). Machine learning in radiation oncology: Opportunities, requirements, and needs. *Frontiers in Oncology*, 8, 110.

13. Field, M., Hardcastle, N., Jameson, M., Aherne, N., & Holloway, L. (2021). Machine learning applications in radiation oncology. *Physics and Imaging in Radiation Oncology*, 19, 13–24.

14. Fiorino, C., Jeraj, R., Clark, C. H., Garibaldi, C., Georg, D., Muren, L., van Elmpt, W., Bortfeld, T., & Jornet, N. (2020). Grand challenges for medical physics in radiation oncology. *Radiotherapy and Oncology*, 153, 7–14.

15. Huynh, E., Hosny, A., Guthier, C., Bitterman, D. S., Petit, S. F., Haas-Kogan, D. A., Kann, B., Aerts, H. J. W. L., & Mak, R. H. (2020). Artificial intelligence in radiation oncology. *Nature Reviews Clinical Oncology*, 17(12), 771–781.

16. Jarrett, D., Stride, E., Vallis, K., & Gooding, M. J. (2019). Applications and limitations of machine learning in radiation oncology. *The British Journal of Radiology*, 92(1100), 20190001.

17. Aggarwal, A. (2002). Light propagation in biological tissue using Monte Carlo simulation. In *Recent Advances in Computational Science and Engineering* (pp. 19–22). Imperial College Press. https://doi.org/10.1142/9781860949524_0004.

18. Aggarwal, A. K. (2014). Rehabilitation of the blind using audio to visual conversion tool. *Journal of Biomedical Engineering and Medical Imaging*, 1(4), 24–31.

19. Beaton, L., Bandula, S., Gaze, M. N., & Sharma, R. A. (2019). How rapid advances in imaging are defining the future of precision radiation oncology. *British Journal of Cancer*, 120(8), 779–790.

20. Kang, J., Thompson, R. F., Aneja, S., Lehman, C., Trister, A., Zou, J., Obcemea, C., & El Naqa, I. (2021). National cancer institute workshop on artificial intelligence in radiation oncology: Training the next generation. *Practical Radiation Oncology*, 11(1), 74–83.

21. Kaur, A., Chauhan, A. P. S., & Aggarwal, A. K. (2019). Machine learning based comparative analysis of methods for enhancer prediction in genomic data. 2019 2nd International Conference on Intelligent Communication and Computational Techniques (ICCT), 142–145.

22. Kiser, K. J., Fuller, C. D., & Reed, V. K. (2019). Artificial intelligence in radiation oncology treatment planning: A brief overview. *Journal of Medical Artificial Intelligence*, 2(9), 1–11.

23. Kocher, M. (2020). Artificial intelligence and radiomics for radiation oncology. In *Strahlentherapie und Onkologie* (Vol. 196, p. 847). Springer.

24. Kumar, A. (2009). Light propagation through biological tissue: Comparison between Monte Carlo simulation and deterministic models. *International Journal of Biomedical Engineering and Technology*, 2(4), 344–351.

25. Kumari, T., Syal, P., Aggarwal, A. K., & Guleria, V. (2020). Hybrid image registration methods: A review. *International Journal of Advanced Trends in Computer Science and Engineering*, 9(2), 1134–1142.

26. Lahmi, L., Mamzer, M.-F., Burgun, A., Durdux, C., & Bibault, J.-E. (2022). Ethical aspects of artificial intelligence in radiation oncology. *Seminars in Radiation Oncology*, 32(4), 442–448.
27. Leary, D., & Basran, P. S. (2022). The role of artificial intelligence in veterinary radiation oncology. *Veterinary Radiology & Ultrasound*, 63, 903–912.
28. Luh, J. Y., Thompson, R. F., & Lin, S. (2019). Clinical documentation and patient care using artificial intelligence in radiation oncology. *Journal of the American College of Radiology*, 16(9), 1343–1346.
29. Luk, S. M. H., Ford, E. C., Phillips, M. H., & Kalet, A. M. (2022). Improving the quality of care in radiation oncology using artificial intelligence. *Clinical Oncology*, 34(2), 89–98.
30. Maini, S., & Aggarwal, A. K. (2018). Camera position estimation using 2D image dataset. *International Journal of Innovations in Engineering and Technology*, 10(2), 199–203.
31. Moore, N. S., McWilliam, A., & Aneja, S. (2023). Bladder cancer radiation oncology of the future: Prognostic modelling, radiomics, and treatment planning with artificial intelligence. *Seminars in Radiation Oncology*, 33(1), 70–75.
32. Mugabe, K. V. (2021). Barriers and facilitators to the adoption of artificial intelligence in radiation oncology: A New Zealand study. *Technical Innovations & Patient Support in Radiation Oncology*, 18, 16–21.
33. Kumar, A. (2006). Near-infrared optical imaging of the breast. *International Journal of Computer Assisted Radiology and Surgery*, 1, 14–16.
34. Kumar, A. (2008). Light propagation through biological tissue: Comparison of Monte Carlo simulation with deterministic models. SCIS \& ISIS SCIS \& ISIS 2008, 1820–1824.
35. Netherton, T. J., Cardenas, C. E., Rhee, D. J., Beadle, B. M., & others. (2021). The emergence of artificial intelligence within radiation oncology treatment planning. *Oncology*, 99(2), 124–134.
36. Parkinson, C., Matthams, C., Foley, K., & Spezi, E. (2021). Artificial intelligence in radiation oncology: A review of its current status and potential application for the radiotherapy workforce. *Radiography*, 27, S63–S68.
37. Rattan, R., Kataria, T., Banerjee, S., Goyal, S., Gupta, D., Pandita, A., Bisht, S., Narang, K., & Mishra, S. R. (2019). Artificial intelligence in oncology, its scope and future prospects with specific reference to radiation oncology. *BJR| Open*, 1(xxxx), 20180031.
38. Scheetz, J., Rothschild, P., McGuinness, M., Hadoux, X., Soyer, H. P., Janda, M., Condon, J. J. J., Oakden-Rayner, L., Palmer, L. J., Keel, S., & others. (2021). A survey of clinicians on the use of artificial intelligence in ophthalmology, dermatology, radiology and radiation oncology. *Scientific Reports*, 11(1), 5193.
39. Teuwen, J., Gouw, Z. A. R., & Sonke, J.-J. (2022). Artificial intelligence for image registration in radiation oncology. *Seminars in Radiation Oncology*, 32(4), 330–342.
40. Thompson, R. F., Valdes, G., Fuller, C. D., Carpenter, C. M., Morin, O., Aneja, S., Lindsay, W. D., Aerts, H. J. W. L., Agrimson, B., Deville Jr, C., & others. (2018). Artificial intelligence in radiation oncology: A specialty-wide disruptive transformation? *Radiotherapy and Oncology*, 129(3), 421–426.
41. Thompson, R. F., Valdes, G., Fuller, C. D., Carpenter, C. M., Morin, O., Aneja, S., Lindsay, W. D., Aerts, H. J. W. L., Agrimson, B., Deville, C., & others. (2018). Artificial intelligence in radiation oncology imaging. *International Journal of Radiation Oncology, Biology, Physics*, 102(4), 1159–1161.
42. Thompson, R. F., Valdes, G., Fuller, C. D., Carpenter, C. M., Morin, O., Aneja, S., Lindsay, W. D., Aerts, H. J. W. L., Agrimson, B., Deville, C., & others. (2018). The future of artificial intelligence in radiation oncology. *International Journal of Radiation Oncology, Biology, Physics*, 102(2), 247–248.
43. Van Dyk, J. (2020). The modern technology of radiation oncology: A compendium for medical physicists and radiation oncologists. Volume 4. *Medical Physics International Journal*, 8(3), 499–509.
44. Vogelius, I. R., Petersen, J., & Bentzen, S. M. (2020). Harnessing data science to advance radiation oncology. *Molecular Oncology*, 14(7), 1514–1528.
45. Wahid, K. A., Glerean, E., Sahlsten, J., Jaskari, J., Kaski, K., Naser, M. A., He, R., Mohamed, A. S. R., & Fuller, C. D. (2022). Artificial intelligence for radiation oncology applications using public datasets. *Seminars in Radiation Oncology*, 32(4), 400–414.

46. Weidlich, V., Weidlich, G. A., & Weidlich, V. A. (2018). Artificial intelligence in medicine and radiation oncology. *Cureus*, 10(4), e2475, 1–6.
47. Wong, K., Gallant, F., & Szumacher, E. (2021). Perceptions of Canadian radiation oncologists, radiation physicists, radiation therapists and radiation trainees about the impact of artificial intelligence in radiation oncology – National survey. *Journal of Medical Imaging and Radiation Sciences*, 52(1), 44–48.
48. Yakar, M., & Etiz, D. (2021). Artificial intelligance in radiation oncology. *Artificial Intelligence in Medical Imaging*, 2(2), 13–31.
49. Zhai, H., Yang, X., Xue, J., Lavender, C., Ye, T., Li, J.-B., Xu, L., Lin, L., Cao, W., & Sun, Y. (2021). Radiation oncologists' perceptions of adopting an artificial intelligence – Assisted contouring technology: Model development and questionnaire study. *Journal of Medical Internet Research*, 23(9), e27122.

10

A Comprehensive Overview of AI Applications in Radiation Oncology

Neel Ghoshal and B. K. Tripathy

10.1 Introduction

The disease of cancer is the foremost cause of death in developed countries while simultaneously contributing as the second leading cause of death in developing countries [1] [2]. Globally cancer is considered as one of the leading causes of death, accounting for nearly 10 million deaths in 2020 [3]. It is also estimated that there is around a 20% risk of an individual of acquiring cancer before the age of 75 and around one in ten people die from the disease [4]. Currently, there exists a consensus that early detection [5] and treatment concerning cancer can have significant effects towards prevention and deterrence of the disease [6].

Radiation oncology, in its essence, can be thought of as an energy-wave–based treatment aimed as a remedy for cancer. The discipline focuses on employing ionization-based radiation to eradicate malignant tumors, either as a primary treatment mechanism or in combination with corresponding surgery and chemotherapy. Many new and significant advancements and breakthroughs have been made towards this domain in recent years [7]. However, there exists a plethora of obstacles and bottlenecks in this endeavour, including technological, clinical, and biological constraints [8]. A considerable amount of these issues is known to involve specific conceptualism, constraints and databases which allow for artificial intelligence technologies to come into play [9] and capitalize on these criterions. Some possible visionary aspects concerning radiation oncology which can be targeted upon by AI systems include identification of target and normal value requirements, optimization and estimation of modalities and arrangements, cohesion and simultaneous inferences via varied medical records [10]. Furthermore, while a patient undergoes this treatment, there is a massive involvement of and requirement for medical records, which often extrapolates itself out to several separate websites and platforms. Allowing for AI to operate hand-in-hand with clinicians and staff will allow for the reduction of redundancy in many of these aspects. The radiation oncology process which in many aspects is image guided, depends upon the acquirement of CT (computed tomography) and repeated CBCT (cone-beam computed tomography) imaging [11]. AI has the potential to play a significant role here via allowing for increasing image quality, ensuring patient safety, administering inferential data to clinicians and assisting in the overall treatment procedure. Oncological treatment, currently, is widely focused on the use of PET imaging [12]. This technology serves a medium for provision of predictive and prognostic markers for evaluation of responsiveness of radiotherapy measures [13]. In these regards as well, AI has the potential to increase effectiveness and accuracy.

DOI: 10.1201/9781003450153-12

Furthermore, in independent studies made by researchers on the topic of medical injuries and mistakes, it was observed that over a quarter of these incidents occur due to possible negligent proceedings on the part of the corresponding professionals [14]. Issues like these can be plausibly dealt with using AI algorithms and streamlining the medical procedures, allowing for a cohesive, efficient and accurate model for assisting medical personnel.

10.2 Background

In recent times, there have been many innovations and developments pertaining to the creation of AI systems and mechanisms for radiation oncology [15], but these tools are yet to be widely accepted into clinical practice [16]. The introduction of deep neural networks (DNN) [17] has revolutionized the application of AI in several fields [18]. These applications are as diversified as audio signal systems [19], noise recognition [20], detection of masks and social distancing [21], healthcare systems [22], image segmentation, image processing [23], detection of COVID-19 [24], detection of confidence in virtual interviews [25], mental health detection [26], determination of gene characteristics [27] and MRI segmentation[28]. Dinkla et al. have developed and evaluated synthetic tomography images which they were able to generate using a convolutional neural network [29], through which they were able to experiment and evaluate accuracy metrics for MR-based dose calculations in the brain [30, 31]. Work has also been carried out concerning organ delineation for dose parameter acquisition requirements; Dijk et al. obtained high accuracy metrics for their model in this regard for contour detections [32]. Software named 'RapidPlan' is another algorithm developed, its purpose being the improvement of treatment outcome with regard to IMRT (intensity modulated radiation therapy) [33]. Recent years have generally seen a noteworthy rise in the interest and performance of deep learning techniques in the radiation oncology field [34]. As the research into processing and on radiation oncological big data has been conducted, it has been found that the data points and cohorts are widely heterogeneous in nature, coupled with unsupervised machine learning methods; a vast amount of intricate detail and nuance can be discovered which would otherwise prove impossible to understand[35]. Work has also been carried out using machine learning methods to recognize and detect potential errors while processing and evaluating the intermittent stages of the overall radiation oncology procedure [36]. Interpretable and explainable AI methods have also been used heuristically for models created for radiation oncology. These inferences, obtained via model training and evaluation, are seemingly crucial and important to provide clinical practice support procedures [37]. Another aspect that is currently being tackled by using AI is motion-tracking requirements during radiotherapy. Radiotherapy basically refers to the monitoring of a patient's internal anatomy while under the process of radiation therapy. Here, AI comes into play, helping in potentially allowing the monitoring of full anatomies and also allowing inferences towards possible future motions [38].

10.3 Electronic Medical Records

Electronic medical records (EMRs) are digitally stored versions of medical information pertaining to individual patients. EMRs generally contain a comprehensive store relating

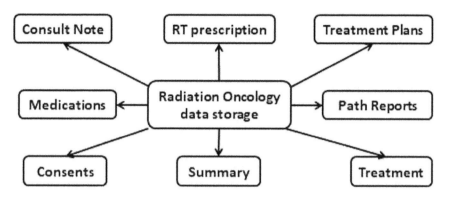

FIGURE 10.1
General categorization of medical information for radiation oncology departments [21].

to a patient's medical history, treatments, diagnoses, medications etc. In radiation oncology, there is a plethora of information that needs to be stored, catalogued and evaluated during the process and before administering radiation-based therapy. Medical institutions generally have a framework-based pattern for storage of radiation oncological data for ease of use and uniformity, a depiction of which is given in Figure 10.1.

10.3.1 AI for Management Purposes in EMR Systems

As already observed, there exists a huge amount of data that needs to be processed before, during and after any radiation oncology procedure. When done manually and without AI assistance, this can lead to high process times, discrepancies, faults etc. Here, the use of natural language processing (NLP) comes into play, allowing for a comprehensive and efficient solution providing many benefits including advantageous mechanisms in the major requirements such as efficient billing, authorization approval and medical policy assessment, among other provisions [39].

Efficient billing using AI in the medical context refers to the leveraging of artificial intelligence technologies to streamline and optimize the overall billing procedures within a healthcare setting. Some main aims are to improve accuracy, lessen manual need, bolster revenue management and other services. Overall, AI can be embedded in data acquisition mechanisms allowing for efficient extractive mechanisms pertaining to patient information from electronic health records (EHRs) and other sources. AI has also demonstrably proven to be effective with respect to CPT (current procedural terminology) billing codes used widely in medical environments [40]. Other than this, AI also provides advantages in newly found functionalities related to ambient speech-recognition for EHRs, medical scribe functionalities etc. [41]. On the other hand, AI also has the ability to provide insights into the realm of financial management prediction for a hospital and their staff, allowing for greater amounts of available funds which can later be used for a plethora of services including researching oncological methodologies, equipment-related research and maintenance, among other things [42]. Another looming issue at hand is the manual-labour and time-constraint factors related to authorization procedures followed for approvals in the radiation oncological departments. AI comes into play in this specific regard and helps increase efficiency with relation to authorization-based matters. For instance, Lenert et al. have proposed a framework for an AI system which has functionalities allowing it to emulate human judgment with respective to administrative medicine ultimately helping in simulating prior authorization (PA) processes [43]. Along with the modern development into increasing efficiencies and advantages with respect to EMRs, there has also been research done into oncology specific databases/EMRs. 'OncoLifeS', developed by Sidorenkov et al., is a hospital databank for oncology allowing for the collection of high-quality data along with inclusion of metrics for patient perspectives and image-based data [44]. AI-based models can also effectively help from a policy perspective in medical records, by providing assistance in regulatory compliance-based matters, policy development issues and review requirements.

10.3.2 AI for Predictive Purposes in EMR Systems

Artificial intelligence has the potential to play a very crucial role in providing insights from EMRs for radiation oncology. Using these specific insights can be of significant help to oncologists, medical physicists, healthcare providers and other related staff in making informed treatment-based decisions. With this in mind, one such scenario is the domain of drug treatment pattern discovery which involves the use of data-driven predictive technology allowing for functionalities adhering to analyzing and predicting the most effective treatment pattern for a specific individual diagnosed as suffering from cancer. Savova et al. have worked on predictive drug treatment pattern discovery in the domain of breast cancer; they have specifically used natural language processing to process EMR data to develop their algorithm [45]. AI has also been extensively used in pre-screening functionalities, basically allowing the prediction of a patient's risk metrics with regard to the development of a specific type of cancer, and hence alleviating the need for diagnostic interventions. Yeh et al. have worked on the prediction of lung cancer risk in this regard, working on non-image EMR data across designated time spans [46]. Similar risk predictive tasks have also been conducted with relation to breast cancer, gastric components and the pancreas [47–49]. Other important insights, particularly concerning mortality, readmission and the duration of hospital stay, have also proved to be a plausible component of AI-use cases [50]. AI in infection prevention and management for cancer patients is also another domain currently being researched and worked upon [51–53]. In addition to simply providing us with various predictive methodologies and functions, currently explainable artificial intelligence is widely being employed, basically providing human understandable and interpretable explanations for the predictions it provides. Explainable AI carries through with its embedded functions using a wide array of mechanisms including explainability techniques, specific feature and characteristic highlighting, rule extraction and visualizations using EMR data [54].

10.4 AI for Image Segmentation and Contouring

Image segmentation in radiation oncology involves the division of medical images, obtained via image acquiring modalities like CT scans, MRI or PET scans, into distinctive regions or segments. Each of the derived segments represents different structures within the body of an individual patient, including organs, tumours, tissues and other anatomical structures. This characterization serves as a crucial step in radiation therapy planning and treatment therapy by accurately providing delineation of target areas and organs at risk. Currently, AI has proved to be extremely beneficial in these specific regards of cancer image segmentation and has been advantageous to medical personnel involved in radiation oncology in terms of effectiveness, efficiency and accuracy. Given below is an example [55] of an individual datapoint present in a variety of cancer segmentation data-sets (Figure 10.2).

Generally, the input used in segmentation models in this case consists of raw images from any number of modalities, which is processed through a previously trained machine learning model, which then yields an output consisting of necessary segmentations. This process is portrayed in Figure 10.3. Image segmentation is carried out in multiple facets of the human anatomy including the brain, head and neck, lungs, abdomen, pelvis among other substructures. Research has been done concerning the use of AI for image segmentation in almost all of the varying substructures. Datasets correlated to manually completed segmentation images have been used and worked upon for these tasks. It is observed that a wide variety of techniques are used for creating efficient and working models for this task including variations of convolutional neural networks, reinforcement learning, among other methodologies.

Many generalized and specific algorithms have been developed and deployed, allowing researchers and medical personnel the freedom and ability to use these models directly in segmentation oncological tasks. Marschner et al. have successfully developed one such algorithm using the concept of 'Autosegmentation with a deep image-to-image network (DI2IN)', which they employ to perform segmentation tasks in and around the region of interest (ROI) of an individual or group of organs instead of the entirety of an image in one go, allowing for a more sophisticated and intricate processing procedure for better results [56]. 'U-Nets', for example, are a variation of convolutional neural networks (CNNs) which

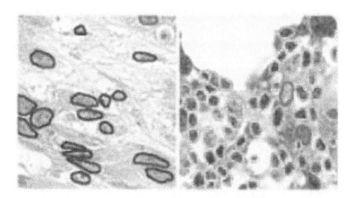

FIGURE 10.2
Sample image of segmentation of cancer cells.

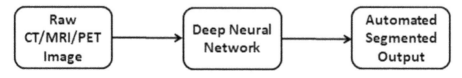

FIGURE 10.3
General overall framework for AI-based image segmentation.

are mainly used for the tasks of image segmentation in oncological subdomains. They work on the principle of encoding and decoding of context and localizations. An input image tile is taken into account, which is then put through dimension changing function-alities and cropping functions, after which a framework is formed until the final output segmentation step is reached. Convolution and pooling mechanisms are employed to form this framework. The encoder functionality allows for precise and proper understanding of the 'context' of an image, that is, basically pointing towards what the image contains; while, the decoder allows for the model to gain precise localization metrics, suggesting accurate predictions of where the object is located. Another important mechanism used by U-Nets is its ability to skip connection points and simultaneously reconstruct an accurate shape of the output segmentation map. A visual conceptual depiction of the U-Net model is given in Figure 10.4.

Other widely used variations and applications for image segmentation tasks are algo-rithms such as fully convolutional networks (FCNs) which are designed for pixel-wise pre-diction, 3D-CNNs which deal with volumetric images, transfer learning which works on pre-trained CNN models and ensemble methods which entail the combination of multiple models or algorithms. Automated segmentation functionalities have been built using the above-mentioned algorithms with a few other variations of them, working towards the goal of volume of interest delineation among other needs. Related work has been carried out for brain-based radiation oncology [57], head and neck image segmentation [58], abdominal image segmentation [59] and image segmentation functionalities for images pertaining to the pelvic area [60], among other organs. Image contouring is another major functional aspect which is crucial when performing the overall procedures related to radiation oncol-ogy. Image contouring specifically refers to the outlining of a surface configuration of a target object present in an image. In AI-based image contouring for radiation oncology, the functionalities revolve around the need for outlining boundaries of specific structures such as tumours and critical organs, thus defining these shapes with the patient's anatomy. Image contouring is an essential pre-step before radiation beams are applied with regard

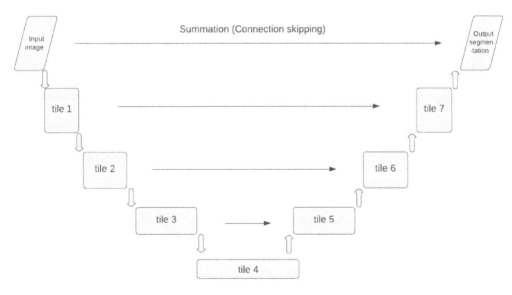

FIGURE 10.4
Framework depiction for U-Net based models.

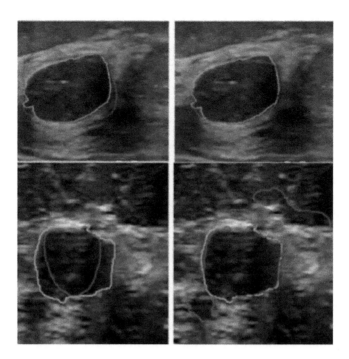

FIGURE 10.5
Example of contouring in relation to tumours/cancer cells.

to a patient, allowing for precise application of radiation beams and avoidance of nearby healthy organs/tissues. Given in Figure 10.5 is an example of an individual datapoint present in datasets aimed at creating models for contouring requirements.

Recently, work has been carried out using AI and applying it to effectively automate image contouring for radiation oncology. For instance, a software namely 'Varian Ethos' has been developed recently which allows for the automation of anatomical contouring among its other functionalities [61]. Many sub-functionalities regarding image segmentation, including identification, segmentation, extraction of features and classifying cancer images, have also been recently worked upon [62]. Udupa et al. have developed a robust auto contouring mechanism for neck and thorax anatomical structures using a combination of natural and artificial intelligence [63]. On the other hand, AI models have also been developed to work hand-in-hand with clinicians allowing for the feasible and effective models for direct assistance [64].

10.5 AI in Image Registration

Image registration in radiation oncology refers to the process of aligning or matching multiple medical images taken at different times or with different equipment or modalities. The primary aim of image registration is to superimpose images of an individual patient's anatomy that allows accurate analysis, treatment planning and comparison. An overall idea of the process followed can be gained from Figure 10.6.

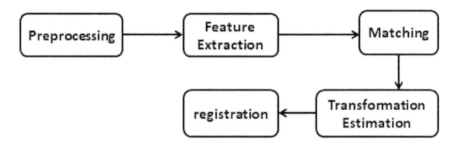

FIGURE 10.6
Steps involved in image registration.

Image registration techniques can be categorized and divided with respect to the workflow it follows:

a. Pre-treatment registration: Before initiating the treatment planning, images acquired at varying timeframes are registered to establish a baseline datapoint to later work upon. This helps radiation oncologists to determine the initial tumour location and surrounding anatomy.

b. Intra-treatment registration: During treatment, imaging is carried out in a repeated manner primarily for monitoring anatomical changes within a patient. These images are put through the process of registration to analyze changes and variations with this regard.

Image registration techniques can also be categorized as:

a. Rigid registration: This involves translation, rotation and scaling for aligning images, and is useful when images have minimal anatomical changes within them.

b. Deformable registration: This is employed when significant anatomical changes occur, allowing for flexible adjustment for matching various shapes and position

Certain DIR (deformable image registration) algorithmic software are currently available for commercial use in the industry, including Velocity AI's automatic DIR software employing the B-Spline and Demons algorithm implementation.

In brief, Velocity AI software follows through with its procedure of DIR via certain inbuilt functionalities inherent to it. For instance, measurement of the volume of the specific structure which is to be imaged is defined as a voxel, which is localized by 3-D grid co-ordinates as required [65]. A displacement vector field (DVF) is also simultaneously obtained which contains information of each specific voxel's movement as compared to its original primary image [52]. For performance assessment, factors like dice similarity co-efficient (DSC) and target registration error (TRE) among other metrics are used.

The dice similarity co-efficient is a metric used to quantify the similarity or overlap between two sets or regions in image segmentation and image registration tasks, essentially providing insight into how well the registered region in one image matches the ground truth in another image. The exact equation for calculating this metric is given below as equation (1) [66].

$$\text{Dice Similarity Coefficient(DSC)} = \frac{2*|A \cap B|}{|A|+|B|} \qquad (1)$$

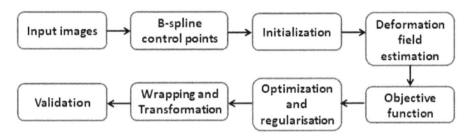

FIGURE 10.7
General framework of the B-spline algorithmic model.

Where $|A \cap B|$ represents the intersection (overlap) of the two regions and $|A|$ and $|B|$ represent the size of the regions. The DSC coefficient yields a value between 0 and 1, 1 indicating a perfect overlap and vice versa [67].

The target registration error is generally used to evaluate the discrepancy between the intended and actual locations of a target point after applying the image registration procedure. The equation that is used to calculate this value is given below as equation (2) [68].

$$TRE = [(x_{actual} - x_{intended})^2 + (y_{actual} - y_{intended})^2$$
$$+ (z_{actual} - z_{intended})^2]^{1/2}$$
(2)

Where $(x_{actual}, y_{actual}, z_{actual})$ is the actual location of the target point or region, and $(x_{intended}, y_{intended}, z_{intended})$ is the intended location

The B-spline algorithm, in particular, represents the deformation field, in lieu of the process of DIR, using B-spline basis functions, which essentially are mathematical functions that have the ability to flexibly describe complex deformations. The overall approach allows for a transformation procedure which is smooth and continuous in nature, which makes it suitable for image registration with images consisting inherent anatomical variations. The process-based steps that are followed in B-spline based algorithms are visually illustrated in Figure 10.7.

10.6 AI for Motion Tracking

As briefly explained earlier, motion tracking in radiation oncology can be thought of as referring to the ability of monitoring and keeping track of a patient's internal anatomy during the process of radiation treatment. The reason for the importance of this subdomain is the fact that the areas which are targeted for radiation may be displaced from their original positions due to biological and physical processes such as digestion, respiration and other bodily processes. Organ motion itself is generally categorized into types such as patient motion, inter-fractional motion occurring between fractions and intra-fractional motion referring to all involuntary movements during a treatment fraction [56]. If movements like these aren't properly accounted for, it can cause unintended radiation exposure to healthy tissues and simultaneous deficiencies in dosages administered to the tumour, essentially adding to heightened risk of undesired dose delivery [60].

The motion detection methodologies and frameworks followed by AI systems can be categorized into the following subparts:

a. Real-time tracking: This refers to the AI algorithms which analyze image sequences in real time to track the motion of anatomical structures simultaneously as the treatment progresses.
b. Predictive modelling: This refers to the specific AI-based algorithms which analyze historical data to create predictive models which pragmatically estimate the future motion patterns of anatomical structures.

Motion tracking algorithms are especially useful when used for the purpose of adaptive radiation therapy, particularly aimed at the dynamic adaption capabilities required for an ongoing radiation treatment planning, essentially allowing for the dose delivery to the location-variant target and avoiding healthy tissues. Currently, there exists a plethora of research and development work concerning motion tracking methodologies and algorithms with AI. Furtado et al. have developed a real-time image pair tracking to monitor tumour tracking using 2-D/3-D registration techniques [69]. On the other hand, ultrasound imaging, based on 2-D image bases, have been used to track intra-fraction respiratory motion for abdominal radiation therapy [70]. Tumour tracking for cancer cells present in the lungs have also seen efficient developments, such as via Homma et al. who have worked using predictive algorithms towards this task and Steiner et al. who have used tomography-based images with predictive lung-target motion algorithms [71, 72]. Markless tumour-tracking algorithms have also been worked on by researchers [73, 74].

10.7 AI for Treatment Plan Optimization and Personalized Therapy

As the name would suggest, AI for treatment plan optimization refers to the use of artificial intelligence techniques to enhance the process of designing optimal treatment plans for patients undergoing radiation therapy. The algorithms work hand-in-hand with medical personnel to assist in improving quality, effectiveness and accuracy of radiation therapy plans by simplifying and resolving the complex processes inherent to the same. On top of this, in the field of radiotherapy, treatment planning and optimization using machine learning and deep learning are possibly the most widely embraced applications at present, which indicates the confidence that physicists have in the capacity of these technologies to enhance the effectiveness of this critical process [75].

Knowledge-based planning (KBP) is a variant of treatment plan optimization techniques, which basically uses pre-existing knowledge and data from historically treated patients for the purpose of optimization and creation of new treatment plans for cancer patients. The procedure entails the application of machine learning and statistical techniques to predict efficient and effective treatment plans when input with data pertaining to previously treated patients. Work has been conducted in this regard in a multi-faceted fashion including dosimetric assessment, treatment validation and performance-based tasks [76, 77]. Wang et al. have worked towards developing a system allowing for ease of use of KBP mechanisms for planners with different experiences [78]. Patient-specific quality control is also something that has been demonstrably shown to be possible and viable via the use of KBP systems [79]. Giaddui et al. have tackled yet another sub-domain

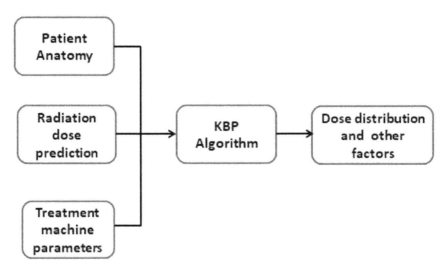

FIGURE 10.8
General framework of a KBP-based algorithm.

of KBP-based offline quality assurance protocols employing the use of a site-specific and multi-institutional KBP model [80].

As depicted in Figure 10.8, a KBP-based algorithm generally takes into consideration the factors related to a patient's anatomy, that is, tumour location, size, its shape, surrounding organ metrics etc., the dose prescriptions including information about the allowable limits of unintended dosages and treatment machine parameters containing information such as collimator settings, beam energy etc. All of this is taken into account via the model as input information, which is thereby processed and the necessary dose distribution factors and other necessary bits of information are output via the model.

Apart from KBP, deep learning has also been used by researchers as a means of investigating and developing automated plan generation software. Fan et al. have developed an IMRT (intensity modulated radiation therapy) based planning strategy for a generative plan generation model [81]. Chen et al. have created dose-distribution predictive models taking into consideration input factors such as planning image and segmented anatomy and using deep learning for the processing procedures [82]. Kajikawa et al. have developed dosimetric eligibility predictive software for patients with prostate cancer using a CNN-based architecture [83].

10.8 AI and Regulatory Considerations in Radiation Oncology

From an ethical point of view, it is essential to understand and tackle a few problems and key factors regarding these matters that come into play. Bias and discrimination are up one such avenue which needs to be tackled, as biases in availability of data or the skewed nature of available input can lead to the created models to inculcate issues such as sub-optimal predictions due to race, ethnicity etc., hence the need for data to be cohesive and evenly representational of all concerned patients. The main reasons for the existence of bias and class imbalance are many, including gender and race imbalance issues in data, limited capture and inclusion of social determinants of health (SDOH) and disabilities, management variability and knowledge transition bias [84]. Apart from this, there also need to be streamlined ways and functionalities for patients to invoke their rights regarding the transparency and accountability of the concerned models and systems. There is precedent for similar work concerning the transparency-based factors; for instance, the American College for Radiology (ACR) has set up principles for AI application stewardship, including the need for public participation towards transparency and accountability and an overall oversight with regard to AI applications. One monumentally important task in this regard is the need for privacy and security of AI systems, as a lot of the data that goes into making medical models and algorithms use sensitive patient information. In regard to this, there have been recent developments towards the creation of a software named 'euroCAT' which focuses on multi-centric machine learning for radiation oncological functionalities implementing privacy preserving practices [85]. Apart from all these necessary considerations, there also need to be mechanisms in place to check and validate the accuracy and safety of the models in use and under deployment in clinical practice, along with overall quality assessment features. With regard to each step followed in the radiation oncological process, work has been carried out for AI systems' quality assessment features regarding case-specific QA, routine QA, RT-application QA and many others [86].

10.9 Case Studies

Let's evaluate the use of artificial intelligence in radiation oncology from a survey- and statistical-based perspective.

The number of papers based on the topic of AI in radiation oncology has risen from 100,000 in 2020 to an expected 200,000 by 2023, as depicted graphically in Figure 10.9.

The division of sub-fields in the use of AI in radiation oncology is depicted in Figure 10.10 [87].

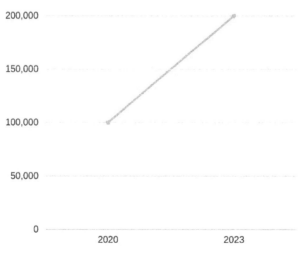

FIGURE 10.9
Comparison graph between number of estimated papers for AI in radiation oncology in 2020 vs 2023.

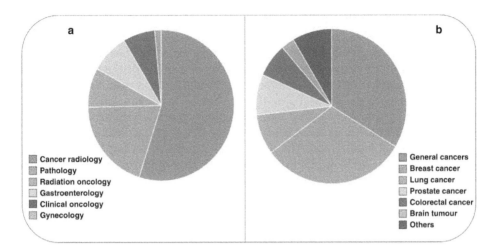

FIGURE 10.10
Pie chart for graphical depiction of percentage divisions of use of AI in oncology and related fields.

A good example of practical implementation-based case study of AI in real-world scenarios would be the case of Manipal Hospitals in India, who have adopted an AI-powered diagnostic system for radiology. This system enables the usage of machine learning algorithms to analyze medical images, which helps radiologists make accurate and timely diagnoses. This has improved the overall efficiency of care-based factors and simultaneously has reduced the risk of errors. [88]

Let us consider a point-of-view based case study to get a bird's eye view on the entire process with respect to a patient diagnosed with cancer and requiring radiation oncology treatment embedded with AI features.

A patient with lung cancer was referred to a radiation oncologist for treatment. The patient had a large tumour in the right lung, and the radiation oncologist wanted to use a technique called intensity-modulated radiation therapy (IMRT) to deliver the radiation to the tumour while minimizing the dose to the surrounding healthy tissue. Here, the clinicians use AI to generate an efficient treatment plan/procedure for the specific patient, according to patterns of already existing patients and their treatments. Then the image-based scans of the patient were processed using AI-based software allowing for automated and efficient segmentation, contouring, registration and motion tracking requirements. Consolidating all these advantages, the radiation oncology team decided to carry forward their procedures and were able to successfully treat the patient with IMRT while simultaneously reducing time and effort and avoiding unnecessary side-effects.

This case study illustrates how AI can be used to improve the quality of radiation therapy for cancer patients. AI-powered software tools can help radiation oncologists to plan more accurate and conformal treatments, which can lead to better outcomes for patients.

10.10 Challenges and Future Directions

Some challenges that researchers and clinicians alike are likely to face mainly concern ethical and regulatory considerations such as ethical concerns, regulatory approvals, widespread acceptance issues, and other technological hinderances. Apart from this, achieving the peak potential of machine learning models may be hindered in part due to the lack of availability of high-quality medical data to be used to make inferences from. Certain other issues like the possible untenability of performance requirements of some of the related models and lack of quantitative metrics for the same can cause hinderances in research efforts as well.

AI is a rapidly evolving field, and it is likely to have a major impact on radiation oncology in the coming years. AI-powered tools have the potential to improve the quality and efficiency of care for cancer patients, and they could also help to make radiation therapy more accessible to patients around the world. Other facets of research such as radiomics and radiogenomics can become crucial as well, providing predictive capabilities for treatments outcomes, disease progression and personal treatment strategies. Acquirement of other bio-data related to the patient can also drastically help in providing necessary inferential data towards treatment goals.

References

1. World Health Organization. *The Global Burden of Disease: 2004 Update*. Geneva: World Health Organization, 2008.
2. Dash, S., B. N. Patra, and B. K. Tripathy. "Study of classification accuracy of microarray data for cancer classification using multivariate and hybrid feature selection method." *International Organization of Scientific Research Journal of Engineering (IOSRJEN)* 2.8 (August 2012): 112–119. ISSN: 2250–3021 (Online), ISSN: 2278-8719 (Print).
3. Ferlay, J., M. Colombet, I. Soerjomataram, et al. "Cancer statistics for the year 2020: An overview." *International Journal of Cancer* (2021). https://doi.org/10.1002/ijc.33588. Epub ahead of print. PMID: 33818764.
4. Ferlay, Jacques, et al. "Cancer statistics for the year 2020: An overview." *International Journal of Cancer* 149.4 (2021): 778–789.
5. Bhandari, A., B. K. Tripathy, K. Jawad, S. Bhatia, M. K. I. Rahmani, and A. Mash. "Cancer detection and prediction using genetic algorithms." *Computational Intelligence and Neuroscience* 2022: 18pages. https://doi.org/10.1155/2022/1871841.
6. Jemal, Ahmedin, et al. "Global cancer statistics." *CA: A Cancer Journal for Clinicians* 61.2 (2011): 69–90.
7. Bernier, Jacques, Eric J. Hall, and Amato Giaccia. "Radiation oncology: A century of achievements." *Nature Reviews Cancer* 4.9 (2004): 737–747.
8. Orth, M., K. Lauber, M. Niyazi et al. "Current concepts in clinical radiation oncology." *Radiation and Environmental Biophysics* 53 (2014): 1–29. https://doi.org/10.1007/s00411-013-0497-2.
9. Jain, Satin, Udit Singhania, B. K. Tripathy, Emad Abouel Nasr, Mohamed K. Aboudaif, and Ali K. Kamrani. "Deep learning based transfer learning for classification of skin cancer." *Sensors* 21.23 (2021): 8142. https://doi.org/10.3390/s21238142.
10. Thompson, Reid F., et al. "Artificial intelligence in radiation oncology: A specialty-wide disruptive transformation?." *Radiotherapy and Oncology* 129.3 (2018): 421–426.
11. Parkinson, C., Matthams, C., Foley, K., & Spezi, E. (2021). Artificial intelligence in radiation oncology: A review of its current status and potential application for the radiotherapy workforce. Radiography (London, England: 1995), 27 Suppl 1, S63–S68. DOI: 10.1016/j.radi.2021.07.012
12. Orth, M., K. Lauber, M. Niyazi et al. "Current concepts in clinical radiation oncology." *Radiation and Environmental Biophysics* 53 (2014): 1–29. https://doi.org/10.1007/s00411-013-0497-2.
13. Yaromina, A., M. Krause, and M. Baumann. (2012). "Individualization of cancer treatment from radiotherapy perspective." *Molecular Oncology* 6.2: 211–21. https://doi.org/10.1016/j.molonc.2012.01.007. Epub 2012 Feb 9. PMID: 22381063; PMCID: PMC5528361.

14. *New England Journal of Medicine* 324 (1991): 370–376. https://doi.org/10.1056/NEJM199102073240604.
15. Huynh, Elizabeth, et al. "Artificial intelligence in radiation oncology." *Nature Reviews Clinical Oncology* 17.12 (2020): 771–781.
16. Netherton, Tucker J., Carlos E. Cardenas, Dong Joo Rhee, Laurence E. Court, and Beth M. Beadle. "The emergence of artificial intelligence within radiation oncology treatment planning." *Oncology* 99.2 (2021): 124–134. https://doi.org/10.1159/000512172.
17. Bhattacharyya, S., V. Snasel, A. E. Hassanian, S. Saha, and B. K. Tripathy. *Deep Learning Research with Engineering Applications*. De Gruyter Publications, 2020. ISBN: 3110670909, 9783110670905. https://doi.org/10.1515/9783110670905.
18. Adate, Amit, B. K. Tripathy, Dhruv Arya, and Aditya Shaha. "Impact of deep neural learning on artificial intelligence research" (Ed: S. Bhattacharyya, A. E. Hassanian, S. Saha, and B. K. Tripathy, *Deep Learning Research and Applications*), De Gruyter Publications, (2020), pp. 69–84. https://doi.org/10.1515/9783110670905-004.
19. Bose, Ankita, and B. K. Tripathy. "Deep learning for audio signal classification" (Ed: S. Bhattacharyya, A. E. Hassanian, S. Saha, and B. K. Tripathy, *Deep Learning Research and Applications*), De Gruyter Publications, (2020), pp. 105–136. https://doi.org/10.1515/9783110670905-00660.
20. Sridhar, Sudershan, Sharmila Banu Kather, and B. K. Tripathy. "Voice recognition system using deep learning" (Ed: S. Bhattacharyya, *Hybrid Computational Intelligent Systems*), CRC Press, (2023), Chapter-19, pp. 279–290.
21. Yagna Sai Surya, K., T. Geetha Rani, and B. K. Tripathy. "Social distance monitoring and face mask detection using deep learning" (Ed: J. Nayak, H. Behera, B. Naik, S. Vimal, and D. Pelusi, *Computational Intelligence in Data Mining. Smart Innovation, Systems and Technologies*), vol 281, Springer, Singapore. https://doi.org/10.1007/978-981-16-9447-9_36.
22. Kaul, D., H. Raju, and B. K. Tripathy. "Deep learning in healthcare" (Ed: D. P. Acharjya, A. Mitra, and N. Zaman, *Deep Learning in Data Analytics- Recent Techniques, Practices and Applications*), Studies in Big Data, vol. 91. Springer, Cham (2022), pp. 97–115. https://doi.org/10.1007/978-3-030-75855-4_6.
23. Adate, A., and B. K. Tripathy. "Deep learning techniques for image processing" (Ed: S. Bhattacharyya, H. Bhaumik, A. Mukherjee, and S. De, *Machine Learning for Big Data Analysis*), De Gruyter, Berlin, Boston, (2018), pp. 69–90. https://doi.org/10.1515/9783110551433-00357.
24. Sihare, Pranchal, Azeem Ullah Khan, Poritosh Bardhan, and B. K. Tripathy. "COVID-19 detection using deep learning: A comparative study of segmentation algorithms" (Ed: A. K. Das et al., *Proceedings of the 4th International Conference on Computational Intelligence in Pattern Recognition (CIPR)*), CIPR 2022, LNNS 480, (2022), pp. 1–10.
25. Rungta, Ravi Kumar, Parth Jaiswal, and B. K. Tripathy. "A deep learning based approach to measure confidence for virtual interviews" (Ed: A. K. Das et al., *Proceedings of the 4th International Conference on Computational Intelligence in Pattern Recognition (CIPR)*), CIPR 2022, LNNS 480, (2022), pp. 278–291.
26. Ghoshal, N., V. Bhartia B. K. Tripathy and A. Tripathy. "Chatbot for mental health diagnosis using NLP and deep learning" (Ed: S. Chinara, A. K. Tripathy, K. C. Li, J. P. Sahoo, and A. K. Mishra, *Advances in Distributed Computing and Machine Learning. Lecture Notes in Networks and Systems*), vol 660, Springer, Singapore, (2023). https://doi.org/10.1007/978-981-99-1203-2_39.
27. Gupta, P., S. Bhachawat, K. Dhyani, and B. K. Tripathy. "A study of gene characteristics and their applications using deep learning, (Chapter 4)," Studies in Big Data, Vol. 103 (Ed: Sanjiban Sekhar Roy, and Y.-H. Taguchi, *Handbook of Machine Learning Applications for Genomics*), Springer Singapore (2021). ISBN: 978-981-16-9157-7, 496166_1_En.
28. Tripathy, B. K., S. Parikh, P. Ajay, and C. Magapu. "Brain MRI segmentation techniques based on CNN and its variants, (Chapter-10)" (Ed: J. Chaki, *Brain Tumor MRI Image Segmentation Using Deep Learning Techniques*), Elsevier Publications, (2022), pp. 161–182. https://doi.org/10.1016/B978-0-323-91171-9.00001-6.
29. Maheswari, Karan, Aditya Shaha, Dhruv Arya, B. K. Tripathy, and R. Rajkumar. "Convolutional neural networks: A bottom-up approach" (Ed: S. Bhattacharyya, A. E. Hassanian, S. Saha, and

B. K. Tripathy, *Deep Learning Research with Engineering Applications*), De Gruyter Publications, (2020), pp. 21–50. https://doi.org/10.1515/9783110670905-002.

30. Singh, Neha, and B. K. Tripathy. "Leukemia cell segmentation from microscopic blood smear image using C-Mode" (Ed: Das, K., Bansal, J., Deep, K., Nagar, A., Pathipooranam, P., Naidu, R. *Soft Computing for Problem Solving*), VIT, Vellore, December (2018), pp. 225–238.

31. Dinkla, Anna M., Jelmer M. Wolterink, Matteo Maspero, et al. "MR-only brain radiation therapy: Dosimetric evaluation of synthetic CTs generated by a dilated convolutional neural network." *International Journal of Radiation Oncology*Biology*Physics* 102.4 (2018): 801–812.

32. Van Dijk, Lisanne V., et al. "Improving automatic delineation for head and neck organs at risk by Deep Learning Contouring." *Radiotherapy and Oncology* 142 (2020): 115–123.

33. Chang, Amy T. Y., Albert W. M. Hung, and Fion W. K. Cheung, et al. "Comparison of planning quality and efficiency between conventional and knowledge-based algorithms in nasopharyngeal cancer patients using intensity modulated radiation therapy." *International Journal of Radiation Oncology*Biology*Physics* 95 (3) 2016: 981–990.

34. Boldrini, Luca, et al. "Deep learning: A review for the radiation oncologist." *Frontiers in Oncology* 9 (2019): 977.

35. Bibault, Jean-Emmanuel, Philippe Giraud, and Anita Burgun. "Big data and machine learning in radiation oncology: State of the art and future prospects." *Cancer Letters* 382.1 (2016): 110–117.

36. Jarrett, Daniel, et al. "Applications and limitations of machine learning in radiation oncology." *The British Journal of Radiology* 92.1100 (2019): 20190001.

37. Cui, Sunan, et al. "Interpretable artificial intelligence in radiology and radiation oncology." *The British Journal of Radiology* 96(1150) (2023): 20230142.

38. Mylonas, Adam, Jeremy Booth, and Doan Trang Nguyen. "A review of artificial intelligence applications for motion tracking in radiotherapy." *Journal of Medical Imaging and Radiation Oncology* 65.5 (2021): 596–611.

39. John, Kirkpatrick, Light Kim, Walker Robyn, et al. "Implementing and integrating a clinically driven electronic medical record for radiation oncology in a large medical enterprise." *Frontiers in Oncology* 3 (2013): 69.

40. Rangasamy, A. S. S., R. Nadenichek, and M. Rayasam. *Natural Language Processing in Healthcare*, mckinsey & company Healthcare (2018). https://www.mckinsey.com/industries/healthcare/our-insights/natural-language-processing-in-healthcare.

41. Kim, J. S., A. Vivas, V. Arvind, et al. "Can natural language processing and artificial intelligence automate the generation of billing codes from operative note dictations?" *Global Spine Journal* (2022). https://doi.org/10.1177/21925682211062831.

42. Avendano, John P., Gallagher DO, Hawes JD, et al. "Interfacing with the electronic health record (HER): A comparative review of modes of documentation." *Cureus* 14(6) (2022): e26330. DOI:10.7759/cureus.26330

43. Leon Sanz, Rafael, and Pilar Leon-Sanz. "Modeling health data using machine learning techniques applied to financial management predictions." *Applied Sciences* 12.23 (2022): 12148.

44. Lenert, Leslie A., Steven Lane, and Ramsey Wehbe. "Could an artificial intelligence approach to prior authorization be more human?." *Journal of the American Medical Informatics Association* 30.5 (2023): 989–994.

45. Sidorenkov, G., J. Nagel, C. Meijer et al. "The OncoLifeS data-biobank for oncology: A comprehensive repository of clinical data, biological samples, and the patient's perspective." *Journal of Translational Medicine* 17 (2019): 374. https://doi.org/10.1186/s12967-019-2122-x.

46. Savova, G. K., and others. "Automated discovery of drug treatment patterns for endocrine therapy of breast cancer within an electronic medical record." *Journal of the American Medical Informatics Association* 19.1 (2012): e83–e89. https://doi.org/10.1136/amiajnl-2011-000295

47. Yeh, M., Y. Wang, H. Yang, K. Bai, H. Wang, and Y. Li. "Artificial intelligence–based prediction of lung cancer risk using nonimaging electronic medical records: Deep learning approach." *Journal of Medical Internet Research* 23.8 (2021): e26256.

48. Yala, Adam, et al. "A deep learning mammography-based model for improved breast cancer risk prediction." *Radiology* 292.1 (2019): 60–66.

49. Bhardwaj, Priya, et al. "An investigational approach for the prediction of gastric cancer using artificial intelligence techniques: A systematic review." *Archives of Computational Methods in Engineering* 29.6 (2022): 4379–4400.

50. Kenner, Barbara J., et al. "Early detection of pancreatic cancer: Applying artificial intelligence to electronic health records." *Pancreas* 50.7 (2021): 916.

51. Cai, Xiongcai, et al. "Real-time prediction of mortality, readmission, and length of stay using electronic health record data." *Journal of the American Medical Informatics Association* 23.3 (2016): 553–561.

52. Chen, Jie, et al. "Use of an artificial neural network to predict risk factors of nosocomial infection in lung cancer patients." *Asian Pacific Journal of Cancer Prevention* 15.13 (2014): 5349–5353.

53. Kuo, Pao-Jen, et al. "Artificial neural network approach to predict surgical site infection after free-flap reconstruction in patients receiving surgery for head and neck cancer." *Oncotarget* 9.17 (2018): 13768.

54. Chen, Jian, et al. "Use of an artificial neural network to construct a model of predicting deep fungal infection in lung cancer patients." *Asian Pacific Journal of Cancer Prevention* 16.12 (2015): 5095–5099.

55. Payrovnaziri, Seyedeh Neelufar, et al. "Explainable artificial intelligence models using real-world electronic health record data: A systematic scoping review." *Journal of the American Medical Informatics Association* 27.7 (2020): 1173–1185.

56. Jevgenij, Gamper, Navid Alemi Koohbanani, Ksenija Benet, Ali Khuram, and Nasir Rajpoot. "Pannuke: An open pan-cancer histology dataset for nuclei instance segmentation and classification." *European Congress on Digital Pathology*.

57. Marschner, S., M. Datar, A. Gaasch, et al. "A deep image-to-image network organ segmentation algorithm for radiation treatment planning: Principles and evaluation." *Radiation Oncology* 17 (2022): 129. https://doi.org/10.1186/s13014-022-02102-6.

58. Tripathy, B. K., et al. "Brain MRI segmentation techniques based on CNN and its variants." *Brain Tumor MRI Image Segmentation Using Deep Learning Techniques*. Academic Press, 2022, 161–183.

59. Yang, Jinzhong, et al. "Auto-segmentation of low-risk clinical target volume for head and neck radiation therapy." *Practical Radiation Oncology* 4.1 (2014): e31–e37.

60. Mittauer, Kathryn, et al. "A new era of image guidance with magnetic resonance-guided radiation therapy for abdominal and thoracic malignancies." *Cureus* 10.4 (2018): e2422.

61. Kuisma, Anna, et al. "Validation of automated magnetic resonance image segmentation for radiation therapy planning in prostate cancer." *Physics and Imaging in Radiation Oncology* 13 (2020): 14–20.

62. Byrne, Mikel, et al. "Varian ethos online adaptive radiotherapy for prostate cancer: Early results of contouring accuracy, treatment plan quality, and treatment time." *Journal of Applied Clinical Medical Physics* 23.1 (2022): e13479.

63. Udapa, Jayaram, K., et al. "Combining natural and artificial intelligence for robust automatic anatomy segmentation: Application in neck and throat auto contouring" *Medical Physics*, 49.11 (2022): 7118–7149.

64. Bai, Ti, et al. "A proof-of-concept study of artificial intelligence–assisted contour editing." *Radiology: Artificial Intelligence* 4.5 (2022): e210214.

65. Sekerak, R. (2011). "Voxel" (Ed: J. S. Kreutzer, J. DeLuca, and B. Caplan, *Encyclopedia of Clinical Neuropsychology*), Springer, New York, NY. https://doi.org/10.1007/978-0-387-79948-3_82.

66. Kuznetsova, Svetlana, et al. "Structure guided deformable image registration for treatment planning CT and post stereotactic body radiation therapy (SBRT) Primovist®(Gd-EOB-DTPA) enhanced MRI." *Journal of Applied Clinical Medical Physics* 20.12 (2019): 109–118.

67. Sahgal, A., D. Roberge, D Schellenberg, et al. "The Canadian Association of Radiation Oncology scope of practice guidelines for lung, liver and spine stereotactic body radiotherapy." *Clinical Oncology* 24 (2012): 629–639.

68. Huertas, A., A. S. Baumann, F. Saunier-Kubs, et al. "Stereotactic body radiation therapy as an ablative treatment for inoperable hepatocellular carcinoma." *Radiotherapy and Oncology* 115 (2015): 211–216.

69. Furtado, Hugo, Elisabeth Steiner, Markus Stock, Dietmar Georg, and Wolfgang Birkfellner. "Real-time 2D/3D registration using kV-MV image pairs for tumor motion tracking in image guided radiotherapy." *Acta Oncologica* 52.7 (2013): 1464–1471.

70. Huang, Pu, Lin Su, Shuyang Chen et al. 2D ultrasound imaging based intra-fraction respiratory motion tracking for abdominal radiation therapy using machine learning, *Physics in Medicine & Biology* 64(18), 185006 (2019). DOI: 10.1088/1361-6560/ab33db.

71. Homma, Noriyasu, et al. "A new motion management method for lung tumor tracking radiation therapy." *WSEAS Transactions on Systems* 8.4 (2009): 471–480.

72. Steiner, E., C. Shieh, V. Caillet, et al. "Both four dimensional computed tomography and four-dimensional cone beam computed tomography under-predict lung target motion during radiotherapy." *Radiotherapy and Oncology* 135 (2019): 65–73.

73. Takahashi, W., S. Oshikawa, and S. Mori. "Real-time markerless tumour tracking with patient-specific deep learning using a personalised data generation strategy: Proof of concept by phantom study." *The British Journal of Radiology* 93.1109 (2020): 20190420.

74. Mori, S., R. Hirai, and Y. Sakata. "Simulated four-dimensional CT for markerless tumor tracking using a deep learning network with multi-task learning." *Physica Medica* 80 (2020): 151–158.

75. Kiser, Kendall J., Clifton D. Fuller, and Valerie K. Reed. "Artificial intelligence in radiation oncology treatment planning: A brief overview." *Journal of Medical Artificial Intelligence* 2:9 (2019): pp. 1–11. DOI: 10.21037/jmai.2019.04.02.

76. Fanou, Anna-Maria, et al. "Implementation, dosimetric assessment, and treatment validation of Knowledge-Based Planning (KBP) models in VMAT head and neck radiation oncology." *Biomedicines* 11.3 (2023): 762.

77. Wu, Binbin, et al. "Cross-institutional knowledge-based planning (KBP) implementation and its performance comparison to Auto-Planning Engine (APE)." *Radiotherapy and Oncology* 123.1 (2017): 57–62.

78. Wang, J., W. Hu, Z. Yang et al. "Is it possible for knowledge-based planning to improve intensity modulated radiation therapy plan quality for planners with different planning experiences in left-sided breast cancer patients?." *Radiation Oncology* 12 (2017): 85.

79. Li, Nan, et al. "Highly efficient training, refinement, and validation of a knowledge-based planning quality-control system for radiation therapy clinical trials." *International Journal of Radiation Oncology* Biology* Physics* 97.1 (2017): 164–172.

80. Giaddui, Tawfik, Huaizhi Geng, Quan Chen, Nancy Linnemann, et al. "Offline quality assurance for intensity modulated radiation therapy treatment plans for NRG-HN001 head and neck clinical trial using knowledge-based planning." *Advances in Radiation Oncology* 5.6 (2020): 1342–1349.

81. Fan, Jiawei, et al. "Automatic treatment planning based on three-dimensional dose distribution predicted from deep learning technique." *Medical Physics* 46.1 (2019): 370–381.

82. Chen, Xinyuan, et al. "A feasibility study on an automated method to generate patient-specific dose distributions for radiotherapy using deep learning." *Medical Physics* 46.1 (2019): 56–64.

83. Kajikawa, Tomohiro, et al. "Automated prediction of dosimetric eligibility of patients with prostate cancer undergoing intensity-modulated radiation therapy using a convolutional neural network." *Radiological Physics and Technology* 11 (2018): 320–327.

84. Tasci, E., Y. Zhuge K. Camphausen and A. V. Krauze. "Bias and class imbalance in oncologic data—towards inclusive and transferrable AI in large scale oncology data sets." *Cancers* 14 (2022): 2897. https://doi.org/10.3390/cancers14122897.

85. Deist, Timo M., A. Jochems, Johan van Soest, et al. "Infrastructure and distributed learning methodology for privacy-preserving multi-centric rapid learning health care: euroCAT." *Clinical and Translational Radiation Oncology* 4 (2017): 24–31.

86. Claessens, Michaël, et al. "Quality assurance for AI-based applications in radiation therapy." *Seminars in Radiation Oncology* 32.4. WB Saunders, 2022.

87. Luchini, C., A. Pea and A. Scarpa. "Artificial intelligence in oncology: Current applications and future perspectives." *British Journal of Cancer* 126 (2022): 4–9. https://doi.org/10.1038/s41416-021-01633-1.

88. https://radiologygroup.manipalhospitals.com/artificial-intelligence.

11

Melanoma Skin Cancer Identification on Embedded Devices Using Digital Hair Removal and Transfer Learning

Shinde Rupali Kiran and Nam Kim

11.1 Introduction

Cancer is a lethal disease in today's world. It is the third leading cause of death in humans, with a 78% mortality rate in later stages. Skin cancer is defined as an abnormal development of skin cells in the body caused by sunshine and UV radiation [1]. If not detected at an earlier stage, it quickly invades surrounding tissues and spreads to other bodily parts. Early detection of skin cancer improves outcomes and is associated with 99% overall survival (OS) [2, 3]. It is suggested that survival prospects are better in the early stages. According to the Skin Cancer Foundation (SCF), the global prevalence of skin cancer is increasing [4]. Over 3 million instances will be discovered worldwide in the year 2021.

One in five Americans may acquire skin cancer in their lifetime, according to SCF figures, since ozone layers are being destroyed [5]. Visual inspection and biopsy are the official methods for diagnosing cancer. Polarised light magnification via dermoscopy is used to assist with the main visual inspection. The important elements taken into account during tests include a patient's history, social habits, skin colour, occupation, ethnicity, and sun exposure. The probable worrisome lesion undergoes a biopsy in the lab. For both patients and doctors, this approach is unpleasant, time-consuming, and expensive. A skin biopsy might cost between $10 and $1000 without insurance [6]. To solve the aforementioned issues, a skin cancer detection system based on artificial intelligence (AI) is urgently needed.

The motivation behind this work is to simplify the skin cancer condition in its early stage; furthermore, the diagnosis process must be economical, user-friendly, and accurate. Visual inspection by an oncologist is challenging; the availability of experts in remote areas is low, moreover the diagnosis by biopsy is expensive. Therefore, with the help of AI in biomedical, the easy solution is developed with a device prototype.

It is suggested that AI-enabled computer-aided diagnostic techniques would revolutionize healthcare and medicine. Numerous studies have demonstrated clinician-level performance for disease diagnosis in medical imaging in the field of dermatology [7]. Deep learning has recently offered many end-to-end solutions for the detection of anomalies, including the detection of COVID-19, lung cancer, skin lesions, brain tumours, breast tumours, stomach ulcers, colon cancer, blood sugar predictions, heart disease predictions, and face mask detection. [8–13]. The last few years have seen advancements in technology

DOI: 10.1201/9781003450153-13

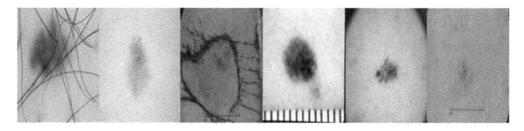

FIGURE 11.1
Challenging skin lesions from the dataset: a) hair artifact, b) low contrast, c) ink marker, d) ruler marker artifact, e) dark corner, f) low illumination.

that have enabled the collection of high-quality digital data on cancer patients all around the world using advanced imaging techniques, 3D imaging, high-resolution cameras, dermoscopy, and digital scanners. Providing a digital dataset of skin lesions for automated diagnosis is the International Skin Imaging Collaboration (ISIC) [14]. It includes melanoma and non-melanoma image datasets with HTTP API to download images and metadata. Some of the images in this dataset are noisy due to hair, ink mark, and ruler marks, as shown in Figure 11.1. Processing those images is challenging for the deep neural network (DNN) model. Therefore, there is a need for adequate dataset preprocessing.

A practising doctor in Solapur, India, named Dr. Anuja Padwal, validated devices from a medical standpoint. Patients have a good chance of surviving in the early stages, the doctor noted. There are fewer oncologists accessible in underdeveloped nations and increased skin cancer risks in India and Africa, where solar UV radiation is severe. As a result, economical medical care is required. If we are successful in commercialising this gadget, a dermatologist or general practitioner will use it for initial analysis.

The following are the chapter's main contributions:

- In order to improve the accuracy of the DNN model, we devised an effective technique for dataset cleaning utilising OpenCV operations. We called this approach the digital hair removal algorithm since it reduces the amount of the dataset while removing noise.
- With the transfer learning method, the MobileNet architecture in conjunction with the head model achieves excellent accuracy (99.36%) and no information loss.
- The model is put into practise and tested on a Raspberry Pi 4 IoT device equipped with a spy camera and NeoPixel 8-bit LED ring. The model is also precise and light, making it ideal for Internet of Things (IoT) applications.
- When compared to other designs like VGG16, MobilenNetV2, and InceptionV3, the DHR-MNet performs better.

11.2 Literature Review

Analysts and researchers have mainly focused on skin cancer classification using OpenCV and the deep learning model. In the early work, Friedman et al. proposed the ABCD abbreviation to offer nonprofessional or naive users a helpful mnemonic to support the early identification of the possibly treatable, most common type of skin cancer melanoma [15]. This ABCD abbreviation stands for asymmetry, border irregularity, color, and diameter of skin lesions. This rule is most appropriate to classify early, thin tumors and moles from benign pigmentation. Later, the ABCD rule expanded to ABCDE by introducing new characteristics evolving the lesion size [16]. Here evolving stands for a new or changing lesion .

Furthermore, Jensen et al. attempted to increase self-screen investigation by joining the ABCDE rule and the ugly duckling mark as the ABCDEF rule [17]. The letter "F" stands for a funny-looking mark. In [18], the authors presented using a genetic algorithm for unique feature extraction in skin images. These acquired features should be classified to see if the input image indicates a disease [19].

Using OpenCV and the deep learning model, analysts and researchers have mostly concentrated on skin cancer classification. The ABCD acronym was initially proposed by Friedman et al. to provide nonprofessional or inexperienced users with a useful mnemonic to facilitate the early detection of the most prevalent and potentially treatable kind of skin cancer, melanoma [15]. Asymmetry, border irregularity, colour, and diameter of skin lesions are all abbreviated as ABCD. The best application of this rule is to distinguish early, thin tumours and moles from benign pigmentation. Later, by adding new variables and evolving the lesion size, the ABCD rule was expanded to ABCDE [16]. Here, evolving refers to a brand-new or developing lesion. Additionally, Jensen et al. joined the ABCDE rule and the ugly duckling mark rule in an effort to increase self-screen investigation as the ABCDEF rule [17]. In [18], the authors presented using a genetic algorithm for unique feature extraction in skin images. These acquired features should be classified to see if the input image indicates a disease [19].

Artificial neural network (ANN) gains an important place among the classifiers [20, 21]. In this domain, researchers focused on architecture design to adapt it to the verification of samples containing a picture of a nervus and the classification of a dataset. In [22], Josue employed ANN with 99.23% accuracy using Fourier spectral information. Currently, convolutional neural network (CNN) has become famous for skin cancer detection. In [23], Marwan presented the CNN model with a novel regularizer to control classification complexity and achieved over 97% accuracy.

Furthermore, Akhilesh et al. improved accuracy by up to 98% using CNN and the color moments and texture feature using HAM10000 dataset with seven different classes [24]. Image segmentation for feature extraction is combined with GAN to improve classification [25]. In this paper, the author used ANN as a classifier. Lidia et al., in [26], used encoder and decoder architecture with CNN to remove hair by segmentation. This work compares the restored image with the original image to calculate performance, but the author ignores model accuracy.

Deep learning requires numerous annotated datasets even though it outperforms handcrafted feature representation in many ways. It is difficult to find a qualified oncologist and takes a lot of time to provide a lot of annotations. Many studies [27] [28–32] have looked into using transfer learning to classify skin diseases in an effort to alleviate this nuisance. There is no need for pricey cost annotation for the target data since transfer learning can filter important knowledge from a prior dataset to a raw target domain. In order to perform transfer learning on the ISIC 2019 dataset, Kessem et al. [29] developed a pre-trained model using the GoogLeNet architecture. They successfully categorized the eight different classes of skin lesions with the inception model and 94.2% accuracy. With the help of the MED-NODE dataset and an AlexNet pre-trained model, Hosny et al. built an automated system for classifying skin lesions. For classification, this model also included a dropout

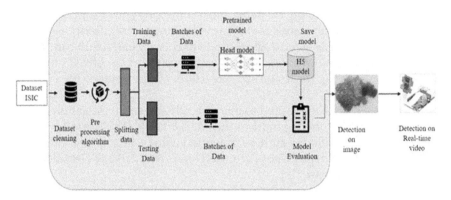

FIGURE 11.2
Dataset preprocessing, training, and evaluation of dataset diagram of the proposed DHR-MNet model.

layer and a softmax activation function. Pre-trained fine-tuning models from Imagenet include MobileNet, InceptionV3, Resnet50, EfficientNet, and MobilenetV2, among others. Researchers in [33] concentrate on those models with an accuracy rate of 84% for skin cancer applications. Furthermore, Hari et al.'s [34] use of the ResNet50 architecture increased accuracy and precision to 90% and 89%, respectively.

IoT is receiving a lot of interest in the 5G/6G internet age. We discovered that the modern world needs AI for healthcare IoT (HIoT) devices during the COVID-19 pandemic. AI for HIoT is difficult because IoT devices have memory restrictions and AI requires vast amounts of memory and computational power. Therefore, using the adjusted dataset and ImageNet, we proposed a simple and effective model for skin cancer as shown in figure 11.2. Here, we split dataset into 80:20 ratio.

11.3 Methodology

In the 5G/6G internet era, IoT is attracting a lot of attention. During the COVID-19 pandemic, we realised that the modern world need AI for IoT (Internet of Things) healthcare equipment. Because IoT devices have memory limitations and AI requires enormous quantities of memory and processing power, AI for IoT is challenging. We therefore suggested a straightforward and efficient model for skin cancer utilising the amended dataset and ImageNet.

11.3.1 ISIC Dataset

The International Skin Imaging Collaboration (ISIC) is an international group to improve skin cancer diagnosis. It is sponsored by the International Society for Digital Imaging of the Skin (ISIC)[35]. It contains dermoscopic images of skin lesions and it is mainly categorized into benign and malignant groups. Further, it is subcategorized into eight different types of skin cancers like carcinoma and melanoma, mole, etc. ISIC provides benchmark 4 different datasets published from the year 2016 to 2020. Here in this study the latest available dataset ISIC 2020 has been used for evaluation.

11.3.2 Preprocessing

Fur, dim lighting, and air bubbles are the main causes of noise in medical pictures [36, 37]. Feature extraction is impacted by the noise and produces erroneous findings when making predictions. Any duplicates and blurry photos should be removed from the dataset, which is then split into roughly an 80:20 training to testing ratio. The distribution of the dataset across two classes is shown in Figure 11.3.

11.3.3 Digital Hair Removal (HDR) Algorithm for Digital Shaving

Despite their importance, hair artifacts have not gotten enough attention in dermatoscopy images, where they are a serious concern. Various segmentation algorithms allow for efficient hair removal without information loss [26, 38, 39]. The suggested algorithm keeps important information while removing noise. We called it a "digital hair removal algorithm" because it shrinks the size of the source photos. This procedure entails thresholding using the morphological Black Hat filter operation and converting to grayscale images. The contour of a hair mask produces a picture. The inpaint() method in OpenCV allows you to restore the chosen area of an image using the surrounding area. In the final step, we took advantage of this function to obtain a consistent image with minimal information loss. Each stage of the algorithm is depicted in Figure 11.4.

11.3.4 Augmentation

This augmentation process is for dataset processing operations such as scaling, shear, resizing, rotation flipping, shear, and zooming on the ISIC dataset. It is necessary when the dataset size is small.

- Rescaling = 1./255 (for normalization),
- Zoom range = 0.15%,
- Shear range = 0.15 degree,
- Horizontal flip = True,

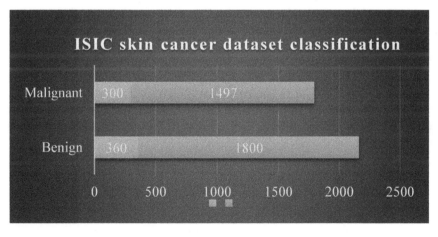

FIGURE 11.3
Dataset distribution.

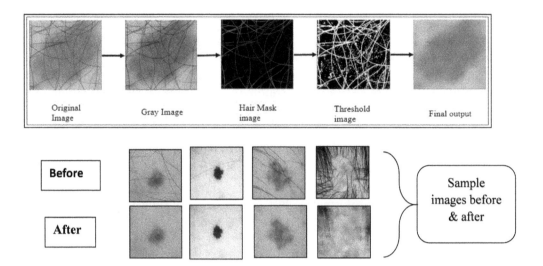

FIGURE 11.4

Digital hair removal algorithm: (a) original image before digital hair removal, (b) grayscale conversion, (c) with thresholding function, (d) inpaint function fills the gaps, and (e) final shaved image.

- Fill mode = nearest,
- Width shift range = 0.2 degree.

11.4 Model Architecture

The proposed model includes a hair removal algorithm and a MobileNet pretrained model with a predefined weight. We use the old weight and training model in the transfer learning approach by adding weights to the tensor. The head model is the output of the base model, which includes flatten layer, dense layers, and Leaky ReLU (Rectifier Linear Unit) activation function. It also helps in avoiding overfitting and underfitting. The flatten layer accepts input from the MobileNet model and feeds forward to the dense network. The Sigmoid is an activation function in the neural network. Detailed architecture of the proposed model is shown below in Figure 11.5. Dense layer sizes are 64, 32, and 2. Binary cross-entropy or log loss is the best-performing loss function for this model because there are just two classes for classification. It contrasts the probabilities predicted with the class output, which can either be 0 or 1. The score that penalizes the probabilities based on how far they are from the predicted value is then calculated [40]. The loss function is expressed in Equation (1). The complete architecture, shown in Figure 11.5, includes a deep, dense network and a backbone model.

$$\text{Log loss} = \frac{1}{N}\sum_{1}^{N}-\left(yi*\log\left(pi\right)+\left(1-yi\right)*log\left(1-pi\right)\right) \tag{1}$$

Here, pi is the probability of class malignant, and (1 − pi) is the probability of class benign.

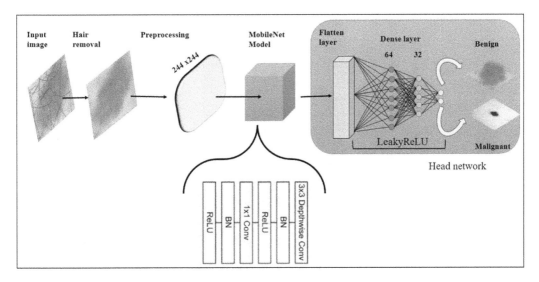

FIGURE 11.5
Proposed model architecture.

The popular deep learning–based library Keras, used on top of the TensorFlow model, is implemented. Spyder IDE integrated with the anaconda environment is used to run this network. All code is in Python, with NumPy, matplotlib, sklearn, and imutils packages used in this experiment.

11.4.1 H5 Model Format

Keras is a high-level neural network API that runs on Tensorflow. It is used to train the model. It builds the model and saves it with tensor weights; this model is in Hierarchical Data format (HDF5) and this is saved with .h5 extension. Hence, saved skincancer.h5 file acts like a .exe file on edge computing. In this study ARM processor is used for edge computing.

11.5 Experimental Setup

The Intel Core i5-7500 3.40GHz processor, Windows 10, 32 GB of RAM, and NVIDIA GeForce GTX 10050Ti graphics processors are used in this experiment. An IoT device to test the model is a Raspberry Pi 4 CPU with a 64-Gb SD card. To the camera port and main board, respectively, are fastened a spy camera and a NeoPixel ring. The ring's function is to capture a crisp image or video at any time, day or night. Three connecting pins—GND, 5V, and D1—are included with this ring and are connected to PINs 1, 6, and 12 of the Raspberry Pi 4 accordingly. The device is 9 × 6.3 × 3.5 cm in size. Figure 11.6 shows the gadget's front, interior, and nighttime views.

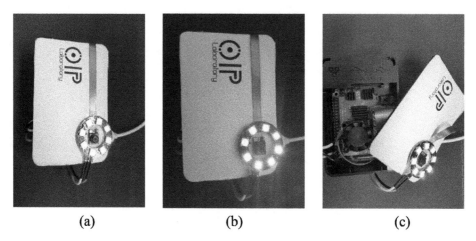

FIGURE 11.6
IoT-based skin cancer detection device: (a) front, (b) in low light, (c) inside view.

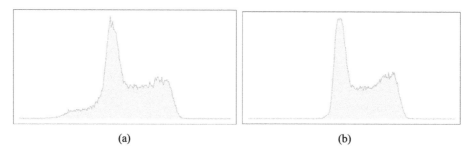

FIGURE 11.7
Histogram (pixel intensity vs. frequency) of the image before (a) and after (b) preprocessing.

11.5.1 Digital Hair Removal (DHR) Algorithm Analysis

The quality and precision of the suggested model are significantly impacted by the hair removal algorithm. To show performance, the learning curve is plotted both with and without a hair removal algorithm. The 162 MB size of the ISIC dataset before preprocessing was reduced to 36 MB. Additionally, the mean square root error (MSE) and peak signal-to-noise ratio (PSNR) values are 8.26 and 38.95, respectively. We noticed a dramatic reduction in dataset size, thus we called the approach a DHR. By removing unnecessary features and only training the model with the important portions of the images, this technique improved model accuracy and decreased training time. The histogram of the random image from the dataset in Figure 11.7 shows it both before and after processing. There is a loss of noise without affecting important information.

Figure 11.7 shows the image's histogram before and after preprocessing using the DHR algorithm. It shows that the image is uniformly dense, and the removal of hairs is because of lower intensity (i.e., black= 0); nevertheless, critical information is not affected much.

11.5.2 DHR-MNet Model Analysis

The following standard metrics have been applied in this manuscript to measure the performance of our system.

Dice similarity coefficient: The similarity measure between two samples of the segmented images.

$$DSC = 2*TP/\{(FP+TP) + (TP+FN)\} \tag{2}$$

Recall (sensitivity): It measures the fraction of retrieved relevant instances.

$$Sensitivity = TP/(TP + FN)$$

(3)Precision: It measures how many positive predictions are correct (true positives), i.e., how precise the model performs.

$$Precision = TP/(FP +TP)$$

(4)F1 Score: This is the harmonic mean of precision and recall.

$$F1Score = 2 * ((Recall * Precision) /(Recall + Precision)))$$

Specificity: It is a measure of how many actual negative predictions made are correct (true negatives)

$$Specificity = TN /(TN + FP)$$

(6)Accuracy: If the measured value is equal to the actual value, it is said to be highly accurate and with low errors.

$$Accuracy = (TN+TP) /(TN +TP FN + FP)$$

(7)ROC curve: An ROC curve (receiver operating characteristic curve) is a graph showing the performance of a classification model at all classification thresholds. It is a curve plot of recall vs. false positive rate.

AUC (area under the ROC curve): It represents the percentage of 2-D area within the entire ROC curve from the origin (0,0) to point (1,1).

All of the model performance matrices are displayed in Table 11.1. Figure 11.8 is a ROC curve, while Figure 11.8(b) shows the confusion matrix. The model is trained with batch size 16 and Epoch 50 for the evaluation. Fewer photos are in the malignant class in the

TABLE 11.1

DHR-MNet Model Performance with ImageNet Pretrained Model

Model	Accuracy (%)	Average Precision (AP)	Recall	F-1 score	Training time(s)	Model Size (KB)	Total parameter	ROC-AUC(%)
MobileNetV2	85	89	87	86	1637.3	56,139	6,273,202	0.937
VGG-16	85	88	86	86	17048.34	76,385	16,321,458	0.94
InceptionV3	80	83	88	83	5272.85	1,24,095	25,080,722	0.908
InceptionResNetV2	84	84	87	85	8945.21	2,42,301	56,795,474	0.929
Xception	82.2	84	84	84	6391.65	157,050	27,285,146	0.51
MobileNet	88	90	88	89	1885.62	50,439	6,441,266	0.949
MobileNetV3Small	74	82	90	79	**1521.64**	**7,074**	1,596,642	0.829
MobilenetV3Large	76	79	86	79	1854.94	17,859	4,309,490	0.844
DHR-MNet(Proposed)	**99.36**	**98.02**	**99**	**96**	2271.60	50,439	6,441,266	**0.989**

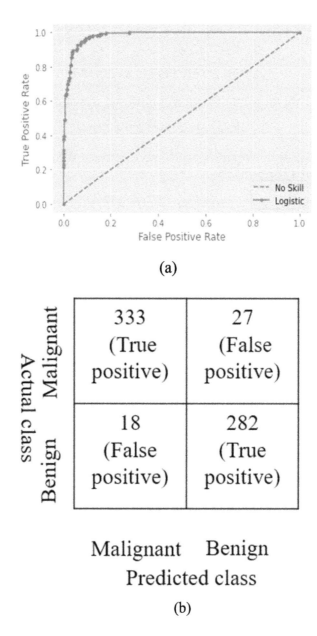

(a)

(b)

FIGURE 11.8
(a) Receiver operating characteristic curve (ROC curve), and (b) confusion matrix of the proposed model.

dataset, which is unbalanced. In this instance, it is required to check the ROC curve for model performance. Figure 11.8(a) displays no skills and improved accuracy as indicated by the blue line. The model's performance is measured by the ROC-AUC, or area under the ROC curve. It is between 0 and 1. The optimum value is 1; however, our model indicates 98.9. Thus, we draw the conclusion that our model is precise and accurate.

A deeper analysis of the learning curve reveals an improvement in accuracy every epoch. Due to Leaky ReLU activation after each dense layer, this curve demonstrates a well tailored model without overfitting or underfitting. Accuracy and loss were plotted

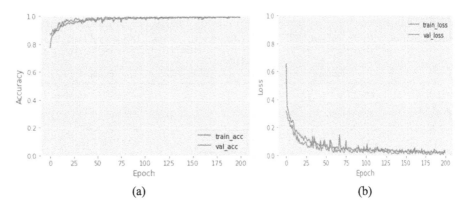

FIGURE 11.9
(a) Accuracy gain, (b) loss reduction per epoch.

each epoch in Figures 11.9(a) and (b). Our model is the greatest option for cancer diagnosis on IoT devices because it is the most accurate, lightest, and fastest model available.

11.6 Comparative Study

In order to conduct a comparison analysis, we examined both current deep AI-based models and conventional approaches. Some characteristics taken into consideration for comparison include methodology, accuracy, precision, IoT interoperability, and ROC-AUC. Table 11.2 contains the detailed analysis.

11.7 Conclusion

This study provides a brand-new DHR-MNet technique for dermoscopy picture hair removal and skin cancer classification on embedded platforms like the Raspberry Pi 4. For dataset preprocessing, we have provided an effective digital hair removal approach built on OpenCV operations. Due to the DHR method, the MobileNet neural network with the head architecture displays excellent result accuracy of 99.36%. In low-powered computing systems where accuracy matters more, this research emphasizes the significance of a lightweight model that keeps model size and training time low. The suggested prototype is accurate, convenient, affordable, and quick. Additionally, the hyperparameters are optimized by varying optimizer type (i.e. Adam/SGD), learning rate, and weighted decay values. Finally, in order to evaluate and contrast their performance, we ran a statistical test.

With the exception of training time, DHR-MNet outperforms MobileNetV3Small the best. The instrument is now based on a Raspberry Pi microprocessor, but we intend to explore other IoT devices like the Jetson Nano or Google Coral Board in future work. AI model implementation is achievable with fog and cloud computing. To lower the edge computational cost, we would assess the optimal cloud computing platform for deep learning. The

TABLE 11.2

Comparative Study with Proposed DHR-MNet Model with Other Traditional and AI Methods

Author	Method	Accuracy (%)	ROC-AUC	Dataset	IoT Compatible
R.Nilkamal et al. [41]	ABCD	90	–	–	yes
T. Dang et al. [42]	ABCD	96.6	–	ISIC	Yes
J. Bandic et al. [43]	ABCDE	81.82	–	121 skin lesions	Yes
K. Kumar et al. [44]	ANN	97.4	–	HAM10000 & PH2	Yes
J. López-Leyva et al. [22]	ANN	99.23	97	Edinburgh Dermofit Library	Yes
Adekanmi et al. [45]	FCN-Densenet	98	99	HAM10000	No
Pham et al. [46]	EfficientNetB4-CLF	89.97	–	CIFAR-10	No
Silvana et al. [47]	IR camera & segmentation	91.5	–	400 images	Yes
Andre et al. [48]	CNN-PA	72.1	91	Edinburgh Dermofit Library	Yes
A.Uzama et al. [1]	GLCM-SVM	95	–	20 images	Yes
Bogdan et al. [49]	Deep uncertainty Estimation for skin cancer	98	–	ISIC	
U. Rehman et al. [50]	K-mean-CNN	97.9 & 97.4	–	DermIS & DermQuest	Yes
A. Saleh et al. [51]	YOLOv4	98.9	–	ISIC 2018&2016	No
S. Parvathaneri et al. [52]	MobilenetV2-LSTM	90.72	–	HAM10000	Yes
Marwan [23]	CNN	97.5	93	ISIC	Yes
Proposed	DHR-MNet	99.56	98.4	ISIC	Yes

suggested approach can identify skin cancer in a photograph, but other skin issues including warts, acne, pimples, and eczema can also be present. The embedded device's next task is to accurately detect more than 25 skin disorders. This approach is exact, simple to apply, reliable, efficient, quick, and advantageous for clinicians. We anticipate that this approach will significantly lessen the strain on the healthcare system in real time.

References

1. U. B. Ansari, "Skin cancer detection using image processing," *International Research Journal of Engineering and Technology (IRJET)*,4 pp. 2875–2881, 2017.
2. M. Goyal, "Artificial intelligence-based image classification methods for diagnosis of skin cancer: Challenges and opportunities," *Computers in Biology and Medicine*, vol. 127, 1–11 2020.
3. U. Leiter and G. Claus, "Epidemiology of melanoma and nonmelanoma skin cancer—The role of sunlight,"Jorg Reichrath *Sunlight Vitamin D and Skin Cancer*. New York, NY: Springer, pp. 89–103, 2008.
4. "S.C. foundation," [Online]. Available: https://www.skincancer.org/. [Accessed 2 June 2022].
5. "Radiation Ultraviolet (UV) radiation and skin cancer," WHO, [Online]. Available: www:// who.int/. [Accessed 6 June 2022].
6. "How much does a biopsy cost?," CostHelper, [Online]. Available: https://health.costhelper .com. [Accessed 6 June 2022].

7. A. Esteva, B. Uprel, R. Novoa, J. Ko, S. Swetter, H. Blau and S. Thrun, "Dermatologist-level classification of skin cancer with deep neural networks," *Nature Letter*, vol. 542, pp. 115–118, 2017.

8. R. Shinde, M. Alam, S. Park, S. Park and N. Kim, "Intelligent IoT (IIoT) device to identifying suspected COVID-19 infections using sensor fusion algorithm and real-time mask detection based on the enhanced MobileNetV2 model," *MDPI Healthcare*, vol. 10, no. 3, 1–18 2022.

9. C. Jacobs and B. Ginneken, "Google's lung cancer AI: A promising tool that needs further validation," *Nature Reviews Clinical Oncology*, vol. 16, pp. 532–533, 2019.

10. S. McKinney, M. Sieniek, V. Godbole and S. Shetty, "International evaluation of an AI system for breast cancer screening," *Nature*, vol. 577, pp. 89–94, 2020.

11. D. Połap, "Analysis of skin marks through the use of intelligent things," *IEEE Access*, vol. 7, pp. 149355–149363, 2019.

12. S. A. Zadeh, E. Fornaciari and N. Bagherian, "DeepSurvNet: Deep survival convolutional network for brain cancer survival rate classification based on histopathological images," *Medical & Biological Engineering & Computing*, vol. 58, pp. 1034–1045, 2020.

13. M. Abràmoff, P. Lavin and M. Birch, "Pivotal trial of an autonomous AI-based diagnostic system for detection of diabetic retinopathy in primary care offices," *NPJ Digital Medicine*, vol. 1, no. 39, 1–8 2018.

14. "ISIC archive," International Skin Imaging Collaboration, [Online]. Available: https://www.isic-archive.com/#!/topWithHeader/wideContentTop/main. [Accessed 3 June 2022].

15. R. J. Friedman, D. S. Rigel and A. W. Kopf, "Early detection of malignant melanoma: The role of physician examination and self-examination of the skin," *A Cancer Journal for Clinicians*, vol. 35, no. 3, pp. 130–151, 1985.

16. N. R. Abbasi, H. M. Shaw, D. S. Rigel, R. Friedman, W. H. McCarthy, I. Osman, A. W. Kopf and D. Polsky, "Early diagnosis of cutaneous melanoma: Revisiting the ABCD criteria," *Journal of the American Medical Association*, vol. 292, no. 22, pp. 2771–2776, 2004.

17. J. D. Jensen and B. Elewski, "The ABCDEF rule: Combining the 'ABCDE Rule' and the 'Ugly Duckling Sign' in an effort to improve patient self-screening examinations," *Journal of Clinical and Aesthetic Dermatology*, vol. 8, no. 2, pp. 15–25, 2015.

18. Q. Ain, B. Xue, H. Al-Sahaf and M. Zhang, "Genetic programming for feature selection and feature construction in skin cancer image classification," in *15th Pacific Rim International Conference on Artificial Intelligence*, Nanjing, 2018.

19. P. Shahi, S. Yadav, N. Singh and N. P. Singh, "Melanoma skin cancer detection using various classifiers," in *2018 5th IEEE Uttar Pradesh Section International Conference on Electrical, Electronics and Computer Engineering (UPCON)*, Gorakhpur, India, 2018.

20. N. Dey, A. Rajinikanth, S. Shour and M. R. Tavares, "Social group optimization supported segmentation and evaluation of skin melanoma images," *Symmetry*, vol. 10, no. 2, pp. 51–60, 2018.

21. T. J. Brinker, A. Hekler, H. Enk, J. Klode, A. Hauschild and C. Berking, "Convolutional neural network trained with dermoscopic images performed on par with 145 dermatologists in a clinical melanoma image classification task," *European Journal of Cancer*, vol. 111, pp. 148–154, 2019.

22. J. A. López-Leyva, E. Guerra-Rosas and J. Álvarez-Borrego, "Multi-class diagnosis of skin lesions using the fourier spectral information of images on additive color model by artificial neural network," *IEEE Access*, vol. 9, pp. 35207–35216, 2021.

23. M. A. Albahar, "Skin lesion classification using convolutinal netral network with novel regularizer," *IEEE Access*, vol. 7, pp. 38306–38313, 2019.

24. A. K. Sharma, S. Tiwari, G. Aggarwal, N. Goenka, A. Kumar, P. Chakrabarti, T. Chakrabarti, R. Gono and Z. Leonowicz, "Dermatologist-level classification of skin cancer using cascaded ensembling of convolutional neural network and handcrafted features based deep neural network," *IEEE Access*, vol. 10, pp. 17920–, 2022.

25. M. U. Rehman, S. H. Khan, R. Danish, Z. Abbas and A. Zafar, "Classification of skin lesion by interference of segmentation and convolotion neural network," in *2nd International Conference on Engineering Innovation (ICEI)*, Bangkok, Thailand, 2018.

26. L. Talavera-Martínez, P. Bibiloni and G.-H. Manuel, "Hair segmentation and removal in dermoscopic images using deep learning," *IEEE Access*, vol. 9, pp. 2694–2704, 2021.
27. J. Bian, S. Zhang, S. Wang, J. Zhang and J. Guo, "Skin lesion classification by multi-view filtered transfer learning," *IEEE Access*, vol. 9, pp. 66052–66061, 2021.
28. A. A. Mahbod, G. Schaefer, C. Wang, R. Ecker, G. Dorffner and I. Ellinger, "Investigating and exploiting image resolution for transfer learning-based skin lesion classification," *arXiv:2006.14715*, 2020.
29. M. A. Kassem, K. M. Hosny and M. M. Fouad, "Skin lesions classification into eight classes for ISIC 2019 using deep convolutional neural network and transfer learning," *IEEE Access*, vol. 8, pp. 114822–114832, 2019.
30. K. M. Hosny, M. Kassem and M. Foaud, "Classification of skin lesions using transfer learning and augmentation with alex-net," *PLoS One*, vol. 14, no. 5, 1–17 2019.
31. A. M. Alqudah, H. Alquraan and I. A. Qasmieh, "Segmented and non-segmented skin lesions classification using transfer learning and adaptive moment learning rate technique using pretrained convolutional neural network," *Journal of Biomimetics, Biomaterials and Biomedical Engineering*, vol. 42, pp. 67–78, 2019.
32. K. M. Hosny, M. A. Kassem and M. Fouad, "Classification of skin lesions into seven classes using transfer learning with AlexNet," *Journal of Digital Imaging*, vol. 33, no. 5, pp. 1325–1334, 2019.
33. S. Jain, U. Singhania, B. Tripathy, E. Nasr, M. Aboudaif and A. Kamrani, "Deep learning-based transfer learning for classification of skin cancer," *Sensors*, vol. 21, no. 23, pp. 8142–, 2021.
34. H. K. Kondaveeti and P. Edupuganti, "Skin cancer classification using transfer learning," in *2020 IEEE International Conference on Advent Trends in Multidisciplinary Research and Innovation (ICATMRI)*, Buldhana, India, 2020.
35. A. Ray, "Skin cancer malignant vs benign," Kaggle.com, 2020. [Online]. Available: https://www.kaggle.com/datasets/abhikray/skin-cancer-malignant-vs-benign?select=test.
36. H. Lee and Y. P. Chen, "Image based computer aided diagnosis system for cancer detection," *Expert Systems with Applications*, vol. 42, no. 12, pp. 5356–5365, 2015.
37. R. Ashraf, S. Afzal, A. U. Rehman, S. Gul, J. Baber, M. Bakhtyar, I. Mehmood, O.-Y. Song and M. Maqsood, "Region-of-interest based transfer learning assisted framework for skin cancer detection," *IEEE Access*, vol. 8, pp. 147858–147871, 2020.
38. D. Kim and B. Hong, "Unsupervised feature elimination via generative adversarial networks: Application to hair removal in melanoma classification," *IEEE Access*, vol. 9, pp. 42610–42620.
39. J. Jaworek-Korjakowska and T. Ryszard, "Hair removal from dermoscopic color images," *Bio-Algorithms and Med-Systems*, vol. 9, no. 2, pp. 53–58, 2019.
40. R. V. Soans and Y. Fukumizu, "Improved facial keypoint regression using attention modules," in *Communications in Computer and Information Science*, Frontiers of Computer Vision, 2022, pp. 182–196.
41. N. Ramteke and S. Jain, "ABCD rule based automatic computer-aided skin cancer," *International Journal Computer Technology & Applications*, vol. 4, no. 4, pp. 691–697, 2013.
42. T. Dang, B. Prasath, L. Hieu and H. Nguyen, "Melanoma skin cancer detection method based on adaptive principal curvature, colour normalisation and feature extraction with the ABCD rule," *Journal of Digital Imaging*, vol. 33, pp. 574–585, 2020.
43. J. Bandic, S. Kovacevic, R. Karabeg, A. Lazarov and D. Opric, "Teledermoscopy for skin cancer prevention: A comparative study of clinical and teledermoscopic diagnosis," *Acta Informatica Medica*, vol. 28, no. 1, pp. 37–41, 2020.
44. K. Manoj, A. Mohammed, A. Rayed, S. Purushottam and D. Vikas, "A DE-ANN inspired skin cancer detection approach using fuzzy C-means clustering," *Mobile Networks and Applications*, vol. 25, pp. 1319–1329, 2020.
45. A. Adegun and S. Viriri, "FCN-based densenet framework for automated detection and classification of skin lesions in dermoscopy images," *IEEE Access*, vol. 8, pp. 150377–150396, 2020.
46. T. Pham, A. Doucet, C. M. Luong, C. Tran and V. D. Hoang, "Improving skin-disease classification based on customized loss function combined with balanced mini-batch logic and real-time image augmentation," *IEEE Access*, vol. 8, pp. 150725–150737, 2020.

47. S. Díaz, T. Krohmer, A. Moreira, S. E. Godoy and E. Figueroa, "An instrument for accurate and non-invasive screening of skin cancer based on multimodal imaging," *IEEE Access*, vol. 7, pp. 176646–176657, 2019.

48. A. Esteva, B. Kuprel and R. Novoa, "Dermatologist-level classification of skin cancer with deep neural networks," *Nature*, vol. 542, pp. 115–118, 2017.

49. B. Mazoure, A. Mazoure and J. Bédard, "DUNEScan: A web server for uncertainty estimation in skin cancer detection with deep neural networks," *Scientific Reports*, vol. 12, no. 179, pp. 1–10, 2022.

50. R. Ashraf, S. Afzal, A. U. Rehman, S. Gul, J. Baber, M. Bakhtyar, I. Mehmood, O.-Y. Song and M. Maqsood, "Region-of-interest based transfer learning assisted framework for skin cancer detection," *IEEE Access*, vol. 8, pp. 147858–147871, 2020.

51. A. Saleh, N. Nudrat, I. Aun, H. Y. Muhammad and T. M. Muhammad, "Melanoma lesion detection and segmentation using YOLOv4-DarkNet and active contour," *IEEE Access*, vol. 8, pp. 198403–198414, 2020.

52. P. N. Srinivasu, G. S. Jalluri, F. I. Muhammad, A. K. Bhoi, W. Kim and J. J. Kang, "Classification of skin disease using deep learning neural networks with MobileNet V2 and LSTM," *Sensors*, vol. 21, no. 8, pp. 1–27, 2021.

12

A Deep Hybrid System for Effective Diagnosis of Breast Cancer

Adyasha Sahu, Pradeep Kumar Das, and Sukadev Meher

12.1 Introduction

Breast cancer is a life-threatening disease that poses a substantial threat to the health of women on a global scale. The World Health Organization (WHO) reports that female breast cancer has a fifth-place fatality rate and ranks second in terms of incidence after lung cancer. It begins in the breast tissue and is characterized by irregular and unregulated cell proliferation, forming a tumor, which may be benign or malignant [19, 23, 2]. Non-cancerous benign breast tumors form inside the breast tissue and grow slowly, with no ability to spread to other regions of the body. In contrast, malignant are cancerous growths characterized by unregulated cell division, with the ability to invade neighboring tissues and spread to other regions of the body. While benign tumors are usually not life-threatening and do not require rigorous treatment, malignant tumors can be deadly if not diagnosed and treated early. It is critical to distinguish between benign and malignant breast tumors since early detection and adequate medical intervention are critical for establishing the best course of action and ensuring optimal patient outcomes [21].

Mammography and ultrasound both serve as important imaging modalities for the early identification of breast cancer, with each providing significant advantages [22]. Mammography, a low-dose X-ray imaging technique, emphasizes detecting small abnormalities and calcifications, allowing malignancies to be detected before they become palpable [23]. However, it is less effective in dense breast tissue. Ultrasound, which uses sound waves to capture breast images, separates the cysts from solid masses. It is very useful particularly when mammograms produce ambiguous results due to dense breast tissue. It helps with further classification of breast cancer and accurate biopsy guidance. These modalities work together to provide a complete strategy for improving diagnostic accuracy, minimizing false positives, and promoting timely treatment, ultimately improving patient outcomes in breast cancer diagnosis [17].

In the last decade, deep learning, especially transfer learning (TL), has grown as a prominent and rapidly increasing medical image processing research area [18, 20, 4, 17, 7]. A number of researchers have focused on automated breast cancer diagnosis employing a computer-aided design (CAD) framework. In 2022, Thawkar [24] came up with an innovative algorithm of hybridization of the Crow search algorithm and Harris Hawks optimization that can handle the convergence challenge with notable breast cancer identification accuracy. In addition, popular ANN and SVM classifiers effectively classify the breast masses. In the same vein, a multimodal approach proposed by Muduli et al. [17]

DOI: 10.1201/9781003450153-14

184

came under the spotlight, which used both ultrasound and mammogram images to detect breast cancer with a five-layered deep CNN architecture (4 convolution layer followed by a fully connected layer). Meanwhile, a comprehensive framework was suggested by Houby et al. [10], which employed several pre-processing techniques like median filter (3×3), contrast enhancement with CLACHE, extraction of ROI, and data augmentation for substantial improvement of the image prior to feeding the CNN module that constitutes 3 convolution, 4 max-pool, and 3 fully-connected layers. Sun et al. [23] suggested a novel multi-view CNN featuring general convolution along with dilated convolution, which efficiently classified mammogram images by regulating the false detection through a penalty term. A modified DenseNet structure, named DenseNet-II, was presented by Li et al. [14] for efficient breast cancer identification and reduction of false detection. An ensemble breast cancer detection technique was suggested by Malebary et al. [16] that dealt with low-contrast images in a great way and validated the performance with different mammogram databases. A number of researchers and scientists have also employed ultrasound pictures to diagnose breast cancer, which is another less costly imaging method [12, 1, 3, 26, 11, 15]. Byra et al. propose a transfer learning framework in 2021 [3]. Here, a pre-trained convolutional neural network (CNN) can effectively reduce the trainable parameters by adding a deep representation scaling (DRS) layer between its component parts while enabling smooth information flow. By tweaking the DRS layer's parameters and improving the underlying pre-trained network, this novel technique enhances the performance of the network.

Substantial developments in machine (ML) and deep learning (DL) have opened the door for more precise and prompt identification [8, 5]. But recently, transfer learning (TL) has emerged as the favored method in medical imaging since it neither needs an additional segmentation phase like ML approaches nor a huge database for training like DL [6, 9]. It performs notably even with small datasets. Though some of these methods give a notable performance, there is still scope for improvement. With this motivation, we came up with a deep hybrid system for effective identification of breast cancer.

12.1.1 Contributions

The primary contributions of the proposed work are listed below.

- A deep hybrid framework is proposed in this chapter for more accurate breast cancer diagnosis. In this case, an efficient deep CNN network is employed to extract deep features along with a random forest classifier to boost performance by using the benefits of each.

- In this work, a lightweight, efficient CNN, ShuffleNet, is used to extract deep features. Pointwise group convolution and Channel shuffling improve the performance and make it faster. In addition, the random forest is used for classification instead of the softmax layer.

- The breast cancer diagnosis process is divided into two steps: abnormality detection (separating abnormal and normal cases) and malignancy detection (separating malignant from normal and benign).

- A 5-fold cross-validation using five performance measuring metrics is presented instead of showing the performance of a single observation for comparative performance analysis in a fair way.

- The proposed work is validated on two different imaging modalities, ultrasound and mammogram, to illustrate the robustness of the suggested scheme.

The subsequent portions of this work are methodically arranged for clarity and cohesion. Section 12.2 describes an efficient deep learning–based system for breast cancer classification integrating ShuffleNet-based feature extraction and RF-based classification. Section 12.3 concisely describes the dataset used in this work. Section 12.4 presents a full exposition of experimental results supported by insightful discussions. Finally, Section 12.5 concludes the chapter's results and contributions in a concise manner.

12.2 Proposed Method

The current section of the chapter illustrates an efficient hybrid framework to diagnose and categorize breast cancer more precisely. TL algorithms have been employed often in recent years for automatic disease identification due to their promising results even with small datasets. The suggested methodology consists of two important stages: ShuffleNet-based feature extraction followed by random forest–based classification. Schematic of the proposed breast cancer detection framework is presented in Figure 12.1.

12.2.1 Feature Extraction

Convolutional neural networks (CNNs) have made important advancements in the field of deep learning. The standard deep learning paradigm and transfer learning are two different paradigms where CNNs are used. In the conventional method, the complete CNN is trained from scratch, requiring a sizable dataset. Due to the small size of breast cancer databases, this strategy is less advantageous. Transfer learning, in contrast, makes use of neural networks that have already been trained in the source domain. With this method, there is no longer a need to start from scratch while training a network. The pre-trained model can be improved by transferring knowledge from a source domain to a target domain, such as medical picture datasets. Here, we have employed ShuffleNet for effective deep feature extraction. ShuffleNet, a small and computationally effective CNN model developed by Zhang et al. [25], uses channel shuffling. Some key characteristics and the detailed architecture of ShuffleNet is explained as follows.

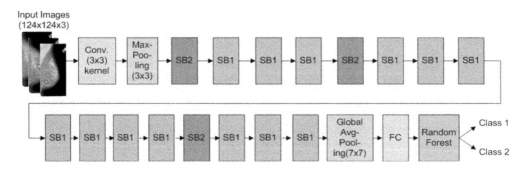

FIGURE 12.1
Proposed breast cancer detection framework.

12.2.1.1 Channel Shuffle for Group Convolution

Group convolution and depth-wise separable convolutions are commonly used building blocks in most network architecture, resulting in an effective trade-off between performance and computational cost.

Depth-wise separable convolutions have not entirely considered 1×1 pointwise convolutions. However, in group convolutions, each input channel can be operated within the respective channel groups, which yields reduced computational complexity. However, when many group convolutions are stacked together, some particular channel outputs are obtained from a small portion of input channels.

Figure 12.2 (a) represents a case where two group convolutions stack together. Here, the output of a specific group relies only on the inputs within the same group, restricting the flow of information within that group. However, the case shown in Figure 12.2 (b) illustrates the group convolution where input and output channels are fully connected to each other. Here, the second layer of group convolution (GC2) receives the information from all the groups after the first layer of group convolution (GC1). To make the process more efficient, each channel is split into different subgroups in a group and then connected to each group with different subgroups in the next layer, as shown in Figure 12.2 (c). Here, the channel shuffling allows the flow of information among the groups. The channel shuffle concept can build efficient structures with several group convolution layers.

12.2.1.2 ShuffleNet Unit

Figure 12.3 represents basic building blocks of ShuffleNet units. Figure 12.3 (a) represents the ShuffleNet unit (SB1) in which pointwise group-convolution and channel-shuffling is applied in place of 1×1 convolution. The second pointwise group convolution is employed so that the channel dimension can be modified accordingly to correlate with the shortcut path. Figure 12.3 (b) shows the structure of the ShuffleNet block (SB2) with stride 2. Here, an average pooling is employed on the shortcut path having size 3. Channel concatenation, which has a minor additional computational expense, is used to increase the channel's dimension rather than element-wise addition.

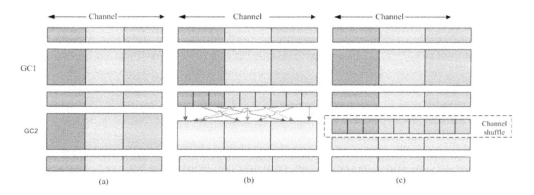

FIGURE 12.2
Channel shuffle with two stack group convolutions (GConv) [25]: (a) two stack convolution layers within a group; (b) the input channels are entirely related to the output channels (GConv2 collects data from various groups); (c) channel shuffling among groups.

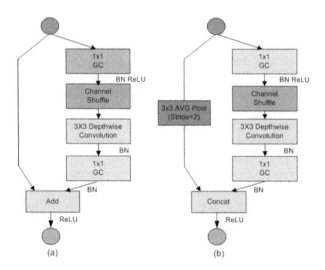

12.2.1.3 Architecture

The ShuffleNet network, as depicted in Figure 12.1, essentially consists of three stages, each of which is made up of a stack of SB1 and SB2. One SB2 block is followed by three SB1 blocks in the first stage, one SB2 block is followed by seven SB1 blocks in the second stage, and one SB2 block is followed by three SB1 blocks in the third stage. The ShuffleNet Unit and channel shuffle for group convolution are two additional features that help this network perform better while requiring less computing effort.

12.2.2 Classification

In TL techniques, the last softmax layer or classification layer is used for classification. Though it achieves commendable performance even with a small dataset, its performance can be improved further by employing any machine learning techniques like random forest for classification, complementing the benefits of both the transfer learning and the machine learning approaches. In this chapter, RF is used in the classification layer of ShuffleNet to efficiently classify breast cancer while preserving the pros of both models. Random forest (RF) is a widely recognized machine learning classification algorithm that combines the decision of numerous trees, as the name implies. To produce a final prediction that is more precise and stable, it combines the predictions of various decision trees. The core idea behind it is to use a variety of different trees' collective expertise to overcome the limitations of a single decision tree. With the help of a randomly selected vector from the input data, each tree is independently formed.

If the dataset contains a total of f_t number of features, RF chooses for fc features at random, where fc < ft. The root node is determined by choosing the feature with the highest information gain out of these features. Subsequently, this root node undergoes branching into child nodes. The result of this iterative process, which repeats T_n times, is a forest made up of T_n trees. After the tree is finished, RF categorizes the input vectors based on the ensemble's average prediction probability. Figure 12.4 shows this procedure in pictorial form. This iterative process recurs T_n times, culminating in a forest comprising T_n trees.

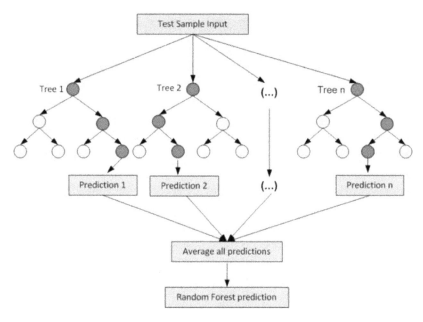

FIGURE 12.4
Schematic of random forest.

FIGURE 12.5
Mammogram images of three different classes taken from [13]: (a) normal, (b) benign and (c) malignant.

Once the tree is constructed, RF classifies input vectors by taking the average of prediction score of all the trees.

12.3 Datasets

Two distinct publicly available standard databases, Digital Database of Screening Mammograph (mini-DDSM) and BUSI are used for performance evaluation for mammogram and ultrasound images, respectively. In this work, for performance evaluation in small dataset, 200 images are taken from each class of benign, malignant, and normal to form a subset of 600 images from mini-DDSM dataset. In the same way, by extracting 130 images from each of three classes of BUSI, a subset is constituted with 390 images for evaluation. Figures 12.5 and 12.6 show the images of three different classes taken from respective datasets.

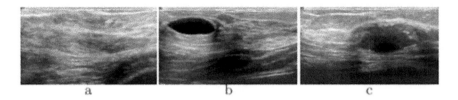

FIGURE 12.6
Ultrasound images of three different classes taken from [2]: (a) normal, (b) benign and (c) malignant.

TABLE 12.1

Performance Evaluation for Abnormality Detection in the Mini-DDSM Dataset

Methods	Specificity (%)	F1 Score	Accuracy (%)	Precision (%)	Sensitivity (%)
Vgg16	96.50	0.9787	97.17	98.24	97.50
ResNet18	97.00	0.9812	97.50	98.49	97.75
ShuffleNet	97.50	0.9824	97.67	98.74	97.75
Vgg16+DT	96.50	0.9812	97.50	98.25	98.00
ResNet18+DT	97.50	0.9837	97.83	98.74	98.00
ShuffleNet+DT	97.50	0.9849	98.00	98.74	98.25
Vgg16+RF	97.00	0.9837	97.83	98.50	98.25
ResNet18+RF	97.50	0.9849	98.00	98.74	98.25
ShuffleNet+RF	**98.00**	**0.9874**	**98.33**	**98.99**	**98.50**

12.4 Results and Discussion

This part presents a thorough comparison analysis of breast cancer detection performance using both mammograms and ultrasound images. We examine the shortcomings by comparing the performance of the suggested hybrid strategy to other well-known transfer learning networks and alternative hybrid approaches using various combinations. Using measures like specificity, F1 score, sensitivity, precision, and accuracy, we determine the quantifiable performance of the suggested strategy and the comparative approaches. A 5-fold cross-validation approach is used to ensure in order to assure fair evaluation for both abnormality and malignancy diagnosis.

To provide a genuine and unbiased comparison, all experimental methods are carried out on a specialized platform. The simulation is run on a machine equipped with an Intel(R) Core(TM) i7-11700 CPU running at 2.50GHz, driven by an NVIDIA T400 GPU with 8GB memory and backed by 16 GB of RAM. The experiments are carried out using the programming tool MATLAB R2020b. The experimentation in this context involves a maximum of 60 epochs as the training cycle, which is regulated by a learning rate of 0.0001. In addition, the minimum batch size is set at 64. We use this platform consistently across all approaches to ensure a fair and authentic comparative assessment.

Tables 12.1 and 12.2 exhibit the results of the studies addressing both abnormality and malignancy identification for the mini-DDSM database, respectively. The extensive study of the tables clearly shows that the suggested strategy regularly outperforms alternative comparison methods across all performance measures. Notably, the suggested technique

TABLE 12.2

Performance Evaluation for Malignancy Detection in the MINI-DDSM Dataset

Methods	Specificity (%)	F1 Score	Accuracy (%)	Precision (%)	Sensitivity (%)
Vgg16	95.50	0.9526	95.25	95.02	95.00
ResNet18	96.00	0.9600	96.00	96..00	96.00
ShuffleNet	97.00	0.9676	96.75	96.52	96.00
Vgg16+DT	95.50	0.9574	95.75	95.98	96.00
ResNet18+DT	96.00	0.9648	96.50	96.97	97.00
ShuffleNet+DT	97.00	0.9700	97.00	97.00	97.00
Vgg16+RF	96.00	0.9600	96.00	96.00	96.00
ResNet18+RF	96.50	0.96740	96.75	96.98	97.00
ShuffleNet+RF	**97.50**	**0.9750**	**97.50**	**97.50**	**97.50**

TABLE 12.3

Performance Evaluation for Abnormality Detection in the BUSI Dataset

Methods	Specificity (%)	F1 Score	Accuracy (%)	Precision (%)	Sensitivity (%)
Vgg16	81.54	0.9119	88.21	90.84	91.54
ResNet18	87.69	0.9405	92.05	93.87	94.23
ShuffleNet	89.23	0.9441	92.56	94.59	94.23
Vgg16+DT	82.31	0.9178	88.97	91.25	92.31
ResNet18+DT	88.46	0.9423	92.31	94.23	94.23
ShuffleNet+DT	90.77	0.9498	93.33	95.35	94.62
Vgg16+RF	83.08	0.9237	89.74	91.67	93.08
ResNet18+RF	90	0.948	93.08	94.98	94.62
ShuffleNet+RF	**91.54**	**0.9557**	**94.1**	**95.75**	**95.38**

obtains exceptional metrics such as 98.99% precision, 98.33% accuracy, 98.00% sensitivity, 98.50% specificity, and 0.9875 F1 score for both abnormality identification. Similarly for malignancy identification, the suggested method exhibits superior performance with 97.50% precision, 97.50% accuracy, 97.50% recall, 97.50% specificity, and 0.9750 F1 score. Similarly, the experimental findings comprising abnormality and malignancy identification utilizing the BUSI dataset (ultrasound images) are methodically displayed in Tables 12.3 and 12.4.

Notably, the results of these tables constantly show that the suggested hybrid strategy outperforms the referenced techniques. The suggested hybrid approach obtains remarkable results in abnormality detection with 95.75% precision, 94.10% accuracy, 95.38% sensitivity, 91.54% specificity, and 0.9557 F1 score, while also excelling in malignancy detection with identical metrics i.e., 92.31% precision, 92.31% accuracy, 92.31% sensitivity, 92.31% specificity, and 0.9231 F1 score.

The ROC curves have also been provided for more effective analysis. The mini-DDSM dataset's ROC curve of the third fold for identifying abnormality and cancer is shown in Figures 12.7 and 12.8. The ROC curve for the BUSI dataset is similarly shown in Figure 12.7 and 12.8, which show abnormality and malignancy, respectively.

TABLE 12.4

Performance Evaluation for Malignancy Detection in the BUSI Dataset

Methods	Specificity (%)	F1 Score	Accuracy (%)	Precision (%)	Sensitivity (%)
Vgg16	85.38	0.8582	85.77	85.5	86.15
ResNet18	90.77	0.9119	91.15	90.84	91.54
ShuffleNet	91.54	0.9154	91.54	91.54	91.54
Vgg16+DT	86.92	0.8735	87.31	87.02	87.69
ResNet18+DT	91.54	0.9154	91.54	91.54	91.54
ShuffleNet+DT	91.54	0.9195	91.92	91.6	92.31
Vgg16+RF	87.69	0.8812	88.08	87.79	88.46
ResNet18+RF	92.31	0.9189	91.92	92.25	91.54
ShuffleNet+RF	**92.31**	**0.9231**	**92.31**	**92.31**	**92.31**

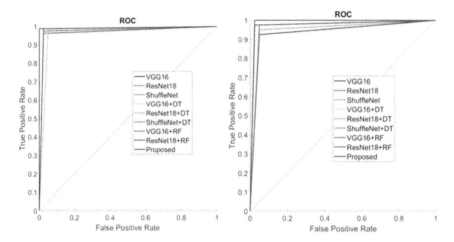

FIGURE 12.7
ROC plot of the third fold for identifying abnormality and malignancy in mini-DDSM dataset.

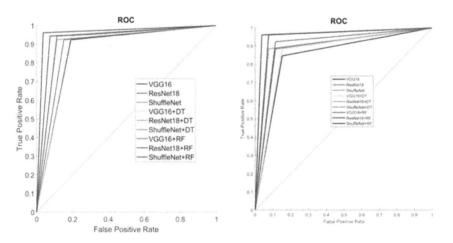

FIGURE 12.8
ROC plot of the third fold for identifying abnormality and malignancy in the BUSI dataset.

12.5 Conclusion

In conclusion, this chapter presents an effective hybrid breast cancer identification framework that capitalizes on the strengths of ShuffleNet and RF. The lack of huge datasets in the medical field is satisfactorily addressed by the implementation of ShuffleNet in this framework. Channel shuffle for group convolution and the basic building blocks maintain a reasonable trade-off between classification performance and computing cost. Thus, the hybrid architecture combining ShuffleNet for feature extraction and random forest for classification proves to be a powerful strategy in detecting breast cancer, offering potential for real-world clinical applications. A comparative performance evaluation is done using 5-fold cross-validation over two distinct datasets: ultrasound (BUSI) and mammogram (mini-DDSM). The experimental research shows that, even with limited datasets, the suggested breast cancer detection framework outperforms other methods presented in the literature in both mammography and ultrasound datasets

References

1. Al-Dhabyani W, Gomaa M, Khaled H, Aly F (2019) Deep learning approaches for data augmentation and classification of breast masses using ultrasound images. *Int J Adv Comput Sci Appl* 10(5):1–11.
2. Al-Dhabyani W, Gomaa M, Khaled H, Fahmy A (2020) Dataset of breast ultrasound images. *Data in Brief* 28(104):863.
3. Byra M (2021) Breast mass classification with transfer learning based on scaling of deep representations. *Biomedical Signal Processing and Control* 69(102):828.
4. Das PK, Meher S (2021) An efficient deep convolutional neural network based detection and classification of acute lymphoblastic leukemia. *Expert Systems with Applications* 183:115311.
5. Das PK, Meher S, Panda R, Abraham A (2019) A review of automated methods for the detection of sickle cell disease. *IEEE Reviews in Biomedical Engineering* 13:309–324.
6. Das PK, Meher S, Panda R, Abraham A (2022) An efficient blood-cell segmentation for the detection of hematological disorders. *IEEE Transactions on Cybernetics.* 52(10): 10615–10626
7. Das PK, Diya V, Meher S, Panda R, Abraham A (2022) A systematic review on recent advancements in deep and machine learning based detection and classification of acute lymphoblastic leukemia. *IEEE Access 10:* 81741–81763.
8. Das PK, Nayak B, Meher S (2022) A lightweight deep learning system for automatic detection of blood cancer. *Measurement* 191(110):762.
9. Das PK, Sahoo B, Meher S (2023) An efficient detection and classification of acute leukemia using transfer learning and orthogonal softmax layer-based model. *IEEE/ACM Transactions on Computational Biology and Bioinformatics* 20(3): 1817–1828.
10. El Houby EM, Yassin NI (2021) Malignant and nonmalignant classification of breast lesions in mammograms using convolutional neural networks. *Biomedical Signal Processing and Control* 70(102):954.
11. Kabir SM, Shihavuddin A, Tanveer MS, Bhuiyan MIH (2020) Parametric image-based breast tumor classification using convolutional neural network in the contourlet transform domain. In 2020 11th International Conference on Electrical and Computer Engineering (ICECE), IEEE, pp 439–442.
12. Lee CY, Chen GL, Zhang ZX, Chou YH, Hsu CC (2018) Is intensity in homogeneity correction useful for classification of breast cancer in sonograms using deep neural network. *Journal of Healthcare Engineering* 2018: 1–10.

13. Lekamlage CD, Afzal F, Westerberg E, Cheddad A (2020) Mini-ddsm: Mammography-based automatic age estimation. *arXiv preprint arXiv:201000494.*

14. Li H, Zhuang S, Li D, Zhao J, Ma Y (2019) Benign and malignant classification of mammogram images based on deep learning. *Biomedical Signal Processing and Control* 51:347–354.

15. Mahmud Kabir S, Tanveer S, Shihavuddin A, Imamul Hassan Bhuiyan M, et al (2021) Weighted contourlet parametric (wcp) feature-based breast tumor classification from b-mode ultrasound image. arXiv e-prints pp arXiv– 2102.

16. Malebary SJ, Hashmi A (2021) Automated breast mass classification system using deep learning and ensemble learning in digital mammogram. *IEEE Access* 9(55):312–55,328.

17. Muduli D, Dash R, Majhi B (2022) Automated diagnosis of breast cancer using multi-modal datasets: A deep convolution neural network based approach. *Biomedical Signal Processing and Control* 71(102):825.

18. Paul I, Sahu A, Das PK, Meher S (2023) Deep convolutional neural network-based automatic detection of brain tumor. In 2023 2nd International Conference for Innovation in Technology (INOCON), IEEE, pp 1-6.

19. Sahu A, Das PK, Meher S (2023) High accuracy hybrid CNN classifiers for breast cancer detection using mammogram and ultrasound datasets. *Biomedical Signal Processing and Control* 80(104):292.

20. Sahu A, Das PK, Meher S, Panda R, Abraham A (2023) An efficient deep learning-based breast cancer detection scheme with small datasets. In Intelligent Systems Design and Applications: 22nd International Conference on Intelligent Systems Design and Applications (ISDA 2022) Held December 12–14, 2022-Volume 4, Springer Nature, vol 717, p 39.

21. Sahu A, Das PK, Meher S (2024) An efficient deep learning scheme to detect breast cancer using mammogram and ultrasound breast images. *Biomedical Signal Processing and Control* 87(105):377.

22. Sahu A, Das PK, Meher S (2023) Recent advancements in machine learning and deep learning-based breast cancer detection using mammograms. *Physica Medica* 114(103):138.

23. Sun L, Wang J, Hu Z, Xu Y, Cui Z (2019) Multi-view convolutional neural networks for mammographic image classification. *IEEE Access* 7(126):273–126,282.

24. Thawkar S (2022) Feature selection and classification in mammography using hybrid crow search algorithm with Harris Hawks optimization. *Biocybernetics and Biomedical Engineering* 42(4):1094–1111.

25. Zhang X, Zhou X, Lin M, Sun J (2018) Shufflenet: An extremely efficient convolutional neural network for mobile devices. In Proceedings of the IEEE Conference on Computer Vision and Pattern Recognition, pp 6848–6856.

26. Zhuang Z, Yang Z, Raj ANJ, Wei C, Jin P, Zhuang S (2021) Breast ultrasound tumor image classification using image decomposition and fusion based on adaptive multi-model spatial feature fusion. *Computer Methods and Programs in Biomedicine* 208(106):22.

13

Identification of Brain Cancer Using Medical Hyperspectral Image Analysis

Aloke Datta and Raj Bahadur Singh

13.1 Introduction

Cancer is the second most significant cause of global mortality, trailing only behind cardiovascular disease. In 2020 alone, it was responsible for an estimated 10 million deaths worldwide [1]. The hallmark of cancer is the abnormal proliferation and division of cells, leading to the formation of tumors or unregulated growth in various regions of the body. This disrupts the normal functioning of organs and various body parts, ultimately resulting in mortality [2]. Cancer encompasses a range of conditions, with some forms being highly treatable while others pose significant challenges. Successful treatment depends on several factors, including early detection, the nature of the cancer (malignant or benign), and its location within the body. These variables play an essential role in determining appropriate therapeutic approaches for managing different types of cancer. Cancer is a formidable disease that physicians and surgeons globally strive to combat daily. Ongoing research in the field of oncology has resulted in the creation of diverse diagnostic and surgical instruments, which play an integral role in identifying cancer with precision and administering effective treatment.

Brain cancer can arise either as primary tumors that originate within the brain tissue or secondary tumors that metastasize to the brain from other parts of the body. These tumors are classified into high-grade and low-grade categories [3]. For this study, we focused on grade IV glioblastoma, which is a particularly aggressive form of high-grade tumor with malignant characteristics. Glioblastoma is typically managed through a combination of chemotherapy, radiation therapy, and surgical intervention. However, the successful complete elimination or precise resection of tumor tissue cannot be guaranteed even with surgery. This uncertainty arises from the difficulty in accurately identifying the boundaries of tumor regions during surgery and relies heavily on the surgeon's proficiency in distinguishing between malignant tissues and normal brain matter [4]. Lara-Velazques et al. [4] emphasize the importance of precise tumor excision and stress the need for improved techniques in identifying tumor regions to aid surgeons in achieving complete removal of all tumor traces, thus reducing the risk of recurrence.

In brain tumor surgeries, advanced imaging techniques such as magnetic resonance imaging (MRI), computed tomography (CT) scan, and fluorescence imaging guided by 5-aminolevulinic acid (5-ALA) have been widely employed for pre-operative planning and intra-operative guidance. In neurosurgery, the use of infrared thermal imaging is also considered as an intraoperative technique [5, 6]. These sophisticated methods aid in improving surgical precision and accuracy during the removal of brain tumors. However, this particular study aimed to explore the potential of hyperspectral imaging techniques in overcoming the limitations associated with these conventional methods [7–13]. HSI offers several advantages, including its non-contact, non-invasive nature that eliminates the need for ionizing radiation exposure or radiological procedures. Additionally, HSI provides a wealth of detailed and high-resolution spectral information [14].

This chapter aims to comprehensively examine the use of hyperspectral imaging in detecting brain cancer through medical image analysis. It will review the relevant literature on medical hyperspectral imaging technology and its applications, specifically focusing on brain cancer detection and diagnosis. The challenges and potential advancements in this field will be discussed, along with an overview of cutting-edge techniques and algorithms used for identifying brain cancer. This chapter is intended for researchers, clinicians, and professionals working in this area who wish to deepen their understanding of current state-of-the-art methods. By consolidating existing research on using medical hyperspectral image analysis to identify brain cancer, this chapter contributes to the ongoing body of literature concerning this topic. The observation has been conducted over the In-Vivo HS Brain Image database, curated by Fabelo et al. [15] as part of the HELICoID demonstrator project. This database comprises 36 hyperspectral cubes from a total of 22 patients obtained from two hospitals.

13.2 Basics of Brain Cancer and Imaging Techniques

13.2.1 Brain Cancer

Cancer remains one of the most prevalent causes of mortality globally, with brain cancer specifically presenting a considerable risk to human well-being [16]. Brain cancer, also called brain tumor, is a condition characterized by the abnormal proliferation of cells within the brain. These anomalous cells have the potential to form a cluster or mass, which can impede the normal functioning of brain tissues. Brain tumors can be classified into two categories: malignant, which is cancerous, and benign, which is non-cancerous. Benign tumors usually exhibit less aggressive behavior and possess well-defined boundaries, facilitating their surgical treatment and removal. On the other hand, malignant tumors display more aggressiveness and infiltrate neighboring healthy brain tissue extensively, thereby posing challenges for complete surgical resection [17].

Brain cancer can be categorized based on the specific type of cell from which it originates, such as gliomas, meningiomas, and metastatic brain tumors. The term "glioma" refers to both low-grade and high-grade brain tumors [18]. Gliomas are tumors that develop from the supportive cells in the brain, known as glial cells. In contrast, meningiomas originate from the protective membranes that cover both the brain and spinal cord. Metastatic tumors refer to cancers that have spread to the brain from other parts of the body. Among these various types, glioblastoma multiforme is a highly aggressive and common primary brain tumor found in adults. Gliomas can be classified as either high or low grade based on factors such as their histopathology, immunohistochemistry, and genetic features [19]. This study primarily focuses on one subtype of glioma known as glioblastoma tumor.

Glioblastoma multiforme (GBM) is a highly aggressive tumor classified as grade IV, known for its rapid growth, invasive nature, and resistance to treatment. It poses substantial challenges during the treatment process due to its high infectivity and poor prognosis [20, 21]. This diffuse infiltration poses challenges in accurately distinguishing between GBM and surrounding normal tissues consisting of white matter, gray matter, and cerebrospinal fluid [22]. The overall survival rate of glioblastoma multiforme is a mere 5–10 %, and this statistic tends to worsen with advancing age [23]. It is to be noted that glioblastoma had a higher prevalence among males, while meningioma was more frequently observed in females [20].

Ensuring timely removal of the tumor is crucial, whether through medical intervention or surgical means. In cases where alternative approaches such as radiation and chemotherapy are not viable, surgery becomes imperative and remains a common course of action for managing such conditions [22]. If the tumor has infiltrated deep into the brain or if it is medically recommended to remove the affected region from the brain, surgeons must possess precise knowledge regarding its localization in order to safeguard healthy tissue during resection. Consequently, this operation assumes great delicacy; hence, various imaging techniques are employed by surgeons to accurately identify regions afflicted with tumors.

13.2.2 Conventional Imaging Techniques to Identify Cancerous Regions

Surgery is the major treatment option for brain tumors, along with radiotherapy and chemotherapy. Due to the invasive nature of brain tumors and their ability to blend into normal brain tissue, surgeons often struggle to visually differentiate between tumor cells and healthy brain tissue. As a result, it is common for some tumor cells to be unintentionally left behind during surgery or for excessive amounts of normal brain tissue to be removed. Numerous studies have highlighted that incomplete removal of tumor cells during surgery is a primary cause of recurrence and leads to significant morbidity and mortality rates [24–26]. Conversely, excessive resection has been found to contribute towards long-lasting neurological impairments, which negatively impact the quality of life for patients [27]. Accurate identification and demarcation of brain tumor boundaries are crucial in ensuring successful surgical removal, making it an essential aspect of neurosurgery. To address the challenges faced by neurosurgeons in differentiating between brain tumors and normal tissue, several imaging techniques have been developed. These include intra-operative neuro-navigation, MRI, CT scan, and the utilization of fluorescent tumor markers like 5-ALA (5-aminolevulinic acid). These methods serve as valuable aids during surgical procedures to enhance accuracy in identifying and demarcating brain tumors.

Although these additional techniques have enhanced the precision of brain tumor excision, they do possess certain limitations. Locating tumor boundaries using neuronavigational becomes less reliable due to the brain shift phenomenon and changes in the volume of tumors during resections [28, 29]. MRI has emerged as a solution for accurately mapping intra-operative tumor margins, even under conditions where there is shifting or movement within the brain. However, this technique is associated with drawbacks such as poor spatial resolution, increased duration of surgery, and high cost [30]. Additionally, since there is a need to interrupt the operation and obtain scans, it provides only a limited number of images at specific time intervals rather than continuous real-time imaging. Fluorescent tumor markers, such as 5-ALA, have proven to be highly efficient in the detection of tumors. However, their applicability is limited to high-grade tumors, and they give rise to significant side effects. Moreover, the markers currently used lack sufficient accuracy in determining the exact boundaries of brain tumors due to their diffuse nature [31, 32]. To address these constraints and improve the precision in identifying and delineating brain tumors during surgical procedures, there has been increasing interest in employing medical hyperspectral image analysis.

13.3 Hyperspectral Imaging: Fundamentals and Principles

13.3.1 Basic of Hyperspectral Imaging

Hyperspectral imaging (HSI) is a spectrally resolved imaging method that captures spectral information across a range of spectral channels, thus allowing the capturing of complex spectrally resolved light-tissue interaction. HSI technique captures and analyzes information beyond the capabilities of the human eye, spanning a wide range of wavelengths from 390 to 700 nm across the electromagnetic spectrum. Usually, a conventional digital color camera employs three bands (red, green, and blue) to capture color information (Figure 13.1a). In contrast, hyperspectral imaging can acquire hundreds of narrow and contiguous spectral bands, allowing for a more comprehensive spectral profile for each pixel in the image (Figure 13.1b).

Hyperspectral imaging acquires data in the form of a 3D hypercube. This dataset contains spatial as well as spectral information within three dimensions. Each pixel in the image is linked to a spectrum that characterizes the wavelength-specific characteristics of the tissue at that particular location (Figure 13.2). Hyperspectral images have varying levels of spectral resolution, which is determined by the number and width of the bands detected by the sensor. A higher level of spectral resolution allows for better discrimination between different wavelengths. Spatial resolution, on the other hand, pertains to pixel size and arrangement in an image. Balancing these two resolutions is important because

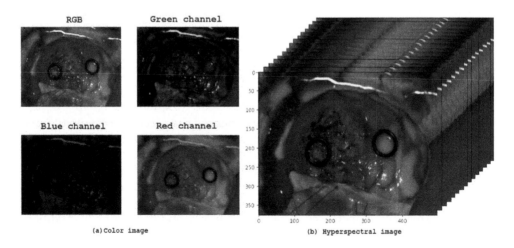

FIGURE 13.1
Illustration of hyperspectral imaging. (a) A standard color image is composed of three spectral channels. (b) A hyperspectral image displays a 3D hypercube containing both spatial and spectral information.

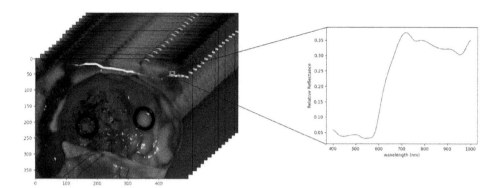

FIGURE 13.2
Diagram illustrating the hyperspectral signature of a pixel.

they are interconnected; improving one may impact the other. The optimal compromise depends on specific application requirements.

Hyperspectral imaging techniques have been widely utilized in a range of applications, including remote sensing, agriculture, geology, environmental monitoring, food inspection, forgery detection, and forensic science. In the biomedical field specifically, HSI has shown promise for various medical applications such as non-invasive optical tissue diagnostics and image-guided surgery [14, 33, 34]. It is particularly valuable for accurately identifying and classifying different materials in these fields. By detecting unique spectral signatures linked to specific substances or objects, hyperspectral imaging enables the differentiation and analysis of visually similar entities. Consequently, the technology can detect targets like pollutants, minerals, vegetation types, or man-made objects even when they lack visual distinctiveness.

Hyperspectral imaging has emerged as a valuable tool in medical imaging, particularly due to its numerous advantages. One significant advantage is that HSI does not pose any potential health risks to patients, as it avoids harmful radiation and physical contact. This non-invasive approach ensures the safety of patients during diagnostic procedures [14, 35]. Moreover, HSI produces reliable, high-quality images that enable accurate analysis and diagnosis. Its non-contact nature makes it suitable for various medical imaging tasks. By capturing data across multiple spectral bands, HSI provides an extensive range of information about biological tissues and structures. This comprehensive dataset facilitates the precise identification of abnormalities by researchers and clinicians alike. In summary, hyperspectral imaging's ability to generate safe images without causing discomfort or side effects to patients highlights its value in advancing medical diagnostics.

13.3.2 Principles of Hyperspectral Imaging Techniques

Hyperspectral imaging is a label-free and non-invasive technique that examines the interaction of reflected light with tissue, allowing for detailed analysis [14]. By examining the changes in light signals at different wavelengths, this method provides valuable information about the structural and spectral characteristics of tissues. The unique absorption properties of biomolecules can be measured using spectrally resolved imaging methods, allowing for predictions to be made regarding the biochemical features of imaged tissues [33].

Variations in the distribution of refractive index within tissue result in light scattering [36]. The composition of tissues varies, with substances ranging in size from nanometers to hundreds of microns. However, as diseases progress, alterations in tissue structure result in different scattering properties throughout the tissue [37–39]. Hyperspectral imaging captures the scattering features of reflected light, which can serve as potential markers for disease diagnosis. This technology provides comprehensive information about the tissue's structural and biochemical characteristics, enabling accurate disease diagnosis and functional analysis during surgical procedures.

Hyperspectral imaging technology operates by measuring the image based on wavelength using spectroscopic techniques. Hence, HSI methods rely on optical components that can detect spectral information from broad-range light signals. Spectral scanning, spatial scanning, and snapshot methods are the three main categories of HSI methods in use. Spectral scanning is a method that involves sequentially scanning different wavelengths of light across the tissue sample, capturing a series of images at each wavelength. Spatial scanning, on the other hand, involves fixing the wavelength and scanning the tissue sample spatially to capture images at different locations. Lastly, snapshot methods capture the entire spectral information at once without the need for sequential scanning or spatial scanning [40]. These different methods of hyperspectral imaging allow for the acquisition of detailed spectral data from tissue samples, enabling the identification and analysis of various diseases and conditions, including brain cancer.

13.3.3 Medical Hyperspectral Imaging Systems

Hyperspectral imaging in the field of medicine can be applied to both microscopic and mesoscopic imaging systems, enabling observation and analysis at various scales, including individual cells and tissue samples. This technique allows for the detailed examination of biological specimens for diagnostic purposes [40]. MHSI involves the utilization of specialized equipment and software for capturing and analyzing spectral information derived from tissue samples. These systems typically consist of a hyperspectral camera capable of capturing images at different wavelengths, as well as a light source that illuminates the tissue sample. The hyperspectral camera captures the reflected or emitted light from each pixel in the sample, enabling the acquisition of its spectral characteristics. This captured spectral data is then processed using dedicated algorithms designed to extract relevant features necessary for disease identification and analysis.

Hyperspectral imaging is a safe and efficient imaging method that does not require contact or labeling, making it suitable for various medical applications. Due to the advantages it offers, hyperspectral imaging is being increasingly used as a valuable tool in clinical trials for disease diagnosis and surgical guidance. The accessibility of HSI systems in the market, and advancements in spectral imaging technology, have accelerated the integration of HSI methods in clinical environments. The utilization of hyperspectral imaging in disease diagnosis is rooted in the concept that modifications in tissue optical characteristics resulting from morphological and biochemical changes during the advancement of a disease can be identified. The utilization of hyperspectral imaging in surgical procedures aims to enhance the surgeon's visual capabilities by providing detailed information at the molecular, cellular, and tissue levels. This enables the identification of subtle variations in tissue composition that may not be noticeable to the unaided eye, thereby improving diagnostic precision and surgical results.

Hyperspectral imaging is an emerging modality with promising potential for medical applications, notably in the field of cancer detection. Numerous studies have demonstrated its potential in improving automated cancer detection methods. In their investigation, Akbari et al. [41] conducted a study on the detection of gastric tumors in human ex vivo tissues utilizing hyperspectral imaging technology that captured images within the wavelength range of 1000 to 1250 nm. Based on their investigation, the authors determined that specific spectral ranges between 1226 and 1251 nm, as well as 1288 and 1370 nm demonstrate effectiveness in distinguishing between healthy gastric tissue and cancerous tissue. Regeling et al. [42] conducted a study on laryngeal cancer using a flexible endoscopy combined with hyperspectral imaging technology. The hyperspectral imaging system acquired a range of wavelengths from 390 to 680 nm in order to capture the hyperspectral cubes. Moreover, researchers like Kester et al. [43] have made progress in this domain by developing a real-time endoscope system for HSI that employs an image mapping method. This HSI system can achieve a frame rate of 5.2 fps and produce hyperspectral cubes with a spatial resolution of 100 μm, covering wavelengths from 450 to 650 nm. Akbari et al. [44] conducted a research investigation into the application of hyperspectral imaging for prostate cancer detection, utilizing an in vivo imaging system to capture images of mice with human prostate tumors. Using a hyperspectral imaging system that operated between wavelengths of 450–950 nm, researchers found that it had a maximum sensitivity of 92.8% and specificity of 96.9% in distinguishing between malignant and non-malignant areas. Hyperspectral imaging has been widely studied for its potential in diagnosing breast cancer. Hou et al. [45] designed a specific HSI system for this purpose, using laser diodes and achieving improved precision, resolution, and processing speed compared to other systems used in diagnosing brain cancer. Moreover, an investigation conducted by Kim et al. [46] aimed to analyze ex vivo breast cancer tissues to identify specific regions of interest and differentiate between tumor and non-tumor tissues. They employed hyperspectral imaging in the wavelength range of 380 nm to 780 nm. This research team also worked to classify ex vivo breast cancer tissues using hyperspectral imaging and achieved impressive sensitivity and specificity rates of 98% and 99%, respectively [47]. Han et al. [48] conducted a study using a versatile hyperspectral colonoscopy system to examine colorectal tumors in vivo and differentiate between malignant colorectal tumors and normal mucosa in human patients. Additionally, Masood et al. [49] carried out an evaluation of colon biopsy samples in a laboratory setting using hyperspectral imaging technology. This involved the use of a specially calibrated light source and a microscope with 40× magnification connected to a charge-coupled device camera. The HSI system covered the wavelength range from 440 nm to 700 nm and achieved an impressive accuracy of 90% in distinguishing between benign and malignant patterns. Furthermore, morphological analysis and wavelet-based segmentation techniques were employed to classify and segment hyperspectral colon tissue images [50, 51]. The utilization of hyperspectral imaging in the examination of skin cancer has also been observed through the application of visible-to-near-infrared data. This approach has shown promising outcomes in accurately distinguishing between melanoma and healthy skin [52, 53]. Hyperspectral imaging is a widely explored technique for studying and analyzing various types of tumors, such as those located in the head and neck region, diabetic foot ulcers, oral tissue, and tongue. However, it is important to note that HSI systems vary as they employ different technologies. For visible-to-near-infrared applications spanning from 400 to 1000 nm, HS cameras generally utilize CCD sensors, while near-infrared applications ranging from 1000 to 1700 nm require indium gallium arsenide sensors due to higher quantum efficiency. In certain cases where a wider spectral range is needed for specific applications, such as creating a library of abdominal organs or detecting intestinal ischemia during surgery, multiple cameras may be utilized [54, 55]. In the field of hyperspectral imaging applications, illumination systems commonly rely on halogen or xenon lamps. In some instances, optical fibers are utilized to transmit light in diffuse reflectance spectroscopy for the timely detection of malignant changes in the oral cavity [56].

Furthermore, hyperspectral imaging has been employed in the domain of pharmaceutical quality assessment. It is effective for detecting counterfeit drugs, analyzing active components, and conducting quality testing on herbal medicines. The combination of spectral information and spatial knowledge offered by HSI makes it indispensable in advanced medical quality inspection procedures.

13.4 Materials and Methods

To achieve the objective of identifying brain tumors using hyperspectral imaging, the researchers involved in the HELICoiD project employed a range of techniques and materials. This section describes the utilization of hyperspectral imaging instruments to acquire a database of in vivo brain cancer-specific hyperspectral images. Additionally, it covers the preprocessing steps that were undertaken on the collected data and describes the classification algorithms that were applied for tumor identification.

13.4.1 Acquisition of Medical Hyperspectral Images

As part of the HELICoiD project, a hyperspectral acquisition system was used to capture in vivo image datasets for brain tumor delineation during surgical procedures [57]. This intra-operative framework provided specific and tailored hyperspectral data for this purpose. The system utilized a pushbroom camera (Hyperspec VNIR A-Series). The camera possessed the ability to capture images within a wide spectrum of wavelengths, ranging from 400 nm to 1000 nm. It was equipped with an extensive array of spectral bands (826 in total) and spatial bands (1004 in total), each exhibiting a significant spectral resolution between approximately 2–3 nanometers. The hyperspectral camera utilizes a pushbroom scanning method to capture the entire hyperspectral cube. This technique enables the 2D CCD detector to capture both spatial and spectral dimensions of the scene. To capture the second spatial dimension, adjustments are made to the camera's field of view during acquisition. Figure 13.3 provides a diagram illustrating this acquisition system. The system is equipped with an illumination device that emits low-intensity cold light within a broad wavelength range spanning from 400 to 2200 nm.

13.4.2 In Vivo HS Brain Image Database

The HELICoiD project resulted in the development of an intraoperative hyperspectral acquisition system, which was employed by Fabelo et al. [15] to create a database of in vivo HS brain images. The dataset consists of 36 hyperspectral cubes obtained from 22 adult patients undergoing neurosurgical procedures at the University Hospital of Doctor Negrin and the University Hospital of Southampton. Table 13.1 presents the summary of the in vivo HS brain image dataset.

Fabelo et al. [15] have provided a detailed methodology for obtaining in vivo data during neurosurgical procedures, which can be summarized as follows. First, after performing the craniotomy and durotomy procedures, the neurosurgeons place rubber ring markers

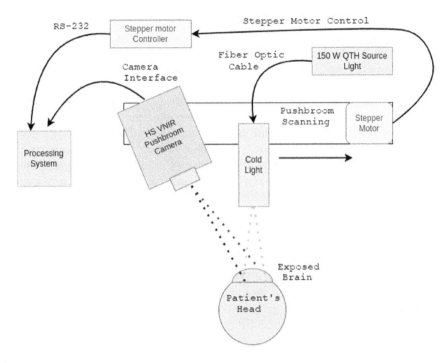

FIGURE 13.3
Diagram illustrating the setup of a hyperspectral acquisition system.

TABLE 13.1

Summary of In Vivo Database

Class	Number of Labeled Pixels
Normal Tissue	117,242
Tumor Tissue	16,328
Blood Vessel	57,863
Background	185,684
Total	**(22 patients – 36 captures)**

on distinct areas of the brain surface that they have determined to be either tumor or normal tissue based on their visual examination of macroscopic characteristics. Additional information from an MRI scan is taken into consideration to aid in this process. These markers serve as reference points for subsequent image acquisition. Following the data collection process, the individual operating the hyperspectral acquisition system proceeds to capture a hyperspectral image. Once obtained, the responsible surgeon then performs a biopsy on the tissue enclosed by identifiable tumor markers. Subsequently, this excised tissue is forwarded to pathologists for additional analysis and verification of its pathological attributes (such as grade and type) as well as confirmation of tumor presence or absence. Since the ability of this technology to penetrate into tissue is limited (especially in the case of near-infrared where it can only penetrate up to 1 mm), samples of resected tumor for pathological analysis are relatively small, measuring approximately 0.5 × 0.5 mm with a depth of 0.2 mm. In order to label these samples, normal tissue markers serve as reference points and are applied after the surgical procedure has been completed. It is important to note that conducting a biopsy on brain tissue known to be normal would be unethical as it could potentially harm the patient's well-being during surgery. By leveraging histopathological data obtained from tissue samples and utilizing the expertise of skilled surgeons who make observations based on normal tissue samples, it is possible to label HS cubes efficiently. This process leads to the creation of a high-quality dataset that can be used in supervised classification algorithms for brain cancer detection.

Manually labeling the hyperspectral data requires visually identifying each sample, a task that is both time-consuming and susceptible to human errors. To overcome these limitations, the HELICoiD project has devised a methodology that utilizes the Spectral Angle Mapper algorithm (SAM) to extract accurate information from hyperspectral cubes, thereby creating reliable gold standard datasets. A specialized tool has been developed to aid in the labeling process by computing the angle between high-dimensional vectors. This computed angle is used as an indicator of spectral similarity between the pixel being analyzed and a reference pixel chosen by an expert in the field. The SAM classification method can be used to compare spectra from pixels within hyperspectral images with a known reference spectrum. After the surgical procedure, surgeons use this tool to create gold-standard maps for each image. A specific procedure was followed to generate the gold-standard map: loading a hyperspectral cube that needs labeling and identifying a reference pixel based on the synthetic RGB representation of the HS cube (Figure 13.4a–c).

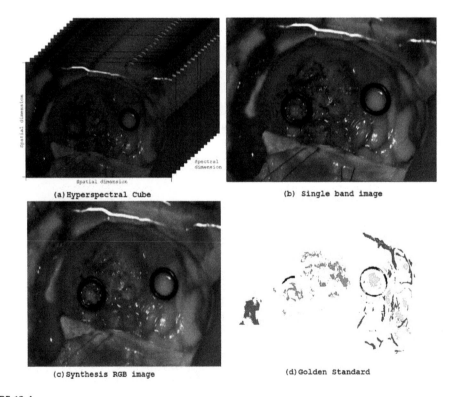

FIGURE 13.4

Datacube for patient ID 015-01 is presented. (a) HSI data cube. (b) An individual band image was extracted from the dataset consisting of 826 bands. (c) RGB image was obtained by applying a tissue marker to the hyperspectral cube. (d) Gold standard map indicating four distinct classes.

The reference pixel is selected either at the biopsy location or at a distance from tumor margins for accurate identification of abnormal tissue in cases involving tumor classification. The surgeon selects reference pixels for normal tissue, blood vessels, and background classes based on their expertise. The system then identifies pixels similar to these references using the spectral angle mapper measurement as a criterion. Users can adjust the threshold to determine which pixels should be emphasized. Finally, the system assigns those selected pixels to a specific class determined by the user (Figure 13.4d) .

13.4.3 Classification Framework

The framework for classifying hyperspectral images was designed to leverage the spatial and spectral characteristics of the image data. This classification scheme consists of several key steps, including data preprocessing, dimensionality reduction, supervised classification based on both spatial and spectral information, unsupervised clustering, and a hybrid approach combining these techniques. Firstly, the hyperspectral cube capturing the surface of the brain is processed to standardize the spectral signatures of each pixel. Then, a dimensionality reduction algorithm is used to obtain a single-band representation of the hyperspectral cube. The establishment of a gold-standard dataset through labeling serves as a reference for developing an efficient classifier model.

13.4.3.1 Pre-Processing

Once the in vivo brain surface hyperspectral cube is acquired, a series of data processing steps are implemented to enhance the spectral characteristics of each pixel and reduce the complexity of the hyperspectral image while preserving its key spectral information. The first step in the process is to perform radiometric calibration on the raw spectral signature of each pixel. This process utilizes black-and-white reference images captured with identical illumination conditions as that at which the final image will be acquired. A standard white reference tile is used for obtaining a white reference image, while a closed camera shutter captures a dark reference image. Figure 13.5a and Figure 13.5b shows the raw and calibrated spectral signature of the patient suffering from grade IV GBM. The second stage involves the application of noise filtering using a method known as the HySIME algorithm. This algorithm incorporates a function known as hyperspectral noise estimation, which allows for the estimation and inference of noise in HS data. It achieves this by assuming that the reflectance at a particular band can be accurately modeled through linear regression on all other bands. Following this, in the third step of this process, certain spectral bands are removed due to their low signal-to-noise ratio. Specifically, bands from 0 to 50 and from 750 to 826 are eliminated (Figure 13.5c). These ranges correspond to regions where the limited performance of the CCD sensor lowers the quality of data. Once these extreme noise-inducing bands have been removed, noise reduction is performed to smooth the spectra (Figure 13.5d). After these, Further reduction is implemented by performing spectral averaging across contiguous bands exhibiting redundancy in information content. As a result, we obtain a reduced representation of our initial hyperspectral cube consisting of only 129 remaining spectral bands. Lastly, in the final step of the preprocessing pipeline, normalization is performed on the samples to mitigate variations in radiation intensities resulting from the non-uniform surface of the brain. This ensures that each pixel within the image is represented consistently and removes any potential biases introduced by unequal illumination.

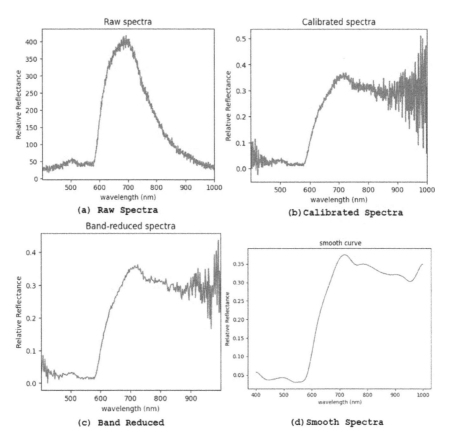

FIGURE 13.5
Spectral signature of patient (patient ID – 015-01) suffering from Grade IV GBM. (a) Raw spectral. (b) Calibrated spectra. (c) Extreme-band reduced spectra. (d) Noise-reduced spectra.

13.4.3.2 *Dimensionality Reduction*

From the perspective of information processing, reducing the inherent complexity of hyperspectral images before conducting further image analysis procedures can be highly beneficial. Dimensionality reduction is critical to hyperspectral image analysis, especially in fields like cancer tissue analysis and identification. Dimensionality reduction is a method used to transform high-dimensional data into a lower-dimensional representation, maintaining the key features of the original dataset. This allows for easier handling and analysis of the data while preserving its essential characteristics. Addressing dimensionality reduction is a complex task due to the lack of knowledge about both the intrinsic dimensions and geometric structure of initial data. In order to overcome this challenge, it becomes necessary to make assumptions about the properties of the data.

Hyperspectral imaging captures both spatial and spectral information from the scene, but the high-dimensional nature of the data poses significant challenges commonly known as the curse of dimensionality. The challenge of handling high-dimensional hyperspectral data, known as the curse of dimensionality, necessitates the development of effective techniques to reduce computational complexity and storage demands [58]. Researchers have devised various approaches for reducing the dimensionality of hyperspectral data while preserving important information.

In the literature, numerous dimensionality reduction algorithms have been developed [59]. One commonly used linear technique is principal component analysis. PCA is a statistical method commonly used in hyperspectral imaging for reducing the dimensionality of data. By transforming the original dataset into a new set of uncorrelated variables called principal components, PCA captures the maximum variation present in the data [60]. This enables a lower-dimensional representation that retains essential information while minimizing redundancy and facilitating efficient storage and pre-processing in cloud computing environments. PCA has certain limitations when it comes to dimensional reduction of hyperspectral images. It relies on a global property, the variance of the data, and is a linear method.

Alongside PCA, independent component analysis and projection pursuit are also viable dimensionality reduction techniques that can be utilized in hyperspectral imaging. Independent component analysis seeks to identify a linear transformation of the hyperspectral data that optimizes the statistical independence of the resultant components. This technique is another effective method for reducing dimensions in hyperspectral imaging applications. In contrast, projection pursuit aims to discover projections of hyperspectral data that uncover noteworthy structures or patterns. These methods allow for reducing high-dimensional hyperspectral data into a lower-dimensional representation while preserving as much information as possible.

In contrast, non-linear methods present certain benefits as they demonstrate effective handling of intricate real-world data. Local linear embedding, Isomap, Hessian-based techniques, and Laplacian are some of the examples that fall under these nonlinear approaches [8]. These methodologies offer an alternative approach to reducing the dimensionality of hyperspectral data by effectively capturing the nonlinear relationships within the dataset.

Fixed Reference t-distributed stochastic neighbors embedding for the dimensional reduction in hyperspectral imaging applications was proposed by Ravi et al. [61]. FR t-SNE is an improved iteration of t-SNE, a nonlinear method that efficiently transforms data from high-dimensional space to a lower-dimensional representation [62]. However, it should be noted that when applying t-SNE to hyperspectral imaging, consistent results are not always guaranteed due to the algorithm's random nature [61]. This randomness can lead to different low-dimensional representations for similar tissues across multiple images during each dimensional reduction step. Consequently, comparable tissues may possess distinct low-dimensional representations in different hyperspectral images, posing challenges in characterizing subsequent tissue samples as there is no consistent coordinate system available. To address these challenges and ensure consistent evaluation of embedded outcomes across different tissue samples, FR-t-SNE integrates a learning procedure that aims to establish a standardized reference coordinate system. The algorithm consists of three primary steps. Initially, a suitable reference system is established to ensure consistent embedding of the manifold in all images and overcome the lack of a fixed coordinate system. Secondly, the training set is systematically tested using this predefined fixed reference. Finally, an efficient embedding for hyperspectral images can be achieved. By incorporating these steps into its framework, FR-t-SNE aims to improve tissue characterization by generating stable embeddings and enabling comparative analysis across multiple samples.

13.4.4 Machine Learning for Cancer Identification

Hyperspectral imaging in detecting brain cancer has emerged as a promising technique with significant potential. Surgeons greatly benefit from the real-time capability of hyperspectral imaging to accurately identify and delineate brain tumors during neuro-surgical procedures, allowing for enhanced precision in tumor removal and improved patient outcomes. However, accurate brain cancer detection and delineation using medical hyperspectral image analysis present challenges that require sophisticated algorithms and techniques. Researchers have explored combining hyperspectral imaging with machine learning methods to classify and identify various types of brain cancer. Machine learning algorithms demonstrate their ability to analyze large volumes of hyperspectral data by extracting meaningful patterns and features that effectively identify cancerous lesions.

Machine learning refers to training artificial intelligence algorithms using a dataset, enabling them to autonomously identify patterns and make predictions or decisions without explicit programming. In the field of hyperspectral data analysis, various machine learning techniques are used. These techniques include supervised and unsupervised learning algorithms, with some approaches incorporating deep learning methods for enhanced classification accuracy.

13.4.4.1 Supervised Learning

Supervised machine learning entails training a model using labeled examples to classify new, unseen data. In the context of identifying brain cancer through hyperspectral imaging, a supervised learning approach involves utilizing pre-labeled hyperspectral images to train a model that can accurately categorize pixels as either cancerous or healthy tissue. This process encompasses three main steps: preprocessing the data, extracting relevant features, and training the model itself. Support vector machines, k-nearest neighbors, and neural networks are commonly employed algorithms in this type of classification task utilizing hyperspectral images. They have proven effective in analyzing the vast amount of detailed information present within these images for accurately discerning regions affected by cancer from normal tissue segments with high precision.

13.4.4.2 Unsupervised Learning

In the field of hyperspectral imaging for brain cancer identification, unsupervised machine learning techniques are employed to analyze unlabeled data and uncover patterns or clusters within the dataset. These methods can effectively identify groups of pixels that may correspond to different types of tissue, even when prior knowledge or training data is lacking. To overcome challenges such as high dimensionality and mixture problems in hyperspectral image analysis, subspace-based clustering algorithms are commonly used in unsupervised learning approaches. These algorithms have shown promising results in effectively analyzing the comprehensive and intricate data obtained from hyperspectral imaging to differentiate cancerous regions from healthy tissue accurately. Notable techniques employed in unsupervised clustering for hyperspectral image analysis include k-means clustering, hierarchical k-means clustering, and principal component analysis.

Semi-supervised learning is a technique that combines the elements of both supervised and unsupervised learning. Semi-supervised learning utilizes a small amount of labeled data along with a large amount of unlabeled data to classify new unseen data. In the context of hyperspectral imaging for brain cancer identification, semi-supervised learning can be used to leverage the limited amount of labeled data available along with the vast amount of unlabeled data to improve the accuracy and efficiency of the classification process.

13.4.4.3 Deep Learning

Deep learning, a branch of machine learning, has gained significant attention in hyperspectral image analysis. With its advanced capability to extract intricate features and patterns from hyperspectral data without directly relying on manual feature engineering, deep learning algorithms offer promising opportunities for accurately identifying brain cancer regions in these images [63]. This automated approach showcases the potential of deep learning models in capturing complex relationships within the data and enhancing levels for cancer classification tasks. Deep learning architectures like deep convolutional neural networks have proven to be effective in extracting significant and distinguishing features from hyperspectral data for the purpose of identifying brain cancer. U-Net, another deep learning model, has also demonstrated promising outcomes in segmenting and detecting regions within the hyperspectral images.

13.4.5 Previous Approaches for Cancer Detection

Numerous studies have illustrated the promise of hyperspectral imaging in detecting brain cancer. Fabelo et al. [7] introduced a methodology for the identification of brain tumors using hyperspectral images. The authors proposed an algorithm known as the brain tumor detection algorithm, which consists of two processes: offline and situ. During the offline phase, machine-learning models were trained using expert-labeled samples. The procedure was conducted in the operating theatre, where a hyperspectral image cube of the patient's brain was obtained. The process is comprised of five steps. Firstly, the hyperspectral image was obtained. Next, data preprocessing was conducted to enhance the accuracy of subsequent analyses. Then, a support vector machine classifier was utilized to assign labels based on supervised data for each pixel in the image. Following that, spatial-spectral homogenization was applied using K-nearest neighbor filtering to improve uniformity across regions within the image. Lastly, supervised and unsupervised techniques were combined using majority voting to generate final classification maps known as TMD (Three Maximum Density) maps.

Fabelo et al. [8] employed a similar methodology as described in the earlier research, introducing their modified BTDA algorithm. Notably, they enhanced the feature extraction and dimensional reduction process by utilizing FR-t-SNE. This modification aimed to simplify the classification of brain cancer identification. Additionally, they adopted a hybrid classification approach that combined supervised and unsupervised classification maps through majority voting, one maximum density, and total maximum density mappings to present their results effectively.

Florimibi et al. [9] conducted a study focusing on optimizing the KNN-filtering method for real-time classification of tumors and non-tumor regions. The proposed optimization aimed to address the time-consuming nature of the KNN algorithm, which involves dividing the image into specific window sizes ranging from two to twenty. The window approach was utilized to search and filter the entire image, implemented through both serial and parallel methods. Additionally, two distance calculation methods were examined for window search optimization. The results were evaluated based on different combinations of window sizes, parallel versus serial implementations, as well as Euclidean versus Manhattan distances. The analysis considered tradeoffs between time consumption and misclassification rates associated with each approach. In their study, the researchers found that using a window size of 8 and employing the Euclidean distance method resulted in optimal outcomes when considering factors such as efficiency and accuracy in tumor identification.

A subsequent study by Florimibi et al. [64] aimed to address the computational challenges in processing hyperspectral image datasets for the identification of brain tumors. The study proposes a system to improve the performance of brain cancer classification processes, aligning with existing detection systems. The framework was implemented using both serial and parallel methods. In the serial approach, preprocessing steps such as principal component analysis, support vector machines, K-nearest neighbors, K-means clustering, and majority voting were implemented one after the other. On the other hand, in the parallel approach, these steps were performed concurrently to achieve faster results. The authors compared and analyzed the performance of different GPUs, including CUDA-enabled GPUs.

In order to achieve real-time performance, Martinez et al. [10] have devised three frameworks with the aim of optimizing and parallelizing the K-nearest neighbors filtering algorithm on a GPU. These frameworks were developed with the goal of extracting pertinent data and facilitating accurate tumor classification into four categories: tumor, normal tissue, hyper vascularized tissue, and background. The aim is to facilitate machine learning models in accurately predicting these classifications for improved diagnostic outcomes. The first framework involved utilizing a dataset consisting of 826 bands and applying various pre-processing techniques commonly used in previous studies. The calculation of the sampling interval was conducted, and, subsequently, SVM classification was applied using leave-one-patient-out cross-validation on both the initial training dataset and a modified version obtained by employing K-means clustering. In contrast, the second framework implemented a genetic algorithm and particle swarm optimization to select channels from a dataset containing 128 channels. This selection process was further refined through additional reduction using K-means clustering. The process of iteratively processing this optimized subset involved utilizing SVM classification, followed by an assessment of its performance using metrics such as overall accuracy and figure of merit. Subsequently, the outcome was enhanced by undergoing iterations involving GA and PSO, with repetition being carried out until reaching either the best possible outcomes or a specified time constraint. Performance evaluations were performed using evaluation criteria such as accuracy, specificity, and sensitivity. Next, the third framework employed in this study involved the use of an ACO algorithm to extract important channels from the image. The process began by optimizing a dataset consisting of 128 channels using the ACO algorithm. The optimized data was subsequently reduced via K-means clustering before applying the SVM classification model identical to previous approaches adopted in this research endeavor. Evaluation of results relied upon assessment metrics, including accuracy, sensitivity, and specificity.

Fabelo et al. [11] introduced an innovative framework that combines deep learning techniques and morphological processes to generate a classification map for the detection of brain tumors. To enhance the dataset, augmentation was performed on 12 images or patches, resulting in 96 input samples for the 2D-CNN classifier. In the training process, they implemented AlexNet, which consists of three convolutional layers, one pooling layer, and one fully connected layer. To optimize the performance during training, we used an AdaDelta optimizer with a learning rate set at 1.0. Two approaches were used: binary (tumor versus non-tumor) and multiclassification (four classes). Additionally, a 1D-DNN with two hidden layers – comprising 28 nodes in one layer and 40 nodes in the other – was employed for both binary and multiclassification tasks. The evaluation of performance included metrics such as accuracy, sensitivity, and specificity to compare the outcomes of proposed methodologies with existing techniques found in previous studies.

In their study, Manni et al. [12] introduced a hybrid classification framework that utilizes both 3D-CNN and 2D-CNN architectures for the classification of brain tumors. The volumetric data was subjected to feature extraction using the 3D-CNN component, which focused on extracting features from multiple image slices. Meanwhile, the 2D-CNN component is specifically aimed at extracting features from each individual image slice. The researchers compared this architecture with other models, including 1D-CNN, simple SVM, and the hybrid model combined with SVM. Various evaluation metrics, such as accuracy, sensitivity, and specificity, were utilized to evaluate the effectiveness of these models. Significantly, the hybrid model combining 3D-2D CNN demonstrated superior performance in terms of classification accuracy compared to other models.

In their study, Leon et al. [13] utilized a combination of VNIR and NIR images to enhance the accuracy of classification. The pixel size of the NIR images was adjusted to match that of the VNIR images through up sampling. Subsequently, the spectral channels were merged together into a unified hyperspectral image. To classify this HS image, they employed machine learning models previously used by Fabelo et al. As a result of this approach, there was an observed improvement in accuracy by 21% compared to previous methods.

Ortega et al. [65] conducted a study where they proposed a deep learning approach to detect GBM brain tumors using analysis of medical hyperspectral images. This approach involved training a deep learning model that combined 2D and 3D convolutional neural networks with deep transfer learning techniques. The aim of this study was to create an effective method for detecting brain tumors using medical hyperspectral image analysis. To assess the performance of their proposed methodology, the authors assembled a dataset comprised of pathological slides from GBM brain tumors. They compared their approach against existing methods found in previous studies and utilized metrics like accuracy, specificity, and sensitivity to evaluate its effectiveness. The findings revealed that the proposed deep learning method attained an impressive overall accuracy rate equivalent to 99.94% on the Salinas dataset. This demonstrates its ability to accurately detect brain cancer utilizing medical hyperspectral image analysis.

13.5 Challenges

Hyperspectral imaging poses several challenges in its application for the detection of brain cancer. One significant challenge is processing the large amount of information and detailed characteristics involved in analyzing hyperspectral images. Additionally, accurate identification and classification of brain cancer are hindered by the uneven distribution of labels in these images. The variations in illumination further complicate the analysis process for identifying brain cancer using hyperspectral imaging. Furthermore, mixed materials present in the background add another layer of complexity to detecting brain cancer accurately. To overcome these challenges, researchers have explored different strategies and algorithms, such as heuristic optimization techniques, to optimize hyperspectral imaging specifically for detecting brain cancer. These approaches aim to identify specific spectral bands that are most relevant for the effective diagnosis of this disease from hyperspectral images.

13.6 Limitations

A potential challenge to take into account when utilizing medical hyperspectral image analysis for the identification of brain cancer is the presence of confounding factors. These factors can include variations in image acquisition, patient characteristics, and tissue preparation techniques. It is crucial to carefully address this potential confounds in order to ensure accurate and dependable analysis of the hyperspectral images. Moreover, interpreting hyperspectral images can be intricate and subjective, requiring expertise in both medical imaging and brain cancer pathology. Additionally, analyzing large amounts of information with detailed characteristics presents a challenge when working with hyperspectral images. Nonetheless, despite these potential limitations, there have been promising outcomes regarding the detection of brain cancer using hyperspectral imaging techniques.

13.7 Conclusions

In summary, the field of medical hyperspectral image analysis shows promise for identifying brain cancer. By employing hyperspectral imaging, researchers can effectively differentiate between cancerous and healthy tissue. However, several obstacles must be addressed to improve the accuracy and reliability of brain cancer detection using medical hyperspectral image analysis. These challenges encompass handling vast amounts of information and intricate characteristics, managing an uneven distribution of labels, addressing variations in illumination conditions, and accounting for mixed materials present in the background. Furthermore, potential confounding factors like differences in image acquisition methods and tissue preparation techniques must be carefully managed to ensure precise analysis. Moreover, interpreting hyperspectral images necessitates expertise in both medical imaging as well as brain cancer pathology knowledge. However, despite the difficulties posed by large amounts of data, uneven-label distribution, varying illumination conditions, and mixed materials in the background, recent progress in hyperspectral imaging technology and the implementation of effective tissue classification algorithms have yielded encouraging results in identifying brain cancer.

References

1. H. Sung, J. Ferlay, R. L. Siegel, M. Laversanne, I. Soerjomataram, A. Jemal, and F. Bray, "Global cancer statistics 2020: Globocan estimates of incidence and mortality worldwide for 36 cancers in 185 countries," *CA: A Cancer Journal for Clinicians*, vol. 71, no. 3, pp. 209–249, 2021.
2. D. Hanahan and R. A. Weinberg, "Hallmarks of cancer: The next generation," *Cell*, vol. 144, pp. 646–674, 2011.
3. D. N. Louis, A. Perry, G. Reifenberger, A. V. Deimling, D. Figarella-Branger, W. K. Cavenee, H. Ohgaki, O. D. Wiestler, P. Kleihues, and D. W. Ellison, "The 2016 world health organization classification of tumors of the central nervous system: A summary," *Acta Neuropathologica*, vol. 131, pp. 803–820, 2016.

4. M. Lara-Velazquez, R. Al-Kharboosh, S. Jeanneret, C. Vazquez-Ramos, D. Mahato, D. Tavanaiepour, G. Rahmathulla, and A. Quinones-Hinojosa, "Advances in brain tumor surgery for glioblastoma in adults," *Brain Sciences*, vol. 7, no. 12, p. 166, 2017.

5. D. Cardone, G. Trevisi, D. Perpetuini, C. Filippini, A. Merla, and A. Mangiola, "Intraoperative thermal infrared imaging in neurosurgery: Machine learning approaches for advanced segmentation of tumors," *Physical and Engineering Sciences in Medicine*, vol. 46, no. 1, pp. 325–337, 2023.

6. R. Thukral, A. K. Aggarwal, A. S. Arora, T. Dora, and S. Sancheti, "Artificial intelligence-based prediction of oral mucositis in patients with head-and-neck cancer: A prospective observational study utilizing a thermographic approach," *Cancer Research, Statistics, and Treatment*, vol. 6, no. 2, pp. 181–190, 2023.

7. H. Fabelo, S. Ortega, R. Lazcano, D. Madroñal, G. M. Callicó, E. Juárez, R. Salvador, D. Bulters, H. Bulstrode, A. Szolna, et al., "An intraoperative visualization system using hyperspectral imaging to aid in brain tumor delineation," *Sensors*, vol. 18, no. 2, p. 430, 2018.

8. H. Fabelo, S. Ortega, D. Ravi, B. R. Kiran, C. Sosa, D. Bulters, G. M. Callicó, H. Bulstrode, A. Szolna, J. F. Piñeiro, et al., "Spatio-spectral classification of hyperspectral images for brain cancer detection during surgical operations," *PloS One*, vol. 13, no. 3, p. e0193721, 2018.

9. G. Florimbi, H. Fabelo, E. Torti, R. Lazcano, D. Madroñal, S. Ortega, R. Salvador, F. Leporati, G. Danese, A. Báez-Quevedo, et al., "Accelerating the k-nearest neighbors filtering algorithm to optimize the real-time classification of human brain tumor in hyperspectral images," *Sensors*, vol. 18, no. 7, p. 2314, 2018.

10. B. Martinez, R. Leon, H. Fabelo, S. Ortega, J. F. Piñeiro, A. Szolna, M. Hernandez, C. Espino, A. J. O'Shanahan, D. Carrera, et al., "Most relevant spectral bands identification for brain cancer detection using hyperspectral imaging," *Sensors*, vol. 19, no. 24, p. 5481, 2019.

11. H. Fabelo, M. Halicek, S. Ortega, M. Shahedi, A. Szolna, J. F. Piñeiro, C. Sosa, A. J. O'Shanahan, S. Bisshopp, C. Espino, et al., "Deep learning-based framework for in vivo identification of glioblastoma tumor using hyperspectral images of human brain," *Sensors*, vol. 19, no. 4, p. 920, 2019.

12. F. Manni, F. van der Sommen, H. Fabelo, S. Zinger, C. Shan, E. Edström, A. ElmiTerander, S. Ortega, G. Marrero Callicó, and P. H. de With, "Hyperspectral imaging for glioblastoma surgery: Improving tumor identification using a deep spectral-spatial approach," *Sensors*, vol. 20, no. 23, p. 6955, 2020.

13. R. Leon, H. Fabelo, S. Ortega, J. F. Pineiro, A. Szolna, M. Hernandez, C. Espino, A. J. O'Shanahan, D. Carrera, S. Bisshopp, et al., "Vnir–nir hyperspectral imaging fusion targeting intraoperative brain cancer detection," *Scientific Reports*, vol. 11, no. 1, p. 19696, 2021.

14. G. Lu and B. Fei, "Medical hyperspectral imaging: A review," *Journal of Biomedical Optics*, vol. 19, no. 1, pp. 010901–010901, 2014.

15. H. Fabelo, S. Ortega, A. Szolna, D. Bulters, J. F. Piñeiro, S. Kabwama, A. JO'Shanahan, H. Bulstrode, S. Bisshopp, B. R. Kiran, et al., "In-vivo hyperspectral human brain image database for brain cancer detection," *IEEE Access*, vol. 7, pp. 39098–39116, 2019.

16. R. L. Siegel, K. D. Miller, and A. Jemal, "Cancer statistics, 2018," *CA: A Cancer Journal for Clinicians*, vol. 68, no. 1, pp. 7–30, 2018.

17. L. Kapoor and S. Thakur, "A survey on brain tumor detection using image processing techniques," in *2017 7th International Conference on Cloud Computing, Data Science & Engineering-Confluence*, pp. 582–585, IEEE, 2017.

18. M. L. Goodenberger and R. B. Jenkins, "Genetics of adult glioma," *Cancer Genetics*, vol. 205, no. 12, pp. 613–621, 2012.

19. C. G. B. Yogananda, B. R. Shah, M. Vejdani-Jahromi, S. S. Nalawade, G. K. Murugesan, F. F. Yu, M. C. Pinho, B. C. Wagner, K. E. Emblem, A. Bjørnerud, et al., "A fully automated deep learning network for brain tumor segmentation," *Tomography*, vol. 6, no. 2, pp. 186–193, 2020.

20. Q. T. Ostrom, G. Cioffi, K. Waite, C. Kruchko, and J. S. Barnholtz-Sloan, "Cbtrus statistical report: Primary brain and other central nervous system tumors diagnosed in the United States in 2014–2018," *Neuro-oncology*, vol. 23, no. Supplement 3, pp. iii1–iii105, 2021.

21. D. N. Louis, H. Ohgaki, O. D. Wiestler, W. K. Cavenee, P. C. Burger, A. Jouvet, B. W. Scheithauer, and P. Kleihues, "The 2007 who classification of tumours of the central nervous system," *Acta Neuropathologica*, vol. 114, pp. 97–109, 2007.

22. M. Havaei, A. Davy, D. Warde-Farley, A. Biard, A. Courville, Y. Bengio, C. Pal, P. M. Jodoin, and H. Larochelle, "Brain tumor segmentation with deep neural networks," *Medical Image Analysis*, vol. 35, pp. 18–31, 2017.

23. J. Choi, G. Kim, S. B. Cho, and H.-J. Im, "Radiosensitizing high-z metal nanoparticles for enhanced radiotherapy of glioblastoma multiforme," *Journal of Nanobiotechnology*, vol. 18, no. 1, pp. 1–23, 2020.

24. N. Sanai and M. S. Berger, "Glioma extent of resection and its impact on patient outcome," *Neurosurgery*, vol. 62, no. 4, pp. 753–766, 2008.

25. N. Sanai and M. S. Berger, "Operative techniques for gliomas and the value of extent of resection," *Neurotherapeutics*, vol. 6, no. 3, pp. 478–486, 2009.

26. K. Petrecca, M.-C. Guiot, V. Panet-Raymond, and L. Souhami, "Failure pattern following complete resection plus radiotherapy and temozolomide is at the resection margin in patients with glioblastoma," *Journal of Neuro-oncology*, vol. 111, pp. 19–23, 2013.

27. W. Stummer, J.-C. Tonn, H. M. Mehdorn, U. Nestler, K. Franz, C. Goetz, A. Bink, and U. Pichlmeier, "Counterbalancing risks and gains from extended resections in malignant glioma surgery: A supplemental analysis from the randomized 5-aminolevulinic acid glioma resection study," *Journal of Neurosurgery*, vol. 114, no. 3, pp. 613–623, 2011.

28. R. E. Kast, G. W. Auner, M. L. Rosenblum, T. Mikkelsen, S. M. Yurgelevic, A. Raghunathan, L. M. Poisson, and S. N. Kalkanis, "Raman molecular imaging of brain frozen tissue sections," *Journal of Neuro-oncology*, vol. 120, pp. 55–62, 2014.

29. M. Reinges, H.-H. Nguyen, T. Krings, B.-O. Hütter, V. Rohde, and J. Gilsbach, "Course of brain shift during microsurgical resection of supratentorial cerebral lesions: Limits of conventional neuronavigation," *Acta Neurochirurgica*, vol. 146, pp. 369–377, 2004.

30. K. Ganser, H. Dickhaus, A. Staubert, M. Bonsanto, C. Wirtz, V. Tronnier, and S. Kunze, "Quantification of brain shift effects in MRI images," *Biomedizinische Technik. Biomedical Engineering*, vol. 42, pp. 247–248, 1997.

31. W. Stummer, U. Pichlmeier, T. Meinel, O. D. Wiestler, F. Zanella, and H.-J. Reulen, "Fluorescence-guided surgery with 5-aminolevulinic acid for resection of malignant glioma: A randomised controlled multicentre phase iii trial," *The Lancet Oncology*, vol. 7, no. 5, pp. 392–401, 2006.

32. F. W. Floeth, M. Sabel, C. Ewelt, W. Stummer, J. Felsberg, G. Reifenberger, H. J. Steiger, G. Stoffels, H. H. Coenen, and K.-J. Langen, "Comparison of 18 f-fet pet and 5-ala fluorescence in cerebral gliomas," *European Journal of Nuclear Medicine and Molecular Imaging*, vol. 38, pp. 731–741, 2011.

33. N. T. Clancy, G. Jones, L. Maier-Hein, D. S. Elson, and D. Stoyanov, "Surgical spectral imaging," *Medical Image Analysis*, vol. 63, p. 101699, 2020.

34. A. Datta, S. Ghosh, and A. Ghosh, "Combination of clustering and ranking techniques for unsupervised band selection of hyperspectral images," *IEEE Journal of Selected Topics in Applied Earth Observations and Remote Sensing*, vol. 8, no. 6, pp. 2814–2823, 2015.

35. M. A. Calin, S. V. Parasca, D. Savastru, and D. Manea, "Hyperspectral imaging in the medical field: Present and future," *Applied Spectroscopy Reviews*, vol. 49, no. 6, pp. 435–447, 2014.

36. H. Yu, J. Park, K. Lee, J. Yoon, K. Kim, S. Lee, and Y. Park, "Recent advances in wavefront shaping techniques for biomedical applications," *Current Applied Physics*, vol. 15, no. 5, pp. 632–641, 2015.

37. T. Collier, D. Arifler, A. Malpica, M. Follen, and R. Richards-Kortum, "Determination of epithelial tissue scattering coefficient using confocal microscopy," *IEEE Journal of Selected Topics in Quantum Electronics*, vol. 9, no. 2, pp. 307–313, 2003.

38. S. Nandy, A. Mostafa, P. D. Kumavor, M. Sanders, M. Brewer, and Q. Zhu, "Characterizing optical properties and spatial heterogeneity of human ovarian tissue using spatial frequency domain imaging," *Journal of Biomedical Optics*, vol. 21, no. 10, pp. 101402–101402, 2016.

39. Z. Volynskaya, A. S. Haka, K. L. Bechtel, M. Fitzmaurice, R. Shenk, N. Wang, J. Nazemi, R. R. Dasari, and M. S. Feld, "Diagnosing breast cancer using diffuse reflectance spectroscopy

and intrinsic fluorescence spectroscopy," *Journal of Biomedical Optics*, vol. 13, no. 2, pp. 024012–024012, 2008.

40. J. Yoon, "Hyperspectral imaging for clinical applications," *BioChip Journal*, vol. 16, no. 1, pp. 1–12, 2022.

41. H. Akbari, K. Uto, Y. Kosugi, K. Kojima, and N. Tanaka, "Cancer detection using infrared hyperspectral imaging," *Cancer Science*, vol. 102, no. 4, pp. 852–857, 2011.

42. B. Regeling, B. Thies, A. O. Gerstner, S. Westermann, N. A. M'uller, J. Bendix, and W. Laffers, "Hyperspectral imaging using flexible endoscopy for laryngeal cancer detection," *Sensors*, vol. 16, no. 8, p. 1288, 2016.

43. R. T. Kester, N. Bedard, L. Gao, and T. S. Tkaczyk, "Real-time snapshot hyperspectral imaging endoscope," *Journal of Biomedical Optics*, vol. 16, no. 5, pp. 056005–056005, 2011.

44. H. Akbari, L. V. Halig, D. M. Schuster, A. Osunkoya, V. Master, P. T. Nieh, G. Z. Chen, and B. Fei, "Hyperspectral imaging and quantitative analysis for prostate cancer detection," *Journal of Biomedical Optics*, vol. 17, no. 7, pp. 076005–076005, 2012.

45. Y. Hou, Z. Ren, G. Liu, L. Zeng, and Z. Huang, "Design of a novel LD-induced hyperspectral imager for breast cancer diagnosis based on VHT grating," in 2011 Symposium on Photonics and Optoelectronics (SOPO), pp. 1–4, IEEE, 2011.

46. B. Kim, N. Kehtarnavaz, P. LeBoulluec, H. Liu, Y. Peng, and D. Euhus, "Automation of roi extraction in hyperspectral breast images," in 2013 35th Annual International Conference of the IEEE Engineering in Medicine and Biology Society (EMBC), pp. 3658–3661, IEEE, 2013.

47. R. Pourreza-Shahri, F. Saki, N. Kehtarnavaz, P. Leboulluec, and H. Liu, "Classification of ex-vivo breast cancer positive margins measured by hyperspectral imaging," in 2013 IEEE International Conference on Image Processing, pp. 1408–1412, IEEE, 2013.

48. Z. Han, A. Zhang, X. Wang, Z. Sun, M. D. Wang, and T. Xie, "In vivo use of hyperspectral imaging to develop a noncontact endoscopic diagnosis support system for malignant colorectal tumors," *Journal of Biomedical Optics*, vol. 21, no. 1, pp. 016001–016001, 2016.

49. K. Masood and N. Rajpoot, "Texture based classification of hyperspectral colon biopsy samples using CLBP," in 2009 IEEE International Symposium on Biomedical Imaging: From Nano to Macro, pp. 1011–1014, IEEE, 2009.

50. K. Masood, N. Rajpoot, K. Rajpoot, and H. Qureshi, "Hyperspectral colon tissue classification using morphological analysis," in 2006 International Conference on Emerging Technologies, pp. 735–741, IEEE, 2006.

51. K. M. Rajpoot and N. M. Rajpoot, "Wavelet based segmentation of hyperspectral colon tissue imagery," in 7th International Multi Topic Conference, 2003. INMIC 2003, pp. 38–43, IEEE, 2003.

52. D. T. Dicker, J. Lerner, P. Van Belle, D. Guerry M. Herlyn, D. E. Elder, and W. S. ElDeiry, "Differentiation of normal skin and melanoma using high resolution hyperspectral imaging," *Cancer Biology & Therapy*, vol. 5, no. 8, pp. 1033–1038, 2006.

53. S. Gaudi, R. Meyer, J. Ranka, J. C. Granahan, S. A. Israel, T. R. Yachik, and D. M. Jukic, "Hyperspectral imaging of melanocytic lesions," *The American Journal of Dermatopathology*, vol. 36, no. 2, pp. 131–136, 2014.

54. H. Akbari, Y. Kosugi, K. Kojima, and N. Tanaka, "Blood vessel detection and artery-vein differentiation using hyperspectral imaging," in 2009 Annual International Conference of the IEEE Engineering in Medicine and Biology Society, pp. 1461–1464, IEEE, 2009.

55. H. Akbari, Y. Kosugi, K. Kojima, and N. Tanaka, "Detection and analysis of the intestinal ischemia using visible and invisible hyperspectral imaging," *IEEE Transactions on Biomedical Engineering*, vol. 57, no. 8, pp. 2011–2017, 2010.

56. J. Jayanthi, G. Nisha, S. Manju, E. Philip, P. Jeemon, K. Baiju, V. Beena, and N. Subhash, "Diffuse reflectance spectroscopy: Diagnostic accuracy of a non-invasive screening technique for early detection of malignant changes in the oral cavity," *BMJ Open*, vol. 1, no. 1, p. e000071, 2011.

57. H. Fabelo, S. Ortega, S. Kabwama, G. M. Callico, D. Bulters, A. Szolna, J. F. Pineiro, and R. Sarmiento, "Helicoid project: A new use of hyperspectral imaging for brain cancer detection in real-time during neurosurgical operations," in *Hyperspectral Imaging Sensors: Innovative Applications and Sensor Standards 2016*, vol. 9860, p. 986002, SPIE, 2016.

58. J. Feng, L. Jiao, X. Zhang, and T. Sun, "Hyperspectral band selection based on trivariate mutual information and clonal selection," *IEEE Transactions on Geoscience and Remote Sensing*, vol. 52, no. 7, pp. 4092–4105, 2013.

59. L. Van Der Maaten, E. O. Postma, H. J. van den Herik, et al., "Dimensionality reduction: A comparative review," *Journal of Machine Learning Research*, vol. 10, no. 66–71, p. 13, 2009.

60. A. Datta, S. Ghosh, and A. Ghosh, "PCA, kernel PCA and dimensionality reduction in hyperspectral images," *Advances in Principal Component Analysis: Research and Development*, pp. 19–46, 2018. https://link.springer.com/book/10.1007/978-981-10-6704-4#bibliographic-information

61. D. Rav`ı, H. Fabelo, G. M. Callic, and G.-Z. Yang, "Manifold embedding and semantic segmentation for intraoperative guidance with hyperspectral brain imaging," *IEEE Transactions on Medical Imaging*, vol. 36, no. 9, pp. 1845–1857, 2017.

62. M. LJPvd and G. Hinton, "Visualizing high-dimensional data using t-SNE," *Journal of Machine Learning Research*, vol. 9, no. 2579–2605, p. 9, 2008.

63. A. Kaur, A. P. S. Chauhan, and A. K. Aggarwal, "An automated slice sorting technique for multi-slice computed tomography liver cancer images using convolutional network," *Expert Systems with Applications*, vol. 186, p. 115686, 2021.

64. G. Florimbi, H. Fabelo, E. Torti, S. Ortega, M. Marrero-Martin, G. M. Callico, G. Danese, and F. Leporati, "Towards real-time computing of intraoperative hyperspectral imaging for brain cancer detection using multi-GPU platforms," *IEEE Access*, vol. 8, pp. 8485–8501, 2020.

65. S. Ortega, M. Halicek, H. Fabelo, R. Camacho, M. d. l. L. Plaza, F. Godtliebsen, G. M. Callic´o, and B. Fei, "Hyperspectral imaging for the detection of glioblastoma tumor cells in h&e slides using convolutional neural networks," *Sensors*, vol. 20, no. 7, p. 1911, 2020.

14

An Efficient Deep CNN-Based AML Detection: Overcoming Small Database Limitations in Medical Applications

Pradeep Kumar Das, Adyasha Sahu, and Sukadev Meher

14.1 Introduction

During the last decade, research in medical images has been trying to develop an automatic and highly precise healthcare facility that aids in disease diagnosis and appropriate treatment plans over the years [9, 16, 11, 23, 10, 17, 6]. The crucial thing to consider is how well the system handles difficulties in a specific medical application. These days, transfer learning has recently emerged as a preferred strategy, particularly for producing good classification results with limited data, which is a prevalent case in the medical area [10, 3, 18, 4, 20].

Acute leukemia, a fast-spreading blood cancer, which begins in bone marrow, has a significant influence on white blood cells (WBCs) [9, 7, 5]. This cancer severely weakens the ability of the human body to resist infections, deteriorating the immune system [9, 16, 8]. The impacts are most noticeable during the stages of childhood and old age. The French-American-British paradigm classifies acute leukemia into two types: acute myeloid leukemia (AML) and acute lymphoblastic leukemia (ALL) [9, 16, 8]. ALL is characterized by the fast proliferation of lymphoblast, which limits the function of lymphocytes. It develops predominantly when these lymphoblasts cluster in the bone marrow, and it can be severe because it can impact organs such as the liver and spleen. Fever, abdominal pain, tiredness, and vomiting are all possible signs [9, 11, 8]. On the contrary, AML attacks the bone marrow and quickly destroys non-lymphocytic WBCs [11, 10, 17]. This type of leukemia causes unusual growth of soft tissue in the bones. Fever, bleeding, and bone pain are common signs and symptoms with the potential for severe consequences affecting the brain and skin if not treated timely. As a result, early detection of this disease, together with access to appropriate treatment resources, has the potential to improve overall health conditions and save lives [11, 10, 17].

During the early stages of research, medical and diagnostic systems extensively relied on traditional machine approaches. Generally, the workflows of these systems begin with the pre-processing of input images, followed by phases such as segmentation, feature extraction, and, finally, classification [11, 10, 17]. On the other hand, modern techniques have embraced convolutional neural networks (CNNs) to improve system efficiency. In contrast to older machine learning approaches, which frequently require manually generated

DOI: 10.1201/9781003450153-16

features for classification, current CNN-based systems may extract significant features directly from raw input images [8, 10, 4, 21].

CNNs are a significant achievement in the science of computer vision, with applications in real life including facial recognition, image categorization, visual search, object identification, and illness diagnosis [6, 8, 10]. Nonetheless, when dealing with CNNs, a substantial challenge arises from the requirement for extensive training data. To achieve accurate feature extraction and classification, training requires a large amount of data. Obtaining labeled datasets, however, is an extremely difficult task, particularly in the field of medical image processing. The most resource-intensive and time-consuming part of the entire process is dataset compilation. Furthermore, many medical organizations are hesitant to disclose patient data due to privacy concerns. As a result, the availability of medical databases is small. The inclusion of a limited dataset in traditional deep learning systems frequently leads to over-fitting and instability difficulties. Transfer learning has developed as a solution to these difficulties. This method uses pre-trained models to extract knowledge from larger, more diversified datasets, successfully solving the limits caused by data scarcity in specialized domains such as medical image categorization.

A number of scientists have lately concentrated their efforts on developing effective approaches for detecting acute leukemia. Das et al. [5] developed one such approach that focuses on discriminating between healthy and diseased lymphocytes affected by ALL. This method involves extracting features based on gray-level run-length matrix (GLRLM) and gray-level co-occurrence matrix (GLCM), which include texture, color, and shape. Following that, principal component analysis is used to determine the most important features and support vector machines (SVM) to classify ALL instances.

Rawat et al. [19] developed a computer-aided classification system for diagnosing AML and ALL based on SVM. Their method begins with nucleus segmentation from myeloid and lymphoid cells, then extracts color and textural information. Agaian et al. [1] described an automated AML diagnostic system. Color correlation, nucleus segmentation from myeloid cells, feature extraction, and classification are all steps in their process. Texture features like local binary pattern (LBP), color, and shape are also extracted resulting in improved classification outcomes. [17] Madhukar et al. used the ASH dataset to successfully apply SVM to classify AML. The strategy employs a K-means clustering algorithm to segment, a LDP to extract features, and ultimately an SVM method to identify anomaly. Employing the ASH dataset, in [12], Goutam and Sailaja proposed a reliable and precise AML detection algorithm. Their method combines the following methods: K-means clustering to segment, LDP to extract features, and SVM to identify cancer. Kumar and Udwadia [16] developed an AML detection technique that is automated. The K-means technique is used to perform nucleus preprocessing and segmentation. Following that, both shape and texture features are retrieved, and the input image is categorized as cancerous or not thorough SVM.

Deep learning advances have motivated researchers to develop novel techniques targeted at improving the effectiveness of systems. Conventional deep learning methods necessitate a large amount of training data in order to extract and classify features effectively. As a result, transfer learning (TL) has emerged as a preferred strategy for robust illness diagnosis, especially when working with small datasets. Das et al. [4] presented an ALL classification technique based on ShuffleNet in 2021, achieving 96.97% accuracy using the ALLIDB1 dataset and 96.67% accuracy with the ALLIDB2 dataset. Das et al. [10] recommended a reliable MobileNetV2-SVM-based blood cancer (AML and ALL) detection algorithm.

According to the explanation above, traditional machine learning-based acute leukemia systems require extra segmentation techniques to produce promising results. Recent advances in deep learning, notably transfer learning, make the identification of AML more reliable since, unlike typical deep learning systems, it can show promising results even in limited datasets. Furthermore, unlike traditional machine learning systems, it does not require additional segmentation schemes. In this work, we have suggested an automatic AML detection system that makes use of a popular model, EfficientNetB0, a cutting-edge deep learning architecture known for its outstanding performance in image recognition tasks. In addition, an augmentation approach has been carried out named RandAugment. Some key contributions of the proposed work are mentioned as follows.

14.1.1 Contribution

The primary contributions of the proposed work are listed below.

- This study deploys a deep learning-based framework for AML diagnosis, based on EfficientNet architecture [25]. Because of its consistent and adaptable scaling of depth, width, and resolution, this technique is especially well-suited for small databases. This adaptability creates a balance between classification performance and computational efficiency, yielding exceptional detection capabilities.

- The addition of a stochastic component to the data augmentation process allows the choice of a mix of augmentation operations at random, instead of applying a fixed set of predetermined augmentation operations to each training image. This randomization adds variation to the enlarged dataset, increasing its robustness and versatility.

- Instead of relying on a single observation, a 5-fold cross-validation process is used to assure fairness and reliable performance assessment. In addition, six separate performance criteria are used for quantitative analysis, allowing a full evaluation of the model's success.

The organization of this work is outlined as follows: Section 14.2 describes the proposed AML detection scheme. Section 14.3 explores the experimental results discussion and presentation. Finally, in Section 14.4, we provide a brief summary and explanation of the work.

14.2 Proposed Method

Transfer learning algorithms have gained significant popularity in the field of autonomous disease identification in recent years due to their ability to give robust results even with minimal data. They overcome the shortcomings of standard deep learning networks, which suffer from performance loss when dealing with small datasets due to a lack of training data. This prompted to development of a reliable transfer learning-based AML detection network, as displayed in Figure 14.1, which is designed to achieve noticeable results even in circumstances with low data availability.

PSEUDO CODE 1: DEEP CNN-BASED AML DETECTION

Input: Microscopic Images
Output: Prediction of Class
Begin
1. Perform data augmentation using RandAugment as a preprocessing step to train the network properly.
2. Adaptively update the scaling parameters: D, W, and R by updating the compound coefficient as presented in Eq. 1 with considering a, b, and c are 1.2, 1.1, and 1.15, respectively.
3. Employs EfficientNetB0 as presented in Figure 14.1 to classify AML and Non-AML more efficiently.

End

Here, the mobile inverted bottleneck, MBConv [24] block, efficiently aids in squeeze-and-excitation updation. It integrates the beneficial features of the inverted residual and the bottleneck structure. A data augmentation approach named Randaugment is employed prior to the CNN structure to train the network properly. The Pseudo Code of the proposed deep CNN-based AML detection approach is presented in Pseudo Code 1.

14.2.1 Pre-processing

RandAugment is a popular data augmentation approach employed in machine learning and deep learning, specifically to train neural networks for image categorization problems. The fundamental purpose of data augmentation is to improve the diversity of the training data by adding numerous transforms to the original images. This improves generalization and lowers over-fitting in the model. Conventional data augmentation strategies require manually picking and applying modifications to the images, such as rotation, scaling, cropping, and flipping.

RandAugment uses a simple yet effective way to automate the process of selecting and executing data augmentation policies. RandAugment randomly picks a series of

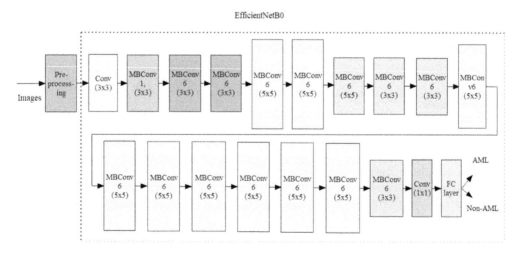

FIGURE 14.1
Proposed AML cancer detection scheme.

augmentation operations from a present set of transformations and parameters rather than manually setting augmentation operations and parameters. Some major elements of RandAugment are as follows:

- RandAugment specifies a collection of augmentation operations, including rotation, translation, shear, and color manipulation (for example, brightness and contrast alterations). A random magnitude or strength is sampled for each selected augmentation process. This magnitude regulates the intensity of the image transformation.
- RandAugment also chooses the number of augmentation operations to apply to each image at random.

The primary feature of RandAugment is that it is an automatic process allowing one to experiment with a variety of augmentation tactics without having to tune them manually. This frequently improves the performance of the AML detection system.

14.2.2 CNN Architecture

The deliberate scaling of specific architectural characteristics, especially depth, width, and resolution, plays a significant role in boosting performance in modern deep-learning networks.

For example, different ResNet architectures are created by increasing the network depth. Various ResNet topologies, for example, have been designed by increasing the depth of the network, resulting in the extraction of more intricate and significant hierarchical features. However, as the network grows deeper, training becomes more difficult due to difficulties such as vanishing gradient problems. Although solutions such as batch normalization and skip connections [13] help to avoid these issues, they can have a negative impact on computing efficiency. The updation of the width term is shown in MobileNetV2 [14]. Expanding the width of a smaller network increases its ability to extract significant features and makes training easy and simple. However, it may offer its own set of training issues, especially in the case of very large but shallow models. The resolution variation is recommended in [25, 15]. Improving the resolution of input images results in better image clarity and sharp visual information to the network, and thus enhances the finer-grained feature extraction ability. This advancement, however, comes at the expense of greater computing needs.

To achieve a well-balanced trade-off between classification performance and computational cost, these three parameters must be carefully adjusted: depth, width, and resolution. A methodical approach is required to achieve this balance effectively. One way, known as compound scaling, suggested in EfficientNet, involves altering the network's depth, width, and resolution all at once and consistently [25]. Here, all three parameters vary uniformly. Figure 14.2 depicts the difference between compound scaling and other scaling methods.

Even if one of these three parameters can be scaled orbitally, the majority of current works concentrate to update a single parameter. Meanwhile, orbitary parameter updation is getting difficult because it requires manual tuning. As a result, in the EfficientNetB0 [25] architecture, an efficient compound scaling strategy is recommended for evenly updating three parameters. As seen in Equation (1), uniform scaling is obtained here.

$$D = a^\gamma; W = b^\gamma; R = c^\gamma; \text{where, } b^2c^2a \approx 2; a \geq 1; b \geq 1; c \geq 1. \tag{1}$$

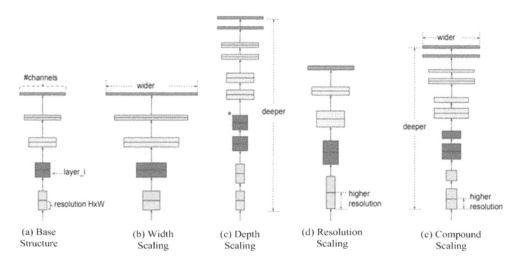

(a) Base
Structure

(b) Width
Scaling

(c) Depth
Scaling

(d) Resolution
Scaling

(e) Compound
Scaling

FIGURE 14.2
Types of scaling [25].

The scaling-up parameters in depth scaling are D = 4, W = 1, and R = 1. The scaling up parameters in width scaling are D = 1, W = 2, and R = 1. The scaling-up parameters in resolution scaling are D = 1, W = 1, and R = 2. The scaling-up parameter is 1, which means the parameter remains constant.

The compound coefficient (γ) scales the resolution, R, width, W, and depth, D, of the network equally. This coefficient is in charge of controlling the availability of additional resources for scaling. c, b, and a, the constant terms successfully employ these additional resources for scaling-up resolution, breadth, and depth, respectively [25]. A small grid search is used to estimate these phrases. In this work, gamma is set to 1, indicating the availability of twice as many resources. As indicated in EfficientNetB0 [25], the values of a, b, and c are 1.2, 1.1, and 1.15, respectively.

Hence, adaptive and uniform scaling of those three terms results in an effective AML detection. Furthermore, the Randaugment improves overall system performance.

14.3 Results and Discussion

Here, we have conducted a comprehensive performance analysis of our suggested technique for detecting AML. First, we present a brief of the employed AML dataset and the performance measures. Then, the performance analysis is performed.

14.3.1 Datasets

In this work, a publicly available dataset, ASH [2] is used for AML detection. It is available at http://imagebank.hematology.org. For the experimentation, 40 images from each class of AML and Non-AML are used. Figure 14.3 shows the AML and Non-AML images from ASH dataset.

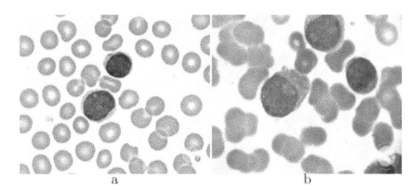

FIGURE 14.3
Two classes of ASH dataset: (a) non-AML and (b) AML.

14.3.2 Performance Measures

We have analyzed the performance quantitatively using five common assessment metrics: accuracy, precision, specificity, sensitivity, and F1 score. Mathematical expressions of these measures [6, 8, 22] are presented below.

$$Accuracy = \frac{TP + TN}{TN + TP + FP + FN} \tag{2}$$

$$Precision = \frac{TP}{TP + FP} \tag{3}$$

$$Sensitivity = \frac{TP}{FN + TP} \tag{4}$$

$$Specificity = \frac{TN}{FP + TN} \tag{5}$$

$$F1\,Score = \frac{2*Precision*Sensitivity}{Precision + Sensitivity} \tag{6}$$

Where TP stands for true positive (AML predicted as AML), TN denotes true negative (non-AML predicted as non-AML), FP stands for false positive (non-AML predicted as AML), and FN denotes false negative (AML predicted as non-AML). These measures provide a complete and deep understanding of how effectively our proposed scheme and the selected transfer learning networks perform in the task of detecting AML.

14.3.3 Performance Analysis

Our goal is to give a comparative analysis by comparing the performance of our proposed approach to that of well-known transfer learning networks such as DenseNet201, InceptionV3, VGG16, GoogleNet, ResNet18, and ShuffleNet. We have used the same data augmentation approach across all of these transfer learning networks to achieve a fair and unbiased evaluation. This consistency is vital for maintaining the results' integrity and comparability. We have used a 5-fold cross-validation strategy over a single cycle to reduce potential biases and improve the dependability of our findings. This cross-validation technique ensures that our research is founded on a robust and representative set of data splits, resulting in a more accurate and unbiased evaluation of the efficacy of the proposed AML detection scheme.

To conduct all experiments, a common experimental platform with the following criteria is used:

Processor- Intel(R) Core (TM) i7-11700;

RAM- 16GB;

Clock speed- 2.50GHz;

GPU: NVIDIA T400 with 8 GB of dedicated memory.

The simulation environment used for the experiments is MATLAB R2020b. The following values are set as the important parameters for the experiments:

Batch sizes – 64;

Number of epochs – 12;

Initial learning rate – 0.0001.

These parameters enable experiment consistency and repeatability, allowing for a thorough evaluation of the suggested AML detection strategy and comparing transfer learning models.

Table 14.1 presents the comparison of the performance of the proposed scheme with the existing schemes in the ASH dataset. The table shows the superiority of the proposed AML detection scheme with the highest accuracy, recall, and specificity.

A detailed performance evaluation is done for both the suggested method as well as the comparing methods for AML detection in Table 14.2. This result represents the mean performance of the 5-fold cross validation. The results of all these models, as presented in Table 4.2, are experimentally obtained in the same environment as that of the proposed method. The table shows that the proposed EfficientNet-based AML detection outperforms its competitors with the best performance values: 96.25% accuracy, 97.44% precision, 97.5% specificity, 95% sensitivity, and 0.9620 F1 score. ShuffleNet gives the second-best AML detection performance with 93.75% accuracy, whereas ResNet18 ranks third with 92.50% accuracy.

The proposed method yields a 2.50% improvement in accuracy, 2.50% improvement in sensitivity, 2.57% improvement in precision, and 2.50% improvement in specificity than

TABLE 14.1

Comparison of Performance of the Proposed Scheme with the Existing Schemes in the ASH Dataset

Method	Accuracy (%)	Recall (%)	Specificity (%)
[17]	93.50	83.00	91.00
[16]	9500	–	–
[10]	95.31	94.38	98.13
Proposed	96.25	95.00	97.50

TABLE 14.2

Performance Evaluation for Identifying AML

Method	Specificity (%)	F1 Score	Accuracy (%)	Precision (%)	Sensitivity (%)
DenseNet201	85.00	0.8780	87.50	85.71	90.00
InceptionV3	90.00	0.8861	88.75	89.74	87.50
VGG16	87.50	0.9025	90.00	88.10	92.50
GoogLeNet	92.50	0.9114	91.25	92.31	90.00
ResNet18	92.50	0.9250	92.50	92.5	92.50
ShuffLeNet	95.00	0.9367	93.75	94.87	92.50
Proposed	97.50	0.9620	96.25	97.44	95.00

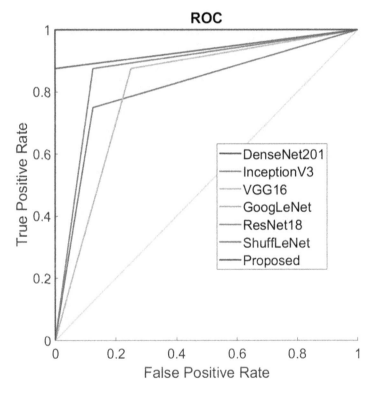

FIGURE 14.4

ROC performances for AML detection.

the second-best model. The proposed method yields the minimum false detection with 1 FP and 2 FN, whereas the second-best ShuffleNet yields 2 FP and 3 FN. The minimum false detection with maximum correct detection helps in achieving the best AML detection performances.

For a better understanding, the ROC curve for the third fold is presented in Figure 14.4. As displayed in the figure, the proposed method gains the best ROC performance, whereas the ShuffleNet achieves the second-best performance. In contrast, GoogLeNet and ResNet18 depict the third-best ROC performance.

14.4 Conclusion

This work describes an effective AML detection method that makes use of the robust EfficientNetB0 deep learning model along with Rand augmentation to deal with the problem of small datasets and over-fitting. RandAugment improves the model's ability to generalize by diversifying the training data, hence reducing the limits of limited data. The CNN structure achieves uniform and adaptive scaling of depth, width, and resolution while maintaining a careful balance between classification efficiency and computing cost, resulting in an efficient detection framework. The combined advantage of RandAugment and EfficientNetB0 makes the proposed AML detection framework perform better than other methods on the ASH dataset. It achieves the best result with 96.50% accuracy, even with a small dataset.

Reference

1. Agaian S, Madhukar M, Chronopoulos AT (2014) Automated screening system for acute myelogenous leukemia detection in blood microscopic images. *IEEE Systems Journal* 8(3):995–1004.
2. Bank AI (2021) Acute myeloid leukemia. *American Society of Hematology*. http://imagebank.hematology.org.
3. Das PK, Meher S (2021) An efficient deep convolutional neural network based detection and classification of acute lymphoblastic leukemia. *Expert Systems with Applications*: 183: 115311.
4. Das PK, Meher S (2021) Transfer learning-based automatic detection of acute lymphocytic leukemia. In: 2021 National Conference on Communications (NCC), IEEE, pp 1–6.
5. Das PK, Jadoun P, Meher S (2020) Detection and classification of acute lymphocytic leukemia. In: 2020 IEEE-HYDCON, pp 1–5, https://doi.org/10.1109/ HYDCON48903.2020.9242745.
6. Das PK, Meher S, Panda R, Abraham A (2020) A review of automated methods for the detection of sickle cell disease. *IEEE Reviews in Biomedical Engineering* 13:309–324.
7. Das PK, Pradhan A, Meher S (2021) Detection of acute lymphoblastic leukemia using machine learning techniques. *Machine Learning, Deep Learning and Computational Intelligence for Wireless Communication*: 749: 425.
8. Das PK, Diya V, Meher S, Panda R, Abraham A (2022) A systematic review on recent advancements in deep and machine learning-based detection and classification of acute lymphoblastic leukemia. *IEEE Access:* 10: 81741–81763.
9. Das PK, Meher S, Panda R, Abraham A (2022) An efficient blood-cell segmentation for the detection of hematological disorders. *IEEE Transactions on Cybernetics* 52(10):615–10,626, https://doi.org/10.1109/TCYB.2021.3062152.
10. Das PK, Nayak B, Meher S (2022) A lightweight deep learning system for automatic detection of blood cancer. *Measurement* 191(110):762.
11. Das PK, Sahoo B, Meher S (2023) An efficient detection and classification of acute leukemia using transfer learning and orthogonal softmax layer-based model. *IEEE/ACM Transactions on Computational Biology and Bioinformatics* 20:1817–1828.
12. Goutam D, Sailaja S (2015) Classification of acute myelogenous leukemia in blood microscopic images using supervised classifier. In: 2015 IEEE International Conference on Engineering and Technology (ICETECH), IEEE, pp 1–5.
13. He K, Zhang X, Ren S, Sun J (2016) Deep residual learning for image recognition. In: Proceedings of the IEEE Conference on Computer Vision and Pattern Recognition, pp 770–778.
14. Howard AG, Zhu M, Chen B, Kalenichenko D, Wang W, Weyand T, Andreetto M, Adam H (2017) Mobilenets: Efficient convolutional neural networks for mobile vision applications. arXiv preprint arXiv:170404861.

15. Huang Y, Cheng Y, Bapna A, Firat O, Chen D, Chen M, Lee H, Ngiam J, Le QV, Wu Y, et al. (2019) Gpipe: Efficient training of giant neural networks using pipeline parallelism. *Advances in Neural Information Processing Systems* 32: 103–112.

16. Kumar P, Udwadia SM (2017) Automatic detection of acute myeloid leukemia from microscopic blood smear image. In: 2017 International Conference on Advances in Computing, Communications and Informatics (ICACCI), IEEE, pp 1803–1807.

17. Madhukar M, Agaian S, Chronopoulos AT (2012) Deterministic model for acute myelogenous leukemia classification. In: 2012 IEEE International Conference on Systems, Man, and Cybernetics (SMC), IEEE, pp 433–438.

18. Paul I, Sahu A, Das PK, Meher S (2023) Deep convolutional neural network-based automatic detection of brain tumor. In: 2023 2nd International Conference for Innovation in Technology (INOCON), IEEE, pp 1–6.

19. Rawat J, Singh A, Bhadauria H, Virmani J, Devgun JS (2017) Computer-assisted classification framework for prediction of acute lymphoblastic and acute myeloblastic leukemia. *Biocybernetics and Biomedical Engineering* 37(4):637–654.

20. Sahu A, Das PK, Meher S, Panda R, Abraham A (2022) An efficient deep learning-based breast cancer detection scheme with small datasets. In: International Conference on Intelligent Systems Design and Applications, Springer, pp 39–48.

21. Sahu A, Das PK, Meher S (2023) High accuracy hybrid CNN classifiers for breast cancer detection using mammogram and ultrasound datasets. *Biomedical Signal Processing and Control* 80(104):292.

22. Sahu A, Das PK, Meher S (2023) Recent advancements in machine learning and deep learning-based breast cancer detection using mammograms. *Physica Medica* 114(103):138.

23. Sahu A, Das PK, Meher S (2024) An efficient deep learning scheme to detect breast cancer using mammogram and ultrasound breast images. *Biomedical Signal Processing and Control* 87(105):377.

24. Sandler M, Howard A, Zhu M, Zhmoginov A, Chen LC (2018) Mobilenetv2: Inverted residuals and linear bottlenecks. In: Proceedings of the IEEE Conference on Computer Vision and Pattern Recognition, pp 4510–4520.

25. Tan M, Le Q (2019) Efficientnet: Rethinking model scaling for convolutional neural networks. In: International Conference on Machine Learning, PMLR, pp 6105–6114.

15

Effective Use of Computational Biology and Artificial Intelligence in the Domain of Medical Oncology

Sameeksha Saraf, Arka De, and B. K. Tripathy

15.1 Introduction

The advent of technology in healthcare has been a progressive journey marked by innovation and breakthroughs. From the simple applications of computer-based record keeping to the sophisticated integration of computational algorithms and artificial intelligence (AI) techniques, the medical field has witnessed a dramatic transformation which has not only enhanced the efficiency of health care but has also provided personalized solutions to intricate medical problems. Among these technological advancements, computational biology and AI stand out as remarkable tools that are shaping the future of medicine. It is an interdisciplinary field that leverages computational methods to analyze and model biological systems and has become a cornerstone in understanding complex biological processes. It assists researchers and medical professionals in predicting biological behaviour, analyzing genetic sequences, and understanding disease mechanisms. Meanwhile AI has brought intelligence to machines, enabling them to learn from patterns and data and thus make predictions and take actions without human intervention. Together, computational biology and AI [1] are paving the way for an era where medical practice is driven by data, intelligence, and precision. Their application spans various medical domains such as diagnostics, prognosis, personalized treatment, and drug discovery. By implementing machine learning algorithms [2], deep learning techniques [3], and predictive modelling, these technologies have revolutionized how diseases are diagnosed, treated, and even prevented.

Computational biology and artificial intelligence (AI) are transforming the field of oncology by enhancing diagnostic precision, personalizing treatment regimens, and expediting drug discovery. AI algorithms excel at interpreting complex medical images and genomic data, enabling earlier and more accurate detection of cancer. AI is also instrumental in developing personalized treatment plans. By leveraging machine learning models that predict individual patient responses to different therapeutic options, clinicians can optimize treatment efficacy and minimize side effects. It has also expedited the drug discovery process. These technologies can examine vast biological datasets to identify potential new drug candidates and interactions, which is invaluable in the urgent quest for innovative cancer therapies. In addition, these computational tools provide a robust framework for data-driven clinical decision-making, refining prognostic evaluations and overall treatment planning.

As computational biology and AI continue to evolve, their application in oncology holds significant promise for transforming patient care and advancing the frontiers of cancer research.

This chapter seeks to explore the multifaceted impact of computational biology and AI on the field of medicine. It provides an in-depth look at their applications, focusing on the potential they hold to redefine healthcare practices. From interpreting medical images with pinpoint accuracy to personalizing treatment strategies based on individual genetic makeup, the chapter will delve into how these technologies are not only enhancing existing medical procedures but also opening new avenues in healthcare delivery. The promise of computational biology and AI [4] in medicine is not merely a scientific curiosity but is a reality that is transforming lives, improving patient outcomes, and shaping a new frontier in health care. A detailed mind map of the chapter has been presented in Figure 15.1. As we move forward into a future where medicine is increasingly personalized, predictive, and precise, the importance of understanding and leveraging these tools will only continue to grow. [5]

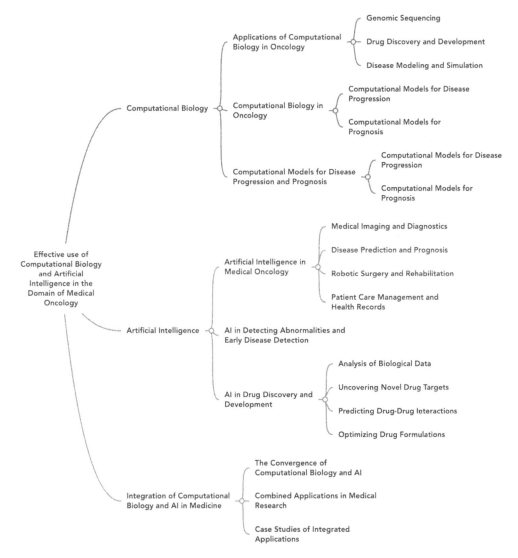

FIGURE 15.1
Computational biology and AI in fields of medical oncology.

15.2 Computational Biology

One of the fields of studies which apply interdisciplinary fields such as computer science, mathematics, and statistics to answer biological questions is computational biology. Due to the development of high-throughput techniques such as automatic DNA sequencing, comprehensive expression analysis with microarrays, and proteome analysis with modern mass spectrometry, its importance has been increased. This has benefited the expert practitioners who utilize it in the survey of computational biology methods by focusing on their applications, including primary sequence analysis, protein structure elucidation, transcriptomics and proteomics data analysis, and exploration of protein interaction networks. For all those scientists who have an interest in pursuing quantitative biology, computational biology serves as a guide. Computational biology is authoritative and easy to use. Computational biology [6] is a multifaceted field that interweaves algorithms, mathematical models, and computational simulation techniques to investigate biological, behavioural, and social systems. Figure 15.2 illustrates the basic make up of computational biology.

By harmoniously blending principles from computer science, mathematics, and physics, computational biology uncovers and deciphers complex biological data. Its integrative approach enables deep comprehension of the underlying mechanisms of life. It is instrumental in understanding genetic sequences, analyzing protein structures, and simulating cellular pathways. The applications of computational biology are vast, encompassing areas such as genomics, proteomics, and medical imaging. In personalized medicine, it allows for the customization of treatments based on an individual's unique genetic makeup. In drug discovery, it aids in identifying novel targets and optimizing formulations, accelerating the development of therapeutics for various diseases, including rare conditions. It also plays a vital role in understanding disease progression at the molecular level, aiding in

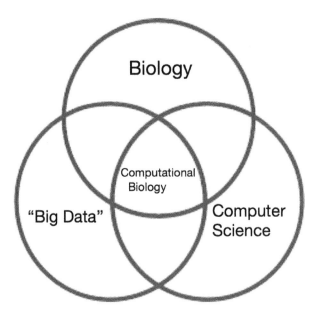

FIGURE 15.2
Components of computational biology.

early detection and prognosis. Moreover, computational biology supports the creation of predictive models for epidemiology, contributing to public health strategies. Its influence in modern healthcare and biological research is profound, as it continually opens new doors to innovation and understanding, aligning with the current trends in technological research and development, and representing a significant leap in scientific exploration.[7]

15.2.1 Computational Biology in Oncology

Computational biology in the fields of oncology and cancer research [8] represents a convergence of biological data along with physical sciences such as physics, mathematics, and engineering with other computational techniques, enabling a profound understanding of complex biological systems and phenomena related to the occurrence, development, as well as treatment of malignant tumours and cancerous cells. In the oncological realm, this integration of fields offers invaluable insights into various aspects of pathogenesis and malignancies with the help of medical imaging, genomic sequencing, biopsy samples, and other clinically available data. By employing mathematical models, algorithms, and statistical methods, computational biology helps in the accurate interpretation of these large-scale biological data. This has led to advancements in early detection of malignancies, personalized medicine, and the efficient development of therapeutic strategies and chemotherapy protocols. Implementation of computational biology [9] with traditional medicine is reshaping healthcare delivery, emphasizing data-driven decisions and precision, and heralding a new era of innovation and improvement in patient outcomes. The concept of computational oncology is serving as a bridge between oncologists and biologists, facilitating close collaboration to develop more effective therapies and diagnostic tools for cancer. Computational biology's imprint on medicine is profound and transformative, be it in cancer research, neurological studies, or infectious disease control and also continues to expand with ongoing research and technological development.

15.2.2 Applications of Computational Biology in Oncology

Computational biology finds diverse and transformative applications in medicine, revolutionizing many traditional processes: from genomic sequencing, where it enables personalized medicine by tailoring treatments to individual genetic profiles, to drug discovery, where it accelerates the identification and development of potential therapeutics. Additionally, computational biology facilitates intricate disease modelling and simulation, providing profound insights into disease mechanisms and progression. By integrating mathematics, physics, and computer science with biological data, computational biology opens new horizons in health care, fostering innovation, enhancing accuracy, and promising a more patient-centric approach to medical practice. Some of the most used applications of computational biology are listed below.[10]

15.2.2.1 Genomic Sequencing

Genomic sequencing [11] has been greatly enhanced by computational biology, allowing for the precise reading and interpretation of genetic code. It has enabled researchers to map entire genomes and identify variations linked to specific diseases or traits. A close computational study of these unique sequences enables the identification of genetic mutations including changes caused in a single nucleotide known as point mutation, which may result in dysfunctional protein and cancer development along with the duplications or deletion of large genomic regions known as copy number variations which may or may not include oncogenes or tumour suppressing genes [12] . Genome sequences of patients are also used in the tumour profiling, identifying the genetic makeups of the tumours and their mutation types which are associated with its ability to metastasize to other parts of the body. Comparative genomics also helps in distinguishing normal cells from cancerous cell and also in cross-cancer comparisons and their evolutionary behaviours. An example of such genomic sequencing used in studies has been presented in Figure 15.3.

15.2.2.2 Drug Discovery and Development

Computational biology plays a crucial role in the modern process of drug discovery and development. By utilizing algorithms, molecular modelling, and virtual screening, it can simulate the interactions between drugs and their target proteins [13]. The first step in the formulation of drugs is the identification of drug targets, which is done through the analysis of high-throughput genomic data. Computational methods such as machine learning algorithms can sift through vast datasets to identify genes or proteins that are aberrantly expressed in cancer cells. Once a potential target is identified, computational docking methods can be used to predict how different drugs will interact with the target. This accelerates the initial screening of drug candidates, saving both time and resources. Computational biology also aids in understanding the complex signalling pathways involved in cancer, which can be targeted for therapeutic interventions [14].Moreover, computational biology helps in predicting drug–drug interactions, optimizing drug formulations, and assessing potential side effects, thus streamlining the development process and reducing the time and cost associated with traditional laboratory methods.

15.2.2.3 Disease Modelling and Simulation

Disease modelling and simulation through computational biology offer invaluable insights into the underlying mechanisms and progression of various diseases [15]. Computational

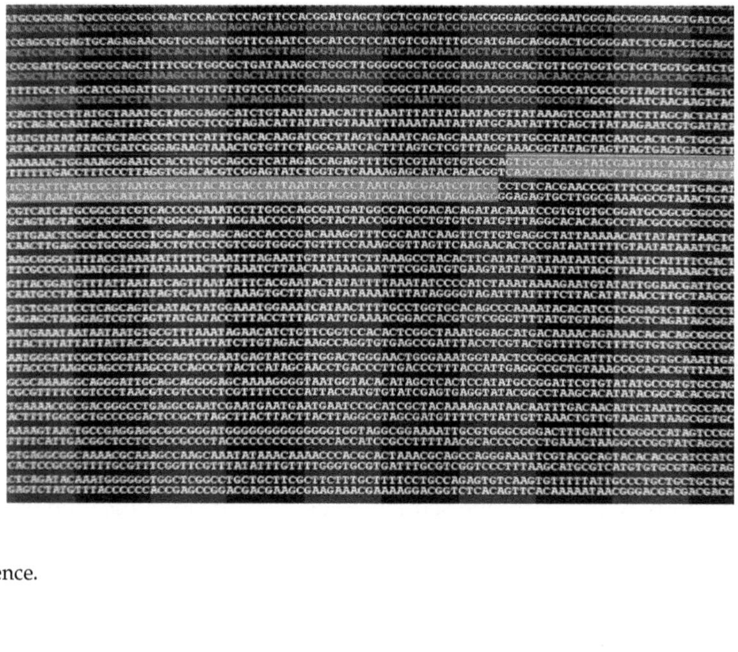

FIGURE 15.3
Genomic sequence.

oncology has been emerging as one of the most pivotal tools in the process of understanding the complex dynamics of cancer progression, treatment, and patient outcomes. The use of mathematics models along with machine learning algorithms and high-performance computation aims to simulate the spatiotemporal evolution of tumours scaling from molecular interactions to tissue and organ-level organizations [16]. Agent-based modelling is one of the key approaches in which individual cells are modelled as agents that are to interact based on a set of predefined rules, thereby mimicking tumour heterogeneity and microenvironmental factors [17]. The use of partial differential equations is another signification method to model the diffusion of nutrients, growth factors, and drugs within the tumour mass [18]. These models are often calibrated and validated using real-world clinical and genomic data, thereby increasing their predictive accuracy.

By creating these virtual representations of biological systems, researchers can mimic the interactions between cells, tissues, and organs in the context of a specific disease, which in turn allows for the exploration of various scenarios, such as the impact of different treatments or the effect of genetic mutations on disease progression. Such modelling enables a deeper understanding of complex disease pathways and the identification of potential targets for therapeutic intervention. Furthermore, it facilitates the design and testing of new treatment strategies in a controlled virtual environment, leading to more focused and efficient clinical trials.

15.2.3 Computational Models for Disease Progression and Prognosis

Computational models are instrumental in the realm of disease progression and prognosis, providing a multifaceted approach to personalized patient care [19]. Through mathematical equations, algorithms, and simulations, these models represent the complex dynamics of disease progression, offering insights that can inform effective interventions and preventive measures. They enable personalized prognosis by considering a patient's unique characteristics, enhancing clinical decision-making, and supporting drug development by simulating drug effects on diseases. Additionally, they play a critical role in public health planning, predicting the spread of infectious diseases, and guiding resource allocation. However, challenges such as data quality, integration, model validation, and ethical considerations must be addressed to fully harness these models' potential. By overcoming these obstacles and leveraging the power of computational modelling, modern medicine stands to gain a nuanced understanding of diseases, more personalized care, evidence-based decision-making, and streamlined healthcare delivery. The integration of computational models into clinical practice promises to transform patient outcomes and herald a new era of precision medicine.

15.2.3.1 Computational Models for Disease Progression

Disease progression modelling through computational techniques provides critical insights into the evolution of illnesses, especially in chronic conditions where progression can be slow and complex. Utilizing algorithms, mathematical models, and vast data analytics, this method simulates how diseases develop and spread within the body. It enables researchers to identify key biomarkers, understand the dynamics of disease pathways, and tailor personalized medical interventions. The application of computational models in understanding disease progression marks a significant advancement in healthcare, allowing for more accurate diagnoses, effective treatments, and a deeper understanding of various diseases.[20]

- **Understanding dynamics:** computational models play a vital role in understanding disease dynamics by analyzing extensive datasets that include patient histories, genetic information, and medical imaging[21]. In the context of cancer, these models simulate tumour growth and metastasis, providing a comprehensive view of the disease's evolution. This complex analysis helps in identifying subtle changes and patterns that may not be apparent through traditional methods. This insight aids medical professionals in designing timely and targeted interventions, thus improving patient outcomes.

- **Predicting pathways:** predicting disease pathways through computational models involves identifying key biomarkers and triggers influencing progression. For instance, in ailments like diabetes or heart disease, these models analyze intricate relationships between genes, proteins, and external factors. By unlocking this information, researchers can predict how a disease might spread and where interventions might be most effective. It provides a roadmap for both prevention and treatment, allowing for strategies that are more proactive rather than reactive.

- **Personalized medicine:** the integration of computational models into personalized medicine is a significant advancement. By modelling how diseases progress in individual patients, healthcare providers can tailor interventions, maximizing effectiveness and minimizing adverse effects. This individualized approach considers a patient's unique genetic makeup, lifestyle, and other factors, allowing for a treatment plan that is highly customized. It ensures that medical interventions are not only focused on treating symptoms but are aligned with the specific characteristics of the disease in each patient, leading to more successful outcomes.[22]

15.2.3.2 Computational Models for Prognosis

Prognostic modelling through computational methods is a sophisticated approach to predicting the likely outcome or course of a disease [23]. By leveraging mathematical algorithms, statistical analysis, and machine learning, these models analyze complex clinical and biological data to forecast disease trajectories. This could include estimating survival rates, predicting responses to treatments, or assessing the risk of recurrence. The precision and insight gained from computational prognosis models assist medical professionals in making informed decisions about treatment strategies, patient care, and resource allocation. It represents a significant advancement in medicine, aligning personalized care with predictive analytics.

- **Risk stratification:** computational prognosis models contribute significantly to risk stratification, categorizing patients based on likely disease progression. By analyzing various factors like genetic information, previous medical history, and current health status, these models can accurately gauge a patient's risk level. This assessment aids clinicians in planning appropriate treatments, ensuring that the medical interventions are aligned with the individual's specific risk factors. It enhances efficiency in healthcare delivery and helps in the timely prevention and management of complications.

- **Treatment response prediction:** treatment response prediction through computational models involves simulating different therapy scenarios to foresee how a patient might respond. By analyzing a patient's unique characteristics, these models predict the effectiveness of various interventions, thereby assisting medical professionals in optimizing therapy plans. This approach leads to more targeted and efficient treatment strategies, reducing unnecessary trials of different therapies and enhancing the overall patient care experience.[24]

- **Survival analysis:** in the context of terminal diseases, computational models are employed to analyze survival rates. This analysis encompasses assessing various factors influencing survival, such as disease stage, treatment options, and patient-specific conditions. By guiding clinical care and patient expectations survival analysis through computational modelling supports informed decision-making, allowing both healthcare providers and patients to plan accordingly.

- **Integration with AI:** the integration of AI[25] algorithms with computational models marks a novel advancement in improving prediction accuracy. Machine learning techniques, specifically, have the capability to find subtle patterns in complex data that human analysis might overlook. This fusion of traditional computational models with AI algorithms results in more precise and actionable insights, allowing for improved risk assessments, treatment predictions, and overall enhanced healthcare delivery.

15.3 Artificial Intelligence

Artificial intelligence (AI) [26] is an interdisciplinary branch within computer science that is dedicated to creating systems that are able to replicate human intelligence as much as possible. The ultimate goal is of building machines that are capable of performing a wide array of cognitive tasks which traditionally require human intellect. AI systems are designed to excel in various domains, such as problem-solving, employing logical reasoning and optimization techniques; speech recognition, interpreting and translating spoken language; planning and decision-making, orchestrating complex tasks; learning from data and experiences; natural language processing (NLP), understanding and generating human languages; perception, recognizing and interpreting sensory inputs like images or sounds; and moving or manipulating objects through robotics.

Machine learning is also a subset of AI which enables systems to adapt to new situations and improve over time. The integration and synergy of these components have led to the remarkable influence of AI across various industries, including health care, finance, transportation, and entertainment. AI is trying to revolutionize the interaction of machines with humans and the possible ways they can assist humans, paving the path for a future where intelligent machines are an integral part of daily life. It is also an attempt to reshape our experience with technology and open new frontiers for innovation with maximum efficiency.

15.3.1 Artificial Intelligence in Medical Oncology

Artificial Intelligence (AI) in medicine [27] is improving healthcare by making machines better at diagnosing illnesses, tailoring treatments to individual patients, and making everything more efficient. AI algorithms are being increasingly integrated into the fields of medical oncology and are assisting in various aspects of cancer care, from diagnosis to treatment planning and monitoring. AI algorithms, mainly deep learning models, are capable of analyzing complex medical radiological images, genomic sequences, and pathological slides to detect malignant tumours and cancer as early as possible and tailor treatments based on the data of each individual patient. Accelerated drug discovery by identifying potential compounds and assisting in predictive analytics to foresee health-care trends are among other features of modern-day intelligent systems. AI, through tele-medicine, extends healthcare access to remote areas, while intelligent wearable systems enable continuous monitoring of health. Though challenges like data privacy and integra-tion complexities still prevail, AI's fusion with medicine is very crucial in transforming medical practices, making healthcare more precise, accessible, and cost-effective.

15.3.1.1 Medical Imaging and Diagnostics

Advanced imaging techniques like MRI, CT scans, PET scans, and ultrasound (Figure 15.4) are often the first line of investigation for suspected cancer cases. These modalities provide high-resolution images that allow for the precise localization of tumours, assess-ment of their size, and differentiation between benign and malignant lesions. In the realm of medical imaging and diagnostics, the integration of AI has brought about transforma-tive change of monumental proportions. Deep learning algorithms lie at the heart of this change, orchestrating a number of analysis and interpretation upon intricate medical images. X-rays, MRIs, and CT scans are analyzed with a degree of accuracy that borders on the extraordinary. These systems are equipped with features of detecting and diag-nosing conditions that range from fractures to tumours, identifying features which are often too subtle to be identified by human practitioners. For example, a decrease in the size of the tumour on successive scans often indicates a positive response to treatment, while an increase or spread to other areas may necessitate a change in therapeutic strategy; these changes are so minute in nature and are often missed by oncologists and health-care professionals but can be accurately tracked and noticed using intelligent systems. The

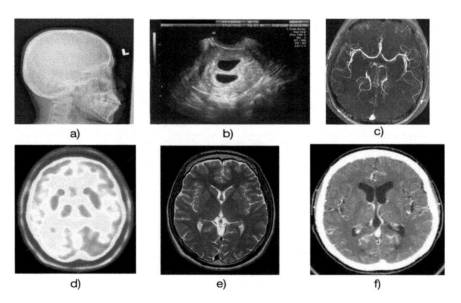

FIGURE 15.4
Several types of medical images: a) brain X-ray, b) ultrasound imagery, c) brain MRA, d) brain PET, e) brain MRI, f) brain CT.

automation and efficiency of these AI systems help reduce human error along with speeding up the diagnostic process and contributing to more personalized care [28].

15.3.1.2 Disease Prediction and Prognosis

By leveraging its data analysis and pattern recognition capabilities, AI is able to identify subtle correlations and risk factors within vast and diverse datasets. These intelligent systems are capable of detecting complex patterns [29] that may elude human observation thus enabling prediction of the likelihood of a patient developing cancer, classifying the type and stage of the tumour, and even forecasting patient outcomes. For instance, convolutional neural networks (CNNs) are commonly used for image analysis in radiology to detect early signs of tumours in MRI and CT scans [30].These predictions enable not only early interventions and preventive measures but also a more informed treatment planning. For instance, when given genetic, lifestyle, and environmental factors, AI is capable of analyzing and predicting the risk of developing breast cancer or prostate cancer, allowing for timely and targeted preventive care.

15.3.1.3 Robotic Surgery and Rehabilitation

Robotic surgery with the assistance of AI is still a young, but cutting-edge, application that has chances of enhancing surgical precision, flexibility, and control. AI-powered robotic systems can assist surgeons in performing minimally invasive procedures, reducing the risk of infection and speeding up recovery times. Surgeons can operate with greater accuracy, removing tumours with minimal damage to surrounding tissues. This is particularly beneficial for complex surgeries, such as those involving the prostate or pancreas [31]. In rehabilitation, AI-driven robots and devices[32] support patients' recovery from injuries or surgeries by constantly monitoring the health chart and predicting any emergencies, also assisting patients to choose suitable activities according to their needs for faster recovery. These systems can also provide personalized therapy exercises and monitor progress accordingly, and they are also able to adapt their treatment methodology if needed, resulting in more efficient and effective recovery pathways. Figure 15.5 displays an image of abdominal surgery being conducted using the assistance of a robotic arm.

15.3.1.4 Patient Care Management and Health Records

In patient-care management and health records, AI has modernized administrative processes and improved patient care. AI algorithms can analyze patient data to identify optimal care pathways, coordinate scheduling, and even predict patient needs for resources like hospital beds or specialized care[33]. In the realm of health records, AI-driven systems enable more secure and efficient handling of vast amounts of sensitive patient data. Automated data entry, categorization, and analysis enhance the accuracy and accessibility of medical records, supporting better-informed clinical decisions

15.3.2 AI in Detecting Abnormalities and Early Disease Detection

Artificial intelligence (AI) has brought about a new era in healthcare by enabling precise detection of abnormalities automatically without any human interaction and also facilitating early disease recognition[34]. The most important ability of intelligent systems, i.e. to examine intricate medical images such as X-rays, MRIs, and CT scans, helps in the

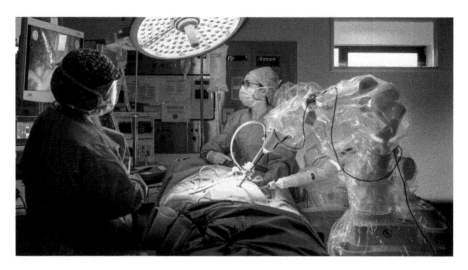

FIGURE 15.5
Surgery using robotic assistance.

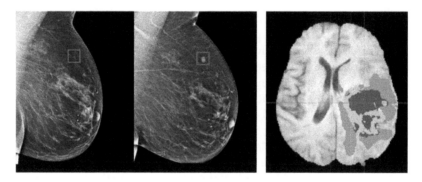

FIGURE 15.6
Intelligent systems used for the detection of tumours and cancerous cells.

identification of subtle anomalies such as fractures, early-stage tumours, etc., which often surpasses human expertise. In the domain of cancer detection, AI models are trained on vast datasets and are made capable of recognizing precancerous changes and early-stage malignancies which significantly enhances the prospects for successful treatment. Today, these systems have become so efficient and intelligent that they are able to predict the risk of chronic conditions such as diabetes, heart diseases, etc., way before the patient starts to develop symptoms, and this is made possible by analyzing and evaluating a multitude of patient data such as their genetic information, lifestyle choices, etc. These early detections lead to timely interventions and more personalized care pathways. Application of these systems has also spread to domains such as genomic analysis and mental health monitoring. The efficient use of AI in detecting abnormalities and early disease detection has not only improved the accuracy of the diagnostics but also holds the key to revolutionizing preventive health care. This paradigm shift underscores the vital and innovative role that AI plays in modern medical practices. Figure 15.6 illustrates such a case of use of AI in the fields of medicine for the detection of tumours and cancerous cells in human body using different medical imagery.

15.3.3 AI in Drug Discovery and Development

The usage of advanced computational techniques in the fields of drug discovery and development has been opening paths to the cure of multiple diseases. In drug discovery [35], the analysis of extremely complex biological data is made possible using artificially intelligent systems. This analysis of data helps to uncover novel targets as well as predict the outcomes of drug interactions. It helps in sifting through vast chemical libraries to find promising compounds and repurpose existing drugs. While developing drugs and their trials, these intelligent systems optimize drug formulations and ensures efficient clinical trials by matching suitable candidates and providing real-time monitoring. These enhancements in precision help to greatly reduce the time taken for the stages of trials to be completed and cut costs. AI offers a transformative approach to pharmaceutical research, aligning with the cutting-edge technological research and solutions that are at the core of drug discovery and development.

15.3.3.1 Analysis of Biological Data

The complexity of biological data, encompassing genomic sequences, protein structures, and cellular pathways are beyond the computational capabilities of the normal human mind. Thus, advanced tools like systems powered by AI are necessary for comprehensive analysis of these data [36]. Deep learning algorithms are now capable of extracting valuable insights, such as the mechanisms of certain diseases and their behavioural patterns, from these data by unravelling intricate biological relationships. In addition, using these relations, potential drug targets are also identified and predictions regarding drug interactions within biological systems are also achieved. AI accelerates the drug discovery process by facilitating the analysis of vast and varied biological data, which leads to more targeted therapeutic approaches, and aligns with the innovative technological exploration in this domain.

15.3.3.2 Uncovering Novel Drug Targets

AI-powered tools are transforming the way novel drug targets are identified. AI, delving into the intricate relationships between genes, proteins, and diseases, can pinpoint specific molecules or pathways that may be targeted with new drugs [37]. Its ability to sift through extensive datasets and detect complex patterns offers opportunities to discover targets that were previously obscured. This not only speeds up the discovery process but also ensures a more precise and personalized approach to treatment.

15.3.3.3 Predicting Drug–Drug Interactions

The prediction of interactions between different drugs is vital for ensuring patient safety and drug efficacy. AI models can meticulously analyze chemical structures, metabolic pathways, and target proteins to forecast how drugs will interact within the body. These insights are essential to avoid harmful combinations and to choose the most effective and safe treatment plans. AI's role in this area represents a critical advancement in personalized medicine, making health care more responsive and precise, and aligning with the cutting-edge technological research on drug interactions .[38]

15.3.3.4 *Optimizing Drug Formulations*

Creating the optimal formulation[39] for a drug is a multifaceted challenge, involving considerations such as solubility, stability, and delivery mechanisms. AI has the power to simulate various formulation strategies, predict their behaviour in the body, and fine-tune them for maximum efficacy and patient comfort. Whether it's developing a slow-release pill or designing a targeted nanocarrier, AI's predictive modelling ensures that drugs are formulated most effectively. This innovative use of technology in pharmaceuticals echoes the interest in technological research in optimizing drug formulation, opening avenues for exploration in a field that bridges technology with practical healthcare solutions.

15.4 Integration of Computational Biology and AI in Oncology

The integration of computational biology and artificial intelligence (AI) has shown us a new era of precision and personalization in health care, particularly in the specialized field of oncology. Computational biology lays the foundation with its algorithms, mathematical models, and computational simulations, offering deep insights into complex biological systems relevant to cancer [40]. On the other hand, AI, with its machine learning capabilities, excels in pattern recognition and predictive analytics. When integrated, these technologies provide actionable insights that significantly impact patient care in oncology. For instance, AI leverages computational biology's in-depth analysis of genomic sequences and protein structures to expedite drug discovery. This synergy enables the prediction of drug interactions, the identification of novel therapeutic targets, and the optimization of drug formulations. Moreover, this integrated approach revolutionizes diagnostic procedures in oncology by enabling the sophisticated analysis of medical images, identifying subtle patterns and abnormalities that may be missed by human observation. The predictive models generated by AI, informed by computational biology's understanding of oncology, allow for treatment plans to be highly personalized, anticipating individual patient responses to various therapeutic options. Additionally, AI algorithms efficiently manage and analyze extensive oncological health records, guided by computational biology's insights into the underlying mechanisms of cancer.

15.4.1 The Convergence of Computational Biology and AI

Chicco emphasizes in his article [41] the growing synergy between computational biology and machine learning. The significance of understanding biological concepts and domain specific knowledge when applying machine learning techniques to biological data has been the main highlight of their work. While working in this field the user or practitioner must be well versed in fields such as biological data formats, such as genomics or proteomics; also knowledge of the unique characteristics of biological data such as the features of high dimensionality and noises is required. Only after grasping these fundamentals are researchers capable of selecting appropriate ML algorithms and pre-processing methods required for case specific challenges with respect to biological data. The complete process of using biological data in ML and DL models can be broken down into a few simple steps described below.

15.4.1.1 *Identification and Selection of Correct Data*

Computational biology is made up of two types of data that include 1) genomic data [42] and 2) proteomic data [43]. Genomic data mainly includes data such as DNA sequences, RNA sequences. DL models are quite efficient in identifying the hidden intricate patterns inside these sequences, aiding in the prediction of gene function, regulatory elements, and even the identification of disease-associated genetic variants. Proteomic data, on the other hand, involves the entire level of proteins present inside an organism's cells and their respective structures; these data help in predicting the functions of uncharacterized proteins, protein structures as well as protein–protein interaction using network analysis and other intelligent methods.

15.4.1.2 *Data Pre-processing*

The accuracy and prediction capabilities of any AI model is directly proportional to its dataset size, properties, and arrangement. First of all, the dataset to be used should be of a minimum size or else training the model properly won't be possible; ideally it is considered that the data instances should be at least ten times the number of the data features [44]. Once the issue of data size has been addressed, the next thing to be prioritized is the arrangement of data; the input features must be clean, scaled into a normalized range, randomly shuffled, and new features must be created or old features may be removed (feature selection) as per the need of the time.

15.4.1.3 *Splitting of Dataset*

The data, once clean and pre-processed, needs to be divided into parts for training and testing purposes. Though traditionally the data set is split into two parts, this method is incomplete: there is yet one more step before applying the model of selecting hyper parameters that is mostly not considered. Thus, the data set must be divided into three parts: training data (roughly around 50%), validation set (around 30%), and testing data (20%). Cross-validation techniques [45] can also be used in the case of small datasets. The training and the validation sets are then used for optimizing the hyper parameters followed by checking the accuracy using a test set.

15.4.1.4 *Categorizing the Biological Problem into the Algorithmic Problem*

It is quite evident that the presence of large amounts of labelled, unlabelled, or raw data for the usage of ML or DL models is extremely necessary. Labelled data can be utilized by the use of supervised ML models that has a final goal of learning a function f(x)=y from data that are paired in a sequence of $(x_1,y_1),(x_2,y_2),\ldots.(x_n,y_n)$, such as a case where profiles of patients has been provided with all their biological features as individual columns along with a ground truth value for each, stating healthy or unhealthy, which can be categorized as labelled data. In this case a supervised method like support vector machines (SVMs) [46] and k-nearest neighbours (kNN) [47] can be employed. Pattern recognition models are used on unlabeled data with real values, such as k means Clustering[48] probabilistic latent semantic analysis (pLSA) [49]. Higher dimensional raw biological data can be dealt using more advanced deep learning methods such as convoluted neural networks (CNN) [50] or recurrent neural networks (RNN) [51].

15.4.1.5 Addressing Imbalance in Data

Computational biology and bioinformatics often faces the problem of data imbalance where one class is over-represented. Taking an example of any normal dataset containing gene ontology data, it can be observed that it has only 0.1% positive data instance and 99.9% negative data instances for a non-negative matrix factorization. In this situation, the model trained on this data will be faster in recognizing negative data instances instead of positive instances. To address this issue different approaches can be followed, such as a heuristic method of averaging [52] or by empirical label distribution using Bayes' rule [53]. Even though there exist many other ways [54] to solve this problem, collecting more data is the best approach. Under-sampling [55] also helps in balancing the data by removing the over-represented data elements, but this restricts the classifier from learning from the excluded data.

15.4.1.6 Hyper Parameter Optimization

Hyper parameter [56] are high-level properties of a given data model that has a strong influence on the complexity and speed of learning. For example, the number of K neighbours in k nearest neighbour, k number of clusters in k means clustering, dimensions of artificial neural networks are hyper parameters of each respective algorithms. When the dataset is divided into the three parts mentioned above, the validation set is employed to calculate the algorithm for a specific hyper parameter and for each of these the values the model is trained and evaluated through the Matthews correlations coefficient (MCC) [57] or precision recall area under curve and these values are then stored. At the end, the parameters leading to the highest accuracy are chosen and the model is finally trained with those hyper parameters.

Algorithm 15.1 Hyper-parameter optimization. h: hyper-parameter. P: maximum value of h. model$_h$: the statistical model having h value as hyper-parameter

    1: Randomly shuffle all the data instances of the input dataset
    2: Split the input dataset into independent *training set, validation set, and test set*
    3: **for** $h= 1,..., P$ **do**
    4: Train model$_h$, on the training set
    5: Save model$_h$, into a file or on a database
    6: Evaluate model$_h$, on the validation set
    7: Save the result Matthews correlation coefficient (MCC) of the previous step
    8: **end for**
    9: Select the hyper-parameter best$_h$, which led to the best MCC value in the previous loop
    10: Load the previously saved model$_{besth}$
    11: Apply model$_{besth}$, to the test set

15.4.1.7 Model Evaluation

Once the model has been successfully trained, the model is then tested on the third division of the dataset, i.e. the test set. The performance of the model is displayed in terms of statistical scores. The algorithm expresses each element of the validation set as positive and negative and basing on these prediction and the gold standard labels, the true negatives (TN), true positive (TP), false positive (FP), and false negative (FN), are categorized (Table 15.1). These categories in turn help in estimating the performance in terms of accuracy (i), F1 scores (ii), and MCC(iii) [57] of the model as:

$$accuracy = \frac{TP + TN}{TP + TN + FP + FN} \tag{15.1}$$

$$F1Score = \frac{2TP}{2TP + FP + FN} \tag{15.2}$$

$$MCC = \frac{TP.TN - FP.FN}{\sqrt{(TP + FP).(TP + FN).(TN + FP).(TN + FN)}} \tag{15.3}$$

We have $0 \le accuracy \le 1$, $0 \le F1 - score \le 1$ and $0 \le MCC \le 1$

Even a precision recall curve and receiver operating characteristic (ROC) [58] can also be constructed using the values mentioned in Table 15.1. The ROC (Figure 15.7) needs two values to be computed: recall (iv) on the y axis and fallout (iv) on the x axis:

$$recall = \frac{TP}{TP + FN} \quad fallout = \frac{FP}{FP + TN} \tag{15.4}$$

Whereas the precision recall curve (Figure 15.7) has precision (v) on the y axis and recall (v) on the x axis:

TABLE 15.1

The Confusion Matrix for Actual Value and Predicted Value

	Predicted Positive	**Predicted Negative**
Actual Positive	TP (True Positives)	FN (False Negatives)
Actual Negative	FP (False Positive)	TN (True Negatives)

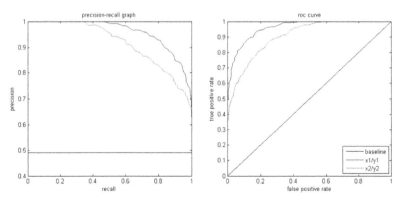

FIGURE 15.7
Examples of ROC and POC.

$$precision = \frac{TP}{TP + FP} \qquad (15.5)$$

15.4.2 Combined Applications in Medical Research

The fusion of computational biology and artificial intelligence (AI) in medical research is driving significant advancements in personalized medicine. Computational biology, with its capabilities in analyzing complex biological systems through algorithms and mathematical models, provides the structural understanding needed for AI's predictive and interpretative functions. Together, they offer a powerful toolset for interpreting genomic data, predicting the behaviour of biological systems, and simulating various disease conditions. Whether uncovering novel drug targets or optimizing drug formulations, their combined applications are revolutionizing the way we understand and treat diseases.

15.4.2.1 Genomic Data Interpretation Using AI

Genomic data interpretation is central to personalized medicine, and the integration of AI with computational biology has significantly advanced this field [59]. AI's machine learning algorithms can sift through enormous genomic datasets, uncovering patterns and connections. Coupled with computational biology's structural understanding, AI allows for accurate interpretation of genetic variations and their implications for disease susceptibility and drug response. This collaborative approach accelerates research and translates to tailored medical interventions, fitting well with interest in genomic data interpretations.

15.4.2.2 AI in Predictive Modelling of Biological Systems

Predictive modelling of biological systems is greatly enhanced by AI's ability to process vast and intricate data. AI algorithms, informed by computational biology's understanding of biological relationships, can predict the behaviour of biological systems under various conditions [60]. Whether forecasting disease progression, modelling drug interactions, or simulating cellular responses, this integrative approach provides valuable insights for medical research and treatment planning. The application of AI in predictive modelling echoes the focus on technological research and development in the field of predictive modelling of biological systems, offering fascinating possibilities for further exploration and innovation.

15.4.3 Case Studies of Integrated Applications

The fusion of computational biology and AI has led to groundbreaking advancements in various medical fields. Through personalized cancer treatments, this integration enables precise targeting of tumours, significantly improving patient outcomes. In Alzheimer's diagnosis, it facilitates early detection, allowing timely interventions. It accelerates drug development for rare diseases by streamlining genetic analyses. During the COVID-19 pandemic, it played a critical role in rapid vaccine development and containment strategies. Furthermore, in the emerging field of precision nutrition, this synergy crafts personalized diet plans. These cases illustrate how the collaboration of computational biology and AI is revolutionizing health care.

15.4.3.1 *Personalized Cancer Detection and Treatment*

Personalized cancer treatment represents a significant advancement in oncology, enabled by the integration of computational biology and AI. Computational biology deciphers the individual genetic makeup of tumours, identifying unique mutations. AI algorithms then process this intricate information to tailor treatment strategies. This precision targets cancerous cells more effectively, sparing healthy tissue and reducing adverse side effects. The ability to analyze each patient's unique tumour characteristics has led to enhanced effectiveness in therapies and improved patient survival rates. This innovative approach aligns with the interest in cutting-edge technological solutions and represents a transformative application of computational biology and AI in medicine.

Nagarajan et al. in [61] introduce us to the intricate intersection of computational biology and artificial intelligence (AI) in the realm of cancer precision-drug discovery. Their study offers a comprehensive exploration of how these advanced technologies synergistically contribute to the identification, development, and optimization of tailored therapies for cancer patients. In the context of computational biology, their work elucidates how modern high-throughput technologies generate massive volumes of biological data, including genomics, transcriptomics, proteomics, and metabolomics data. These intricate datasets hold the key to unravelling the complex molecular mechanisms underpinning different types of cancer. Through innovative computational techniques, such as data mining, machine learning, and network analysis, researchers gain unprecedented insights into the genetic mutations, dysregulated pathways, and potential biomarkers specific to individual cancer cases. This empowers the identification of novel therapeutic targets that could be exploited to design more effective treatments. They then navigate into the realm of artificial intelligence, showcasing how AI algorithms play a transformative role in decoding the intricate biological information embedded within these data landscapes. AI-powered predictive models and algorithms sift through the intricate data patterns to identify potential drug targets and therapeutic candidates with high precision. They also explain how AI algorithms can analyze an individual patient's genetic makeup and molecular profile to tailor treatment strategies based on their unique biological characteristics. This individualized approach maximizes treatment efficacy while minimizing adverse effects, reflecting a shift from a one-size-fits-all model to a precision medicine paradigm.

15.4.3.2 *Early Alzheimer's Diagnosis*

Early detection of Alzheimer's disease has become feasible through the combined power of computational biology and AI. By analyzing complex data sets, including genetic markers, brain imaging, and cognitive performance, early-stage Alzheimer's can be identified. Computational biology aids in understanding the biological factors, while AI's pattern recognition identifies subtle early signs. This early diagnosis allows for interventions that can delay or mitigate the progression of the disease, profoundly impacting patient care and family planning. It's an inspiring example of how technology can significantly influence health care, reflecting focus on technological innovation and research.

Hampel et. al. presents a comprehensive perspective on the potential of precision medicine for Alzheimer's disease (AD)[62], focusing on biomarker-guided disease modelling. The paper emphasizes the significant role of artificial intelligence (AI) and computational biology in the detection and prediction of Alzheimer's disease. The study underscores how AI and computational biology contribute to advancing early detection and prediction of Alzheimer's disease. These technologies enable the integration of diverse data types, such as genetic information, biomarker measurements, neuroimaging data, and clinical assessments. Through sophisticated algorithms, AI analyzes these complex datasets, identifying patterns, correlations, and subtle changes that may precede clinical symptoms. This early-stage analysis aids in the identification of potential biomarkers that can serve as indicators of disease progression, enabling more accurate and timely diagnosis. They also outline the role of AI and computational biology in constructing integrative disease models. By combining data from various sources and modalities, these models provide a holistic view of the disease's underlying mechanisms. AI-driven predictive modelling plays a pivotal role in simulating disease progression and predicting outcomes based on individual patient profiles. These models allow for the exploration of different treatment strategies and their potential impacts on disease trajectories.

15.4.3.3 Drug Development for Rare Diseases

The development of treatments for rare diseases has historically been a slow and expensive process. The fusion of computational biology and AI is changing this landscape. Computational biology uncovers the genetic interactions underlying these conditions, and AI accelerates the process of identifying potential drug candidates. This targeted approach streamlines the development process, reducing both time and cost. For patients with rare diseases, this means more accessible and effective treatment options, underscoring the real-world impact of these combined technologies. This synergy echoes the pursuit of innovative solutions in technology and healthcare.

Alves et. al. in [63] delve into the pivotal role of computational biology and artificial intelligence (AI) in revolutionizing drug discovery for rare diseases. They present a study that illustrates how AI-driven knowledge-based approaches can effectively address the unique challenges associated with developing treatments for rare and often understudied conditions. In their study, AI serves as the backbone of a multi-faceted approach to drug discovery for specific rare diseases. Firstly, their approach involves data integration from various sources, including genomic databases, biomedical literature, and molecular interaction networks. Through AI algorithms, these diverse datasets are harmonized and analyzed, creating a comprehensive knowledge base that highlights potential disease-associated genes, pathways, and molecular targets. Secondly, AI predictive modelling takes centre stage, utilizing machine learning techniques to prioritize potential drug candidates. These models leverage the integrated knowledge to predict the likelihood of specific compounds interacting with the identified targets and potentially modulating disease mechanisms. This enables researchers to narrow down the vast chemical space to a focused set of compounds with high therapeutic potential. Overall, the case study exemplifies how AI empowers drug-discovery efforts for rare diseases by intelligently harnessing available data to accelerate target identification, compound screening, and treatment optimization, thereby offering a beacon of hope for patients and families affected by these challenging conditions.

15.4.3.4 Pandemic Response

The COVID-19 pandemic showcased the essential role of computational biology and AI in rapid vaccine development and containment strategy. Computational biology enabled an understanding of the virus's genetic structure, while AI modelled potential immunological responses. This collaboration allowed researchers to quickly design vaccine candidates and proceed to trials. Additionally, AI-driven analyses of global spread patterns informed containment measures, providing governments with critical insights. This comprehensive response illustrates the broader societal benefits of integrating computational biology and AI, a cutting-edge application that would likely resonate with technological aspirations and research focus.

A detailed study has been done on role of contemporary technologies in addressing the COVID-19 pandemic [64], with a special emphasis on artificial intelligence (AI) by Kumar et. al. in [65]. A procedure for the automatic report of an X-ray test is in [66]. An approach to detect COVID-19 using deep learning technology is presented in [67]. Besides using a vaccine, one of the key factors in maintaining COVID-19 effectively is social-distancing monitoring. A method to measure social-distancing and hence see that it is maintained is carried out in [68]. During the prevalence of COVID-19, lockdown was an effective precautionary measure to avoid contamination of the disease. An effective study in this direction for determining the lockdown period was proposed in [69]. Several pandemic situations occurred in the world before COVID-19. One such pandemic was the spread of the Zika virus in 2016. A study on the spread of the Zika virus is presented in [70]. An analysis of the spatial epidemiology of literature is carried out in [71]. A study of the patterns to explore incidence-prevalence in spatial epidemiology using an uncertainty based model is carried out via neighbourhood rough sets in [72]. Another pandemic situation had arisen due to the spread of West Nile Virus. An approach to measure the similarity subzones affected by the virus was presented in [73] by using neighbourhood rough sets. One of the key roles of AI highlighted in their work is its central contribution to early outbreak detection and surveillance. By analyzing real-time data from sources like social media, news reports, and healthcare records, AI plays a crucial role in identifying potential hotspots and emerging patterns, aiding in the rapid response to outbreaks [74]. Additionally, AI-driven diagnostic tools enable remote symptom assessment, streamlining the triage process and providing individuals with a better understanding of their risk factors. Kumar et. al. in their work accentuate AI's broader impact in pandemic response, extending to drug discovery and vaccine development. AI's predictive capabilities expedite drug repurposing efforts by simulating interactions between existing drugs and the virus's molecular structures, thereby identifying potential treatment candidates more rapidly [75]. Beyond this, AI's predictive modelling assists in epidemiological forecasts, guiding resource allocation decisions, lockdown measures, and travel restrictions. Also, AI's proficiency in sentiment analysis and misinformation tracking enhances public health communication, enabling tailored strategies to combat the spread of inaccurate information.

In Figure 15.8, we see how developments were made in the field of medicine using AI, from scientists just discussing the idea in the 1950s to actually implementing them for the first time in 1970 to using them flawlessly in the 2000s.

15.5 Challenges and Future Potential

The integration of artificial intelligence (AI) and computational biology brings forth a complex interplay of opportunities and challenges. On the challenges side, concerns about data security and privacy have become even more critical given the sensitive nature of cancer-related data, especially with the reliance on extensive datasets. Issues of bias and ethical dilemmas are equally pressing, and computational resource requirements add to the complexity. The lack of transparency in some AI models can cause interpretability

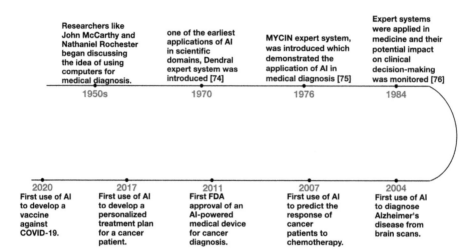

FIGURE 15.8
Timeline showing the progression of AI in medical oncology.

problems, while the integration with existing systems poses logistical challenges. Despite these hurdles, the future potential is immense. Personalized medicine could be revolutionized by combining AI with computational biology, tailoring treatment plans to individual needs. AI's capacity to create energy-efficient solutions supports sustainability, and its ability to enhance human decision-making frees up creativity and innovation. The potential democratization of health care through AI and computational biology could make advanced care accessible and affordable globally. Lastly, the ability to handle complex data unlocks new scientific frontiers, from understanding life's fundamentals to space exploration. In essence, while the challenges are substantial, with careful management and strategic research and development, the convergence of AI and computational biology may fundamentally reshape our world, balancing ethics, innovation, governance, and collaboration. To conclude, while the challenges of integrating AI and computational biology in oncology are non-trivial and require careful ethical and logistical considerations, the potential for improving patient outcomes and advancing the field is enormous [76].

15.6 Conclusions

The combination of artificial intelligence (AI) and computational biology in oncology is a major breakthrough with the potential to revolutionize personalized cancer care, making targeted therapies more affordable and accessible, and paving the way for groundbreaking research. However, this promise comes with its own set of challenges, such as protecting patient data, meeting computational requirements, and addressing ethical concerns specific to cancer care. Addressing these challenges will require a collaborative effort from technologists, biologists, ethicists, and healthcare policymakers. As we venture beyond this new frontier, we must focus on harnessing the transformative power of AI and computational biology to improve oncological outcomes, while ensuring ethical and equitable progress. The effective utilization of these technologies in oncology is a testament to the limitless possibilities at the intersection of technology and biology. However, realizing this potential will require careful planning, ethical oversight, and collaborative innovation to truly transform the field of oncology.

References

1. Chaddad, A., Peng, J., Xu, J., & Bouridane, A. (2023). Survey of explainable AI techniques in healthcare. *Sensors*, 23(2), 634. https://doi.org/10.3390/s23020634. PMID: 36679430; PMCID: PMC9862413.
2. Beaulieu-Jones, B. K., Yuan, W., Brat, G. A., Beam, A. L., Weber, G., Ruffin, M., & Kohane, I. S. (2021). Machine learning for patient risk stratification: Standing on, or looking over, the shoulders of clinicians?. *NPJ Digital Medicine*, 4(1), 62.
3. Ching, T., Himmelstein, D. S., Beaulieu-Jones, B. K., Kalinin, A. A., Do, B. T., Way, G. P., ... Greene, C. S. (2018). Opportunities and obstacles for deep learning in biology and medicine. *Journal of the Royal Society Interface*, 15(141), 20170387.
4. Rundo, L., Tangherloni, A., & Militello, C. (2022). Artificial intelligence applied to medical imaging and computational biology. *Applied Sciences*, 12(18), 9052.
5. Combi, C., Amico, B., Bellazzi, R., Holzinger, A., Moore, J. H., Zitnik, M., & Holmes, J. H. (2022). A manifesto on explainability for artificial intelligence in medicine. *Artificial Intelligence in Medicine*, 133, 102423.
6. Noble, D. (2002). The rise of computational biology. *Nature Reviews Molecular Cell Biology*, 3(6), 459–463.
7. Angermueller, C., Pärnamaa, T., Parts, L., & Stegle, O. (2016). Deep learning for computational biology. *Molecular Systems Biology*, 12(7), 878.
8. Lefor, A. T. (2011). Computational oncology. *Japanese Journal of Clinical Oncology*, 41(8), 937–947. https://doi.org/10.1093/jjco/hyr082
9. Fenyö, D. (Ed.). (2010). *Computational biology*. Humana Press.
10. Huang, Z., & Gu, R. X. (2019). Development and application of computational methods in biology and medicine. *Current Medicinal Chemistry*, 26(42), 7534–7536.
11. Waterman, M. S. (2018). *Introduction to computational biology: Maps, sequences and genomes*. Chapman and Hall/CRC.
12. Silva, F. C., Lisboa, B. C., Figueiredo, M. C., et al. (2014). Hereditary breast and ovarian cancer: Assessment of point mutations and copy number variations in Brazilian patients. *BMC Medical Genetics*, 15, 55. https://doi.org/10.1186/1471-2350-15-55
13. Materi, W., & Wishart, D. S. (2007). Computational systems biology in drug discovery and development: Methods and applications. *Drug Discovery Today*, 12(7–8), 295–303.
14. Murga, M., & Fernandez-Capetillo, O. (2022). Emerging concepts in drug discovery for cancer therapy. *Molecular Oncology*, 16(21), 3757–3760. https://doi.org/10.1002/1878-0261.13325. PMID: 36321722; PMCID: PMC9627784.
15. Germain, R. N., Meier-Schellersheim, M., Nita-Lazar, A., & Fraser, I. D. (2011). Systems biology in immunology: A computational modeling perspective. *Annual Review of Immunology*, 29, 527–585.
16. Bellomo, N., Li, N. K., & Maini, P. K. (2008). On the foundations of cancer modelling: Selected topics, speculations, and perspectives. *Mathematical Models and Methods in Applied Sciences*, 18(4), 593–646.
17. Zhang, L., Wang, Z., Sagotsky, J., et al. (2009). Multiscale agent-based cancer modeling. *Journal of Mathematical Biology*, 58, 545–559. https://doi.org/10.1007/s00285-008-0211-1
18. Ramis-Conde, I., Chaplain, M. A., & Anderson, A. R. (2008). Mathematical modelling of cancer cell invasion of tissue. *Mathematical and Computer Modelling*, 47(5–6), 533–545.

19. Bearer, E. L., Lowengrub, J. S., Frieboes, H. B., Chuang, Y. L., Jin, F., Wise, S. M., ... Cristini, V. (2009). Multiparameter computational modeling of tumor invasion. *Cancer Research, 69*(10), 4493–4501.

20. Heijman, J., Sutanto, H., Crijns, H. J., Nattel, S., & Trayanova, N. A. (2021). Computational models of atrial fibrillation: Achievements, challenges, and perspectives for improving clinical care. *Cardiovascular Research, 117*(7), 1682–1699.

21. Helikar, T., Cutucache, C. E., Dahlquist, L. M., Herek, T. A., Larson, J. J., & Rogers, J. A. (2015). Integrating interactive computational modeling in biology curricula. *PLOS Computational Biology, 11*(3), e1004131.

22. Collin, C. B., Gebhardt, T., Golebiewski, M., Karaderi, T., Hillemanns, M., Khan, F. M., ... Kuepfer, L. (2022). Computational models for clinical applications in personalized medicine—Guidelines and recommendations for data integration and model validation. *Journal of Personalized Medicine, 12*(2), 166.

23. Rigney, G., Lennon, M., & Holderrieth, P. (2021). The use of computational models in the management and prognosis of refractory epilepsy: A critical evaluation. *Seizure, 91*, 132–140.

24. Pappalardo, F., Russo, G., Pennisi, M., Parasiliti Palumbo, G. A., Sgroi, G., Motta, S., & Maimone, D. (2020). The potential of computational modeling to predict disease course and treatment response in patients with relapsing multiple sclerosis. *Cells, 9*(3), 586.

25. Chakravarty, K., Antontsev, V., Bundey, Y., & Varshney, J. (2021). Driving success in personalized medicine through AI-enabled computational modeling. *Drug Discovery Today, 26*(6), 1459–1465.

26. Winston, P. H. (1984). *Artificial intelligence*. Addison-Wesley Longman Publishing Co., Inc.

27. Hamet, P., & Tremblay, J. (2017). Artificial intelligence in medicine. *Metabolism, 69*, S36–S40.

28. Gore, J. C. (2020). Artificial intelligence in medical imaging. *Magnetic Resonance Imaging, 68*, A1–A4.

29. Jiang, F., Jiang, Y., Zhi, H., Dong, Y., Li, H., Ma, S., ... Wang, Y. (2017). Artificial intelligence in healthcare: Past, present and future. *Stroke and Vascular Neurology, 2*, 230–243.

30. Chattopadhyay, A., & Maitra, M. (2022). MRI-based brain tumour image detection using CNN based deep learning method. *Neuroscience Informatics, 2*(4), 100060. https://doi.org/10.1016/j.neuri.2022.100060

31. Hashizume, M., & Tsugawa, K. (2004). Robotic surgery and cancer: The present state, problems and future vision. *Japanese Journal of Clinical Oncology, 34*(5), 227–237. https://doi.org/10.1093/jjco/hyh053

32. Yip, M., Salcudean, S., Goldberg, K., Althoefer, K., Menciassi, A., Opfermann, J. D., ... Lee, I. C. (2023). Artificial intelligence meets medical robotics. *Science, 381*(6654), 141–146.

33. Matheny, M. E., Whicher, D., & Israni, S. T. (2020). Artificial intelligence in health care: A report from the National Academy of Medicine. *JAMA, 323*(6), 509–510.

34. Kumar, Y., Koul, A., Singla, R., & Ijaz, M. F. (2022). Artificial intelligence in disease diagnosis: A systematic literature review, synthesizing framework and future research agenda. *Journal of Ambient Intelligence and Humanized Computing, 14*, 1–28.

35. Paul, D., Sanap, G., Shenoy, S., Kalyane, D., Kalia, K., & Tekade, R. K. (2021). Artificial intelligence in drug discovery and development. *Drug Discovery Today, 26*(1), 80.

36. Ataş Güvenilir, H. (2023). *INTEGRATION AND ANALYSIS OF BIOLOGICAL DATA FOR COMPUTATIONAL DRUG DISCOVERY* [Ph.D. - Doctoral Program]. Middle East Technical University.

37. Mak, K. K., & Pichika, M. R. (2019). Artificial intelligence in drug development: Present status and future prospects. *Drug Discovery Today, 24*(3), 773–780.

38. Zhang, Y., Deng, Z., Xu, X., Feng, Y., & Junliang, S. (2023). Application of Artificial Intelligence in Drug-Drug Interactions Prediction: A Review. *Journal of chemical information and modelling*, 10.1021/acs.jcim.3c00582. Advance online publication. https://doi.org/10.1021/acs.jcim.3c00582

39. Landin, M., & Rowe, R. C (2013). Artificial neural networks technology to model, understand, and optimize drug formulations. In Aguilar, J.E. (Ed.).*Formulation tools for pharmaceutical development* (pp. 7–37). Woodhead Publishing.

40. Mathew, J. P., Taylor, B. S., Bader, G. D., Pyarajan, S., Antoniotti, M., Chinnaiyan, A. M., ... Mishra, B. (2007). From bytes to bedside: Data integration and computational biology for translational cancer research. *PLoS Computational Biology, 3*(2), e12.

41. Chicco, D. (2017). Ten quick tips for machine learning in computational biology. *BioData Mining, 10*(1), 35.

42. Ramanan, V. K., Shen, L., Moore, J. H., & Saykin, A. J. (2012). Pathway analysis of genomic data: Concepts, methods, and prospects for future development. *Trends in Genetics, 28*(7), 323–332.

43. Colinge, J., & Bennett, K. L. (2007). Introduction to computational proteomics. *PLoS Computational Biology, 3*(7), e114.

44. Haldar, M. (2017). How much training data do you need?https://malay-haldar.medium. com/how-much-training-data-do-you-need-da8ec091e956

45. Refaeilzadeh, P., Tang, L., & Liu, H. (2009). Cross-validation. In L. Liu & M. T. Özsu (Eds.) *Encyclopedia of database systems* (pp. 532–538).

46. Ben-Hur, A., Ong, C. S., Sonnenburg, S., Schölkopf, B., & Rätsch, G. (2008). Support vector machines and kernels for computational biology. *PLoS Computational Biology, 4*(10), e1000173.

47. Nasibov, E., & Kandemir-Cavas, C. (2009). Efficiency analysis of KNN and minimum distance-based classifiers in enzyme family prediction. *Computational Biology and Chemistry, 33*(6), 461–464.

48. Frandsen, P. B., Calcott, B., Mayer, C., & Lanfear, R. (2015). Automatic selection of partitioning schemes for phylogenetic analyses using iterative k-means clustering of site rates. *BMC Evolutionary Biology, 15*(1), 1–17.

49. Masseroli, M., Chicco, D., & Pinoli, P. (2012, June). Probabilistic latent semantic analysis for prediction of gene ontology annotations. In *The 2012 international joint conference on neural networks (IJCNN)* (pp. 1–8). IEEE.

50. Bhardwaj, P., Guhan, T., & Tripathy, B. K. (2022). Computational biology in the lens of CNN. In *Handbook of machine learning applications for genomics* (pp. 65–85). Springer Nature Singapore.

51. Raza, K., & Alam, M. (2016). Recurrent neural network based hybrid model for reconstructing gene regulatory network. *Computational Biology and Chemistry, 64*, 322–334.

52. Tarekegn, A. N., Giacobini, M., & Michalak, K. (2021). A review of methods for imbalanced multi-label classification. *Pattern Recognition, 118*, 107965.

53. Wilkinson, D. J. (2007). Bayesian methods in bioinformatics and computational systems biology. *Briefings in Bioinformatics, 8*(2), 109–116.

54. He, H., & Garcia, E. A. (2009). Learning from imbalanced data. *IEEE Transactions on Knowledge and Data Engineering, 21*(9), 1263–1284.

55. Yu, H., Ni, J., & Zhao, J. (2013). ACOSampling: An ant colony optimization-based undersampling method for classifying imbalanced DNA microarray data. *Neurocomputing, 101*, 309–318.

56. Andonie, R. (2019). Hyperparameter optimization in learning systems. *Journal of Membrane Computing, 1*(4), 279–291.

57. Chicco, D., & Jurman, G. (2020). The advantages of the Matthews correlation coefficient (MCC) over F1 score and accuracy in binary classification evaluation. *BMC Genomics, 21*(1), 1–13.

58. Giglioni, V., García-Macías, E., Venanzi, I., Ierimonti, L., & Ubertini, F. (2021). The use of receiver operating characteristic curves and precision-versus-recall curves as performance metrics in unsupervised structural damage classification under changing environment. *Engineering Structures, 246*, 113029.

59. Dias, R., & Torkamani, A. (2019). Artificial intelligence in clinical and genomic diagnostics. *Genome Medicine, 11*, 70. https://doi.org/10.1186/s13073-019-0689-8

60. Bhardwaj, A., Kishore, S., & Pandey, D. K. (2022). Artificial intelligence in biological sciences. *Life, 12*(9), 1430. https://doi.org/10.3390/life12091430. PMID: 36143468; PMCID: PMC9505413.

61. Nagarajan, N., Yapp, E. K., Le, N. Q. K., Kamaraj, B., Al-Subaie, A. M., & Yeh, H. Y. (2019). Application of computational biology and artificial intelligence technologies in cancer precision drug discovery. *BioMed Research International, 2019* 8427042. https://doi.org/10.1155/2019/8427042

62. Hampel, H., O'Bryant, S. E., Durrleman, S., Younesi, E., Rojkova, K., Escott-Price, V., ... Alzheimer Precision Medicine Initiative. (2017). A precision medicine initiative for Alzheimer's disease: The road ahead to biomarker-guided integrative disease modeling. *Climacteric, 20*(2), 107–118.

63. Alves, V. M., Korn, D., Pervitsky, V., Thieme, A., Capuzzi, S. J., Baker, N., ... Tropsha, A. (2022). Knowledge-based approaches to drug discovery for rare diseases. *Drug Discovery Today, 27*(2), 490–502.

64. Jain, A., Goel, I., Maheshwari, S., & Tripathy, B. K. (2022). Contemporary technologies to combat pandemics and epidemics. In B. K. Tripathy, P. Lingras, A. K. Kar, & C. L. Chowdhary (Eds.), *Next Generation Healthcare Informatics, Studies in Computational Intelligence*, vol 1039. Springer. https://doi.org/10.1007/978-981-19-2416-3_11

65. Kumar, A., Gupta, P. K., & Srivastava, A. (2020). A review of modern technologies for tackling COVID-19 pandemic. *Diabetes & Metabolic Syndrome: Clinical Research & Reviews, 14*(4), 569–573.

66. Sai, R., Kather, S. B., & Tripathy, B. K. (2023). Automated medical report generation on chest X-Ray images using co-attention mechanism. In S. Bhattacharyya (Ed.), *Hybrid computational intelligent systems: Modeling, simulation and optimization.* (pp. 111-122). CRC Press

67. Sihare, P., Khan, A. U., Bardhan, P., & Tripathy, B. K. (2022). COVID-19 detection using deep learning: A comparative study of segmentation algorithms. In A. K. Das, et al. (Eds.), *Proceedings of the 4th International Conference on Computational Intelligence in Pattern Recognition (CIPR)* (pp. 1–10). CIPR 2022, LNNS 480.

68. Yagna Sai Surya, K., Geetha Rani, T., & Tripathy, B. K. (2022). Social distance monitoring and face mask detection using deep learning. In J. Nayak, H. Behera, B. Naik, S. Vimal, & D. Pelusi (Eds.), *Computational intelligence in data mining.* Smart Innovation, Systems and Technologies, vol 281. Springer. https://doi.org/10.1007/978-981-16-9447-9_36

69. Mohanty, R. K., Tripathy, B. K., & Parida, S. C. (2022). Decision making on Covid-19 containment zones' lockdown exit process using fuzzy soft set model. In J. Nayak, H. Behera, B. Naik, S. Vimal, & D. Pelusi (Eds.), *Computational intelligence in data mining.* Smart Innovation, Systems and Technologies, vol 281. Springer. https://doi.org/10.1007/978-981-16-9447-9_29

70. Tripathy, B. K., Thakur, S., & Chowdhury, R. (2017). A classification model to analyze the spread and emerging trends of the Zika virus in Twitter. In H. Behera & D. Mohapatra (Eds.), *Computational intelligence in data mining.* Advances in Intelligent Systems and Computing, vol 556. Springer. https://doi.org/10.1007/978-981-10-3874-7_61

71. Kather, S. B., & Tripathy, B. K. (2016). Data analytics in spatial epidemiology: A survey. *Jurnal Technology, 78*(10), 159–165.

72. Kather, S. B., & Tripathy, B. K. (2017). Exploring incidence-prevalence patterns in spatial epidemiology via neighborhood rough sets. *International Journal of Healthcare Information Systems and Informatics, 12*(1), 30–43.

73. Shah, K., Tripathy, B. K., & Kather, S. B. (2019). Neighborhood rough set based similarity measurement of subzones affected by West Nile Virus. *2019 Second International Conference on Advanced Computational and Communication Paradigms (ICACCP)*, Gangtok (pp. 1–6).

74. Lindsay, R. K., Buchanan, B. G., Feigenbaum, E. A., & Lederberg, J. (1993). DENDRAL: A case study of the first expert system for scientific hypothesis formation. *Artificial Intelligence, 61*(2), 209–261.

75. Van Melle, W. (1978). MYCIN: A knowledge-based consultation program for infectious disease diagnosis. *International Journal of Man-Machine Studies, 10*(3), 313–322.

76. Fieschi, M. (2013). *Artificial intelligence in medicine: Expert systems.* Springer.

16

Computer-Aided Ensemble Method for Early Diagnosis of Coronary Artery Disease

Arkashree P. Mishra and Suvasini Panigrahi

16.1 Introduction

With growing environmental and social change, unexpected evolution of diseases, rising stress levels, abnormal food habits, and lack of physical activity, diseases which used to develop in the later stages of life have now become common among the younger generation, leading to a spike in premature death rate. As per the World Health Agency, around 17.9 million people have lost their lives due to CVDs. And this condition has worsened since the eruption of Covid-19 pandemic. Not only is there an alarming increase in cases of heart failure but also a deepening of co-morbid conditions and development of other complications, resulting in neurological and oncological emergencies. So, health has become the pivotal focus of all the developed, as well as the developing, nations, in the post-Covid period, especially in the middle to low-income countries, where people live in remote areas, are hardly aware of the disease, have minimal access to advanced medical facilities, and are still striving for basic health amenities. Such a situation re-enforces the need for up-to-date research and development to be carried in the field of medicine and, simultaneously, the improvement of response for early detection and diagnosis of disease, which can reduce further risks. Figure 16.1 depicts the leading causes of death globally (2019) as provided by the WHO.

CVDs are a group of heart and blood-vessel related disorders which include CAD, congenial heart disease, stroke, rheumatic heart disease, cerebrovascular diseases etc. In this chapter, we have basically studied CAD, otherwise known as ischemic heart disease (IHD) or coronary heart disease (CHD), which develops when coronary arteries find it difficult to provide nutrients and oxygen to the heart. The blood supply is interrupted due to accumulation of plaque or cholesterol in the coronary arteries. In due course, these deposits intensify in the artery resulting in narrowing of the arteries and sometimes complete blockage. This gradual process, called atherosclerosis, if not checked in time may lead to cardiac arrest and ultimately death of the patient. The severity of the disease depends on the stenosis, that is, the extent to which the artery is narrowed. CAD is defined as at least one vessel with stenosis greater than 50%. Figure 16.2 shows the slow deposition of plaque leading to blockage of the artery.

CHD cannot be cured once its acuteness increases but early treatment can help in reducing the chances of heart attacks. So, it is necessary to predict the disease at the earliest opportunity to avoid further complications. Detection of heart ailments is done through a blood test, a treadmill test, CT scan, X-ray, MRI scan, coronary angiography,

DOI: 10.1201/9781003450153-18

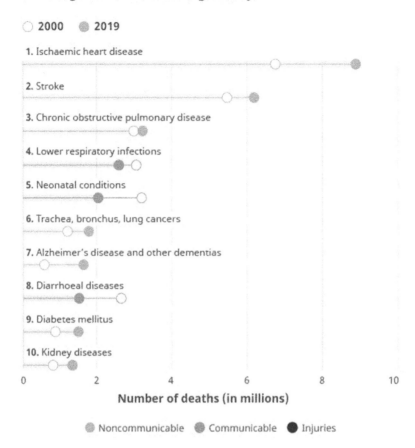

FIGURE 16.1
The leading causes of death as per WHO.

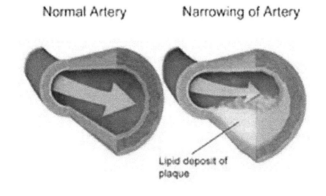

FIGURE 16.2
Atherosclerosis.

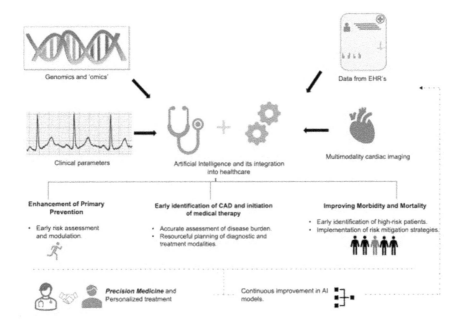

FIGURE 16.3
Role of AI in improving CAD diagnosis.

and electrocardiography (ECG). Coronary angiography is the most common technique for detecting the disease, but it is invasive, risky, and costlier. ECG, though a non-invasive technique, does not always produce correct results and conceals underlying heart problems. The introduction of artificial intelligence (AI) [1] and its applications, with different ML and deep learning (DL) algorithms, means that raw data is used to discover hidden knowledge. Such methods have proved to be highly beneficial in the efficient detection of CAD and other diseases. The clinical data from electronic health records (EHR), echocardiography images, MRI images, CT images, and ECG signals have been used by researchers for further pre-processing, feature extraction, and application of computer-enabled algorithms to produce suitable results, that can help clinicians and medical experts to analyze the disease easily. Figure 16.3 shows the application of AI in improving CAD diagnosis.

16.2 Cardio-Oncology

The concept of cardio-oncology or onco-cardiology is critical to CVD. The term cardio-oncology is defined as identifying, treating, and monitoring cardiovascular diseases in a patient after receiving cancer therapies. Cancer can bring about major cardiac dysfunctionalities within a system, reducing the longevity of the patient, which is another cause of growing morbidities among oncological population. The prime objective of this branch of medicine is to reduce the side effects of cancer treatment and to preserve the normal working of the cardiovascular system. The rising incidence of CVD in cancer patients is due to symptoms like diabetes, hypertension, unhealthy lifestyle, obesity etc. Along with this, sometimes cardiotoxicity arising from anti-cancer treatment plays a key role in

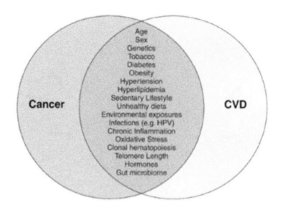

FIGURE 16.4
Common conditions of cancer and CVD.

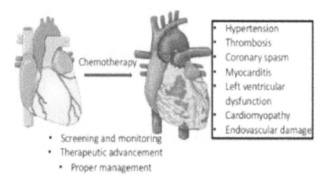

FIGURE 16.5
Cardiac vulnerabilities post chemotherapy.

diminishing the health status of a cancer patient. Figure 16.4 shows the common conditions of cancer and CVD, which has been proved to be deadly.

Certain cancer-related drugs and therapies result in heart damage known as cardiotoxicity. The radiation therapy used in cancer treatment will automatically increase the risk of cardiotoxicity [2]. Basically, it develops after several years of cancer treatment, especially in patients who have undergone the treatment during childhood. Therefore, cardiological assessment is vital before taking up the treatment for cancer that is chemotherapy or radiotherapy [3]. For patients with high vulnerabilities, a comprehensive management strategy should be developed during and post medication. The foremost step is to identify serious patients who have abnormal lifestyle like minimal physical exercise, obesity, and smoking. Also, the morbidities should be checked like history of CAD, angina, hypertension etc. Both hematological as well as ECG and echocardiographic tests should be considered. Figure 16.5 shows cardiac vulnerabilities post chemo treatment.

Malfunctioning of the heart might manifest during or after the cancer treatment. Therefore, it is highly essential to safeguard the normal functioning of the heart by diagnosing as early as possible. The contribution of this chapter is as follows. Firstly, we have considered the Z-Alizadeh Sani dataset [4] and rigorously applied pre-processing strategies to streamline the existing data and have used various ML and DL methods to accurately classify the target label. Secondly, we have applied an ensemble technique that is hybrid 'improved CNN-SVM' algorithm to aid the efficacy of the proposed model. The chapter also encompasses the various relevant works carried out by researchers on CAD.

16.3 Related Work

Researchers have been looking into various ML and DL [5, 6] paradigms for over a decade to enhance the decision-making process of the algorithms.

Traditional data mining practices and the feature formation algorithm used in [7] show 94.08% accuracy. Many algorithms like bagging, sequential minimal optimization (SMO), naïve Bayes, and neural networks have been tested on the dataset [4] and to enrich it a feature creation algorithm has been proposed. However, the paper can be modified to include cost-sensitive algorithms. Along with that, extensive datasets and advanced data mining algorithms could be used. On the same lines, a hybrid data mining framework mentioned in the paper [8] has attained 98.99% accuracy. In this paper, local configuration pattern (LCP) features have been extracted from an echocardiography image dataset. Further, the attributes are exposed to marginal Fisher analysis (MFA), resulting in scaling-down of the dimension, followed by a ranking method established on fuzzy entropy. Moreover, a unified index called the myocardial infarction risk index (MIRI) is also developed for recognition of the infarcted myocardium at three levels, that is, normal, moderate, and severe. MIRI shall also assist the healthcare experts in rapid diagnosis and estimation of the intensity of myocardial infarction using echocardiography images as shown in Figure 16.6.

Ensembled strategies like bagging, boosting, and stacking are known for displaying better behaviour when compared with those of traditional baseline methods. K-nearest neighbor (KNN), binary logistic classification, and naïve Bayes used in [9] are combinedly studied. The model consisting of KNN, random forest and support vector machine (SVM) has proved to be competent with 75.1% accuracy. However, the model shows lower recall value. A two-tiered stacking model [10] has been designed to find the best-performing classifiers for combining and producing top results. It has at most two levels; the first one is base level and the second one is meta level which receives the input in the form of predictions given by the classifiers of the first level. The stacked model performs exceptionally well, with 95.43% accuracy. The proposed model has two limitations. The first is that the considered parameters are not optimal and second is cost and time overheads.

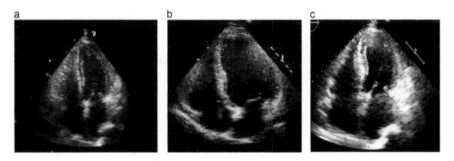

FIGURE 16.6
Echocardiography images: (a) normal, (b) moderately infarcted and (c) severely infarcted myocardium.

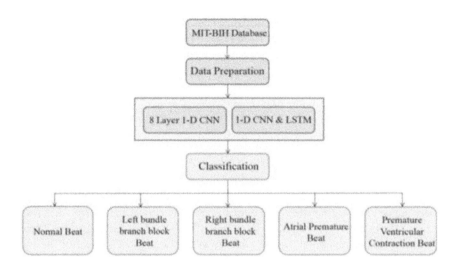

FIGURE 16.7
Block diagram of the model [12].

A detailed analysis of cardiac signals is vital to diagnose CAD. ECG signals are one of the prominent ones that give an idea about the electrical activity of the heart. Moreover, the heart rate and rhythm can also be deduced from the ECG signals. As these signals are sensitive to minor changes, wavelet transform techniques have been used to examine the characteristics of the signals. A new method proposed in [11], implements tunable-Q wavelet transform (TQTW) to extract correntropy based features from heart rate signals, which are then exposed to least-squares support-vector machine (LS-SVM) for automated CAD detection. Likewise, in [12] a deep neural network model using CNN and LSTM has been applied on ECG signals to assist physicians to promptly detect abnormalities in the signal, with 99% accuracy. The proposed model of [12] is shown in Figure 16.7. Also, in certain papers, researchers have taken CT image datasets for the application of deep neural network models. In [13] a CNN framework has been proposed along with convolutional autoencoder (CAE) which highlights the local ischemic changes. This is followed by classification of patients as per the presence of stenosis through SVM, which would help patients to avoid other invasive diagnosis methods.

The process of feature selection and reduction can be simplified also through some meta heuristic methods. In [14], fusion of emotional neural networks (EmNNs) and particle swarm optimization (PSO) produces superior performance as EmNNs enhance the training ability of the network by using emotional parameters, thereby showing 88.34% accuracy. The proposed model also surpasses PSO-based adaptive neuro-fuzzy inference system (PSO-ANFIS). N2Genetic optimizer demonstrated in [15], has produced accuracy of 93.08%. Moreover, the paper uses a hybrid optimization model of genetic algorithm and PSO which competes well with the traditional ML algorithms.

16.4 Method and Simulation

The proposed model's flow diagram is shown in Figure 16.8.

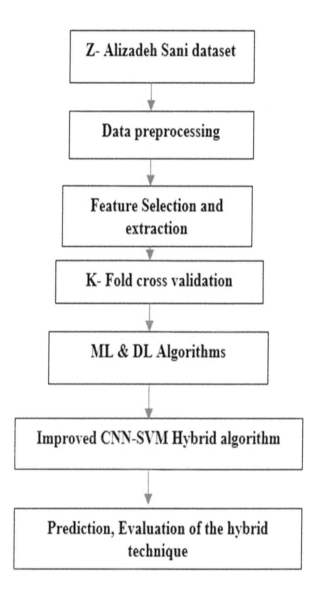

FIGURE 16.8
Proposed model.

- The dataset [4] of our model consists of 303 patients along with 54 attributes.
- These 54 attributes are broadly based on demographic attributes, clinical symptoms and examination, ECG and laboratory and echocardiographic features.
- The target label of the dataset is divided into two major classes: normal and CAD. The dataset is shown in Figure 16.9.
- The number of patients under the normal class is 87 and that under the CAD class is 216. The complete simulation is done using Jupyter notebook of Anaconda Navigator.
- The data pre-processing part is the key to producing the final output of any model. The dataset consists of various types of heterogeneous attributes like numerical

Feature Type	Feature Name	Range
Demographic	Age	30-86
	Weight	48-120
	Sex	Male, Female
	BMI (Body Mass Index Kg/m²)	18-41
	DM (Diabetes Mellitus)	Yes, No
	HTN (Hyper Tension)	Yes, No
	Current Smoker	Yes, No
	Ex-Smoker	Yes, No
	FH (Family History)	Yes, No
	Obesity	Yes if MBI>25, No otherwise
Symptom and Examination	CRF (Chronic Renal Failure)	Yes, No
	CVA (Cerebrovascular Accident)	Yes, No
	Airway Disease	Yes, No
	Thyroid Disease	Yes, No
	CHF (Congestive Heart Failure)	Yes, No
	DLP (Dyslipidemia)	Yes, No
	BP (Blood Pressure: mmHg)	90-190
	PR (Pulse Rate) (ppm)	50-110
	Edema	Yes, No
	Weak peripheral pulse	Yes, No
	Lung Rales	Yes, No
	Systolic murmur	Yes, No
	Diastolic murmur	Yes, No
	Typical Chest Pain	Yes, No
	Dyspnea	Yes, No
	Function Class	1, 2, 3, 4
	Atypical	Yes, No
	Nonanginal CP	Yes, No
	Exertional CP (Exertional Chest Pain)	Yes, No
	Low Th Ang (low Threshold angina)	Yes, No
ECG	Rhythm	Sin, AF
	Q Wave	Yes, No
	ST Elevation	Yes, No
	ST Depression	Yes, No
	T inversion	Yes, No
	LVH (Left Ventricular Hypertrophy)	Yes, No
	Poor R Progression (Poor R Wave Progression)	Yes, No
Laboratory and Echo	FBS (Fasting Blood Sugar) (mg/dl)	62-400
	Cr (creatine) (mg/dl)	0.5-2.2
	TG (Triglyceride) (mg/dl	37-1050
	LDL (Low density lipoprotein) (mg/dl)	18-232
	HDL (High density lipoprotein) (mg/dl)	15-111
	BUN (Blood Urea Nitrogen) (mg/dl)	6-52
	ESR (Erythrocyte Sedimentation rate) (mm/h)	1-90
	HB (Hemoglobin) (g/dl)	8.9-17.6
	K (Potassium) (mEq/lit)	3.0-6.6
	Na (Sodium) (mEq/lit)	128-156
	WBC (White Blood Cell) (cells/ml)	3700-18000
	Lymph (Lymphocyte) (%)	7-60
	Neut (Neutrophil) (%)	32-89
	PLT (Platelet) (1000/ml)	25-742
	EF (Ejection Fraction) (%)	15-60
	Region with RWMA * (Regional Wall Motion Abnormality)	0,1,2,3,4
	VHD (Valvular Heart Disease)	Normal, Mild, Moderate, Severe

FIGURE 16.9
Dataset.

and categorical (nominal and ordinal), which affect the final classification and prediction result.

- Under data processing, we have adopted different feature scaling methods like normalization and standardization for numerical data and encoding for categorical data to convert the data into a homogeneous set.
- The dataset noise is reduced by checking on the redundant values, missing values, and null values. The target label class balancing, known as data balancing,

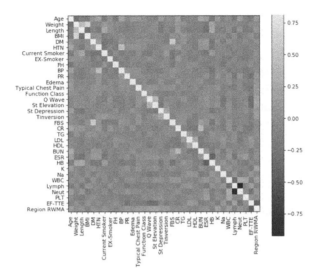

FIGURE 16.10
Correlation features.

is done to minimize any class-bias by using the synthetic minority oversampling technique (SMOTE) algorithm.

• Under the feature engineering, important features have been selected through feature selection techniques like correlation based, chi2, feature importance, mutual information, random forest, and selectkbest techniques.

Figure 16.10 shows feature correlation matrix which quantifies the relation among any two features. The features which are highly correlated are insignificant and any of the them can be dropped selectively.

• The features are integrated according to their rank and a final dataset is obtained with twenty significant features.

• Five-fold cross validation (with K = 5) has been applied to validate the data preprocessing and feature selection. The cross-validation method uses a decision-tree classifier to maintain the consistency and randomness of the data. A validation accuracy of 85.24% has been achieved. The training-to-testing split ratio is taken as 7:3.

• Different ML and DL algorithms have been used to classify the target label. A hybrid 'Improved CNN-SVM' algorithm has been proposed to classify the data into CAD and normal.

• We have considered one-dimensional CNN as having convolution layers followed by a dropout layer, a pooling layer, a flatten layer, and dense layers. The first layer does all the major calculations of the network. The dropout layer acts as a mask and directs data overfitting and underfitting. The flatten layer does the mapping of data, whereas the dense layer classifies the data based on the inputs from the convolution layers. We have chosen adam and binary cross-entropy as our CNN parameters.

• We have added an extra layer that is the batch normalization layer to the above CNN model for faster learning and solving the overfitting issue. This improved

CNN model gives better training as well as validation accuracy which is better than that of a simple CNN model.

- The SVM classifier takes the training and testing features of the improved CNN model for further processing to produce the final output that is to predict the presence of CAD in a person.
- Finally, the predictions and evaluations are done and the performances of different algorithms are compared.

16.5 Results and Discussions

The results of the classification can be analysed in terms of five aspects. They are as follows:

1. Precision
2. Recall
3. F1 score
4. Support
5. Accuracy

The four aspects that play a crucial role in this model are described below in a brief manner.

1. **Precision: (*P*)** Precision is defined as the number of true positives (*T_p*) over the number of true positives plus the number of false positives (***F_p***)

$$P = \frac{T_P}{T_P + F_P} \tag{1}$$

2. **Recall: (*R*)** Recall is a measure of how many truly relevant results are returned. Recall is defined as the number of true positives (*T_p*) over the number of false negatives (***F_n***)

$$R = \frac{T_p}{T_p + F_n} \tag{2}$$

1. **F1 score: (*F_1*)** The harmonic mean of Precision and Recall.

$$F1 = 2\frac{P*R}{P+R} \tag{3}$$

3. **Support:** It is the number of samples of true response that a class contains.
4. **Accuracy (A):** The ability of the classifier to label as positive, a sample that is positive and to label as negative, a sample that is negative.

$$A = \frac{T_P + T_N}{T_P + T_N + F_P + F_N} \tag{4}$$

TABLE 16.1

Prediction Accuracy of the Algorithms

Algorithms	Accuracy in percentage
Logistic regression	84.61
Naïve Bayes	57.54
SVM	83.81
KNN	81.31
Artificial neural network (ANN)	83.61
Multi-layer perceptron (MLP)	82.00
CNN	83.00
Proposed hybrid model (Improved CNN -SVM)	86.00

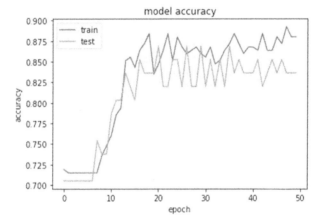

FIGURE 16.11
Model accuracy.

As shown in Table 16.1, the proposed hybrid 'Improved CNN-SVM' model achieves significant results in terms of training accuracy (88.84%) and validation accuracy (86%), which is better than the individual ML and DL algorithms mentioned (logistic regression, KNN, naïve Bayes, SVM, ANN, MLP, CNN).

The model accuracy and loss (training and validation) are depicted in Figure 16.11 and Figure 16.12 respectively. The evaluation metrics and confusion matrix are shown in Figure 16.13 and Figure 16.14. From the confusion matrix we can infer that the number of true positives and true negatives are higher than the number of false positives and false negatives, which indicates a sound performance of the hybrid algorithm.

Our model performs at parallel with the ensemble method based on majority voting [16] as well as the hybrid model mentioned in [17] and excels that of [9] with respect to accuracy as mentioned in Table 16.2.

16.6 Conclusions and Future Directions

CAD is one of the life-threatening diseases that might result in other complications in the body if not treated early. This prediction model shall reduce the response time of the

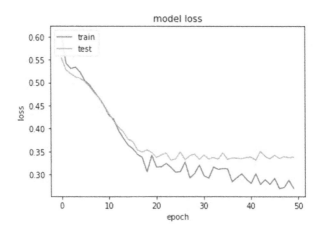

FIGURE 16.12
Model loss.

```
Accuracy   0.8852459016393442
                precision    recall   f1-score    support

        0.0        0.79       0.83       0.81         18
        1.0        0.93       0.91       0.92         43

    accuracy                             0.89         61
   macro avg       0.86       0.87       0.86         61
weighted avg       0.89       0.89       0.89         61
```

FIGURE 16.13
The evaluation metrics.

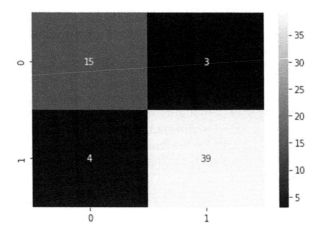

FIGURE 16.14
Confusion matrix.

TABLE 16.2

Comparison with Some of the Existing Works

Papers	Accuracy	Precision	Recall	F1 score
[9]	75.1	–	–	–
[10]	95.43	–	95.84	–
[14]	88.34	92.37	91.85	92.12
[16]	90	–	–	–
[17]	88.4	–	–	–
Proposed hybrid model (Improved CNN –SVM)	86.00	86	87	86

clinicians by accurately detecting the disease in least amount of time. With a validated accuracy of 86% and training accuracy of 88.84%, this is one of the best non-invasive models to easily forecast the presence of the disease in a person. Our contribution stands apart from other research works in terms of the major pre-processing strategies that we have carried out on the dataset which has been explored limitedly till now. However, this model can be extended to image datasets, which would show better results if integrated with other deep learning techniques. A larger dataset can be used with other refined pre-processing techniques to improve the performance of the model. Also, this proposed method can be extended to detect other critical diseases like cancer and neurovascular diseases. Hence, this work would facilitate a health expert to detect the CAD disease efficiently (Figures 16.7–16.14).

References

1. Nitesh Gautam, Prachi Saluja, Abdallah Malkawi, Mark G. Rabbat, Mouaz H. Al-Mallah, Gianluca Pontone, Yiye Zhang, Benjamin C. Lee, Subhi J. Al'Aref, "Current and future applications of artificial intelligence in coronary artery disease.", Artificial Intelligence (AI) and Machine Learning (ML) in Human Health and Healthcare, January 2022.
2. Robert A. Hong, Takeshi Iimura, Kenneth N. Sumida, Robert M. Eager, "Cardio-oncology/ onco-cardiology," Internal Medicine Residency Program, The Queen's Medical Center, Honolulu, Hawaii, December 2010.
3. Kostakou, P.M., Kouris, N.T., Kostopoulos, V.S. *et al.* Cardio-oncology: a new and developing sector of research and therapy in the field of cardiology. Heart Fail Rev **24,** 91–100. (2019).
4. Z-Alizadeh sani dataset, Kaggle Repository. https://www.kaggle.com/code/kerneler/starter-z-alizadeh-sani-dataset-27270969-2
5. R. Alizadehsani, A. Khosravi, M. Roshanzamir, M. Abdar, N. Sarrafzadegan, D. Shafie, F. Khozeimeh, A. Shoeibi, S. Nahavandi, M. Panahiazar, A. Bishara, R. E. Beygui, R. Puri, S. Kapadia, R.-S. Tan, U. R. Acharya, "Coronary artery disease detection using artificial intelligence techniques: A survey of trends, geographical differences and diagnostic features 1991–2020," in *Computers in Biology and Medicine*, vol. 128, January 2021.
6. Roohallah Alizadehsani, Moloud Abdar, Mohamad Roshanzamir, Abbas Khosravi, Parham M. Kebria, Fahime Khozeimeh, Saeid Nahavandi, Nizal Sarrafzadegan, U. Rajendra Acharya, "Machine learning-based coronary artery disease diagnosis: A comprehensive review," in *Computers in Biology and Medicine*, vol. 111, August 2019.
7. Roohallah Alizadehsani, Jafar Habibi, Mohammad Javad Hosseini, Hoda Mashayekhi, Reihane Boghrati, Asma Ghandehariouna, Behdad Bahadorian, Zahra Alizadeh Sani, "A data

mining approach for diagnosis of coronary artery disease," in *Computer Methods and Programs in Biomedicine*, vol. 111, pp. 52–61, July 2013.

8. Vidya K. Sudarshan, U. Rajendra Acharya, E. Y. K. Ng, Ru San Tan, Siaw Meng Chou, Dhanjoo N. Ghista, "Data mining framework for identification of myocardial infarction stages in ultrasound: A hybrid feature extraction paradigm (PART 2)," in *Computers in Biology and Medicine*, vol. 71, pp. 241–251, April 2016.

9. V. Shorewala, "Early detection of coronary heart disease using ensemble techniques," in *Informatics in Medicine Unlocked*, vol. 26, 2021.

10. Jikuo Wang, Changchun Liu, Liping Li, Wang Li, Lianke Yao, Han Li, Huan Zhang, "A stacking-based model for non-invasive detection of coronary heart disease," in *IEEE Access*, vol. 8, pp. 37124–37133, February 2020.

11. Shivnarayan Patidar, Ram Bilas Pachori, U. Rajendra Acharya, "Automated diagnosis of coronary artery disease using tunable-Q wavelet transform applied on heart rate signals," in *Knowledge-Based Systems*, vol. 82, pp. 1–10, July 2015.

12. S. Ghousia Begum, Esha Priyadarshi, Sharath Pratap, Sharmistha Kulshrestha, Vipula Singh, "Automated detection of abnormalities in ECG signals using deep neural network," in *Biomedical Engineering Advances*, vol. 5, June 2023.

13. Majd Zreik, Nikolas Lessmann, Robbert W. van Hamersvelt, Jelmer M. Wolterink, Michiel Voskuil, Max A. Viergever, Tim Leiner, Ivana Išgum, "Deep learning analysis of the myocardium in coronary CT angiography for identification of patients with functionally significant coronary artery stenosis," in *Medical Image Analysis*, February 2018.

14. A. H. Shahid, M. P. Singh, "A novel approach for coronary artery disease diagnosis using hybrid particle swarm optimization based emotional neural network," in *Biocybernetics and Biomedical Engineering*, vol. 40, pp. 1568–1585, December 2020.

15. Moloud Abdar, Wojciech Książek, U. Rajendra Acharya, Ru-San Tan, Vladimir Makarenkov, Paweł Pławiak, "A new machine learning technique for an accurate diagnosis of coronary artery disease," in *Computer Methods and Programs in Biomedicine*, vol. 179, October 2019.

16. Rahma Atallah, Amjed Al-Mousa, "Heart disease detection using machine learning majority voting ensemble method," IEEE Conference, 2019.

17. Luxmi Verma, Sangeet Srivastava, P. C. Negi, "A hybrid data mining model to predict coronary artery disease cases using non-invasive clinical data," in *Transactional Processing Systems*, 2016.

Index

For Product Safety Concerns and Information please contact our EU
representative GPSR@taylorandfrancis.com
Taylor & Francis Verlag GmbH, Kaufingerstraße 24, 80331 München, Germany